2 .

Chamber Music

Chamber Music

HOMER ULRICH

SECOND EDITION

Columbia University Press

NEW YORK

Homer Ulrich is Professor of Music and Head of the
Music Department at the University of Maryland

Copyright © 1948, 1966, Columbia University Press
Library of Congress Catalog Card Number: 66–17909
Printed in the United States of America
ISBN 0-231-08617-2 Paperbound

20   19   18   17   16   15   14   13

TO MY WIFE

Preface to the Second Edition

THE FIELD of chamber music has undergone consistent development since this book was first published eighteen years ago. Historical researchers have discovered many new facts and provided new insights into the earlier periods. A new generation of contemporary composers has introduced new styles and style elements into the field. The standard repertoire itself has been enlarged even as the sheer number of chamber-music performances and recordings has increased.

The second edition of this book seeks to reflect the increasing impact of chamber music on concert life everywhere. The chapters dealing with its growth to about 1730 have been completely re-arranged, and much new material has been incorporated. Sections on composers treated sketchily or not at all in the first edition—notably Vivaldi and Boccherini—have been enlarged or added in the second. The very definition of chamber music has been broadened to include violin sonatas and cello sonatas, and many works in these categories have been discussed. The chapter on contemporary music has been rewritten and expanded to take into account the most recent developments. Finally, the bibliography has been enlarged to include the most important items that deal with chamber music and its composers. One omission may be noted in the second edition: the lists of chamber-music publications and recordings. Such lists are inevitably out of date even when they first appear; and the existence of comprehensive catalogues today makes the music and long-playing phonograph recordings generally available in any case.

I have been greatly pleased on many occasions to learn that the first edition of this book has served the needs of general readers, teachers, and students. I dare to hope that the improved second edition will continue to do so. The place of chamber music in concert life and in the home is probably more solidly fixed now than ever before. If this book has played a small part in bringing this about, it has succeeded in its purpose.

HOMER ULRICH

Silver Spring, Maryland
April 28, 1966

Preface to the First Edition

THIS BOOK lays no claim to being a history, nor does it pretend to be an essay in music appreciation. A history presents all the pertinent facts about the subject, uncovers principles and trends, and accounts for the phenomena it brings to light. An "appreciation," on the other hand, concentrates on a few significant works, tells its readers what to look and listen for in them, and in so doing becomes a guide to musical understanding. But while this book is neither one nor the other exclusively, it does contain elements of both. What, then, is its purpose?

No major field of musical literature is as little known as chamber music. True, certain works in the repertoire are widely performed, and many persons have heard that Haydn fathered the string quartet. In general, however, its history has remained obscure, its importance to the whole literature of music has been misunderstood, and many laymen whose contact with the field has been limited consider it highbrow. To introduce chamber music to the wider public which admires it from afar and to remove misconceptions about its quality and appeal, two things are necessary: an orderly account of its evolution to the point where the contemporary concert repertoire begins and a survey of the works which form the bulk of that repertoire. Those things this book hopes to supply.

Its first seven chapters, having to do with music that is seldom heard today, are designed to introduce the principal musical events, works, and tendencies of the two centuries before 1750. Subsequent chapters, beginning with the account of Haydn, are concerned with orienting the reader in the extensive and important chamber-music literature by major composers since 1750.

Chamber music is one of the oldest of instrumental literatures. While the book has been planned to illustrate, at times merely by implication, the continuity of that literature, it has been impossible to include all composers. For example, Luigi Boccherini, Ludwig Spohr, Ernest Chausson, Alexander Glazounow, and many other composers of similiar stature are scarcely mentioned. One may with justification omit accounts of such men and their works, largely because they have been of little influence upon their successors. The essential composers and the essential works, however, have been discussed in detail.

With sincere gratitude I record the part Mr. Ferdinand Volk played in my student days, in stimulating my first interest in chamber music and in helping to provide the solid musical background out of which this book has emerged. Likewise, the efforts and sacrifices of my mother to enrich that background went far beyond parental responsibilities. Such debts, while they may be publicly acknowledged, are not easily repaid.

The book itself owes its existence to my erstwhile colleague Dr. Donald Grout. His many helpful suggestions, his constant stimulation, and his patient reading of preliminary chapters are gratefully remembered. Without his encouragement the book might not have been written; nevertheless, he is not to be held responsible for its defects. Dr. Paul Henry Lang's interest in the work began when it was still in its early stages. His great help at crucial steps in its path from desk to press is deeply appreciated. To Dr. Warren D. Allen, Dr. J. M. Coopersmith, Dr. Karl Geiringer, Dr. Wiley Housewright, Mr. Kent Kennan, Mr. William Kroll, and Dr. Paul Pisk, all of whom read portions of the manuscript, I am indebted for factual corrections and stylistic improvements. In all matters of bibliography I acknowledge with thanks the technical assistance of Miss Jean Cassel, whose patience and good will seem inexhaustible. Finally, my sincere thanks go to Mr. John Scabia, for his help in preparing the musical examples; and to the individuals who are the Columbia University Press, particularly to Miss Ida M. Lynn, for their help at all stages of the book's progress. The professional skill and great interest Miss Lynn exhibited in the final preparation of the manuscript are especially appreciated.

My thanks are extended to Music Press, Inc., New York, and to the editor of the Alessandro Scarlatti *Sonata a quattro*, Dr. Hans Theodore David, for permission to quote a phrase from that work. An extended quotation in the text is reprinted from *Music in Western Civilization*, by Paul Lang, by permission of W. W. Norton & Company, Inc., New York, copyright, 1941, by the publishers. The passage from the Arnold Schoenberg Suite, Opus 29, appears by kind permission of Universal Edition, Vienna. The example drawn from the string quartet of Anton von Webern is reprinted by permission of the copyright owners, Boosey & Hawkes, London and New York.

The list of chamber-music publications and recordings found as an appendix to the book has been compiled from a purely practical standpoint. I venture to hope that the reader, stimulated by the textual account, will wish to become better acquainted with chamber music itself. He will then turn to that list for information about the availability of a particular composition, and will go further along the path of musical enjoyment with the score or the records in his possession. If that should be the case and the music should thus become a vital part of his musical life, the book will have served its purpose.

HOMER ULRICH

Austin, Texas
March 27, 1948

Contents

Tables and Charts

Musical Examples

Chamber Music

1. Backgrounds

SINCE ABOUT 1950 interest in the performance of old music has been a striking characteristic of the concert world. Many performers and listeners have discovered the charm and beauty of works composed as early as the 1400s or as late as the 1700s. This is in sharp contrast to the situation that prevailed a few decades earlier, when the year 1750 seemed to mark a point beyond which performers and performing groups dared not often venture. As a consequence, a wealth of pre-Haydn, pre-Bach, and even pre-Palestrina music has become familiar through recordings and live performances.

While this renewed interest in Renaissance and Baroque music—that composed between about 1450 and 1750—has opened the doors to new areas of musical enjoyment, it has not always been consistently developed. Large quantities of music in many forms and by many composers remain virtually unknown. Except when preparing "historical" recordings, orchestras today seldom perform works earlier than the late symphonies of Haydn, even though an occasional Bach or Handel masterpiece is played. Opera companies do not often reach further into the past than a Mozart performance requires. And in the field of chamber music, relatively few of the many pre-1750 works have been performed or recorded. This might lead to the erroneous conclusion that the string quartet, one of the greatest musical achievements of western civilization, had no ancestors, that it emerged from the mind and pen of Haydn as a new invention.

The first portion of this book will attempt to give an account of the hundred fifty years of chamber music that preceded the quartets of Haydn, describe the many forms that flourished during those years, trace the many threads that lead from the earliest instrumental forms to the latest, and indicate how greatly every age is indebted to that which went before. Later sections will attempt to guide the reader to the rich and extensive literature that constitutes the bulk of the present-day repertoire, namely, that from Haydn to the present.

THE NATURE OF CHAMBER MUSIC

Chamber music is a bountiful source of pleasure to those who know the field. It is at once one of the most enjoyable and the most dignified of literatures. The musical amateur often makes it his hobby and considers it the mainspring of his musical existence. The experienced layman finds himself richly rewarded for his intelligent listening. The professional musician turns to it for relaxation and for a kind of pleasure that no other field offers.

It has challenged the greatest composers to their best efforts. A list of the chamber-music works of the masters from Haydn to Hindemith includes their finest compositions. The string quartets of Mozart and Beethoven, for example, and the quartets and quintets of Brahms are among the most profound and moving works in the entire literature of music, though only a few instruments are required for their performance. "E'en little things can yield a perfect pleasure, e'en little things may be supremely dear"—so run the lines of a Tuscan love song beautifully set to music by Hugo Wolf. And of nothing is that so true as of the "little things" of chamber music. One finds in this field no necessary correlation between size and quality.

Again, chamber music provides a medium for the expression of particularly intimate musical ideas. Many listeners grow weary of bombast and pretension and appreciate some degree of subtlety and refinement in their musical fare. Chamber music is for them, since it does not depend for its effects upon great splashes of sound, great variety of tone color, or great virtuoso display. In chamber music there is room only for essentials; mere padding is avoided. One is aware of the musical essence, of the composer's inmost intentions, and is not distracted by extraneous glamour.

Until well into the nineteenth century chamber music was amateur music, confined to small rooms and private homes. In a day when every cultured person played an instrument and professional musicians played several, chamber music provided the natural outlet for their activities.[1] Every home of any size or pretension to culture harbored a chamber-music group; the sounds of trio sonatas, quartets, and even flute duets were heard throughout Europe.[2] In the time of Beethoven, however, professional chamber-music players became active,[3] and the two classes of musicians—performers and listeners— took a long step away from each other. It became more fashionable to listen than to play, and the amateur status of the field deteriorated somewhat. As the music became more difficult to play (there can be no question but that each new composer made greater demands upon the player) it became more and more a specialized field; consequently fewer amateurs played it and knew it as a living literature.

But it is true that the finest musicians, the most enthusiastic amateurs, and the most cultivated listeners had not lost sight of chamber music. Concerts were well attended, the most competent amateur groups throve, and the field not only remained alive but continued to draw new admirers in the decades just preceding and following 1900. Since the turn of the century the advent of phonograph re-

[1] Baldassare Castiglione (1478–1529) wrote a treatise on manners, social problems, and general behavior, *Libro del cortegiano*, for the sixteenth-century courtier. Here one can learn how important musical skills were to the well-being of educated persons of that age. Similar accomplishments at the Elizabethan court are too well known to need comment.

[2] Among the first public concerts of chamber music were those presented by John Banister, from 1672 to 1678, at his home in London.

[3] Ignaz Schuppanzigh (1776–1830), friend of Beethoven and Schubert, became active in the Rasoumowsky Quartet in 1808. The Koella Quartet, composed of four brothers of Swiss parentage, played during the 1820s. The four Mueller brothers (b. 1797–1808, d. 1855–75) began their quartet playing in 1830. Confining themselves to Haydn, Mozart, and Beethoven and traveling in all parts of western Europe (and Russia in 1845), they did much to create interest in and to set standards for chamber-music playing. The quartet founded by Joseph Helmesberger, Jr. (1829–93), played from 1849 to 1887 and was influential in making the last quartets of Beethoven widely known. In 1869 Joseph Joachim founded his quartet, perhaps the most famous of all nineteenth-century ensembles. To these must be added the name of the Kneisel Quartet as the first well-known American chamber-music group, active from 1885 to 1917. The Flonzaley Quartet (1903–c. 1930), the London Quartet (1910–c. 1935), and the Kroll, Budapest, and Juilliard quartets of the present decades have maintained the high standards set by the earlier groups.

cordings and radio broadcasts has contributed to the general awakening of a larger music audience and has done much to make chamber music better known to the public at large. Nothing more has been needed. To know chamber music is to revere it; to hear chamber music is to enjoy it. It is fast returning to the favored position it held throughout the seventeenth and eighteenth centuries. The prejudices and misconceptions that surrounded it in the past are rapidly disappearing; they are being replaced by honest appreciation and real understanding. Chamber music, long known to musicians and some listeners as the source for the finest music in western civilization, is again being recognized as one of the most satisfying manifestations of the human spirit.

It is true that the approach to chamber music was once clouded by prejudices and misconceptions. Some laymen, even today, mistrust the field. This may be because chamber music, like every other branch of music, has certain limitations along with its positive characteristics. One thing is true of all branches of music: each has a particular function to perform, and each has peculiar possibilities and particular disadvantages. Sacred music, for example, is well adapted to contribute to church services, to help establish an attitude of reverence, to testify to the presence of the divine in the human; sacred music is unsuitable as a source of dance tunes. An orchestral piece gives the composer ample opportunity to develop a musical idea with great variety of tone color and to create effects that depend upon tonal mass for their success; an orchestral piece cannot succesfully meet the requirements of intimacy and economy in music. So with the other branches: each does one thing well, other things less well or badly. A single composition or literature cannot be all things to all men; to this the field of chamber music is no exception.

The character of chamber music makes its limitations follow as a matter of course. Since it is a medium for expressing subtle musical ideas, it cannot serve more general or obvious musical purposes. It is not a medium for elaborate display or extensive verbosity. It does not lend itself to vivid color effects or to dazzling passages that impress one sheerly by a large number of players or mass of tone. It is not a medium for storytelling, for delineation of this or that extramusical effect. It is not often suited to the purposes of the virtuoso, whose effectiveness depends as much upon technical facility as upon musical worth. Since there is only one player for each part, certain types of writing that can afford to ignore human frailty and the limitations of physical endurance are not successful in it. These are the limiting aspects of chamber music.

The person who looks for the color of an orchestra, the pomp and display of an opera, the rhythmic vitality of a military band, looks vainly for these things in chamber music. Disappointed or disillusioned, he calls it dull or austere or colorless. He is bored by it and considers it a subject fit only for the music historian. But he must not listen negatively and look for characteristics that properly belong to other branches of music.

In chamber music one can find complete clarity of texture. The listener to an orchestra is often so lost in a maze of sound, in variety of tone color, and in the great number of tonal lines that he is aware of only a formless mass; in a musical sense, he cannot see the trees for the forest. His enjoyment of the finer points is greatly hampered, and his over-all appreciation of the work is made difficult. He who listens to a string quartet, on the other hand, seldom has to follow more than three tonal lines, the mass of tone is never so great as to overwhelm him, and he is able to look within the music, to hear between the notes, much as one learns to read between the lines. This quality, often and aptly called "transparence," is one of the great assets of the genre.

In chamber music is found an economy of resources that eschews all padding and flamboyance. The extramusical effects that impress the naïve listener through sheer novelty or sheer weight, the kaleidoscopic colors whose appeal is mainly sensuous—these are seldom found in chamber music. And their absence allows the music to stand on its own feet, with all its beauties and strengths revealed. The result is that its shams and weaknesses are also uncovered. Chamber music is honest music if it is successful. No insincerity is possible in good chamber music, for the characteristics of musical insincerity go hand in hand with noise, bluster, and confusion; and these are, of course, lacking.

Chamber music is based upon flawless balance and ensemble, a selfless teamwork, the achievement of which is one of the finest manifestations of the human spirit. Loyalty to the composer's intentions requires the perfection of ensemble that the chamber musician strives for and only the chamber musician can hope to achieve. In chamber music a feeling of intimate contact with the music itself is developed. Undistracted by sensuous appeals, undisturbed by flamboyant delivery, unencumbered by overstuffed detail, the listener can give himself up to the pure enjoyment of the tonal lines themselves, can follow their paths and their encounters, and can come close to realizing the composer's ultimate intention. Let the person who mistakenly looks for the color and pomp of an orchestra in a string quartet address himself to the positive values that chamber music has to offer. He will not be bored or disappointed.

INSTRUMENTAL COMBINATIONS

In the original sense of the term, *chamber music* refers to any music designed for home performance, as opposed to performance in the church, concert hall, or opera house. From this point of view both vocal and instrumental forms may be identified as chamber music if they are suited to performance in a chamber or small room. In this book, however, we must concern ourselves only with the instrumental branch of the field. And even after excluding the repertoire of vocal chamber music, the remaining quantity of instrumental music is too large to be discussed adequately in a single book. Many divertimentos for string and wind instruments composed by minor masters of the early Classical period approach orchestral works in size and may properly be placed in a "chamber orchestra" category. A wide repertoire of ensemble pieces for wind instruments, extending from the sixteenth century to the twentieth, exists also; this music can best be considered by a specialist in the field and will necessarily be omitted here. Therefore a more restricted definition is called for, one that will determine which works are to be discussed in the pages that follow. Thus we arrive at the following interpretation.

Chamber music is, for our purposes in this book, instrumental ensemble music written in the largest forms available to the composer, for groups of two to eight players, having one player to a part, and in which piano or string instruments supply the principal interest. The limit as to the number of players is not made arbitrarily. Chamber music implies ensemble music, and two is the minimum number to qualify under this definition. Then again, it is rarely feasible for more than eight players to remain in good ensemble without a conductor. Since players must sit some distance apart, even eight players can produce so large a tonal volume that the end men cannot clearly hear each other; and more than eight different musical natures make compromise rather difficult and accurate ensemble almost impossible. Thus the upper limit of size is arrived at.

What remains of the field if vocal chamber music, wind ensemble music, and solo works are not to be included? Table I (see p. 8) gives the combinations of instruments engaged in chamber music in the sense of the above definition. In addition to these most common combinations a few works exist in which a wind instrument is substituted for a string, as in the Mozart and Brahms quintets for clarinet and strings and in the Brahms trio for violin, horn, and piano. Other exceptions include combinations of winds and strings, such as the Beethoven septet and the Schubert octet. The forms listed in the table as flourishing in the Classical and later periods are among the post-1750 combinations to which contemporary chamber-music groups customarily address themselves. The Baroque *sonata a tre,* on the other hand, represents the chief instrumentation for the great majority of pre-1750 forms; these include the *sonata da chiesa, sonata da camera,* the trio sonata itself, and to a large extent the *canzone,* the form in which the first true chamber music was written.

EARLY INSTRUMENTAL MUSIC

For about three centuries before 1600 composers had concerned themselves largely with vocal contrapuntal music. The expressive

TABLE I

USUAL COMBINATIONS IN CHAMBER MUSIC

BAROQUE PERIOD

Sonata
  Violin (or oboe, flute, etc.)
  Sometimes cello or bass
  Harpsichord

Sonata a tre (Trio Sonata)
  Violin I and II
  Cello and/or bass
  Harpsichord

CLASSICAL AND LATER PERIODS

Sonata
  Violin (or cello, flute, clarinet,
    etc.)
  Piano

String Trio
  Violin
  Viola (or Violin II)
  Cello

Piano Trio
  Violin
  Cello
  Piano

String Quartet
  Violin I and II
  Viola
  Cello

Piano Quartet
  Violin
  Viola
  Cello
  Piano

String Quintet
  Violin I and II
  Viola I and II
  Cello

Piano Quintet
  Violin I and II
  Viola
  Cello
  Piano

String Sextet
  Violin I and II
  Viola I and II
  Cello I and II

possibilities and the economy of means employed are to be seen in the work of a long line of composers from Machaut through Obrecht and Josquin to Palestrina and Lasso. The purity and stylistic consistency of that music suffered a rather rapid decline in the decades after about 1600, at which time instrumental music slowly began to emerge as an independent branch of the art. This historical development has often obscured the fact that instrumental music was well established and assiduously cultivated as early as the thirteenth century.

While there are few manuscripts giving direct evidence, numerous paintings testify to the number and variety of instruments in common use.[4] Lute, zither, vielle, guitar, and harp are among the string instruments played in those years; the recorder, flute, oboe, and horn are the wind instrument contemporaries. Chaucer and Boccaccio give added evidence that instrumental music was a part of everyday life among certain classes of people. Especially in the *Decameron* do the characters make use of instruments, both in solo playing and to accompany singing. Professionally, too, instrumental music was on a firm basis; guilds of trumpeters, pipers, and fiddlers were established late in the thirteenth century.

From the fourteenth century through the sixteenth, instruments gradually encroached upon vocal music. One of the early great French composers, Guillaume de Machaut (c. 1300–1377), set the pattern for secular music in France until well into the fifteenth century. Machaut seized upon the old Gothic motet, a sacred choral piece in contrapuntal style with a Latin text, and by substituting French love lyrics and performing it with one part played (probably on viol or lute) and the others sung began the process of transforming vocal into instrumental music. This method of performance underwent certain changes in the course of many decades: at times an improvised instrumental part was added; in the absence of a singer an instrument played the missing part; occasionally a drone bass was added. The end result was that vocal music, which is to say choral music, was often performed by instruments alone. In such performances viols predominated; but other instruments were there in abundance, not in families of similar tone color, but in as great a variety of color and sonority as possible.[5] The organ and lute also took part in these transformed vocal pieces to a great extent; the large number of collections containing lute transcriptions of instrumental music that itself was derived from vocal music testify to the popularity of this form of activity. This type of arrangement, the lute transcription of a vocal piece, remained in favor for more than two centuries. We shall see it again in Italy about 1550.

[4] Leichtentritt, "Was lehren uns die Bildwerke des 14ten–17ten Jahrhunderts," *Sammelbände der Internationalen Musikgesellschaft,* VII [3] (May–June, 1906), 315–64.

[5] Adler, *Handbuch,* I, 383.

Toward the middle of the fifteenth century a similar step was taken in Germany; there, too, instrumental music was freed from the position of merely supporting the voices. The German folk song had been popular since the twelfth century; it was sung on many occasions and often provided the music for dancing. About 1450 it became the basis for a new type of composition.[6] Certain folk-song melodies (called "tenors") were supplied with two or three accompanying countermelodies and were otherwise expanded and ornamented. These three- or four-part contrapuntal arrangements of folk songs were then given over to groups of instruments for performance. In addition to these popular arrangements, designed for home (that is, chamber) music use, a number of leading composers of the time applied the same devices to original tunes. Conrad Paumann, a famous blind Bavarian organist (c. 1410–1473), was among the best known of these men. Three sources for music of this kind are the *Lochamer, Berliner,* and *Münchener Liederbücher,*[7] all from the period about 1450–60. The arrangements contained in these books are perhaps the earliest recorded music for amateurs—*Hausmusik,* which large numbers of Europeans have held in esteem up to the present day. The *Münchener Liederbuch* contains trios by Paumann, along with many arrangements of "tenors" similar to those described.

Again following these models is a set of arrangements by Hans Gerle (1532) for *Grosz- und Kleingeigen Quartet.* These are still folk-song transcriptions, but arranged with more regard for instrumental style and with less slavish adherence to the vocal originals. Still later, in 1561, *Duo libri musices,* a work composed by Martin Agricola (c. 1486–1556), was published by Rhau in Wittenberg; it contains sixty-seven textless trios and quartets for groups of viols.[8]

[6] New, that is, to Germany. A discussion of the similar French motets of the thirteenth century, as found in the Montpellier *Codex* (modern edition published as *Polyphonies du XIII° siècle,* ed. Yvonne Rokseth [Paris, 1935–39]), would lead too far afield.

[7] *Das Locheimer* (Lochamer) *Liederbuch,* prepared in facsimile edition by Ameln. Cf. Moser, *Geschichte der deutschen Musik,* I, 349–54.

[8] Moser, *Geschichte der deutschen Musik,* I, 429.

Meanwhile Heinrich Finck had written, in 1520, "songs . . . lustily to be sung, and suitable for instruments."

From the fourteenth century to the seventeenth there existed, principally in Germany, a branch of music that owed nothing to vocal models—tower music. Brass ensembles employing *Zinken*,[9] natural horns, and trombones had many functions in the German Medieval and Renaissance towns. Their activities were varied: playing short concerts from the town hall tower at stated hours, taking part in religious and municipal ceremonies, playing for town dances, alarming the town at the approach of the enemy, and giving fire warnings. Regulations concerning instrumentation of the group, behavior, terms of service, and the like, are common in the Acts of the burgomasters of the several towns as late as 1650.[10]

The dance had, of course, been accompanied by music since ancient times. During the Middle Ages the duty of playing for dancers was assigned to the *jongleur;* the Medieval chanson provided the music, the *estampie* was the step. Throughout the fourteenth and fifteenth centuries dance music remained in the humble hands of the itinerant *Musikant* or the performing musician of the courts. It did not enter into the purview of the "composer" or into the realm of art music (as opposed to folk music) until the beginning of the sixteenth century. From that point its influence on chamber-music forms of the seventeenth century can be traced. An account of dance music thus belongs more properly in a later chapter of this book, hence need not be elaborated here.

On the basis of considerable evidence, of which the foregoing paragraphs are only a fragment, it is no longer permissible to think of the years from 1400 to 1600 as a purely vocal, *a cappella,* period. The view borne out by the results of modern research is that instrumental music was at first a substitute for vocal music, that it grew in importance during the fifteenth and sixteenth centuries, and that it finally emerged as a separate branch of music in the seventeenth.

[9] A type of conical wood or ivory instrument with a cup mouthpiece, provided with holes to produce notes lying between the natural overtones; also called *cornetto.*
[10] Moser, *Geschichte der deutschen Musik,* I, 304–7.

It is true that it came into the light of day about 1600 without a true style of its own. Instrumental melodies remained within the easy range of the human voice, contained no intervals that the voice could not sing easily, and had no awkward or rapidly shifting rhythmic patterns. Above all, the characteristic melodic shapes that today identify a melody as being suitable for the violin or the trumpet or the piano were completely missing from early instrumental music. Organ music, as well as that for strings, employed the same general texture found in vocal contrapuntal music; indeed, many of the early instrumental forms (the *ricercari* and the *canzoni*) have the appearance of textless motets and chansons—which is, after all, what they were. It was one of the great accomplishments of the seventeenth century to create separate musical styles for the organ, harpsichord, and the violin and to make each of these styles an eminently satisfactory medium for carrying its wealth of musical ideas.

FROM CHANSON TO *Canzone*

The ensemble *canzone* was one of the earliest of a long line of musical forms in which the first independent instrumental music appeared late in the sixteenth century in Italy. It had begun as an instrumental (lute or organ) arrangement of a French vocal form, the chanson. From about the fourteenth century to the seventeenth the chanson had enjoyed a highly regarded place in French musical life. Composers had taken the short lyric poems of their day, poems of a secular nature, poems full of love and springtime and pining away and rosebuds, and the like, and set them to music; the resultant musical form was the chanson. Much of the time the chanson was set for four voices, in contrapuntal style; in phrase structure and general form it always mirrored the form and the rhyme scheme of the poem. And since repetition and recapitulation of verses were characteristic of the poetry, the musical forms ABBA and ABA became characteristic of the chanson.

During its three hundred years of popularity the chanson underwent many changes in length, style, and general content. By the time it began to serve as a model for the Italian *canzone* it had resolved itself into a composition of twenty to sixty measures in length, well separated into sections marked by a change from contrapuntal to note-against-note style. In addition to the change in style of succeeding sections, there was often a change in meter: a duple-meter section would be succeeded by one in triple meter, where the change in textual rhythm made such a metrical change necessary (see Example 1). The chansons were distinguished by a considerable

Example 1   Crequillon, *Quand me souvient*

use of quarter notes (eighth notes in modern notation), which provided a certain amount of bustling rhythmic vitality. Finally, they so frequently began with a dactylic motive that the motive almost became a trademark for the form.

The extreme popularity of the chanson is made evident by the hundreds of publications and dozens of collections appearing in Paris, Antwerp, and Venice before 1550.[11] But equal in popularity to

[11] Attaignant, at Paris, published several hundred chansons in a half dozen collections between 1527 and 1549. Other Parisian publishers, imitating his example, were similarly active: Jacques Moderne published 1538–43; Le Roy et Ballard, 1552–99. In Antwerp, Tilman Susato published c. 1540; in Venice, Andrea Antico, 1520–36, and Antonio Gardano, 1531–48. The latter was joined later in the century by Vincenti, who was still publishing chansons in 1588. See the unpublished dissertation by Crocker, "An Introductory Study of the Italian Canzona for Instrumental Ensembles," I, 80–83. Hereafter this work will be cited as "Italian Canzone."

the chansons as a four-voiced contrapuntal piece of vocal music was the instrumental arrangement of the chanson. It will be remembered that in the absence of the required singers one of the practices of the sixteenth century was to substitute instruments for the lower voices of a vocal work and to perform it with one part sung and the others played. Viols were so used, and to some extent other instruments. But whereas string and wind instruments could play the missing voices directly from the part books (which were like present-day orchestra parts in that they contained only the part for one voice), a "harmony" instrument, such as the lute, required that the parts to be used be combined and if necessary arranged for it. Thus one finds arrangements of chansons for solo voice and lute, with the original lower voices written in the lute tablature of that period. Publishers, with an eye to increasing their sales through "plugging" their best sellers, often undertook to make these lute and voice arrangements themselves or had them made.[12] Another type of arrangement, which is perhaps more important than the voice and lute version for the subsequent history of chamber music, is that for lute or keyboard instrument alone. Chansons were arranged for lute by many mid-century Italian lutenists. The form appears arranged for the virginal in the *Fitzwilliam Virginal Book*,[13] one of the important sources of Elizabethan music in England.

The transcriptions for organ, however, had the greatest influence on the later history of the instrumental version of the chanson. We must note the use of the word *transcription* in place of *arrangement* here. The practice of ornamenting a melody, improvising embellishments, runs, and the like, was an established part of the organist's calling. When this practice was applied to a work previously existing in a vocal form, the piece was so greatly altered by the florid ornamentation that it ceased to be an arrangement, made merely to

[12] One such work was published by Attaignant in 1529 and contains chansons by Creqillon, Clemens non Papa, Gombert, and others, many of which he had published in the original form a few years earlier. This work was republished in modern notation by the Société Française de Musicologie (Paris, 1934) and includes also publications of Phalèse (1553) and Le Roy et Ballard (1571).

[13] In modern edition by Fuller-Maitland and Squire.

facilitate its performance in some other medium, and became in effect a piece recomposed by the ornamentor. We must henceforth speak of transcriptions, for many sixteenth-century examples of the chanson adapted to the organ show to a great degree the results of this practice.

The first transcriptions of chansons for organ appeared in Italy in 1523 in a collection of organ tablatures by Marcantonio (Cavazzoni) de Bologna. Girolamo Cavazzoni followed his father in including two "canzoni alla francese" in his *Intavolatura, cioè recercari, canzoni, himni, magnificat*, published in 1542.[14] The younger Cavazzoni's teacher, Andrea Gabrieli (c. 1510–1586), continued in the same tradition with many similar transcriptions, most of which were published posthumously in two books in 1605.[15] Many of the *canzone* transcriptions by these three composers bear as subtitles the names of the chansons on which they were based. Those of Marcantonio and Gabrieli do nothing more than "color" (that is, ornament with runs and flourishes) the original chansons. Those of Girolamo, on the other hand, are much freer; contrapuntal parts are changed, some are omitted, and some new material is added.[16]

One of Gabrieli's *canzoni* may be singled out for closer attention;[17] it is based on a chanson by Crequillon. The latter is typical, in that it begins with a section in imitative counterpoint and is followed by other sections in note-against-note style; true to form, a short section in the middle of the chanson is set in triple meter, as opposed to the duple meter of the remainder. Faithful to the model, Gabrieli retains the triple-meter fragment in the midst of the contrasting duple, and does nothing more than embellish that section with running scale figures.

It should be noted that an apparently unimportant detail such as the one given in the paragraph above may be of vital significance in

---

[14] Published in 1543, according to Eitner, *Quellen-Lexikon;* reprinted in Torchi, *L'arte musicale in Italia*, Vol. III.

[15] *Canzoni alla francese—per sonar sopra istromenti da tasta; Lib. V e VI* (Venice: Gardano, 1605).

[16] Crocker, "Italian Canzona," I, 90.

[17] In Torchi, *L'arte musicale in Italia*, Vol. III.

the future evolution of musical forms. The reader will remember that a *canzone* usually contained a short section of triple meter in the midst of the prevailing duple. In a later chapter it will be seen that this triple-meter fragment is the germ out of which the entire second movement of the later four-movement form grew. It is not too much to say that had the fragment not existed, the forms we know as the string quartet and the symphony might have taken other shapes entirely.

To return to Gabrieli: he did not, however, confine himself to mere elaborations or "colorings" of preexisting chansons. He wrote other transcriptions as free as some of the young Cavazzoni's, and he wrote original *canzoni* for the organ, perhaps the first original works in this form.[18] In these works the same formal scheme of sections in contrasting meter was adhered to: the same imitative beginning and the same dactylic motive. The subsequent history of these keyboard works cannot occupy us here; it is sufficient to mention that the original organ *canzoni* (that is, not the transcribed ones) of Gabrieli provided the models for the next development in instrumental music.

As the sixteenth century ran its course, transcribed and original *canzoni* became well established in all parts of Italy. We can imagine that string and wind players became envious of this growing literature, in the unfolding of which they had no part. As a matter of fact, string and wind instruments began to amplify the organ and even to substitute for it, just as they had long accompanied and substituted for voices. In line with the Baroque feeling for tone color, and with such diversity of color as viols, *cornetti*, trombones, and woodwind instruments supplied, it was natural that the whole group of available instruments should be called to take part. Thus arose the development that followed hard on the heels of the original organ *canzoni* mentioned above: the *canzone* form written for string or wind groups appeared, modeled on the organ *canzoni* of Gabrieli. And it is with these ensemble works that instrumental music attained the status of a separate branch.

The first instrumental *canzone* of which there is any bibliographi-

[18] Crocker, "Italian Canzona," I, 91.

cal record did not see the light of day until 1572, when Nicolà Vicentino published *La Bella (canzone da sonar)* at Milan.[19] A host of other works followed in short order.[20] Among the innovations this new development brought in its wake was a new version of the name, the *canzone da sonar,* mentioned above. We have seen in the younger Cavazzoni's publication of 1542, for organ alone, the name *canzone alla francese,* which is obviously the Italian form of chanson plus the modifying phrase, "in French style." Now, with Vicentino we meet the new version, *canzone da sonar,* or *canzone* to be played —that is, played instead of sung. The distinction is an important one. It points first to the fact that music up to this time could have been performed by either a vocal or an instrumental group, or by both, that the composer henceforth found it necessary to specify which group he had in mind, and that the possibility of distinguishing between vocal and instrumental style was at hand.

Many other works of this period included the phrase *da sonare o cantare* or *da sonare e cantare:* they could be sung and/or played. Works so designated were obviously not independently instrumental, but were hybrids, partly in vocal style and yet not sufficiently removed from vocal to be in instrumental style. The chief difference between these hybrids and the purely *da sonar* works was that the latter were tending toward a type of workmanship that took into account the mechanics, characteristics, and sonorities of the viols, *cornetti,* or woodwinds for which they were meant. Hence the former, the "and/or" variety, are on a side path, so to speak, and do not lead to the independent instrumental style, the development of which is one of the great achievements of the Baroque period.

The original *canzoni* for organ written in the period from 1523

[19] Most histories credit Maschera's publication of 1584 as being the first in this category. The latest authority, Eunice Crocker (ibid., p. 109), has uncovered much valuable information about the early history of the *canzone.*

[20] Vincenti at Venice, in 1596, published a collection containing *canzoni* by Merulo, Guami, and others. Amadino, also at Venice, published a work of Banchieri's that contains several *canzoni alla francesa a quattro voci per sonar.* Floriano Canale composed nineteen *canzoni da sonar a quattro,* published by Vincenti in 1600. These are only a few items drawn from Miss Crocker's extensive bibliography of *canzoni* ("Italian Canzona," Appendix, Vol. II).

to about 1597 were of three different types, the characteristics of which were quickly taken over by the composers of instrumental *canzoni* of the type just mentioned. The three were: (1) those whose chief appeal lay in florid, elaborate ornamentation or coloring, a type that lost ground when the form was transferred to instrumental ensembles and that had little influence on the evolution of subsequent forms; (2) those that were in imitative style throughout and were closely related to another form, the *ricercare*, which turned out to be the ancestor of the fugue; (3) those characterized by many short sections in contrasting duple and triple meter, in a diversity of styles very much akin to the French chanson discussed above. The two latter types, one largely contrapuntal and in one meter throughout, the other homophonic to some extent and characterized by many short sections in contrasting meter, existed side by side throughout the late sixteenth and the early seventeenth centuries. The first of these, the formally unified type, is less significant here; its later history, however, leads to Henry Purcell, and it will be taken up again when that composer is reached. The other, the type with many short and diversified sections, was of immediate and great importance in the further evolution of chamber-music forms and will be discussed as a characteristic of the later Venetian school of composers, of which Giovanni Gabrieli is an outstanding exponent.

This younger Gabrieli (1557–c. 1612), a nephew of the Andrea Gabrieli mentioned earlier, was, like his uncle, an organist at St. Mark's in Venice. He was another of the long line of famous Venetian organists and composers that had begun with Adrian Willaert early in the sixteenth century, that included such men as Cipriano de Rore, Claudio Merulo, Andrea Gabrieli, and that was later to number Claudio Monteverdi among its members. To the Venetian school is ascribed the first general use of the antiphonal principle in western Europe, a principle that makes use of two organs or two choirs heard alternately. Giovanni Gabrieli, as one of the most distinguished composers of this school, inherited the traditional use of the double organ and the choir. And he inherited the instrumental *canzone da sonar*, to whose literature he contributed a number of works. His collection,

Sacrae symphoniae, published by Gardano at Venice in 1597, contains forty-five motets, fourteen *canzoni da sonar*, and two sonatas. This collection was one of the most important works of the early period of *canzone* composition (1572–1600). The *canzoni* included in it are typically Baroque in their brilliant writing and display; in them Gabrieli carried the antiphonal principle at least as far as any of his predecessors. They are full of great masses of sound, and they show the first extensive use of the sectional principle characteristic of the third type of *canzoni* mentioned above, a principle that was to be of great importance in the early years of the seventeenth century.

Another innovation of Gabrieli's was the use of more than four voices (*voice* is here used in the contrapuntal sense, meaning a separate musical line or part, and does not refer to the singing voice). Some of his later *canzoni*, in a posthumous publication of 1615, are for as many as twenty-two voices.[21] The dramatic impact of this music when heard for the first time must have been tremendous. It is small wonder that the music of Gabrieli contributed to the speedy decay of the pure, reserved style we associate with the works of Palestrina.[22]

The main element of expressiveness in works of this type is to be found in some manifestation of the principle of alternation. An eight-voice *canzone da sonar*, with unspecified instrumentation,[23] from Gabrieli's *Sacrae symphoniae* of 1597, may serve as an example.[24] The work contains seven sections ranging in length from three to twenty-four measures, and an alternation of two dissimilar elements

[21] *Canzoni et sonate—per sonar con ogni sorte di istrumenti.*

[22] So quickly was that style outmoded and misunderstood that Giovanni Francesco Anerio (c. 1567–c. 1620) provided some of Palestrina's Masses with instrumental accompaniment; a similar fate befell some of Lasso's motets. And the famous Palestrina *Missa Papae Marcelli* was enlarged, provided with a *basso continuo*, and transcribed for a gigantic polyphonic chorus (quoted by Lang, *Music in Western Civilization*, p. 324). See Arnold, *The Art of Accompaniment from a Thorough-Bass*, p. 90n.

[23] Particular instruments were rarely specified in sixteenth-century compositions. Crocker ("Italian Canzona," I, 233) mentions the fact that a few of Gabrieli's *canzoni* have a specified instrumentation, but that this was unique in the early litterature.

[24] Reprinted in Riemann, *Old Chamber Music*, Vol. I.

is manifested in several ways (see Table II, A). Additional manifestations of this principle appeared in the seventeenth and eighteenth

TABLE II

A. MANIFESTATIONS OF ALTERNATION IN A GABRIELI *Canzone*

Tempo	slow	fast
Meter	duple	triple
Instrumentation	first group	second group
Texture	four-voice	eight-voice
Dynamics	loud	soft
Style	contrapuntal	note-against-note
Mood	strongly rhythmical	introspective, lyrical

B. LATER MANIFESTATIONS

Theme (in rondo)	A theme	B theme
Mass (in concerto)	concertino	ripieno
Harmony (in sonata)	tonic group	dominant group

centuries to contribute to still more varied expression (Table II, B).

Gabrieli was among the first to employ the sectional principle consistently and among the leaders in writing for more than four parts.[25] Until his works became generally known, other composers in other localities wrote *canzoni* in the old way, with four voices and a rather unified formal scheme (that is, in one meter and one tempo throughout). Among them were Floriano Canale in Brescia, Gaspar Costa and Agostino Soderino in Milan, and Aurelio Bonelli and Adriano Banchieri in Bologna.

Even in the old form, that is, in the *canzoni* written in one meter throughout, there were sections well marked by cadences and by shifts from contrapuntal to a more homophonic style. In the truly sectional type the consecutive sections were, of course, marked by the most obvious of contrasts, a contrast brought about by a change from

[25] In both these innovations, members of the earlier Venetian school had led the way. Francesco Spongia and Claudio Merulo, Gabrieli's predecessors, had occasionally written sectional *canzoni,* and occasionally a texture for more than four voices had appeared. But what were tendencies in the older Venetians became characteristics in Gabrieli, and it was the latter's work that influenced later composers. See Crocker, "Italian Canzona," I, 181, 244, 246 ff.

duple to triple meter, or vice versa. Thus in both types composers adhered to a structure that originally had been necessary (in the French chanson) because of the strophic text, but now was merely a matter of traditional usage. Consequently in none of the *canzoni* from 1572 to those appearing in the first decades of the seventeenth century was real unity of form possible. That development had to wait until composers attacked the problem from the other side. Instead of attempting to achieve unity within the many sections of the *canzone,* they expanded each individual section to greater length. Finally, through sheer size the *canzone* fell apart into a number of separate movements of contrasting style, tempo, and meter. We shall see the course of that development in the chapters that follow.

THE FLORENTINE CAMERATA

The Renaissance had been largely successful in rediscovering the art, architecture, and to some extent the literature of classic Greece. From the fourteenth century through the seventeenth the forms, aesthetic purposes, and styles of those fields became known to educated Europeans, were widely imitated, and became the bases upon which the new forms of the Renaissance were constructed. A rebirth of Greek music had not fared as well. It was suspected that music had been combined with speech to form the Greek drama, but detailed knowledge was lacking.

In the 1580s, at Florence, steps were taken to effect this rebirth of Greek music. A group of noblemen, poets, and musicians met at the home of Count Bardi to engage in aesthetic discussions about the classic arts. The members of this group, called the Camerata, felt keenly that however successful artists in other fields had been in reviving classic forms and practices, musicians had not realized anew the supposed union of speech and music. The Camerata, among whose members were Ottavio Rinuccini, a poet, and Vincenzo Galilei, Emilio del Cavalieri, Jacopo Peri, and Giulio Caccini, musicians, experimented to restore the supposed connection. But instead of realizing their aim of rediscovering the past, they stumbled upon an entirely new mode of expression and gave birth to a new style—

accompanied recitative. The particular part of their accomplishments that concerns us here centers in their development, out of this new style, of the principle of monody: the use of a solo vocal line accompanied by a bass instrument. The new principle is of basic importance in the great bulk of seventeenth-century music and of great influence on the future course of all music.

Vincenzo Galilei, the father of the astronomer, was one of the Camerata's leading figures. He felt that the union of speech and music must be achieved by subordinating the music—in other words, by letting a sort of singing speech carry the textual idea. The singing was to mirror the actual speech rhythm and be supported at appropriate places by chords having the dual function of enhancing the punctuation of the text and relating the melody to a particular mode or tonality. To illustrate his principles Galilei set to music parts of the Lamentations of Jeremiah and portions of pastoral poems written by fellow Camerata members. Others of the group, notably Peri and Caccini, followed the same principles and emerged with the style that was to make opera possible.

The monodic principle consists of several factors. First there is the essential idea that the function of the music is to carry the text, and nothing more. There should be no preoccupation with making the music expressive in its own right, no concern with lyric melody, no formal ideas of balance or symmetry in the musical form that results. The words of the text are recited to music, and out of that idea grows the second factor.

The second factor is concerned with the melodic shape implied in the word *recitative*—a melodic shape whose contour follows to some extent the natural inflections of the speaking voice, whose rhythm reflects the natural rhythm established by the text itself. Now, when the inflections of the dramatic speaking voice, with its natural cadences and rhythms, its rise and fall in intensity, its very punctuation, are all mirrored in the music, it becomes possible for the music to transmit the emotions implicit in the text. The second factor is also concerned with the proper proportion between melody and accompaniment, insuring that the melody will always be more important than the lowly accompaniment—this in keeping with Galilei's idea that the music (that is, the accompaniment) must always be subordinated to the text.

The third factor, the accompaniment itself, includes the bass line, the choice of chords implied by the interaction of melody and bass, and the manner of performing the chords; this aggregate is brought together in the term *basso continuo*, or continuous bass. In its simplest form the bass was a continuous line of long notes corresponding to whole and half notes in modern notation. The function of the bass line was not to provide a pleasing countermelody below the superior reciting melody but simply to act as a foundation upon which chords could be erected. Actually the idea of using a bass line to accompany a melody was not an innovation of the Camerata. As early as 1553 Diego Ortiz had published at Rome a treatise dealing with this problem.[26] During the course of time (we are dealing with the years between 1580 and about 1600) several other kinds of bass line had come into use; these are distinguished by the terms *basso generale, basso seguente,* and *basso ostinato.*[27] While the new bass types all played their part in seventeenth-century music, and while they differ to some extent from the *basso continuo,* we shall ignore their special characteristics and treat them all together under the term *basso continuo*—which is exactly what seventeenth-century musicians did with them. But one related new term must be introduced at this point—figured bass, a device for indicating chords in these two-voice (melody and bass) compositions.

The origin of the figures to indicate chord intervals is not very clear. In the earliest preserved works that first show the *basso generale* type (1594) sharps and flats had appeared above certain bass notes

---

[26] *Trattado de glosas sopra clausulas y otro generos de puntos en la musica de violones* ("Treatise on Ornaments over Cadences and Other Kinds of Notes in Music for Bass Viols").

[27] For more exact details about these types of basses see Kinkeldey, *Orgel und Klavier in der Musik des 16ten Jahrhunderts,* p. 198; Arnold, *The Art of Accompaniment from a Thorough-Bass;* and the general reference books.

to indicate that the corresponding chords were to have major or minor thirds.[28] At any rate, the figured bass did appear in two of the earliest operas,[29] and in the course of the next decades was widely copied. Many divergent practices existed side by side in those early years, some composers indicating every chord, some figuring more sparsely, and some not at all. For more than one hundred fifty years (as late as 1765) theoretical works appeared that gave instructions for using unfigured basses but recommended that composers use the figured type.[30]

There were, then, these four main forms of bass, the device of figuring being common to all. Many of these main forms were loosely grouped together under the common term *basso continuo*. Later, when tradition had settled upon a keyboard instrument to carry the bass line and fill in the indicated or implied chords (with doublings of the bass line by a cello and/or bass viol, trombone, or bassoon), this whole factor of the accompaniment was called *continuo*, and it was incorrectly spoken of (and still is) as "playing the *continuo*," as if it were an instrument.

Composers of the Camerata created the opera by setting pastoral poems to music in the new monodic recitative style. But they also applied the style to other media, and one result of this activity is Giulio Caccini's collection of madrigals and canzonettas published in 1601, which he proudly entitled *Le nuove musiche*. These are solo songs with a figured *basso continuo*, true enough; but they are not all in the recitative style. It is apparent that even the innovators themselves realized that the new monodic principle need not be confined to recitation, but could become the vehicle for lyric melody as well.

It is argued by some historians that the Camerata achieved little that was really new. They point to the close union of text and music

[28] Arnold, *The Art of Accompaniment from a Thorough-Bass*, pp. 7–9.
[29] Both named *Eurydice*, one by Peri and the other by Caccini.
[30] Arnold, *The Art of Accompaniment from a Thorough-Bass*, pp. 66–67. Arnold mentions Werckmeister's *Harmonologia musica*, Gasparini's *L'armonico practico al cimbalo*, Heinichen's *Der General-Bass in der Composition*, and K. P. E. Bach's *Versuch über die wahre Art das Klavier zu spielen*.

in the French chanson; they remind us that long before the 1590s madrigals, motets, and chansons had emerged as solo song accompanied by a bass line; they point to the appearance of an independent accompanied solo in the musical illustrations given by Diego Ortiz in his treatise of 1553; they find that figured bass was known in a rudimentary form to many late sixteenth-century organists. All that remains of the Camerata's efforts, according to this view, is the particular outline of the melody. We might even demolish this remaining achievement by pointing out that plainsong, too, is a kind of recitation, and *its* origin is ancient indeed. Even if one grants that this view has some truth, one essential feature remains.

While the union of text and music had been achieved in the chanson, it was essentially the intellectual aspect of the text that was satisfied. It remained for the Camerata's compositions to satisfy the emotional aspect; not necessarily the emotion expressed by the words, but the emotion implicit in the situation out of which a singer (or speaker) was acting. There is a vast difference between the two. Because of the latter feature it became possible to portray dramatic situations in music even when the text was absent—that is, in instrumental music. The Camerata, in establishing the monodic principle to bring about a union of dramatic text and music, provided the means for dispensing with the text entirely and establishing the possibility of dramatic instrumental music.

The practical results of the new principle of monody were far-reaching. (1) The contrapuntal style, with its short motives and imitative developments, was virtually abandoned by those composers who championed monody. A new style resulted, a style in which only melody and bass were indicated, in which inner voices were created only to complete the harmonies, and in which a note-against-note accompaniment predominated. (2) A new type of melody appeared, a type not dependent upon contrapuntal associates to complete its significance. The melody was self-contained (that is, it had a beginning and an end), was cast in phrase or period form of four or eight measures; and, not being bound by modal restrictions of range and intervals, it contained the possibility of all kinds of emotional expression. This the contrapuntal melody had had only rarely, for it was always one part merely of a polyphonic texture that depended upon the interaction of several melodic fragments for its emotional appeal. (3) The corpus of harmony became more vigorous as the figured-bass notation made convenient and practical the use of a greater variety of chords. At first largely restricted to triads and the few passing dissonances typical of modal harmony, it gradually acquired unprepared dissonances, employed chromatically altered chords, and the like, until the modal aspects of the music were so much weakened that we can speak of the breakdown of modality and the emergence of the tonal system.

2. From Canzone to Sonata da Chiesa

THE CONCEPT of monodic style as defined by its Florentine inventors late in the sixteenth century was broadened considerably early in the seventeenth. The earliest works in this style, composed about 1585, were recitatives with *basso continuo*, and they had led to the creation of opera a decade later. Caccini in his collection of madrigals and canzonettas (1601) had written solo songs also with *basso continuo*, but in a style that approached lyric melody. And in 1602 Viadana published a set of songs entitled *Cento concerti ecclesiastici a 1, 2, 3, 4 voci*, in which the monodic principle was expanded to include multivoiced works.

INSTRUMENTAL ENSEMBLE *Canzone*

Evidence is lacking about the exact steps through which the monodic style was first adopted by instrumental composers; solo instrumental works that correspond to the solo songs of the period do not appear until 1610. The appendix to Viadana's *Cento concerti*, however, contains an instrumental ensemble piece in broadened monodic style written for four instruments. This small piece, tucked away at the end of a set of more pretentious vocal works, may be singled out as the first that conforms to our definition of chamber music. It is designed for instruments alone, not for instruments and/or voices, and its title is *Canzone francese a quattro, a riposta.*[1]

Lodovico Grossi da Viadana was born at Viadana, on the Po River, in northern Italy, about 1564. From 1594 to 1609 he served as chapel-master in the cathedral at Mantua, during which time he joined the

[1] Reprinted in modern notation in Riemann, *Old Chamber Music*, Vol. I.

Franciscan Order (1596) and published the *Cento concerti ecclesiastici* (1602). He held posts as chapelmaster in other cathedral towns in northern Italy (Concordia, 1609; Fano, 1612; Piacenza, 1615; etc.) and died in a Franciscan convent at Gualtieri in 1645. Viadana wrote many psalms, canticles, and other religious music, but he is remembered primarily for the *Cento concerti*. To him is ascribed the invention of the term *basso continuo*, although the device itself and its related forms (for example, *basso generale* and *basso principale*) were in use in the sixteenth century.

The title of the piece may be translated "French Chanson for Quartet, in Responsive Style," the quartet in this case being a violin, a *cornetto*, and two trombones, with an unfigured *basso continuo*. It is interesting to observe, and important to remember, that the *continuo* was never included in the numbering of the voices. According to the practice of the times, which practice soon became traditional, this work was performed by the four instruments just mentioned plus a keyboard instrument. Similarly, duo sonatas for violin and bass, let us say, often turn out to be trios in performance (we shall meet such works later in the century) when the keyboard instrument is added. It should not be surprising, then, on examining the Viadana *Canzone francese* to find that we have to do with a quintet. Nor is the combination of instruments as strange as would appear at first sight, for a *cornetto* is not a cornet. The former, known as *Zink* in Germany, was an instrument made of wood or ivory like a flute or recorder, but with a cup mouthpiece like a trumpet or horn. Its tone was closer to a woodwind than to a brass instrument, and it provided a quality between the violin and the trombone. As late as 1670 it was often substituted for the violin.

The *Canzone* contains several stylistic innovations. As indicated above, it is probably the first instrumental ensemble work that is written in monodic style; all earlier *canzoni*, including the transcriptions of vocal chansons, were in polyphonic style. Its inclusion of *basso continuo* implies a dominant melody and a subordinate non-melodic bass line. And although written for four instruments, it is in effect for two pairs of two each; one melody and one accompanying

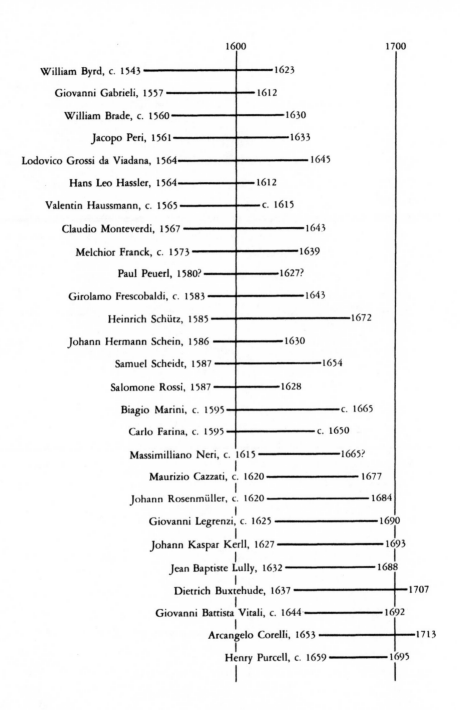

1600   1700

William Byrd, c. 1543 ———————— 1623

Giovanni Gabrieli, 1557 ——————— 1612

William Brade, c. 1560 ———————— 1630

Jacopo Peri, 1561 ————————— 1633

Lodovico Grossi da Viadana, 1564 ———————————— 1645

Hans Leo Hassler, 1564 ———————— 1612

Valentin Haussmann, c. 1565 ——————— c. 1615

Claudio Monteverdi, 1567 —————————— 1643

Melchior Franck, c. 1573 —————————— 1639

Paul Peuerl, 1580? ——————————— 1627?

Girolamo Frescobaldi, c. 1583 ——————————— 1643

Heinrich Schütz, 1585 ——————————————— 1672

Johann Hermann Schein, 1586 ————————— 1630

Samuel Scheidt, 1587 ———————————————— 1654

Salomone Rossi, 1587 ——————————— 1628

Biagio Marini, c. 1595 ——————————————— c. 1665

Carlo Farina, c. 1595 ————————————— c. 1650

Massimilliano Neri, c. 1615 ——————————— 1665?

Maurizio Cazzati, c. 1620 ———————————————— 1677

Johann Rosenmüller, c. 1620 ——————————————— 1684

Giovanni Legrenzi, c. 1625 ———————————————— 1690

Johann Kaspar Kerll, 1627 ——————————————— 1693

Jean Baptiste Lully, 1632 ————————————— 1688

Dietrich Buxtehude, 1637 ———————————————— 1707

Giovanni Battista Vitali, c. 1644 ——————————— 1692

Arcangelo Corelli, 1653 ——————————————— 1713

Henry Purcell, c. 1659 ———————— 1695

LIFE SPANS OF PRINCIPAL SEVENTEENTH-CENTURY COMPOSERS

instrument are grouped, announce the themes, and are then echoed by the other similiar group. The piece turns out to be essentially a series of accompanied phrases for two pairs of instruments and may be considered an early representative of a long line of *canzoni* for less than four instruments, a line that will later be seen to be of great importance. In these respects Viadana's work is of considerable historical interest.

As indicated by its title, the *Canzone* is antiphonal (that is, in responsive style) throughout. The melodic material consists of a large number of motives ranging in length from two to eleven beats; each motive is accompanied by a differently styled bass motive. We speak of beats (single half notes) rather than measures here, because the diversity of 2/2, 3/2, and 3/4 measures in the modern transcription would not permit the comparative lengths of the motives to be shown accurately.

No bass motive is quite like another. Sometimes it consists of a few whole notes; sometimes it is in the same rhythm but in contrary motion to the melody; often it is purely contrapuntal and provides a brief bit of countermelody. On two occasions it serves merely as a harmonic bass, and in one place it forms a canon at the octave for three measures. This example of canonic imitation between bass and melody is strong evidence that very soon after its inception the monodic style began to take up again elements of the discarded polyphony of the sixteenth century.

There is thus a strange mixture of old and new in this work, a mixture of melodic and harmonic association between the two voices of each pair that points to both the sixteenth and the seventeenth centuries at once. The shape of the melodies, too, is worthy of attention, and again represents a mixture of the two periods (see Example 2).

The first melody, for example, is a typical *canzone* type, with the familiar dactyl *canzone* trademark. The second and ninth are self-contained melodic units that would not, except for their typically modal cadence patterns, sound out of place in an eighteenth-century work. Others are scale fragments; still others are merely rhythmic figures with no melodic contour to speak of.

Example 2   Viadana, *Canzone francese*

This *canzone* consists of three well-defined parts, with the first part roughly as long as the other two (53–27–22 measures, respectively, in the three parts). But the third part contains an exact recapitulation of the first ten measures of the first part. There is thus a distinct and recognizable three-part form, in spite of the unequal lengths of the first and third sections. In all three parts one characteristic is very prominent: the difference in the spacing of the responsive entrances, of the entrance of the second pair of voices carrying the same melody as the first. For example, in the first section one pair of voices is heard in the first melody, the second pair "answers" with the same melody after eleven beats; the same melody is heard again in the first pair, but this time the answer in the second pair comes after seven beats; then five melodies, each one shorter than the previous one (ten, eight, five, three, and two beats, respectively) are heard, first in one pair of voices, then in the other. That characteristic appears throughout the entire *canzone*. Why is this difference in distance important?

One of the ways in which the listener to music is moved, one of the ways in which an emotional effect is achieved, is by altering the degree of the listener's attention to the music. Let any particular texture or style or melodic device be continued for a considerable length of time; the listener will be attentive at first, less attentive as the music goes on, and finally become inattentive. But let the texture, style, or melodic device be changed and his attention is restored; he again listens. In this alternation between attention and the relaxation of attention, between different states of emotional tension, lies one of music's powers to affect the emotional interest of the listener. Now, if it be realized that in any pair of antiphonal entrances the second one of the pair momentarily reattracts the listener's attention and provides an emotional accent through the mere fact of entering the tonal structure, it will be seen how a closer series of entrances increases the attention and thereby the emotional interest of the listener. Further, if the texture is changed from a two-voice to a four-voice section, with the temporary abandonment of the antiphonal device, the emotional interest is increased.

Both these devices are present in the Viadana *Canzone* and give evidence of intelligent planning of musical effects. The antiphonal entrances come closer together as the end of each of the three sections is approached, and at each section's end the four instruments are heard together in the cadence that terminates the section. Thus the interest of the listener is increased, and he experiences the three-part form; for after each cadence a pair of more distant entrances is heard, and he may momentarily relax again. The degrees of emotional tension and relaxation may be diagramed in somewhat the following

A: 53 measures   B: 27 measures   C: 22 measures

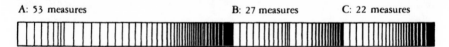

way. A greater degree of shading represents a thickening of texture, or closeness of entrance, or both. It is not to the point here to discuss whether Viadana was the first to achieve this expressive device. But the device is of considerable importance here and later in the century as one means of making a rather amorphous texture able to convey musical interest and emotional excitement to the listener, and to provide a degree of aesthetic pleasure.

In another *canzone* of the period a completely different procedure for obtaining musical coherence is found. *Capriccio a 4, canzone da sonar* by Giovanni Grillo[2] employs a sectional structure to a greater extent than do the *canzoni* of Giovanni Gabrieli (see p. 19). But a form that is symmetrical in large and small detail results nevertheless (see Table III). In this work the ten sections—one might almost call them fragments—are brought into relationship through the use of symmetry alone.

TABLE III

FORM OF A *Canzone* BY GRILLO

Sections	Type	Number of measures	First chord and cadence	Form	
1	Imitative	7	G–G	a	
2	Galliard	11	G–D	b	A
3	Imitative	21	G–G	a	
4	Pavane	4 & 6	C–C	introduction and c	
5	Galliard	8	C–C	d	B
6	Pavane	6	F–G	c	
7	Galliard	8 & 4	G–D	e and extension	
8	Imitative	7	G–G	a	
9	Galliard	11	G–D	b	A
10	Imitative	5	G–G	a	

THE ENGLISH FANCY

The practice of transcribing and "coloring" preexistent vocal works for an ensemble of instruments, which gave rise to the instrumental *canzone* in Italy, led to a somewhat different result in England. There, in place of French chansons, polyphonic motets provided source material for such transcriptions. A mid-sixteenth-century repertoire of instrumental ensemble arrangements based on motets exists in large

[2] Published by Raverii in a collection of *canzoni*, Venice, 1608, and reprinted by Riemann, *Handbuch der Musikgeschichte*, II², 116–38. Hereafter the latter work will be cited as *HM*.

quantities.[3] An outgrowth of this practice in turn led to a specifically English form: an original polyphonic composition for instruments, in which a single plainsong melody served as a *cantus firmus*. That melody, "Gloria tibi Trinitas," used in a Mass by John Taverner (c. 1495–1545), was employed by scores of composers for over a century in a new form that came to be known as an *In nomine*. An ensemble of two to six instruments was most often called upon.

More than a hundred fifty works in this form are known. Tallis, Tye, Parsons, Byrd, Ferrabosco, Purcell, and many other English composers from about 1530 to the 1680s composed *In nomines*. The earliest of these works resemble textless motets in form and texture. They are most usually written in one long and continuous part, characterized by overlapping of voices and sections. Little evidence of instrumental style is found; scalewise passages and small leaps in an essentially vocal idiom are most usual. Later *In nomines*, roughly after 1560, are closer to an instrumental idiom in their use of repeated notes and wide leaps; and occasionally an *In nomine* is composed in the metrical pattern of a pavane or a galliard.

The Fantasy (Fancy). The *In nomine* was in effect a special type of a larger class of English instrumental ensemble music written in contrapuntal style. Based on its relationship to the Italian *canzone*, which was sometimes called *ricercare* or *fantasia*, the English version became known as a *fantasy* or a *fancy*. It differed from the *In nomine* in not being based on a *cantus firmus* melody but in being freely composed in all respects; and the overlapping of sections characteristic of the older *In nomine* was given up in favor of a clearly sectional structure. The earliest fantasies for consorts of viols date from a few decades before 1600 and were composed by such men as William Byrd, Alfonso Ferrabosco, Sr., and Thomas Morley.

At the beginning of the seventeenth century the sectional structure represented in the fantasies of Morley was maintained, but successive sections were often given melodic material different in character from the material of the first section. Fantasies by Thomas Lupo, Giovanni

---

[3] Meyer, *English Chamber Music*, pp. 82, 83, gives composers and titles.

Coperario (Cooper), and Alfonso Ferrabosco, Jr., are of this type,[4] and some of them add an element of dramatic contrast to the sections as well. Later fantasies, especially those by Orlando Gibbons (1583–1625), the greatest master of the period about 1620, carry the sectional principle to the point of setting successive sections in contrasting meter and in extending them to such lengths that miniature movements result (the relationship of this to parallel developments in the Italian sonata is close [see p. 47]); and the later movements are often cast in dance rhythms. But at the same time other fantasies reveal a reduction of contrast between sections and employ the same thematic material in each section; the result is a form resembling a fugue, in which each section corresponds to a fugal exposition.[5]

Side by side with these developments came a tendency to remove elements of vocal style from the melodic material itself. Earlier fantasies, based largely on undulating scale passages, had been modeled on vocal forms such as the motet, as indicated above. By the first quarter of the seventeenth century instrumental idioms had become

Example 3

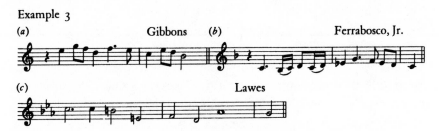

characteristic; melodies such as those seen in Example 3 appeared in greater number, and often the individual parts exceeded two octaves in range.[6] And finally, a degree of brilliance approaching the concertante style was achieved (see Example 4).

A decline in the general progress of English chamber music took place after about 1620 that parallels the general decline of madrigal composition at that time. A few isolated compositions, notably by William Lawes (1602–45), kept the genre alive. Somewhat influ-

[4] Ibid., p. 132.   [5] Ibid., p. 158.   [6] Ibid., p. 163.

Example 4   Gibbons, *Fantasia a 3*

enced by Italian madrigalisms and expressive dissonance in general, Lawes brought a subjective, experimental air to the fantasy. His relaxed contrapuntal style often approached homophony, and on a few occasions he employed *basso continuo*. Further, several of his fantasies served as first movements in sets of dances; this also parallels Italian developments, as we shall see below (see p. 71).

Lawes's older and longer-lived contemporary, John Jenkins (1592–1678), essentially a conservative composer at first, was able to adopt a more modern style at an advanced age. More than a hundred fantasies for two to six viols, many of them written in a polyphonic and imitative style, represent a manner that had become old-fashioned by the middle of the seventeenth century. Another group of fantasies for five and six viols are essentially homophonic in style and are probably adapted to a more popular taste. And another set, possibly from the 1660s or later, are for violins rather than viols, and some include parts for *basso continuo*.

Younger composers include Christopher Simpson (?–1669) and Matthew Locke (1630–77). Locke absorbed some of the bold harmonic style of Lawes and wrote with equal facility for groups of viols or of violins; but much of his work is in the form of the dance suite, and his fantasies are relatively few. Among the last fantasies to be written were sixteen by Henry Purcell (c. 1659–1695) about 1680, in the general harmonic style of Lawes and without *basso continuo.* The majority of Purcell's chamber-music compositions were in the field of the *sonata da chiesa,* however; they will be discussed below (see p. 53).

EARLY BAROQUE STYLE ELEMENTS

The Canzone. The differences that had distinguished various *canzone* types early in the history of the form became more pronounced toward 1610. About that time three types of *canzoni* existed. One type, written for more than four voices under the influence of Gabrieli's *canzoni a* 8, traveled far afield and emerged in Germany in the works of Hans Leo Hassler, Samuel Scheidt, Hermann Schein, and others. Hassler's *Sacri concentus* of 1601,[7] for example, includes three *canzoni a* 8 modeled on those of Gabrieli. These larger works were in general inclined toward chord masses and homophonic style. The *basso continuo* was of small importance in them and resembled the *basso seguente* type, with figuring sparsely employed. This type went into a decline shortly after 1620.

A second type, for the traditional four voices, attracted conservative composers in general, tended to remain somewhat contrapuntal, and often appeared without *basso continuo.* Representative composers of this type were Salomone Rossi (Mantua, 1608), Tarquinio Merula (Venice, 1615), and Francesco Lucino (Milan, 1617); the latter's collection was among the last to be devoted mainly to the *canzone a* 4. This traditional type also began to decline about 1620.

A third type, for fewer than four voices, became the most important in its influence on later developments. *Canzoni* of this type, for two or three instruments, provided the greatest amount of innovation and progressive change; and composers of this type showed considerable interest in the possibilities of varied instrumentation. Independent instrumental style came closer and a specific instrumentation was often called for. In the use of the *basso continuo,* too, the smaller *canzoni* differed from their larger relatives. The bass line approached a melodic contour, took a greater part in thematic imitations, and

[7] Reprinted in *Denkmäler deutscher Tonkunst, erste Folge,* Vols. XXIV and XXV. Hereafter this work will be cited as *DDT.*

tended to be more completely figured. The last characteristic was probably made necessary by the incomplete triads in the two parts above the bass. Finally, in general content the *canzone a* 2 and *canzone a* 3 found it desirable to provide for particular instrumental effects, because the thinness of the tonal structure brought simple chord progressions and routine imitations close to the point of monotony. Giulio Belli (1613), Giovanni Battista Riccio (1614 and 1620), and Biagio Marini (1617) were among the many progressive contributors to the literature of the smaller *canzoni*.

A considerable amount of confusion is attached to the naming and instrumentation of works with less than three or four instruments. In a composition (whether *canzone* or the later sonata) referred to as a "solo" one could expect to find the solo instrument accompanied by a *basso continuo* that in turn was doubled by another bass instrument. But the same piece could also be called a "duo." Conversely, a duo or *canzone a* 2 could take at least three forms: (1) the version just described, for solo plus *basso continuo;* (2) solo with *basso continuo,* in which the accompaniment was doubled by a bass instrument that took some part in the thematic work; (3) two solo instruments (two violins, say, or violin and viol da gamba) unaccompanied.[8]

The Sonata. Even while the *canzone* was undergoing these external stylistic changes, still other changes were taking place within the form itself. The internal changes became marked after about 1608 and shortly thereafter crystallized into a new and separate form, the sonata. From about 1610 one may justifiably speak of both the sonata and sonata style, even though a lack of uniformity in labeling forms in this period was most characteristic. A number of terms were used almost interchangeably and often meant different things to different composers. The terms *sinfonia, concerto, fantasia,* along with

[8] The symbols suggested by Newman (*The Sonata in the Baroque Era*, pp. 52, 53), if generally adopted, would end this confusion. In his system the three types listed here would be shown as S/bass, SB/bass, and SS- or SA- or SB-, respectively. The letters themselves refer to soprano, alto, etc., and indicate the relative ranges of the participating instruments. The trio sonata, the most usual instrumentation of Baroque chamber music until about 1700 (to be discussed at length in the following pages), is most usually SS/bass or SSB/bass, depending on whether or not the *basso continuo* was doubled.

canzone and *sonata,* appeared in a great variety of pieces near the beginning of the century. In time they took on their specialized meanings, and by 1650 the confusion had disappeared to a considerable degree.

Elements of sonata style can be traced back well into the sixteenth century, in the organ *canzoni* of Andrea Gabrieli (about 1575) and in the instrumental *canzoni* as well as the sonata *Pian e forte* (1597) of Giovanni Gabrieli. Sonata style elements are found in the *canzone* long after the sonata had achieved a separate form; and at that time many sonatas still contained elements of *canzone* style. Much of the confusion in accounts of early seventeenth-century music history comes from the fact that the two styles were at first so closely bound. The elements of sonata style may perhaps be seen most clearly if they are compared to those of *canzone* style in schematic fashion (see p. 40).

EARLY SONATAS

The collections of sonatas in the period under discussion (about 1600 to 1620) include works by Giovanni Gabrieli, Giovanni Paolo Cima, Salomone Rossi, Biagio Marini, and many others, most of whom also composed collections of *canzoni*. *Concerti . . . e sei sonate,* by Cima (Milan, 1610), includes probably the first work composed for solo violin and bass.[10] Idiomatic string figures—leaps, undulating scale passages, and the like—in both parts of one of the sonatas suggest that the lower part was not to be realized at the harpsichord and that this is a true instrumental duet.

Rossi. Another new feature introduced into the sonatas of this period is the set of variations, perhaps the earliest of which is found in the sonatas of Salomone Rossi (1560?–1630?). Two sonatas that contain variation sets are found in his set of *Varie sonate* (1613),[11]

---

[10] Reprinted in Beckmann, ed. *Das Violinspiel in Deutschland vor 1700: 12 Sonaten.*

[11] Riemann, HM, II², 87–94. The full title of this work is *Il 3 lib. de varie sonate, sinfonie, gagliarde, brandi e corrente per sonar 2 viol da braccia & un chittarone, o altro stromento simile* (Venice: Vincenti, 1613). Further information is given in Newman, *The Sonata in the Baroque Era,* pp. 111–13.

COMPARISON OF STYLE ELEMENTS[9]

	Canzone	Sonata
FORM	Most often continuous, without tempo alteration or metrical change.	Often broken by change of tempo and meter. The triple-meter fragment in the early *canzone* was itself an element of sonata style. Sometimes the piece is in the form of a set of variations.
TEXTURE	Derived from a contrapuntal, imitative style. Equality of voices was typical.	Largely homophonic or in note-against-note style; instrumental figurations often were characteristic. Upper and lower voices took on added importance, with a consequent decline of the importance of inner voices.
MELODIC MATERIAL	Short, motivelike phrases, with repeated notes much in evidence. Dactylic motive at beginning most usual. No great rhythmic diversity; scalewise passage work common.	A distinct effort to lengthen melodic lines and to achieve expressiveness in four- or eight-measure phrases. Greater range in the melody and greater care in melodic details, often accompanied by phrasing indications and a tendency to employ instrumental idioms.
METRICAL UNIT	Quarter-note dominated, giving the effect of a moderately fast tempo.	Note values ranged from a half note to a sixteenth, with half note the prevailing unit, thus giving the effect of a slow tempo.
RHYTHM AND METER	Definite beat was typical, and duple meter was most usual.	More diverse in rhythm; being primarily expressive, it avoided the regular pulse typical of the *canzone*.
INSTRUMENTAL MEDIUM	Not greatly concerned with medium; the traditional *canzone a 4* did not specify instrumentation.	Viols or (later) violins most usually specified for the two voices above the bass.

[9] This summary of elements of the two opposing styles is based on Crocker, "Italian Canzona," I, 375–83, where numerous examples are given.

for two viole da gamba and *basso continuo.* One is "On the Romanesca Air," the other "On the Air of Ruggiero." The two tunes that
supply the themes for these variation sets were extremely popular in
their day and inspired many composers, both vocal and instrumental,
to treat them as Rossi did. Rossi, however, was the first to set them
for instrumental groups.[12] Each sonata contains eight variations over
a *basso ostinato;* each variation is confined to one type of figuration.
The figurations found here grow naturally out of the instrumentation
Rossi employed. This type of trio setting became the most widely
used chamber-music combination throughout the seventeenth century.

Rossi's first experiments with string instrument trios date back to
1607 and 1608, to two collections, *Sinfonie e gagliarde a 3, 4, et 5
voci . . . per sonar 2 viole, oueri 2 cornetti, et un chittarone.* The
first *sinfonia* of the second book[13] is entirely homophonic, with the
two viols playing in thirds above an angular bass line. By 1622, the
date of his fourth collection, he has specified violins instead of viols
and indicated the bass simply as *basso continuo.* This is among the
earliest examples of that instrumental combination in the century;
other early trios had been optionally for viole da braccio or violins, or
else had permitted the substitution of *cornetti.*

The "Romanesca" and "Ruggiero" variation-sonatas of 1613 still
employ two violas, as indicated above. Parallel thirds are basic to the
style; but with them appears a new device that contributed much to
the future of instrumental style—the figuration is distributed between the two instruments. Example 5 will show the device (taken
from the "Ruggiero" sonata).

Example 5   Rossi, "Ruggiero" Sonata

The antiphonal or responsive style, the principle of alternating two
opposing groups, is again at work here, even if in a miniature way.

[12] Crocker, "Italian Canzona," I, 395.
[13] Reprinted in Haas, "Die Musik des Barocks," p. 90.

We saw the principle at work in the massive *canzoni* of Gabrieli, in the alternation of two large tonal masses; we saw it again in the *Canzone francese* of Viadana, where it became a factor of the monodic style and was concerned with the alternation of two pairs of instruments and several pairs of long melodies. Here we see it again, this time in the multivoiced sonata, and we see it used to divide a single melodic figuration between two instruments, producing the effect of a single instrument. The type of figuration, the rapid repetition of broken-chord patterns, marks a decided step forward in the evolution of violin style. A comparison of this passage with, let us say, one of Corelli's later in the century will show how the latter was derived from such humble beginnings. Salomone Rossi stands at the very beginning of the line of composers who gradually developed violinistic music. Because of his consistent use of parallel thirds in his trio sonatas as well as in his *sinfonie* and in the variations discussed above, his use of dialoguelike passages between the violins, and his use of note-against-note writing in his instrumental music generally, Rossi must be considered one of the foremost champions of instrumental monody. Further, he was among the earliest composers to employ the instrumentation of the trio sonata.[14]

Marini. The excellent writing and fertile imagination of Biagio Marini (c. 1597–1665) did much to influence the music of the later seventeenth century. Marini was a composer of progressive *canzoni* and, following the lead of Cima (see p. 44), one of the founders of the solo-violin literature; he was also active after the middle of the century in writing in the new forms of that time. His importance lies largely in his contributions to bithematic composition, to the development of two- and three-note chord writing for the violin, and to the evolution of violin technique generally. Marini published his first work, *Affetti musicali*, at Venice in 1617 while he was a violinist in the orchestra of St. Mark's in that city. This work contains two pieces that Marini calls *sinfonie;* both are for solo violin or *cornetto*, with *basso continuo,* and the first includes also an optional part for bass

[14] Riemann, *HM*, II², 139.

viol. Both have subtitles—"La Orlandina" and "La Gardana," respectively.[15]

"La Orlandina" consists of five sections, ranging in length from seven to sixteen measures, containing duple meter in two sections, triple in three, and having a variety of tempos from slow to very fast. It would almost serve as a model for the summary of sonata style given above. The piece begins in homophonic style, with a lyric melody; the metric unit is a half note. Succeeding sections employ more rhythmic diversity. The most obvious difference between this work and a sectional *canzone* is that in the former the imitative section based on the manipulation of the *canzone* dactyl motive is missing. On closer inspection the piece is not nearly as broken up as the formal description would imply. The second, third, and fifth sections all contain figures found in the first section, and the second actually grows out of the first (see Example 6).

Example 6   Marini, "La Orlandina"

[15] "La Orlandina" reprinted in Riemann, *HM*, II², 96–99; "La Gardana" reprinted in Schering, *Geschichte der Musik in Beispielen*, No. 182.

The effect of these works of Marini (published 1617) is quite different from that of the *canzoni* of Gabrieli (1597), Viadana (1602), and Grillo (1608), to mention only those we have examined in detail. In Marini one feels the attempt to establish a longer melodic line—rudimentary, it is true, and characterized by extreme changes of tempo and meter. But the dead stop between sections is not present here, and melodic material used in one section appears in another.

"La Orlandina" and "La Gardana" are important for other reasons also. The reader will recall that few instrumental works representative of solo monody are known in the years immediately following the Camerata's first achievements. In the years since Galilei's experiments took definite shape (c. 1581), there are operas (the two versions of *Eurydice*, 1600), solo monodic songs (Caccini's *Nuove musiche*, 1601), group songs utilizing the monodic principle (Viadana's *Canzone francese*, 1602), and two sonatas for violin and bass (Cima, 1610). These works of Marini mark the real beginning of solo instrumental monody, even though Cima's are a bit earlier. In them is definite evidence of the growth of instrumental style. Types of figuration and passage work found in them are eminently playable on the violin and are entirely unsuited to the voice; broken-chord figures and scale passages that have been stock in trade among string composers ever since the seventeenth century emerge in Marini's work. We saw similar devices above when we examined the trios of Salomone Rossi; those works antedate Marini's by a few years, so we cannot speak of the latter as having established the instrumental style. But Marini's importance in helping at its birth cannot be denied, especially if other works of his are considered.

Among such works are "La Foscarina," another of the *Affetti musicali* of 1617. Here is found probably the first use of the tremolo in violin music, seven years before Monteverdi's more famous use of that device in *Il combattimento di Tancredi e Clorinda*.[16] Later, in his *Sonate, sinfonie, canzoni* . . . (1629), Marini wrote a "caprice in which two violins play in four parts" and a "caprice for solo violin with three strings in the manner of a lyre." [17] Thus Marini, among

[16] Riemann, *HM*, II², 100.   [17] Fragments reprinted ibid., pp. 101–2.

the earliest composers of solo instrumental monodic pieces, is also the first to use the tremolo as well as double and triple stops throughout long passages.

EXPANSION OF FORM

In the second quarter of the seventeenth century a tendency to reduce the number of sections in the sonata became marked. It will be recalled that the *Capriccio a 4* by Grillo (1608) contained ten sections, and Marini's sonata "La Orlandina" (1617) had five. Eventually the sections became longer and ended with definite closing cadences. The result was a compound form consisting of three to five movements in contrasting tempo, meter, and style. That development extends from about 1617 to 1649.

Frescobaldi. A step in this direction is seen in the five *canzoni da sonar* (1623, 1628) by Girolamo Frescobaldi (1583–1643), perhaps the most eminent Italian organist of his time. In his early years Frescobaldi enjoyed an excellent reputation as a singer and organist. He journeyed to Antwerp early in the seventeenth century, and his first madrigals were published there in 1608. In that year he returned to Italy and was appointed organist at St. Peter's in Rome, probably the most honored position in the musical world at that time. He retained the post for twenty years, and after a five-year absence in Tuscany returned to St. Peter's for nine more years, from 1634 until his death.

The mixture of style characteristics in the early seventeenth century is reflected in the *canzoni* of 1623; old-fashioned *canzoni* in imitative style, sectional sonatas, and combinations of the two stand side by side. One of the works is a forerunner of the *sonata da chiesa* and may be examined in detail.[18] The piece is for *due canti e basso*, in five sections: slow triple, fast duple, slow duple, fast triple, and moderate compound, respectively. The third section is simply a phrase five measures long, heard in the bass and imitated once by each of

---

[18] One of the five is reprinted in Riemann, *HM*, II², 142; two others are in Riemann, *Old Chamber Music*, Vol. I.

the upper voices. It is reproduced here as an example of how great beauty is achieved with economy of means (see Example 7).[19]

Example 7   Frescobaldi, *Canzone da sonar*

The features that attract our attention here are found in the first four sections: (1) the use of homophonic style in the first, second, and fourth sections, and the retention of polyphonic style in the second; (2) the slow tempo of the first section, with a consequent lack of *canzone* characteristics; (3) and most important for the future, whereas contrasts between the other sections are introduced abruptly (either through a change from triple to duple meter, or from slow to fast tempo, or both), no such contrast exists between the fourth and the fifth sections. The fifth grows out of the fourth (see Example 8), and the piece as a whole gives the effect of being virtually in four sections. And this Frescobaldi work is not alone in thus relating sections to one another. Many other pieces of the time exhibit the same device, and a work with more than four sections is seldom found after the 1630s.

Nicolas à Kempis. The sections themselves become longer and increasingly independent. For an example of this development we turn to the *Symphoniae 1, 2, 3 violinarum*, by Nicolas à Kempis (c. 1610–60), published in 1644. In these works the tendency is seen to separate the sections entirely and to let each stand alone. The thirteenth *symphonie*,[20] for one violin and bass, is typical of the set. It is in four sections. The first is in slow duple meter and consists merely of

[19] In this place, as in many others, Riemann's overelaborate realization of the *continuo* destroys the charm of Frescobaldi's inspiration.

[20] In Riemann, *Old Chamber Music*, Vol. I.

Example 8   Frescobaldi, *Canzone da sonar*

last two
measures

a broad lyric melody with its repetition. The second section, in fast duple meter, is concerned largely with the development of a short rhythmic motive:

The third section, in slow triple, has a similar motive that is similarly developed; a five-measure extended cadence intervenes between the third and the fourth sections. The fourth section, again in fast duple, has yet another version of the rhythmic motive. Each of the four sections of this work gives the impression of being longer than it really is, because of the skillful avoidance of cadences, the spun-out nature of the phrases, and the sequential treatment of the various motives. Obviously, when cadences appear only two or three times in an extended section (the four sections range from nine to twenty-one measures in length), when they lead to new sections in greatly contrasting tempo and meter, and when a feeling of unity within sections is achieved, the four-movement form is close at hand.

Uccellini. The next decided step forward in the direction of four-movement form can be seen in a work by Marco Uccellini (c. 1605–80), *Delle sonate ovvero canzoni da farsi a violino solo e basso continuo*, Opus 5 (1649).[21] It is now time to speak of separate movements rather than sections. The four parts of this work are extended considerably beyond any we have examined previously. And Uccellini is consistent in his use of one device for achieving this greater length in these monothematic structures: he depends upon sequence repetition of a fairly long phrase, then allows the phrase to dissolve into running scale figures. In this manner he is able to write a piece three

[21] The second sonata reprinted ibid., Vol. IV.

of whose parts (first, second, and fourth) are forty-four, sixty-five, and forty-one measures long, respectively. Only in the third part does he revert to the older practice, for here the part breaks off after six measures. Thus each of the longer parts is more than twice as long as corresponding parts or sections of earlier works in this form. And the feeling of length is enhanced here, as it was in the Nicolas à Kempis work above, by skillful use of cadences, mainly at the end of each part. Further, the use of a well-marked cadence only at the end of a part does more than strengthen a feeling of the part's length; it also serves to separate that part from what follows. Of all the works examined in these pages this is the first that can be said to have separate movements. And what was achieved in this work, and in other contemporary works in which the same tendency is to be observed, became common property in the years following 1649. From that date forward we are no longer justified in speaking of sections in this type of sonata; we shall refer entirely to movements.

Uccellini's earlier works (three books containing *canzoni*, sonatas, and dance pieces), published between 1639 and 1645, had included many works for trio instrumentation. The set under discussion here (Opus 5, 1649), on the other hand, consists of twelve solo sonatas and only one trio sonata. This suggests a tendency to favor the solo type over the trio, and toward the end of the century this tendency became a trend. Possibly the earliest set to contain only solo sonatas is the *Compositione . . . fatto per sonare col fagotto solo* (1645), by an obscure composer named Giovanni Antonio Bertoli; the bassoon part makes virtuosic demands upon the performer.[22] And a large collection of thirty-one sonatas for violin and *basso continuo*, by the equally obscure Giovanni Antonio Leoni (1652), is the first known set to be dedicated entirely to the solo violin. From this point forward, collections tended to be confined to one or the other instrumental combination.

Legrenzi. Giovanni Legrenzi (1626–90), eminent composer of operas, cantatas, and chamber music, was active at Venice as the director of the Conservatory of the Mendicants and during the last

[22] Newman, *The Sonata in the Baroque Era,* p. 117.

five years of his life as chapelmaster of St. Mark's. His Opus 2, published in 1655, contains eighteen *sonate a due e tre;* the thirteenth of the set, entitled "La Valvasona," is for two violins and cello. It contains four movements in the expected fast and slow tempos and in the expected duple and triple meters. The first movement, thirty-three measures long, contains elements reminiscent of the old *ricercare,* yet is in an open, transparent style in which nothing more involved than imitations of previously heard phrases is attempted. The second movement, consisting of sixteen measures in slow tempo, contains a broad lyric melody accompanied in part in homophonic style, in part by bits of countermelody. The third movement, forty-seven measures long, is almost entirely in note-against-note style. The last movement, of twenty measures, is again fugal; the contrapuntal lines accompanying the principal motives are derived from the motives themselves.

The noteworthy features of this sonata are: (1) the four-movement form, with the greatest emphasis put on the first movement (even though the third is a few measures longer); (2) the intrusion of so many contrapuntal elements in a style that is essentially homophonic. These features are found also in other chamber-music works of Legrenzi, notably in another work from Opus 2, "La Savorgnana." [23] But in that work the third movement is extremely short, as in the Nicolas à Kempis sonata discussed above, and serves merely as an introduction to the fourth. Thus, hardly a decade after the sonata had been enlarged and quartered, so to say, it began to lose its third quarter. We shall see in the following paragraphs that the next step in the evolution of chamber-music forms is in the direction of a three-movement form—for a few years at least.

SONATA DA CHIESA

Toward the middle of the seventeenth century, following the death of Frescobaldi (1643), many of the duties of church organists devolved upon instrumental groups. Portions of the musical part of the

[23] A fragment is reprinted in Riemann, *HM,* II², 156–64.

Roman Catholic service were given to string ensembles for performance, with appropriate music drawn from the sonata literature existing
at the time. A name for the appropriate selections from this literature
had appeared in 1637, with Tarquinio Merula's trio *Canzoni, ovvero
sonate concertante per chiesa e camera* ("for church and chamber"),
to be followed in 1655 by Marini's *Diverse generi di sonata da chiesa
e da camera.* These works are essentially *canzoni* (of several movements or sections) with some added dance movements. For church
use the dance movements were omitted, and a church sonata (*sonata
da chiesa*) resulted.[24]

Vitali. A distinct separation of the sonata literature into two func-
tionally different types, however, was not immediately forthcoming.
Not until 1667, with the publication of Opus 2 of Giovanni Battista
Vitali (c. 1644–1692), did the *sonata da chiesa* as such appear with
name and content pointing to its sacred function. The tendencies
shown in the works of Frescobaldi, à Kempis, Uccellini, and Legrenzi
became characteristics in Vitali's *sonate da chiesa.* The characteristics
that this type developed until it began to fuse with its relative, the
sonata da camera, are in general as follows: (1) three separate movements, often with a short slow movement before the second or third;
(2) the first and last movements in fast duple meter and contrapuntal
style, with a degree of thematic relationship between them; (3) the
second movement a slow lyric piece in triple meter, rather homophonic in style. Vitali's *Sonate a 2 violini col suo basso continuo per
l'organo,* Opus 2, published in 1667, show these characteristics.

The first sonata of this set[25] contains a first movement in fast duple
meter, with a fugue subject that would do credit to any eighteenth-
century composer, so far has Vitali traveled along the path of instrumental style; the texture is contrapuntal throughout. The second
movement, in slow, broad duple meter, is largely note-against-note,
with the violins in parallel thirds most of the time. The third movement is in fast duple meter, largely in homophonic style, but with a

---

[24] Riemann, *HM*, II², 419. But whereas Riemann calls them *canzoni*, they should
be called sonatas in the light of modern research.

[25] In Riemann, *Old Chamber Music*, Vol. IV.

contrapuntal section in which the initial portion of the first movement's fugue theme is employed. So far this sonata conforms. But then there follows another slow section in duple meter and homophonic style, leading directly into a fourth movement, again in fast duple meter and contrapuntal in style. Here the second half of the first movement's fugue theme is much in evidence. It is as though the two halves of one large movement were separated by an interpolated slow section; the halves are unified by giving to each half a portion of a single theme employed in an earlier movement. The form of the entire sonata might be diagramed A—B—aca′; and the general characteristics mentioned in the preceding paragraph are seen to hold true for this sonata also.

Corelli. There comes a time in the history of every musical medium when one composer, more gifted than his fellows, arrives on the scene to summarize, clarify, and in a sense give a new impulse or a new direction to the evolution of that medium. In the early history of chamber music that composer was Arcangelo Corelli (1653–1713). At the age of seventeen Corelli was an accomplished violinist and a member of a famous orchestra in Bologna. Moving to Rome in his early twenties, he soon established a reputation as an outstanding virtuoso and an excellent conductor. He was employed by popes, honored by royalty, and died universally admired and respected. His system of violin teaching was copied in all parts of Europe and forms the basis for modern methods. Corelli has rightly been called the "father of violin playing," both for his solid accomplishments in the field of teaching and for his achievements in clarifying and perfecting a true violin style in his compositions. His work in the latter field brought to an end a century of experimenting with the problems of violin style.

Corelli's complete works total no more than six sets of sonatas and concertos, with twelve compositions in each set. On these seventy-two works Corelli spent almost thirty years.[26] He paid little attention

---

[26] A number of other works attributed to Corelli exist, but opinion is divided about the authenticity of many. See Pincherle, *Corelli et son temps* (Paris: Plon, 1954), pp. 177 ff.

to experimenting with form and structural details; instead he was pre-occupied with new expressive devices, new ways of making the violin to sound, and new concepts of melodic beauty. The complete works, with their original titles, follow.[27]

XII Suonate a tre, due violini e violoncello, col basso per l'organo, Opus 1 (Rome, 1681).

XII Suonate da camera a tre, due violini, violoncello e violone o cembalo, Opus 2 (Rome, 1685).

XII Suonate a tre, due violini e arcileuto col basso per l'organo, Opus 3 (Modena, 1689).

XII Suonate da camera, due violini e violone o cembalo, Opus 4 (Bologna, 1694).

XII Suonate a violino e violone o cembalo, Opus 5 (Rome, 1700). Of these, six are *sonate da chiesa,* five are *sonate da camera,* and the last is a set of variations, "La Follia."

Concerti grossi con duoi violini e violoncello di concertino obbligato e duoi altri violini, viola, e basso di concerto grosso . . . , Opus 6 (Rome, 1714). Eight of these are *sonate da chiesa* and four are *sonate da camera.*

The *sonate da chiesa* of Opera 1, 3, and 5 are much alike; a tabulation of the characteristics of Opus 3 will apply to the others as well. *First movements:* mixed homophonic and imitative style. Ten of the twelve are in slow tempo. *Second movements:* nine of the twelve begin with fugal expositions. Eleven of the twelve are in fast tempo and in duple meter. *Third movements:* homophonic style in general. Eleven of the twelve are in slow tempo, and triple meter is most common. *Fourth movements:* eight are homophonic, four are contrapuntal. All twelve are in fast duple meter. Five are dancelike, three have quasi-fugal beginnings, three consist of broken-chord figurations, and one contains series of short phrases played in parallel thirds.

It is at once obvious that Corelli has added a movement at the head of the sonata as represented by Vitali. The other movements conform to the model. The second movements (Vitali's first) are fast, in duple meter, and largely contrapuntal; the third movements (Vitali's second) are slow, generally in triple meter, and almost always homo-

---

[27] *Œuvres,* modern edition by Joachim and Chrysander. The *sonate da camera* will be discussed in the following chapter.

phonic. In the fourth movements (Vitali's third) a new element appears: while they are all fast, and either in duple or compound meter, they are not in the main contrapuntal. Instead of fugal movements Corelli writes dancelike tunes, idealized and stripped of dance characteristics. Through skillful and charming employment of dotted rhythms, occasional syncopations, and considerable use of the bass in antiphonal passages (where the bass answers the two violins, which are playing in parallel thirds), Corelli succeeds in introducing an air of lightness and charm in place of the sometimes stodgy contrapuntal movements of his predecessors.

Another important difference between Corelli and Vitali comes to light when one considers the former's addition of a first slow movement. Vitali had established a sequence of forms that ran to a fast-slow-fast pattern. Corelli, by adding a new first movement, established a slow-fast-slow-fast arrangement. The dualism that had existed earlier in the century returns again: the *canzone*-sonata conflict is again apparent. For where the *canzone* had begun fast and contrapuntally, the sonata had begun in slow tempo and in homophonic style. Vitali's *sonate da chiesa* represent a late flowering of *canzone* elements, concealed and considerably altered, it is true, but still conforming in general to the *canzone* pattern. Corelli, on the other hand, with his slow homophonic beginning movements, held to sonata elements; yet his *sonate da chiesa* contain within them (in their last three movements) what is left of the *canzone*. We shall see in later chapters that Corelli's scheme, or rather shall one say the scheme of the sonata, had longer life. One has only to look at the French opera overture, or even at the slow, homophonic introductions of eighteenth-century symphonies, to see how long-lasting was this particular aspect of sonata style.

Purcell. England had one bright moment in the musical history of the late seventeenth century, centered around the work of one of her greatest composers. In 1683, two years after Corelli's Opus 1 appeared, Henry Purcell published in London his *Twelve Sonnatas of Three Parts*. Purcell, the son of a violinist in the Royal Band (of violins) of Charles II, was born about 1659. At an early age he came under the influence of French music, for his teacher, Pelham Hum-

frey, had been sent to Paris to study with Lully and remained an
avid and successful imitator of that master's style. Purcell became
organist at Westminster Abbey in 1680, at the age of twenty-one,
and remained in that position until his death in 1695. He wrote vast
quantities of church music, more than fifty works for the theater,
including the well-known opera *Dido and Aeneas,* many secular songs,
pieces for keyboard instruments, fantasies for strings (three to eight
parts), perhaps the earliest solo sonata by an English composer, and
two sets of chamber-music sonatas, the set of twelve mentioned above
(1683) and a set of ten, published by his widow in 1697. All this,
and he died when he was thirty-six! Although much of his work is
uneven in quality, he remains one of England's greatest composers
and one of the great masters of all time.

But not only the French style was influential in England in Purcell's day. Italian works circulated widely, Italian musicians held
honored positions in London's musical life, and Italian influences
were felt in church and chamber music. It is not surprising, then,
to discover that Purcell acknowledges the Italian influence in the
preface to his first set of sonatas. He says "he has faithfully endeavor'd
a just imitation of the most fam'd Italian Masters" and "he is not
mistaken in the power of the Italian Notes, or elegancy of their Compositions, which he would recommend to the English Artists." There
is no direct evidence as to which Italian models Purcell had before
him; the editor of the composer's complete works, J. A. Fuller-Maitland, surmises that Giovanni Battista Vitali's Opus 5, *Sonate a 2, 3, 4,*
e 5 stromenti (Bologna, 2d ed., 1677), may have served, for that work
contains sonatas strongly resembling Purcell's.

The two sets of sonatas,[28] the twelve of 1683 and the ten of 1697,
may be considered together, for they are much alike. Most of them
have five movements, the others either four or six, except Number
6 of the second set. The latter is a one-movement chaconne, consisting of forty-four variations of a five-measure phrase. Of the twenty-
one sonatas having from four to six movements, all but two of the
first movements are slow and in duple time, and all but three are

[28] In Purcell's *Complete Works,* Vols. V and VII.

contrapuntal in style. Sixteen of them contain movements marked
"canzona," most usually (eleven out of the sixteen) appearing as the
second movement. The rest of the movements do not lend themselves to generalizations; there is no system apparent in placing them
in the sonatas. While about half of them are arranged in accordance
with tempo alternations of slow-fast-slow-fast, the other half seem
to overlook this principle of contrasting tempos. In two cases three,
and in one case four, slow movements follow one another, with no
fast tempo intervening. True, there are differences between an adagio,
a largo, and a grave, and Purcell was aware of these differences, for
in the preface to the 1683 set he defines them thus: "*Adagio* and
Grave, which import nothing but a very slow movement: *Presto
Largo, Poco Largo,* or *Largo* by It Self, a middle movement." In the
order of meters, too, there is a similar lack of regularity. Two or three
movements in duple time are followed by one or two in triple, in
most cases. Only in one sonata, Number 7 of the 1697 set, is there a
regular alternation of duple, triple, duple, triple, and duple. Purcell
does make this concession to the god of contrast, however: he does
not allow two movements to follow each other without changing
either tempo or meter. Again there is an exception: the fifth sonata
of the 1683 set has four consecutive slow movements, of which the
first two are both in duple time. This lengthy paragraph forces one
to the conclusion that one cannot generalize successfully about the
sequence of movements in these two sets. Let us try once more, this
time examining the contrasts of style.

The sonatas indicate that Purcell was at home in both the lyric
French and the dramatic monodic Italian styles. But he was also of
the nationality that had produced William Byrd a few generations
earlier, that had been so successful in developing the contrapuntal
arts of the thirteenth and fourteenth centuries. Purcell's style, in these
two sets of sonatas and in much of his church music, is essentially
contrapuntal (see Example 9). And to indicate the quality of his contrapuntal writing, a *toccata* of Purcell's, copied out in admiration by
Bach himself, was included in the great edition of the Bachgesellschaft as being probably that master's own work.

Example 9   Purcell, Sonata VIII

We should expect to find, then, and we do find, that the great majority of the movements in these sonatas are in contrapuntal style. Of the more than one hundred separate movements more than three-quarters are contrapuntal. The nature of the counterpoint ranges from a "canon in twofold augmentation in the 5th and 8ve above" (first movement of the sixth sonata of 1683) through the magnificent chaconne that is the sixth sonata of the 1697 set, through movements that contain true fugal expositions, through movements that are full of skillful imitations of one phrase, to movements made up of chains of countermelodies. Purcell is equally competent in fast, moderate, and slow movements, and his skill and imagination in the chaconne are masterful. He succeeded to a great degree, as Bach did to a greater, in casting his contrapuntal ideas into regular phrases of four or eight measures, thus avoiding the feeling of formlessness one so often experiences in less successful contrapuntal music.

The noncontrapuntal movements (twenty-six of them) are about equally divided between slow in triple meter and slow in duple, with two others in fast triple meter. Nine additional movements, scattered throughout the two sets of sonatas, are in mixtures of note-against-note and contrapuntal styles; these include three in slow triple, two in slow duple, and four in fast triple meter. It is the twenty-nine slow movements that give these sonatas their strongest link with the Italian *sonate da chiesa*. The triple-meter largo and adagio movements especially are close to the corresponding movements of Corelli, in the lyric beauty of their melodies, the freshness of their cadences, and at times their resemblance to sarabandes.

The last-mentioned characteristic, insignificant as it may seem in an over-all view of Purcell's sonatas, is of great importance to the future of this sonata type. We saw the tendency in Corelli to depart from contrapuntal last movements (as they were in the case of Vitali) and write dancelike tunes in a light and airy manner. This tendency appears again in Purcell, for the last movement of the ninth sonata in the 1683 set is practically a siciliano. The rhythmic figure typical of that dance form (𝅘𝅥𝅭 𝅘𝅥𝅮𝅘𝅥𝅮 𝅘𝅥𝅭 𝅘𝅥𝅮𝅘𝅥𝅮) is never long absent; the movement flows along in a lively manner and must have pleased Purcell's patron, Charles II, who is said to have found much church music entirely too dull. Another movement, the fourth movement of the seventh sonata of 1697, one can easily mistake for an eighteenth-century minuet, so dainty, lilting, and charming are the melodic and rhythmic aspects of the piece.

In neither of these two sets of 1683 and 1697 did Purcell indicate the type of sonata he was writing. But the evidence is overwhelmingly in favor of calling them *sonate da chiesa*. The differences between these and other sonatas of that type are largely in sequence of movements and the quantity of contrapuntal writing. And, as we have seen from a comparison of Vitali and Corelli, a hard and fast formula for sequence of movements was not characteristic in the great Italian masters either. The similarities between these three composers lie closer at hand, for there is in all of them an outward adherence to formal models, coupled with a desire to make melodies expressive and suited to the character of the violins for which they were written.

Each in his own way was successful; if Purcell's way is more contrapuntal, nothing is lost and the literature of chamber music has
gained much.

In the last decades of the seventeenth century the *sonata da chiesa*
branched out into other instrumental fields. Three sonatas by Gregorio
Strozzi (1687) and a sonata (1692) and a set of seven works bearing
the title *Frische Klavierfrüchte* ("Fresh Fruits of the Keyboard,"
1696) by Johann Kuhnau (1660–1722) were among the first keyboard works in this form.[29] Also during these years the chamber-music
version of the form adopted stylistic elements drawn from a parallel
form, the *sonata da camera,* that had itself developed out of the dance
suite of the early seventeenth century. A discussion of those developments will form the content of the following chapter.

[29] A set of keyboard "sonatas" by the obscure Italian Gioanpietro Del Buono,
about 1641, consist of melodic elaborations over a *cantus firmus,* hence do not come
into account here. Similarly, an organ sonata by Christian Ritter, probably composed
between 1680 and 1688, is in sections rather than movements, hence is not a *sonata
da chiesa.* See Newman, *The Sonata in the Baroque Era,* pp. 126 and 231, for
details.

3. From Dance Suite
to Sonata da Camera

THE EVENTS described in the previous chapter, concerned with the transformation of the *canzone* and the early sonata into the *sonata da chiesa*, occupied all of the seventeenth century. The *Canzone francese* by Viadana (1602) and the six *sonate da chiesa* in Corelli's Opus 5 (1700) may be taken as the first and last items in that series of events. Another line of development, running virtually parallel to that series, took place within the field of dance music and culminated in the *sonata da camera*, or chamber sonata. Its beginnings lie somewhat further back in time than the beginnings of the instrumental *canzone* development, but its ending corresponds exactly, for the five *sonate da camera* also contained in Corelli's Opus 5 mark the completion of the development. The present chapter, then, will return to the sixteenth century and carry the series of events up to 1700.

THE DANCE SUITE

Early sixteenth-century dance tunes, whether designed for people of aristocratic birth or for commoners, usually appeared in pairs of two contrasting parts or movements. The first part of the pair was a relatively slow and stately dance, usually in duple meter; the second was a lively dance in triple meter and had a strong melodic similarity to the first. This pair of melodically related dances was common to all countries of western Europe and was the germ out of which the seventeenth-century dance suite grew.

The most common of the duple-meter dances was called, with great variety of spelling, *paduana, padouana, padovana, paduan, pavane, paven,* and *pavin,* in Italy, France, Germany, and England. Its triple-meter associate, that is, the second of the pair, was most usually a *galliard* (also *gaillarde, gagliarda*), *saltarello,* or *courante.* In Germany the distinctive names of the pair often disappeared, and the pair was called *Dantz und Nachdantz* or *Hofdantz und Nachdantz.* In Italy the *passamezzo,* closely related to the pavane in steps and music and often substituted for it, was popular. In France the pair of dances named *basse danse* and *tourdion* was often used; here, however, both dances were in triple meter.

Arrangements of dance music were among the very first musical works to be printed. As early as 1508, in Venice, Ottaviano dei Petrucci, the inventor of the process of printing music with movable metal type, published several sets of dances arranged for the lute. The dances appeared in sets of three: the pavane and saltarello are joined by another lively dance in triple meter, called *piva.* In other countries, too, arrangements for the lute appeared, in addition to similar arrangements of dance tunes for keyboard instruments. In 1531 Pierre Attaignant, the foremost Parisian publisher, issued a set of dances for lute under the title *Quatorze gaillardes, neuf pavennes, sept branles, et deux basses danses.*[1] These are all short dances of twenty-four to thirty-two measures each, with repeated sections and well-defined periodic structures; both homophonic and polyphonic styles are represented. A German publication of 1571, by Elias Ammerbach, contains several sets in the usual duple-triple pairing as well as one set that contains three movements.[2]

The dances and dance pairs mentioned in the above paragraph are typical of the bulk of sixteenth-century music in this form. Large collections such as the Attaignant set, with its thirty-two single dances, and small ones such as the Ammerbach, with its few pairs, were published throughout the century. But a tendency to arrange dances in groups of three to eight or more movements—in a word, to create a suite of dances—also was present. This tendency is first to be observed in works for keyboard instrument or lute and only later in instrumental ensemble works.

---

[1] Facsimile reproduction in *Chansons und Tänze,* ed. Bernouilli; modern reprint in *Klaviertänze des 16ten Jahrhunderts,* ed. Halbig.

[2] Reprinted in *Klaviertänze des 16ten Jahrhunderts.*

The Suite in England. English keyboard music for a few decades before and after 1600 is based largely on the variation forms. The application of the variation principle to dance forms enabled composers such as William Byrd (1543–1623), John Bull (c. 1562–1628), and Orlando Gibbons (1583–1625) to organize dance music into larger forms. The "Spanish Paven" by John Bull, for example, composed for the virginal, consists of a dance tune and seven variations.[3] Each variation is sixteen measures long, corresponding to the theme, and all but two of the variations follow the theme in being in duple meter. Nowhere during the variations is the form or harmonic structure of the theme altered. The variations are purely ornamental figurations of the theme, and as such are characteristic of the great bulk of virginal music in the variation form.

In a pavane by William Byrd [4] another type of procedure is seen. The pavane has three distinct and melodically unrelated sections; each is sixteen measures long, and each is followed by one variation. Thus a form of AÁBBĆĆ results. Another piece by Byrd, a galliard with five variations,[5] is formally akin to the Bull "Spanish Paven" but is filled with melodious inner voices and other bits of counterpoint to a degree that the Bull piece is not.

Judging by these and other dance pieces found in the three principal collections of virginal music, one gathers that the polyphonic and homophonic styles existed side by side in England through the first quarter of the seventeenth century. Along with strongly contrapuntal pieces, such as the examples by Byrd mentioned above, are others by the same composer (for example, "A Gigg," "Rowland," and "Wolsey's Wilde") and by his contemporary John Bull ("Pavana" and "Duke of Brunswick") that are equally homophonic. Nor is there great uniformity of style and tempo within dance pieces of the same type. Byrd's "Sir John Grays's Galliard," for example, is moderately slow and rather somber; his galliard with the five variations mentioned above is animated and filled with lively figurations.

---

[3] Reprinted by Schering, *Geschichte der Musik in Beispielen*, No. 147.

[4] From the *Fitzwilliam Virginal Book;* reprinted and ed. by Bantock, *Three Dances of William Byrd.*

[5] Ibid.

As early as 1599 suites of dance tunes written for groups of viols had appeared in England: Thomas Morley's *Consort Lessons, for Six Instruments to Play Together* (1599); John Dowland's *Lachrymae; or, Seven Teares, Figured in Seaven Passionate Pavanas, in Five Partes* (1605); Phillip Rosseter's *Lessons for Consorts* (1609), for five voices. A number of manuscripts from this time exist also, among them "Fancies for Viols" and the "Great Consort," by John Cooper (Giovanni Coperario, ?–c. 1575). It was in this form, as music for groups of viols, that English music greatly influenced the German in the years after 1600.

After James I assumed the English throne (1603) many English musicians fled to the Continent of Europe and continued to compose in the style they had brought with them. William Brade (c. 1560–1630), as a forerunner of these composers, lived in several north German cities, enjoyed a high reputation as a violinist and composer, and published several dance suites, mostly for five and six voices, in the years between 1607 and 1621. John Dowland (1563–1626) and Thomas Simpson (?–1669) were two of the better-known expatriates to follow Brade. These composers had great influence on their German contemporaries and opened a new epoch in German music, the epoch of the suite for orchestra and chamber ensemble. William Young (?–1671), too, composed sets of dances (1653) for two, three, and four violins and *basso continuo* while active at Innsbruck. While the south German and Austrian centers were more influenced by the Italians, north German composers adopted the style and instrumentation of the English, seized enthusiastically upon the consort, and transferred their attention to that vehicle. Thus in the instrumental field the school of Elizabethan composers split into two lines: the emigrants to Germany carried with them instrumental dance music, to the great advantage of Continental musicians; the composers who remained in England stayed largely within the framework of the suite for virginal and the fancy for sets of viols.

The Suite in France. The lute and clavecin remained the favorite instruments for the dance suite in France, and steps leading to the development of the French suite are largely to be found in music for those instruments. Dances for the lute retained the melodically related pair pavane-galliard or pavane-courante until well into the seventeenth century. Instrumental composers writing for the staged *ballet de cour* toward the end of the sixteenth century added a second pair melodically unrelated to each other and in the sequence of triple and duple meter; but this version, written for the ballet theater, properly lies outside the scope of this book.

In the seventeenth century, especially in suites written for the lute, the typical order of movements was allemande, courante, sarabande, and gigue. Denis Gaultier (c. 1597–1672) was the most important composer of lute suites. The same form appeared in suites for the clavecin composed by Louis Couperin (c. 1626–1661) and Jacques de Chambonnières (c. 1600–c. 1670). The most usual metrical and tempo scheme was moderate duple, fast triple, slow triple, and fast duple. The dance suite in this form was destined, later in the century, to remove all other forms of the suite from the field; but up to the 1690s it appeared primarily for keyboard or for string orchestra.

The Suite in Italy. Steps leading toward the development of a unified suite were also being taken in Italy. The popularity of the lute extended to that country in the sixteenth century, and a number of the usual pairs of dances as well as occasional larger sets appeared for the lute. Keyboard suites are represented a bit later by a set of dances by Frescobaldi from 1637.[6] Here is a set consisting of four melodically related courantes, a ballet I with its triple-meter variant, a passacaglia, and a ballet II with related courante II—nine movements in all. This is obviously not a dance suite in the sense of the French version of the form, but it serves to show that in Italy, too, composers were concerned with combining single dances into larger sets having some inner thread—in this case, melodic relationship.

Dance music for ensembles is found in Italy as early as 1607, in the first book of sonatas by Salomone Rossi, who was discussed in Chapter 2. That book and three succeeding books (1608, 1613, and 1622) contain a variety of galliards, courantes, and other sets of

[6] In Tagliapietra, *Antologia di musica antica e moderna,* Vol. V.

dances, usually with a *sinfonia* as introductory movement (see below, p. 71). Sets of dances by Giovanni Battista Buonamente (?–1643) appeared in four books published between 1626 and 1637. In the 1637 set of eight sonatas, each sonata consists of *sinfonia, branda, gagliarde, e corrente.* The last three are dance forms, of course; the *sinfonia* in these cases is a nondance form in three parts: slow in duple meter, fast in triple, and slow section that often recapitulates the first section.[7]

In many of the dance collections to about 1670 several dances of each type were placed together. The four courantes in the Frescobaldi set (1637) mentioned above provide a simple early example; and six courantes, six ballets, and three sarabandes in Legrenzi's set of Opus 4 (1656) offer a more extensive and later example. It was taken for granted that performers would select from those sets the dances that met their requirements for a specific occasion and thus establish their own suites. Beyond this point Italian composers seldom ventured.

The Suite in Germany. In 1601 Hans Leo Hassler (1564–1612), perhaps the greatest German composer of the late Renaissance, published a collection of thirty-nine vocal and eleven instrumental pieces under the title *Lustgarten* ("Garden of Pleasure"). Many of the vocal pieces are actually dance tunes with text. Each piece consists of a duple-meter section and its triple-meter variant, and successive verses have their own music; thus miniature vocal suites, or dance-song cycles, are created.

Other composers of the time followed more orthodox procedures and wrote dances for instruments alone. Among the more important composers after Hassler were Melchior Franck (1573–1639) and Valentin Haussman (c. 1565–c. 1615). These men still wrote dances in which duple-triple and melodic relationships were present. Many of the composers of Hassler's generation, Franck and Haussman among them, followed a practice whereby the same piece could be played on brass instruments by the tower musicians, on wind and

[7] Riemann, *HM,* II[2], 530–31.

string instruments for dances, and on strings and lute for chamber-music purposes. In regard to sequence, Franck remained true to the old tradition and issued his dances in sets of similar type (several pavanes and several galliards in one set, for example), out of which the players made their own suites.[8] Haussman, on the other hand, experimented with his own sequences of dances; the usual pair of pavane and galliard served as a nucleus to which other pairs were attached. One finds a passamezzo and reprise, or a Polish dance and fugue, or an occasional set of variations.[9]

The distinction of adding a second pair of dances melodically re-lated to the first pair, thus creating a unified whole based on the use of the variation principle, falls to Paul Peuerl (Bäurl) (1580?–1627?) with his *Newe Paduan, Intrada, Dantz, und Galliarda,* pub-lished in 1611. From the beginning of German activity in this field, including that of Hassler and Franck, the dance forms had been given to an ensemble of strings—five or six voices in the case of the older composers, four in the case of Peuerl.

One of Peuerl's suites may serve as an example.[10] The four dances are respectively in duple, triple, duple, and triple meter. There is no longer evidence of mere melodic relationship; these dances are actually variations of the motive on which the pavane is based (see Example 10). Each of the four movements is in three parts, and each part is repeated. But the movements are not all the same length: The pavane contains thirty-two measures; the others range from sixteen to twenty. This is the result of the unique way in which phrases are elided, omitted, or expanded during the course of the respective dances. There is a respectable amount of "development" of the basic motive throughout the suite, yet the harmonic relationship of each movement to the others is never lost sight of. Contrapuntal writing, too, is more evident here than in Hassler's and Franck's *intrade,* and the demands made on the lowest instrument, bass viol in this case, are greater than in the works discussed previously. In the pavane, for

---

[8] Moser, *Geschichte der deutschen Musik,* I, 509.   [9] In *DDT,* Vol. XVI.
[10] Reprinted in Riemann, *Old Chamber Music,* Vol. II.

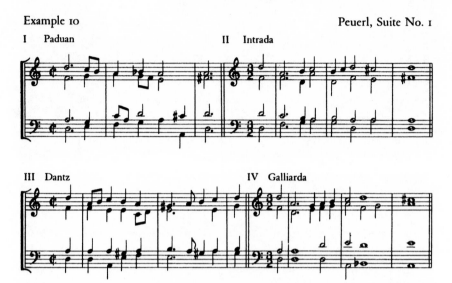

Example 10   Peuerl, Suite No. 1

I   Paduan   II   Intrada

III   Dantz   IV   Galliarda

example, the bass takes part in the contrapuntal imitations of the basic motive and engages in rapid parallel-third motion with the alto viol.

The variation suite thus originated by Peuerl was carried further a few years later with the publication by Johann Hermann Schein (1586–1630) of his *Banchetto musicale* (Leipzig, 1617). The tenth of the twenty suites contained in this publication is for five instruments, and Schein specifically mentions that these are meant to be violins, not viols.[11] In this he follows the innovation of Haussman, who had introduced the violin into Germany in 1604. There are five movements in this suite instead of the usual four: pavane, galliard, courante, allemande, and *tripla*. The variation principle is employed somewhat more freely here than in Peuerl's works. The galliard is almost independent of the pavane; in only one or two passages is there a sign of melodic similarity between the two dances. The other movements do show, however, a considerable amount of relationship to the first. The lengths of the five movements are forty, twenty-four, twenty-eight, twelve, and twenty-four measures, respectively. It will be noticed that with regard to length in both the

[11] Moser, *Geschichte der deutschen Musik,* I, 509.

Schein suite and the Peuerl the pavane is the most important movement. Even at the beginning of the seventeenth century the first
movement was taking on some of the characteristics that were to
lead to its domination of the sonata structure in the middle of the
eighteenth century.

The next important step in the development of the dance suite was
taken by Samuel Scheidt (1587–1654)—namely, the addition of the
figured bass. A "Paduana und Courante dolorosa," from Scheidt's
set of *Paduana, Galliarda, Couranta* (1621) are for two violins, viola,
and figured *basso continuo*.[12] Scheidt has here returned to the custom
of melodically relating the pair of dances, for the courante is a
triple-meter variant of the pavane. Each of the dances has three sections, totaling forty measures in one and fifty-five in the other. The
pavane shows several unique features; each of the three sections is
in a completely different style. In the first section the first and second
violins run in parallel thirds and sixths, but they are in counterpoint
with the viola, while the bass is in the conservative *continuo* style.
In the second section all the instruments, including the bass, break
out into rapid figurations, syncopations, and considerable rhythmic
diversity. In the third section the figuration ceases, the middle voices
harmonize a descending scale melody, and the bass resumes a *continuo* role. The courante is largely in mixed homophonic and note-
against-note style, with the first and third sections following rather
closely the corresponding sections of the pavane; the middle section
deviates, both in melody and harmonization, from the second section
of the previous movement.

Scheidt's inclusion of the *basso continuo* in his instrumental works
seems to have met with approval in Germany. In 1626 Carlo Farina
(c. 1595–c. 1650) published at Dresden *Pavane, gagliarde, brandi,
mascherata, arie francese, volti, balleti, sonate, canzone,* in two books.
This collection, as the title indicates, comprised German, French, and
Italian works. Dances in four-voice counterpoint appear next to trio
sonatas for two violins and figured bass. These are, perhaps, the first
trio sonatas printed in Germany.

[12] Reprinted in Riemann, *Old Chamber Music,* Vol. II.

The New French Suite. While this work of assembling the dances into suites was going on, the single dances themselves were undergoing considerable internal transformation. In the early years of the seventeenth century the pavanes, *intrade,* and galliards had been solidly rhythmical. Based largely on note-against-note texture, the regular pulse of the dance tune was clearly perceived. During the course of the century's first half, several factors caused the dance to lose its pristine rhythm and take on a stylized character. Among such factors were (1) the use of contrapuntal devices, imitations, and the like, which tended to obscure the rhythm; (2) the adoption of the *basso continuo,* which allowed a greater degree of rhythmic diversity and figuration to develop in the upper parts; (3) the development of self-contained melody to such a degree that lyric expression became a part of instrumental style and appeared in dances to the detriment of the prevailing rhythm. The end result of this was that the pavane to a great extent became a piece of pure music in two- or three-part form and lost its connection with dance music. Further, a variety of tempos served the same dance; there were slow, fast, and moderate pavanes; courantes could be sprightly, *dolorosa,* moving, and so forth. With the dance characteristics of unpretentious melody and straightforward rhythm obscured, the erstwhile dance tune was now virtually a piece of concert music.

These new developments took place largely in the post-1650 French suite, which had become popular in much of western Europe. The sequence allemande, courante, and sarabande had appeared in Copenhagen in 1626, whence it had migrated to France.[13] Those three movements plus a gigue were adopted by the lutenists (Denis Gaultier) and clavecinists (Louis Couperin and Jacques de Chambonnières in France and Johann Jacob Froberger in Germany). The inclusion of an allemande and sarabande in several ensemble suites by Johann Neubauer, (1649) in Germany[14] gives further evidence of the gradual spread of the favored French sequence. From 1650 on,

[13] Norlind, "Zur Geschichte der Suite," in *Sammelbände der Internationalen Musikgesellschaft,* VII[2] (Feb.–March, 1906), 186.
[14] One is reprinted in Riemann, *Old Chamber Music,* Vol. II.

that sequence became increasingly popular. Johann Kaspar Kerll (1627–93) and Dietrich Becker (1623–79) in Germany, Matthew Locke (c. 1630–1677) and Benjamin Rogers (1614–98) in England, and Johann Rosenmüller (a transplanted German whom we shall meet again) in Italy were among the first composers outside France to write ensemble suites in the new form.[15]

The tendency toward stylization of individual movements became almost a characteristic in these new French suites. The allemande, for example, took on the nature of a prelude, with fast passages in eighth and sixteenth notes. The courante and the sarabande acquired a degree of rhythmic diversity and motive manipulation, all within the framework of the homophonic style. The gigue alone retained a bit of contrapuntal imitation; its fast, two-part form usually included a fugal type of exposition complete with episodes and the motive-overlapping structure known as "stretto." Each of the four movements exhibited the combination of a harmonically three-part form within a formally two-part form; in general the diagram

$$||: \text{tonic-dominant} :||: \text{dominant-tonic} :||$$
$$\underbrace{\quad}_{A} \quad \underbrace{\quad\quad\quad}_{B} \quad \underbrace{\quad}_{A}$$

was characteristic. Just in those countries where the suite was dominant, namely, France and Germany, no collective name for the set of dances was available. In Italy the term *partita* had been in use as early as 1603; Tarquinio Merula had introduced the term *sonata da camera* in 1637. In France and Germany on the other hand the suite appeared either with a fanciful title—Schein's *Banchetto musicale* is an example—or as a collection, such as Neubauer's "Newe Pavanen, Galliarden," or with a general term, as *pièces de luth*. In Germany the term *partita*, or *partie*, became general; not until just before 1700 was the term "suite" adopted in France. In the eighteenth century such terms as *ordre*, as in François Couperin, 1713, or *ouverture*, referring to the predominant position of the suite's first movement, came into general use as collective names for the dance suite.

In the period after 1650 new dances and nondance movements

[15] Adler, *Handbuch*, I, 566.

were inserted into the suite in ever-growing numbers. Two types may be distinguished:[16] one, usually placed between the sarabande and the gigue, often called *intermezzo;* another, placed at the head of the suite as a prelude or introduction.

(1) Among the *intermezzi* various movements were in common use. The most usual were dances of other nations, or regional dance tunes that had found no place in the suite heretofore, or revivals of obsolete dances. Polonaise, hornpipe, rigaudon, siciliano, minuet, gavotte, bourrée, and passepied were among the more popular new-comers. One of the last four usually appeared paired with another of the same type (for example, minuet I and II, or bourrée I and II), with the second in a different key, after which the first was repeated. It became customary in the orchestra suite to set the second dance (minuet II, for example) with a smaller instrumentation than the first (three voices in many instances). Thus arose the *trio,* which in the form of minuet-trio-minuet *da capo* persisted in sonata, quartet, and symphony until well into the nineteenth century. And the appearance of the trio in a related key was the first breakdown in unity of tonality that the suite had suffered; heretofore, of course, all movements had been in the same key.

Others among the *intermezzi* were of several types. (a) Airs, or arias, were sometimes dances whose names had been lost or simply pieces in two-part form without particular dance characteristics. (b) Rondeaus were, in French suites, movements whose principal characteristic was an alternation of solo and chorus episodes (of course, in an instrumental sense), each consisting of an eight- or sixteen-measure period. The melody of the rondeau was usually cast in a particular dance rhythm; hence hybrid movements such as *minuet en rondeau* and *gavotte en rondeau* are sometimes found in French suites. (c) Variations of previously heard movements were sometimes included, either in the form of *double,* which might be a contrapuntal variant of the preceding dance, or *agrément,* which was an ornamented version of the dance heard just before it. (d) *Basso ostinato*

[16] The following is based on Fischer, in Adler, *Handbuch,* I, 568–70.

forms existed, the best known of which were the chaconne (*ciaccona*) and passacaglia (*passacaille*). These dances were characterized by a constantly reiterated short phrase in triple meter heard in the bass, over which a series of contrapuntal variations of that phrase was played.

(2) The other group of nondance forms was attached to the beginning of the suite. The tendency to begin the dance suite with a nondance form can be seen before 1650. It reveals itself in three ways: the nondance form (a) replaces the first movement, (b) is attached before the first movement, and (c) influences the alteration of the first movement itself. We have called attention to the degree of stylization found in the pavane in the 1620s and 1630s. A similar change took place in the allemande about 1650; it, too, lost a great deal of its dancelike character and took on the character of an introduction. As early as 1650 Johann Rudolf Ahle (1625–73) and Johann Martin Rubert (c. 1614–1680) had written what they called "trio sonatas," in which the first movement bore the title *sinfonia;* Johann Jakob Löwe (1628–1703) had done likewise in 1658.[17] Movements of the toccata type, but variously called *toccata, praeludium,* or *praeambulum,* appeared in the works of Esajas Reusner (1667) for lute and Johann Kaspar Kerll (undated) for harpsichord.

SONATA DA CAMERA

Perhaps the most influential type of first movement added to the head of a dance suite was the early sonata, as described above (see p. 38). Many collections dating as far back as 1607 (Rossi, Book I) had carried titles such as *sinfonie, gagliardi, brandi,* and so on; the *sinfonia,* as we have seen, was an alternate term for the sectional *canzone.* In the earliest of such cases—including Buonamente's Book IV (1626) and many similar works composed during the next two or three decades—the sets consisted simply of dance forms and nondance forms combined under a single opus or "book" number. After

---

[17] One *sinfonia* is reprinted by Riemann in *Sammelbände der Internationalen Musikgesellschaft,* VI⁴ (July–Aug., 1905), 505 ff.

the middle of the century, however, the practice became general of employing a sectional sonata as the first movement of a set of dances. Matthias Kelz, in his *Primitiae musicales* (1658), was perhaps the first in this field.[18] Each of the four dance suites in this set contains such an introductory sonata.

Rosenmüller. One composer may be singled out for being most consistent in the type of introductory movement he employed, for introducing the German form of the dance suite to Italy, and for attaching to the transplanted suite a functional term, *sonata da camera,* or chamber sonata. Johann Rosenmüller (c. 1620–1684) was born near Leipzig and received his early employment there. Imprisoned for moral lapses, he escaped in 1655 and shortly afterward arrived in Italy. He remained there until 1674, when he was pardoned, recalled to Germany, and given the post of chapelmaster at Wolfenbüttel. He had written much church music and a number of dance suites before his imprisonment, but the portion of his work that is significant here was written in Italy. It consists of a publication of eleven works, *Sonate da camera cioè sinfonie* ("Chamber Sonatas, That Is, Sinfonie") at Venice about 1667.[19]

The sequence of movements in eight of the eleven sonatas is identical: *sinfonia, alemanda, correnta, ballo,* and *sarabanda.* In two more cases an *intrata* is inserted after the *correnta,* and in one case an *intrata* plus an extra *alemanda* and *correnta.* The *sinfonia* as Rosenmüller writes it deserves to be examined; the introductory movement from the second sonata is typical.

The movement is characterized by ten short sections, all note-against-note and contrasting in tempo and meter. All sections are in duple meter except the sixth and the tenth, and the two latter are identical in all respects. The ten sections can be placed in four groups (labeled A, B, C, B, respectively) as follows:

A. $\frac{4}{4}$ Adagio—Allegro—Adagio—Allegro—Adagio—

    3 meas. 5 meas. 3 meas. 9 meas. 4 meas.

[18] Newman, *The Sonata in the Baroque Era,* p. 223.
[19] Reprinted in *DDT,* Vol. XVIII. The date is sometimes given as 1670.

B. $\frac{3}{2}$ Adagio—

  19 meas.

C. $\frac{4}{4}$ Adagio—Allegro—Adagio—

  11 meas. 11 meas. 7 meas.

B. $\frac{3}{2}$ Adagio

  19 meas.

This arrangement into four groups of sections or parts is seen to be justified if the other sonatas of the set are examined. In every one of the eleven *sinfonie* in this set, (1) the second and fourth parts are always in triple meter, and the fourth is an exact repetition of the second, (2) the third part always contains an adagio-allegro-adagio group, (3) all parts and sections except the second and the fourth are in duple meter. In every case an ABCB form results.

The adagio sections of parts A and C have several points in common. The style is always note-against-note, and the content is always a chord progression, nothing more. A few measures taken from the eleventh sonata's beginning will show the style that is typical of all the A and C slow sections (see Example 11). Rarely does a phrase

Example 11   Rosenmüller, *Sonata da camera* No. 11

consist of more than five or six chords. Each phrase comes to a cadence, either perfect or Phrygian, a hold is placed over the last chord, and after an empty half measure a new phrase is begun. And this is not an isolated construction; it is found in practically all the adagio sections of the A and C parts in all eleven sonatas.

Many histories give Rosenmüller credit for attaching the *canzone* at the head of the suite; this attribution originated in the period when the distinction between the *canzone* and the early seventeenth-century sonata was not well understood. Thanks to recent research in that field, that distinction can now be made.[20] One may indicate that these *sinfonie* of Rosenmüller are not *canzoni* but sonatas, as a comparison of their style elements with those of the sonata type described on page 40 will show.

The slow chordal sections in the sonatas may have provided the violinist with a harmonic background upon which to improvise. It is well established that slow movements of many seventeenth- and early eighteenth-century instrumental works contained only the harmonic and melodic outlines of the composer's ultimate musical intentions. A melodic line of a few long notes, unrelieved by any rhythmic vitality or great melodic charm, was written with the understanding that the performer would improvise an appropriate ornamental variant of the phrase. A judicious selection of mordents, trills, scale runs, figurations, and the like, were inserted as the good taste and creative imagination of the performer dictated. We see the results of that practice in the florid, highly ornamented adagios of the Haydn string quartets a century later, except that there the ornaments and embellishments are all specifically indicated by the composer. It seems likely that musicians and public alike would have been dissatisfied with the austere chord progressions of Rosenmüller and would have demanded the same type of improvised embellishments they were hearing in the solo sonatas of Vitali and many other composers.

The combination of sonata and dance set also appeared in Germany. In 1668 Dietrich Becker (1623–79) published, in Hamburg, *Musikalische Frühlingsfrüchte* ("Musical Fruits of Spring"), which contained, among other works, four suites having Italian sonatas as first movements.[21] These are expanded beyond Rosenmüller's dimensions, for they often consist of separate short movements rather than sections and are more contrapuntal and tighter in form.[22] The *Leipzigischen Abendmusiken* (1669), by Johann Pezel (n.d.), con-

---

[20] See footnote, p. 13, in reference to Crocker, "Italian Canzona."
[21] Nef, *Geschichte der Sinfonie und Suite*, p. 64.
[22] Riemann, *HM*, II², 419.

tains twelve suites, eight of which make use of sonata first movements. The fifth part of *Parergon musicum* (1676), by Johann Kaspar Horn (n.d.), contains five suites on the same model as those mentioned.[23] And a number of other works published between 1670 and the end of the century are similarly built.

Kusser. With the publication of six sets of dances called *Composition de musique selon la méthode française,* in Stuttgart (1682), by Johann Sigismund Kusser (or Cousser, 1660–1727) a new type of first movement found its way into the *sonata da camera;* also the work itself was written for a larger ensemble. The new first movements are modeled on the French overture introduced into the opera by Jean-Baptiste Lully (1632–88). This was a two-part form: a slow section of large dimensions built on a dotted rhythmic figure was followed by a fugal allegro that often ended with a few measures in slow tempo. The whole was characterized by the high degree of pathos expected of a piece that was to introduce and set the mood for the opera. The French overture was not only used successfully by Lully's followers in Paris but found wide application in Germany, in orchestra suites, oratorios, and operas. The style derived from that form is an important part of the familiar Handel style. As late as 1750 its rhythms and sequence of tempos were influential in shaping the new Classical symphony.

This type of first movement, however, most often appeared in works designed to have several players on a part; orchestral music emerges and takes a path of development away from chamber music and toward the symphony. A number of orchestral suites or "overtures," consisting of a first movement based on the French overture and several later movements in dance forms, were composed after 1682. That development culminated in the four orchestral suites of Bach. Similarly, the suite of dances for keyboard instrument, with a first movement of this type or another, emerged to lead to the innumerable suites or "partitas" by later Baroque composers. Here again the suites and partitas of Bach virtually end the development.

In the field of chamber music the version introduced by Kusser

[23] Nef, *Geschichte der Sinfonie und Suite,* pp. 68–70.

played little part, as did the sectional sonata represented in the works
of Rosenmüller. The majority of later chamber-music works, for
whatever instrumentation, took a form in which the first movement
was simply an introductory prelude—sometimes containing contrasting tempos and meters, and sometimes not—and later movements
were drawn from the various dance types then available.

Corelli. The thirty-four *sonate da camera* of Arcangelo Corelli are,
like his *sonate da chiesa* (see p. 52), among the most successful
compositions of the late seventeenth century in Italy. They include
works for violin and *basso continuo,* for *concerto grosso,* and for two
violins and *basso continuo,* and are found in the following: twelve
trio sonatas in Opus 2 (1685) and twelve[25] in Opus 4 (1694); Nos.
7–11 of Opus 5 (1700; for violin and *basso continuo*) and the last
four of Opus 6 (1712; these are *concerti grossi*). The difference in
instrumentation seldom carries with it a difference in form or style.
The twelve sonatas of Opus 4 are typical of all of Corelli's *sonate da
camera.*

The sonatas in general are short; one has two movements, eight
have three, and three have four. There are in each of the sonatas a
prelude and one, two, or three of the following dances: allemande,
courante, sarabande, gavotte, and gigue, placed in no special order.
Six of the dances (one each in sonatas 1, 2, 4, 7, 9, and 10) are preceded by short introductory movements varying in length from five
to seventeen measures. The introductions are slow in duple time,
and without dance characteristics. Each of them is attached to the
dance that follows by means of a Phrygian cadence. Throughout the
seventeenth and the eighteenth centuries this old modal device was
used to indicate a half close and show that the movement in which
it was found was to proceed directly into the next. Furthermore, the
introductions are of two kinds: three are in note-against-note style;
three are contrapuntal. But all are similar to the internal slow movements of Corelli's *sonate da chiesa* and would not be out of place in
those works, except that they are all in duple meter, whereas two

---

[25] Not six, as Riemann asserts in *HM,* II², 421.

thirds of the slow movements in the church sonatas of Opus 3 and Opus 5 are in triple meter.

An interesting relationship to past centuries comes to light here. In the twelfth and thirteenth centuries, at the time when metrical notation was being established, the only possible meter was a triple one. Based on its analogy to the Trinity, it seemed the obvious meter for the sacred music of that time. When one observes the rise of secular music in the fourteenth century, one finds that a duple meter became possible. To distinguish between the two meters, the terms of *perfect* (referring to the Trinity) for the triple meter, and *imperfect* (symbolizing the worldly aspects of the music) for the duple, came into use. It seems quite likely that in Corelli's choice of triple meter for the sacred slow movements (in the church sonata) and duple meter for the secular slow movements (in the chamber sonata) we see a faint, idealized reminiscence of this ancient practice. That this practice was not consistently carried out goes without saying; there is probably as much duple-meter church music in the period from 1400 to 1700 as there is music in triple meter. One can, however, account for the appearance of the old *tempus perfectum* in the *sonata da chiesa* and *tempus imperfectum* in the *sonata da camera* by pointing out these metrical characteristics of Medieval sacred and secular music.

The dance movements themselves, which make up the body of these sonatas, do not differ essentially from their German and French counterparts. They are almost entirely in homophonic style and are based largely on broken-chord figurations (see Example 12). The tempo indications are not invariably in the expected relationship to the dances, however; we find that out of three sarabandes one is in the usual slow tempo, one is in 3/4 meter and marked vivace, and one is in 6/8 marked allegro. Several of the courantes are marked vivace instead of the more sedate allegro, and two of the seven allemandes are marked presto. Of these last dances, only one of the seven begins with the up-beat characteristic of older and more northern allemandes. Finally, throughout all the dances the bass part has be-

Example 12   Corelli, Opus 4, No. 1

come much more animated, takes part in imitations of violin figures, and requires a degree of technical proficiency comparable to the violin parts.

In *sonate da camera,* as in *sonate da chiesa,* the first movements are always the most important, for they exhibit the greatest changes from one period to another. They best show the prevailing trend of forthcoming changes, and they carry the style elements of the seventeenth century most directly to eighteenth-century sonata-form. The first movements of Corelli's Opus 4 are similar to the first movements of the twelve *sonate da camera* of Opus 2 and the five of Opus 5. They are in a mixed homophonic and imitative style, averaging about twenty-four measures in length, and the majority are slow and in duple meter. Several are based on broad chordal figurations, a few have lyric melodies, but almost all have beautifully moving and expressively melodious bass lines. These characteristics they share with the *sonate da chiesa* of Opus 3 that we have looked at.

One feels that everywhere in these first movements there is a successful attempt to write dignified, melodious pieces of music, free of formal restrictions and free of pomp and empty display. This is also true of the other slow movements, in *chiesa* and *camera* alike. Lyric charm and expressive melody are found everywhere that the tempo of the music permits. While the fast movements seldom can have lyric moments, because of their speed and dance characteristics, they are like the slow movements in that in both classes every trace of the domination of vocal style elements is removed. The figurations, scale passages, and in general all the melodic contours are those that grow out of the nature of the string instrument and are those that we have associated with instrumental style ever since Corelli's day. The long road from the *da sonare o cantare* works of the early 1600s, through the attempts of Rossi and Marini, reaches its terminus in these sonatas of Corelli. The patterns for violin style were laid down for all to see, for all to admire, and for all to imitate. Corelli, almost unique among seventeenth-century composers, is as much respected today as he was in his own time.

Composers active in the field of chamber music continued to flourish in the early years of the eighteenth century. The *sonata da chiesa* and the *sonata da camera* began to influence each other mutually, to take on characteristics one from the other. Soon the formal distinction between the two types disappeared and we can speak of one combined form—the trio sonata. Details of that development will form the content of the next chapter.

4. The Solo and the Trio Sonata

LET US review briefly the chief characteristics of the two sonata types existing at the end of the seventeenth century. The *sonata da chiesa,* whose four movements were derived from the four sections of the *canzone,* was essentially a serious work, contrapuntal in style, and well adapted to its function of contributing to the church service. Even though the second and the fourth movements of the sonata were in fast tempo, they were still felt to be suitable for sacred use. As much as seventy-five years later Charles Burney reports his visits to churches in Paris in these words: "When the Magnificat was sung he [the organist] played likewise between each verse several minutes [minuets?], fugues, imitations, and every species of music, even to hunting pieces and jigs, without surprising or offending the congregation, as far as I was able to discover." And about a visit to St. Roque's church to hear M. Balbastre: "great latitude is allowed the performer in these interludes; nothing is too light or too grave, all styles are admitted." [1] Thus we can account for gay and dancelike movements in some of Corelli's *sonate da chiesa,* and we must realize that they were suited to the needs of the church of his day.

The *sonata da camera,* regardless of whether its first movement was derived from a French overture, from a Venetian opera overture, or from an early *sinfonia,* was still largely a set of dances, usually homophonic in style. During the course of several decades the separate dances had become stylized, their dance rhythms had become obscured through the addition of bits of imitation and bits of lyric melody, and, finally, many nondance movements had been inserted into the sonata.

[1] *The Present State of Music in France and Italy,* pp. 37, 41.

The most obvious of such added movements was, of course, the overture or *sinfonia* or prelude found at its beginning. Notably in the *sonata da camera* of Corelli, the first movement was in the nature of an introduction; typical violin figures were exploited, or broad passages in homophonic style were presented. Movements within the sonata were often slow in tempo, again in homophonic style and lyric in character.

We have, then, in the *sonata da chiesa* a type of movement that is light and dancelike, and in the *sonata da camera* a type of movement that is slow and serious and consequently nondancelike. The differences between the two sonata types were minimized still further in the early decades of the eighteenth century, and the similarities became more pronounced. But the terms distinguishing the opposing types continued in use long after the essential differences in the types themselves had disappeared, much as the terms had existed long before the two types had achieved separate status (for example, in Merula's *Canzoni, ovvero sonate concertate per chiesa e camera* of 1637). Although a number of composers, both German and Italian, continued to use the old terms, an equal number adopted the more inclusive term *sonata* (primarily in works for one melody instrument and *continuo*) or *sonata a tre* (two melody instruments with or without bass, and *continuo*). Among some Italian composers the term *balletto* was adopted to identify works that contained dance movements, or at least dance titles. Since the dance-derived movements (that is, the erstwhile *sonata da camera*) gradually gave way to forms without dance characteristics, the history of chamber music in the first half of the eighteenth century is essentially the history of the *sonata* and the *sonata a tre*.

Another characteristic of the sonata in the early eighteenth century is that unity of tonality was no longer observed. Originally all the movements of the early-seventeenth-century dance suite had been in the same key. After 1650, when it became customary to add to the suite two related movements in the same form (in the sequence minuet I, minuet II, minuet I repeated), the second of the two was placed in a different key, usually the dominant (see p. 70, above).

In the latter half of the century this practice was extended, in the sonata types, to other movements as well. In Corelli, for example, we find that thirty of his seventy-two sonatas and concertos have one movement in a related key; it is usually the slow movement of the major sonatas that is placed in the relative minor key. By the turn of the century (c. 1705) the practice was general, and any sonata containing all movements in the same key must be looked upon as archaic.

BUXTEHUDE

It is likely that the most significant chamber-music developments —and probably the greatest amount of music—appeared first in Italy. Composers such as Dall' Abaco, Albinoni, and Vivaldi, to name only those to be discussed below, were Italians and for the most part active primarily in Italy. Contemporary with them were the great and small Italian masters composing at all the courts of Europe. The Italian gift for melody and the traditions of Vitali, Torelli, and Corelli were alive in these composers and established the style of the first half of the eighteenth century. But northerners were not idle during this period. In 1696 Dietrich Buxtehude published his fourteen trio sonatas for violin, viol da gamba, and *basso continuo.*

Buxtehude was born at Helsingborg, near the southern tip of Sweden, in 1637. In 1668 he succeeded Franz Tunder at the organ of St. Mary's Church at Lübeck. There, in 1673, he instituted the *Abendmusiken,* church concerts for the several Sundays before Christmas. These elaborate concerts, replete with soloists, chorus, and orchestra, for which Buxtehude composed many cantatas, became famous throughout Europe. Bach journeyed on foot from Arnstadt to Lübeck in 1705, drawn thence by the great reputation of the concerts and their founder. Buxtehude died at Lübeck in 1707.

In these few lines is condensed the essential biography of one of the great composers of the generations before Bach. Famous as an organist and master of improvisation at that instrument throughout his lifetime, Buxtehude was an important figure in the line from Heinrich Schütz (1585–1672) to Bach. In his music, Italian dramatic and lyric elements and north German seriousness and technical skill are brought together and illuminated by his own vivid imagination and typically Baroque enthusiasm and humor. Here is no mere predecessor of Bach but a great composer in his own right, without whom a Bach might not have been possible.

Among Buxtehude's chamber-music works are two sets, with seven sonatas in each, entitled *Suonate à doi, violino e viola da gamba, con cembalo*, Opus 1 and Opus 2, respectively, both published in 1696.[2] In these fourteen sonatas we are immediately faced with a form that contains elements of the German suite of the 1650s, the Italian *canzone* of the same period, and the *sonata da camera* of the 1670s. The influence of the German suite is suggested by the dance movements scattered here and there in the sonatas. A notable example is Opus 2, No. 4, originally containing four melodically related dance movements; this suite was discarded when Buxtehude prepared the sonatas for publication.[3] We are reminded of the Italian *canzone* by the apparent lack of an organizing principle in either the type, the order, or the length of the movements. The sonatas range from three to twelve movements or sections, the length of which varies from a four-measure adagio to a hundred-thirty-four-measure allegro. As an echo of the *sonata da camera*, there is a short phrase structure broken by pauses, a mixture of homophonic and contrapuntal style, and a use of virtuosic elements. Let us examine the first sonata of Opus 1 in detail. The choice is justified, for all fourteen are of the same amorphous type.

The formal and stylistic elements of the sonata may be shown as in Table IV (see p. 84). It is seen that there is no regular alternation of fast-slow or of duple-triple, nor is there regularity of any other sort. Key relationships of various movements are likewise impossible to classify, and this is true of the other sonatas as well. In one case (Opus 2, No. 1) keys of B flat, D major, F major, G minor, and D minor are found; in another (Opus 1, No. 6, with twelve move-

---

[2] Reprinted in *DDT*, Vol. XI, together with a suite for trio and two sonatas for other combinations.

[3] According to Stiehl, writing in the foreword to Vol. XI of *DDT*.

TABLE IV

BUXTEHUDE, TRIO SONATA, OPUS 1, NO. 1

Tempo	Meter & length	Tonality	Style
Vivace	⁴⁄₄ 27 meas.	F, cadence in C	Contrapuntal
Lento	⁴⁄₄ 6 meas.	F major	Homophonic
Allegro	⁴⁄₄ 40 meas.	F, cadence on the dominant of D	3-part fugal with counter-themes
Adagio	⁴⁄₄ 12 meas.	D minor, cadence in F	Mixed contrapuntal and homophonic
Andante	⁶⁄₈ 40 meas.	F major	Homophonic 3ds & 6ths
Grave	⁴⁄₄ 11 meas.	B flat, cadence in F	Homophonic
Presto	⁴⁄₄ 47 meas.	F major	Fugal-homophonic

ments) one finds the keys of D minor, B flat, C minor, F major, and A minor. On the other hand, in other sonatas of five to seven movements one finds only one or two movements in different keys. Harmonically, Buxtehude is much closer to modal writing than are many of his predecessors—Corelli and Rosenmüller, for example. Many cadences and many chord sequences sound harsh to an ear accustomed to the tonal progressions of eighteenth-century Vienna. And in the mixture of styles, Buxtehude is unique. One has come to expect an alternation between counterpoint and homophony in successive movements. But Buxtehude changes style radically within movements. The last movement of Opus 1, No. 1, for example, begins with four measures in homophonic style, followed by a fugal exposition; this gives way to a section in imitative counterpoint, with material unrelated to the fugue; this in turn, to a homophonic section that employs repeated note figures; finally there is a return to fugal construction, with a few homophonic measures added to close the movement. All this occurs within forty-seven measures.

The forms encountered in the various movements are of great interest. There is a large proportion of fugal movements, but as indicated above, not consistently in fugal style. There are many improvisatory, cadenzalike movements, for violin alone or for viol da gamba alone. There are several sets of variations over a *basso ostinato* motive. There are a few quasi sarabandes and gigues. In practically all these various forms the element of brilliance is present, along with dramatic surprises, unexpected turns of phrase, and sudden style changes. This music is exciting, to a degree not encountered previously in any of the earlier Italian or German chamber-music works.

The elements of excitement and enthusiasm are especially evident in the fugal movements. The fugue, derived from the Italian *ricercare*, had up to this time been a rather staid and reserved movement, even when in fast tempo. In Buxtehude we encounter a new type of fugue theme and a new type of fugal treatment. Short rhythmic motives, characterized by many repeated notes, separated by short pauses, full of effervescent humor, are typical of Buxtehude's fugues. A selection of his themes is given to illustrate the characteristic humor and sparkle of these movements (see Example 13).

These themes are treated in a great variety of ways, used in homophonic as well as contrapuntal contexts, always with energy and liveliness. The slow movements that surround these fast fugal ones (and all the fugues in these fourteen sonatas are fast) serve as interludes or transitions; rarely are they extensive enough to develop lyric melodies in the style of the Italian sonatas. The over-all impression one receives from the sonatas is one of speed, virtuosity, and humor, so large is the proportion of fast movements. The rhythmic treatment Buxtehude affords all his musical material is especially noteworthy. There are no dull moments, no feeling of something about to happen; things happen all the time, and there lies the particular charm of these sonatas.

In summary, one must conclude that while these two sets of sonatas, published in 1696, are in themselves valuable as music and delightful as repertoire material, they are somewhat off the line that leads from Corelli through Dall' Abaco to Haydn. Buxtehude has more in common with his predecessors than with those who come after him. His use of viol da gamba in place of a second violin is a case in point.

Example 13   Buxtehude, Fugue Themes

While his contemporaries were writing trios for two violins and bass, Buxtehude retained a member of the viol family, a family that was well on the way to obsolescence in his day. Earlier north German works, notably the dance suites, had employed five string instruments —violins and viols of various sizes. Buxtehude is among those writing for the trio, but he prefers the darker tone color that only the viol can provide. He stands at the crossroads, musically, harmonically, formally, and instrumentally.

DALL' ABACO

Innumerable Italian composers were active in the early 1700s. Many were better known for their contributions to the operatic field than to the instrumental, however, and their chamber music has not yet been adequately examined. Among the noteworthy instrumental composers in the generation immediately following Corelli's we may mention

Antonio Caldara (1670–1736), Francesco Geminiani (1687–1762), and Nicola Porpora (1686–1768). But among the most significant of them was Evaristo Dall' Abaco. This eminent violinist was born at Verona in 1675. In his twenty-sixth year he moved to Munich, and shortly thereafter he entered the employ of the Elector of Bavaria, in whose service he remained active until 1740. His works include the following: twelve *sonate da camera*, Opus 1, c. 1705; twelve *concerti a 4 da chiesa*, Opus 2, c. 1712–14; twelve *sonate da chiesa e camera*, Opus 3, c. 1712–15; twelve *sonate da camera*, Opus 4, c. 1714–16.[4] Opus 5 (c. 1717) and Opus 6 (c. 1730) are concertos for various instruments. Dall' Abaco died in 1742 in Munich.

The works of Opera 1, 3, and 4, all for two violins and *basso continuo*, give evidence that Dall' Abaco was a composer second only to Corelli in melodic invention, purity of style, and nobility of expression; and in contrapuntal skill he often overshadowed his predecessor. They exhibit a regularity of form found in few of the works of earlier composers, and we shall see later that sonatas by Telemann, Handel, Bach, and many other composers share this characteristic. Almost invariably the sonatas contain four movements in slow-fast-slow-fast sequence; almost invariably the third movement is in triple meter. This is true in trio sonatas of both the *chiesa* and the *camera* types. Gone are the interpolated introductions to fast movements in the *chiesa* sonatas; gone are the added fifth and sixth movements in the *camera* sonatas. Rather than an arbitrary inclusion of any number from two to six movements, one finds the regularity of number that proceeds in an almost unbroken line down to the end of the genre.[5]

[4] The works of Dall' Abaco were published without date; consequently they can be related to particular years only approximately. Sandberger, in the preface to *Denkmäler deutscher Tonkunst, zweite Folge: Denkmäler der Tonkunst in Bayern* (hereafter *DTB*), Vol. I, gives the dates as shown here. He bases his surmises on hints in the prefaces of the sonatas, Dall' Abaco's nearness (in Belgium or France) to places of publication, and similar evidence.

All but one of the thirty-six trio sonatas of Opera 1, 3, and 4 are available: Opus 3, Nos. 4, 5, and 9 are in Riemann's *Collegium Musicum* series, Nos. 41–43; all the rest, except Opus 3, No. 7, are found in *DTB*, Vols. I and IX, which also includes four of the concertos of Opus 2.

[5] The following exceptions to these general statements must be noted: Of the thirty-nine available works of Dall' Abaco (see n. 4, above), twenty-seven contain

Three sonatas from Dall' Abaco's Opus 3 may be examined: Nos. 4 and 5 are *sonate da chiesa*, No. 9 is a *sonata da camera*; and the sonatas are so labeled by the composer. One sees, however, a continuation of the trend first noticed in the sonatas of Corelli and Purcell: the inclusion of dancelike movements in the *chiesa*, and a considerable use of counterpoint and rhythmic diversity in the *camera* type. *Sonata da chiesa* No. 5, in D major, contains, for example, a third movement that is in all respect a sarabande; and on the other hand, the allemande and the gigue of *sonata da camera* No. 9 are almost entirely imitative, with a consequent lessening of dance characteristics. One expects *sonate da chiesa* to be written in a contrapuntal style; but when a *sonata da camera* contains passages like the following, the essential differences between the two types have practically disappeared (see Example 14).

Example 14   Dall'Abaco, Trio Sonata, Opus 3, No. 9

four movements, and all but two of them are in slow-fast-slow-fast tempo sequence; nine of the remainder have either two, three, or five movements; one has a five-measure interpolated introduction to the fourth movement; two have similar short introductions to the third movements.

In the slow movements of these sonatas Dall' Abaco succeeds in establishing an atmosphere of beauty and reverence that for purity and charm is not exceeded even by the great Corelli. There is no longer any experimenting with violinistic effects. Corelli had for all time laid the foundations of violin style, and Dall' Abaco is content to write pure music in that style. The following shows the kind of lyric expression of which he was capable (see Example 15).

Example 15   Dall'Abaco, Trio Sonatas

The fast movements are in general in a mixed homophonic and contrapuntal style. All begin either fugally or imitatively but dissolve into homophonic passages in thirds and sixths after a few measures. Counterpoint is never long absent, however, and in the imitations the cello plays an important part. A typical device of Dall' Abaco's is to employ two voices (usually one violin and the cello) in parallel motion and write the third voice in counterpoint to them. Thus even in the homophonic passages, skillful bits of imitation, small canons, and the like are introduced. Neither the labeled dances of sonata 9 nor the contrapuntal fast movements of sonatas 4 and 5 exhibit any regularity of phrase structure. Elisions, extensions, sequences, and the like, combine to produce phrases of seven, ten, or any number of measures. Thus the dances—in this case allemande and gigue—have lost the characteristic that was evident earlier in the century, namely, standardized phrase lengths of four or eight measures, and have come still closer to being idealized dance forms rather than functional ones. The sonatas as a whole have come to be regarded as largely of historical interest; yet their value as repertoire material remains high. They deserve to be revived.

ALBINONI

Tommaso Albinoni (1671–1750) may be taken as representative of Venetian composers in the early decades of the eighteenth century. Some ten sets of instrumental works occupied him up to about 1720, after which he turned primarily to the composition of operas. About equally divided between trio and solo settings, more than fifty sonatas by Albinoni have survived. The earlier sets (1694 and c. 1704) show the formal plans, textures, and even melodic patterns made familiar in the works of Corelli. The four-movement sequence (slow-fast-slow-fast) is met most often, and the same general types of harmonic devices (consecutive sixth chords, series of seventh chords, etc.) are found on occasion.

In later works, however, Albinoni inclined toward a poignant, intense, and personal kind of writing. The smooth rhythmic flow of the music was broken by dramatic pauses between short phrases. Leaps as large as an octave or tenth added range and variety to the melodic line, and profuse ornamentation added elegance. Altered chords and occasional bits of chromaticism marked the harmonic scheme of these later works; the slow harmonic rhythm of earlier works gave way to expressive harmonic changes presented in close order (see Example 16).

Example 16   Albinoni, Sonata, Opus 6, No. 11

The titles of Albinoni's works, whether for trio or solo setting, call attention to a change in the naming of sonata types, a change that became general in the early decades of the eighteenth century. The

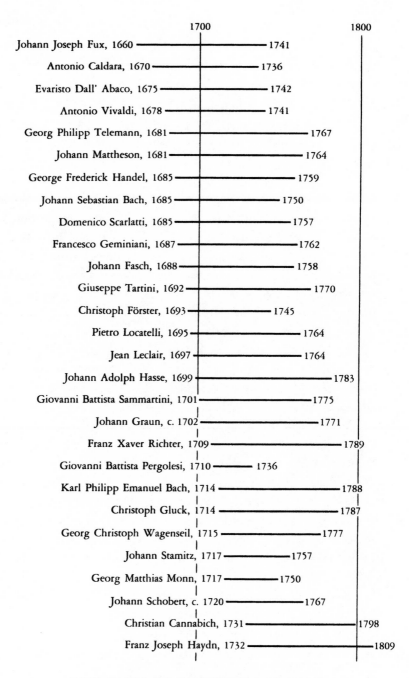

Johann Joseph Fux, 1660 ———————— 1741

Antonio Caldara, 1670 ———————— 1736

Evaristo Dall' Abaco, 1675 ———————— 1742

Antonio Vivaldi, 1678 ———————— 1741

Georg Philipp Telemann, 1681 ———————— 1767

Johann Mattheson, 1681 ———————— 1764

George Frederick Handel, 1685 ———————— 1759

Johann Sebastian Bach, 1685 ———————— 1750

Domenico Scarlatti, 1685 ———————— 1757

Francesco Geminiani, 1687 ———————— 1762

Johann Fasch, 1688 ———————— 1758

Giuseppe Tartini, 1692 ———————— 1770

Christoph Förster, 1693 ———————— 1745

Pietro Locatelli, 1695 ———————— 1764

Jean Leclair, 1697 ———————— 1764

Johann Adolph Hasse, 1699 ———————— 1783

Giovanni Battista Sammartini, 1701 ———————— 1775

Johann Graun, c. 1702 ———————— 1771

Franz Xaver Richter, 1709 ———————— 1789

Giovanni Battista Pergolesi, 1710 ———————— 1736

Karl Philipp Emanuel Bach, 1714 ———————— 1788

Christoph Gluck, 1714 ———————— 1787

Georg Christoph Wagenseil, 1715 ———————— 1777

Johann Stamitz, 1717 ———————— 1757

Georg Matthias Monn, 1717 ———————— 1750

Johann Schobert, c. 1720 ———————— 1767

Christian Cannabich, 1731 ———————— 1798

Franz Joseph Haydn, 1732 ———————— 1809

LIFE SPANS OF EIGHTEENTH-CENTURY
COMPOSERS BEFORE HAYDN

term *sonata* was confined to works of the *da chiesa* type, whereas the term *balletto* was used to identify those that had earlier been called *sonate da camera*. Thus Albinoni's church sonatas of Opus 1 (1694) are called simply *Suonate a 3*, the chamber sonatas of Opus 3 (1701) are *Balletti a tre*, and a mixed set of twelve (with six of each type) in Opus 8 (c. 1720) is entitled *Balletti e sonate a tre*.

VIVALDI

Although Antonio Vivaldi (c. 1678–1741) was well known and highly esteemed during his lifetime, and a fair proportion of his enormous musical output was published, he became little more than a name in the nineteenth and early twentieth centuries. A revival of interest in his music, accompanied by (or perhaps set in motion by) the early volumes of a new scholarly edition of his works,[6] has led to a reevaluation of him as one of the most important composers of the Baroque period.

Of the approximately six hundred fifty known compositions by Vivaldi (including some four hundred fifty concertos of various types) about seventy-five lie in the field of chamber music. Forty-two solo and trio sonatas were published in five sets in 1705, 1709, c. 1717, c. 1737, and c. 1740, respectively; the remaining thirty-odd were left in manuscript. The solo sonatas (fifty-three—either for violin and *continuo* or cello and *continuo*) considerably outnumber the trio sonatas (eighteen), again illustrating the tendency of later Baroque composers to favor the solo genre. Whether for solo or trio setting, however, the influence of the *sonata da camera* is still strong. Twelve trio sonatas in Opus 1 (c. 1705), twelve violin sonatas in Opus 2 (1709), and four violin sonatas plus two for trio in Opus 5 (c. 1717) consist mainly of preludes, allemandes, sarabandes, and gigues; and the movements are so named. The set called *Il Pastor fido* ("The Faithful Shepherd"), which consists of six violin sonatas, Opus 13 (c. 1737), occupies an intermediate position, in that only seven of the twenty-six movements in the set are dance movements and bear dance

[6] Published by Ricordi, Milan, 1947—. About four hundred compositions have been issued to date.

titles. In the later sets, however, including six sonatas for cello, Opus 17 (c. 1740; Opus 14 in some sources), and four trio sonatas, Opus 19 (not dated), dance movements have disappeared entirely.

Vivaldi's chamber-music works, taken as a whole, are representative of a type. Individual differences tend to disappear in them, and the early and late sets (*camera-* and *chiesa*-influenced, respectively) approach each other closely, except in the naming of movements. Certain standard devices—the sequence, for example—appear to a greater or lesser extent in virtually every work (see Example 17).

Example 17   Vivaldi, Trio Sonata, Opus 19, No. 2

Consistency of style is not to be considered a negative trait of Vivaldi's music, however. Within the self-imposed limitations of that style Vivaldi developed tremendous rhythmic drive in the fast movements and pathos or poignancy in the slow. Virtuosic brilliance is characteristic of much of his instrumental music; routine harmonic sequences take place within passages made up of dazzling string figurations. Concentration upon one melodic or rhythmic idea through long sections gives his music an intensity and unity that are among its most attractive features. Harmonic mannerisms—a series of diminished seventh chords in one case—are accompanied by imaginative passage work that charms the listener by its very simplicity (see Example 18). Above all, the momentum and inexorable drive that are developed in the best of Vivaldi's fast movements are equaled in the period only by the rhythmic quality of the music of Bach, whose admiration for Vivaldi's work was made evident in his many concerto transcriptions.

Example 18   Vivaldi, Trio Sonata, Opus 19, No. 2

HANDEL

George Frederick Handel was born at Halle in 1685, the birth year of Bach and of Domenico Scarlatti as well. Destined (by his father) to be a lawyer, he entered the University of Halle in 1702, but in the following year he went to Hamburg and immediately became interested in opera. Within two years, by 1705, he had had his first two operas performed, and a year later he journeyed to Italy. During the years of his stay there (1706–10) he wrote several operas and oratorios, was honored by distinguished personages in Venice, Florence, and Rome, and became acquainted with eminent musicians, notably the two Scarlattis and Corelli. The latter had great influence on the young German master, for the nobility of Corelli's ideals and the purity of his style struck answering chords in Handel's heart. After returning from Italy in 1710, Handel remained in Germany for a

short while before moving permanently to London. Dozens of operas
(1712–36) and many oratorios (1732–51) were his main contributions to the musical literature. Organ works, orchestral suites, and
instrumental concertos, along with the chamber music we are about
to examine, complete the list. Handel died in 1759 and was buried
in Westminster Abbey.

The amount of his chamber music is not large in comparison to
his enormous output of operatic and choral works. There is first a set
of trio sonatas for two oboes and *basso continuo* attributed to 1696,[7]
when Handel was in his eleventh year. Next, published as Opus 1
in 1724, is a set of fifteen solo sonatas (one instrument and *basso
continuo*), some for violin, others for recorder, flute, or oboe.[8] Opus 2,
published in 1733, consists of nine trio sonatas for two violins (or
flutes or oboes) and *basso continuo*.[9] Opus 5, from 1739 or 1740,
contains seven more for the same combination. A few scattered works,
including an excellent sonata for viol da gamba and *basso continuo*
and a transposed version of one of the sonatas of Opus 1, exist also.[10]

Like the trio sonatas of Dall' Abaco, Handel's six sonatas of 1696
are in a four-movement form, in the order slow-fast-slow-fast. The
first movements, all marked adagio, are in contrapuntal style, imitative
but not fugal. The difference between these two is, of course, that in
the latter the imitations regularly occur on tonic and dominant, while
in the former the interval chosen for the imitation is most often the
unison, and the imitation is in general neither complete nor exact.
Occasionally, as in sonatas 4 and 6, the counterpoint in the two upper

---

[7] By Chrysander in Vol. XXVII of Handel's *Werke*. Moser, *Geschichte der
deutschen Musik*, II[1], 279, and Leichtentritt, *Händel*, p. 820, believe the sonatas
to have been written much later.

[8] The first edition, published by Witvogel at Amsterdam in 1724, contained twelve
sonatas. Several later editions, by Walsh at London, between 1732 and 1740, contain fifteen. This may explain Eric Blom's assertion (in Williams, *G. F. Handel*,
pp. 106, 226) that Handel began composing these sonatas (the last three?) in 1732.

[9] The first and second editions, published by Walsh at London, contained six
sonatas. When, later, Chrysander found three isolated sonatas at Dresden, he added
them to the original six and introduced them, in Vol. XXVII of the *Werke*, as Nos.
3, 8, and 9 of Opus 2.

[10] All are published in Handel's *Werke*, Vols. XXVII and XXVIII. It may be
well to point out that in Handel's music only the instrumental works bear opus
numbers, of which Opus 7 (organ concertos published posthumously) is the last.

parts gives way to passages in thirds and sixths; in these cases the imitations are carried out by the bass—a device we also found in Dall' Abaco. The style in general is majestic, with considerable use of dotted rhythms reminiscent of the French overture of Lully and characteristic of Handel throughout his lifetime. Obviously there can be no lyric melodies in a style compounded of short motives heard contrapuntally and many dotted rhythmic figures; hence the appeal of these movements must be found in their consistency of style, neat turns of phrase, and inexorable progression toward the cadences.

The second movements are, on the other hand, fugues of quite definite construction; they are complete with expositions in related keys, stretto (a stretto in a fugue is a condensed, overlapping section leading to the climax of the movement), and coda. So large do the dramatic and melodious aspects of Handel's style loom when one considers his operatic and choral works that one sometimes loses sight of the fact that his contrapuntal skill was second to none. These movements should do much to remind one that contrapuntally, too, Handel was one of the great masters. The melodic invention of the majority of these fugues is not outstanding. Some themes are angular; some remain tied to one spot. But the effectiveness of the development of the themes cannot be denied; good proportion, musical excitement, and well-defined climax are all there to a great degree. In all except sonata 5 the bass is equal in importance to the two oboes; three-voice fugues result. The fifth sonata's second movement is two-voiced, the bass providing a homophonic accompaniment.

In the third movements also, sonata 5 provides an exception, which it shares with sonata 1. In these two cases the third movement is merely a short duple-meter interpolation between second and fourth, has as its first chord the resolution of the dominant chord with which the second movement closed, and proceeds directly to the fourth by means of a Phrygian cadence. The third movements of the other sonatas, however (Nos. 2, 3, 4, and 6), are fairly long (averaging thirty measures), are complete in themselves, and have the further distinction of being in a key different from the tonality of the other movements. When the sonata is in major, the third piece is in the relative minor (No. 3: E flat—C minor; No. 4: F major—D minor; No. 6: D minor—B minor); in the minor sonata the relationship is reversed (No. 2: D minor—F major). Furthermore, these slow movements are all in triple meter, as opposed to the duple-meter slow first movements. While contrapuntal style prevails, there is a noticeable absence of the dotted rhythmic figure characteristic of the first movements; in its place are melodic fragments that occasionally combine into lyric phrases of no remarkable beauty.

The fourth movements are all fast, all in imitative contrapuntal style, and full of bustling scale figures that require a certain virtuosity to play successfully. It is interesting to observe that in these works (for oboes) there is a complete absence of the broken chords and string alternations so typical of violin style. These devices one does find in many of the solo sonatas of Opus 1 and the trio sonatas of Opus 2 and Opus 5, which, be it remembered, are for violins *or* flutes *or* oboes. One can be sure that Handel actually had the oboe in mind when writing this first set of trio sonatas; the "or flute or oboe" phrase must have been added to the three sets of violin works either as an afterthought or at the publisher's suggestion. When one remembers how freely Handel's publishers, particularly Walsh in London, approached the works, one may assume that the alternate instruments were included on the title page merely to increase the sale of the Opera 1, 2, and 5 sonatas.

The fifteen solo sonatas of Opus 1 include six for violin, two for oboe, four for flute, and three for recorder—all with *basso continuo*. Again the four-movement form predominates, the exceptions being Nos. 5, 7 (each with five movements), and 9 (seven movements). The added movements in each case bear dance titles (bourrée, minuet, etc.), and they are less contrapuntal than the movements that surround them; we may see here a brief intrusion of the *sonata da camera* influence. In many cases the bass forms a real counterpoint to the solo part; imitative passages several measures in length occur often, and short bits of true countermelody are common. In other movements the bass provides no more than a harmonic support, all the melodic beauty then being provided by the solo instrument.

With a few exceptions, what has been said about the six trio sonatas of 1696 applies to the nine trio sonatas of Opus 2, for two violins and *basso continuo*.[11] Here again is the four-movement alternation of slow-fast-slow-fast, except in sonata 5, which contains a fifth movement in fast tempo. In about half of the first movements the dotted rhythmic figure is not found; the style remains contrapuntal, however, and the prevalence of figures with repeated notes may be mentioned. In several of the second movements the regular fugue writing characteristic of the 1696 sonatas is absent. In these cases there is a return to the imitative style of the first movements, and the fugal relationships of tonic-dominant are not present in the sequence of the imitations. The third movements of the two sets most resemble each other: the same change of key is at hand (relative minor or major), the same near approach to lyric melody, the same use of triple meter.

Looking at these two groups of trio sonatas together (those ascribed to 1696 and the set of Opus 2), one is struck by the remarkable technical skill Handel exhibits in them. Granted that the melodic materials are not exceptional, the total effect produced is one of great maturity in handling the materials. The dramatic moments and the great lyric breadth one finds in the operas are missing, for the most part. But these factors are not components of early eighteenth-century chamber music, and one does wrong to look for them here. What one does have is music entirely suited to the trio sonata instrumentation, music in which every detail is clear and well proportioned, and music that is delightful to play. One often suspects that Handel improvised on paper in writing his dramatic works, thereby achieving a certain spontaneity at the cost of well-proportioned forms. These trio sonatas are definitely not improvised; yet, strangely enough, the spontaneity is not lost in the process of composing them. They are not world-shaking, but they are excelled in musical worth only by the really great instrumental works of the period, notably those of Dall' Abaco.

The two sets of trio sonatas examined thus far, the set attributed

[11] Leichtentritt, *Händel,* p. 823, unaccountably lists the third of this set in D minor. Three movements are in F major, and only the third movement is in D minor.

to 1696 and that of Opus 2, are related to the line of the *sonata da chiesa*, without, however, being so named. The prevalence of counterpoint, the absence of dance rhythms, the fugal second movements— these are all *da chiesa* characteristics. The next set of Handel's works we shall examine, the seven trio sonatas of Opus 5 (1739), are just as obviously related to the *sonata da camera*, again without being specifically so named. One cannot generalize about the form or style of these works; each has several unique features, and no two are exactly alike. Thus only sonata 1 has five movements; No. 7 has five movements plus a short introductory adagio of five measures before the third movement; No. 4 has five movements, the second containing two different tempos; No. 5 has six movements; No. 2 has six also, but the fourth is a recapitulation of the second; No. 3, with six movements, contains an ..lternate version of the second movement; No. 6, with six movements, includes a variant of the fifth.

In content, too, the sonatas show considerable diversity. It is as though Handel only gradually became reconciled to the idea of writing *sonate da camera*, for in sonata 1 only the last movement is a dance form, in No. 2, three movements are dances, in Nos. 3 and 4, four and three movements, respectively, are dances. Then the dances decrease in number, for sonatas 5, 6, and 7 contain only one each. Nor is there regularity in the order: the last four movements of sonata 3 are a sarabande, an allemande, a rondeau, and a gavotte; sonata 4 contains a *passacaille*, a gigue, and a minuet as the last three movements. The *passacaille* is noteworthy in that variations 1–12 and 18–20 are in major, while only variations 13–17 are in minor, thus contradicting the textbooks that describe this form as being predominantly in the minor mode. The three dances of sonata 2 are a musette and its *da capo* (separated by a lengthy allegro in duple meter with brilliant passage work for the first violin), a march, and a gavotte. A bourrée, two minuets, and two gavottes are scattered elsewhere in the sonatas. All these fifteen dances are predominantly in homophonic style, with passages in note-against-note or in parallel thirds and sixths. Even the *passacaille* of sonata 4 is largely homophonic, contrary to the nature of most dances in this form.

Of the twenty-odd nondance movements remaining, two-thirds are
in homophonic style. All seven of the first movements are included
in this group (six slow, one fast); here they differ greatly from the
corresponding movements of the first two sets of sonatas, for the Lully-
like dotted rhythm is present only in a few passages, and the skillful
imitations characteristic of the sets of 1696 and Opus 2 are noticeably
absent. In many of the nondance movements, slow and fast alike,
rapid and brilliant passages for the first violin abound. The virtuoso
element is present in these sonatas to a great degree, and the demands
made upon the third instrument (bass or cello) are as great as those
upon the violins. Finally, the remaining eight movements—the other
one-third of the twenty-odd—are fugues of the same quality as those
found in the 1696 set. The same completeness as to dominant and
subdominant expositions, logical episodes, stretto, and coda is found,
and the themes themselves contain much more melodic interest.

This last point is in general true of the entire set of Opus 5. While
the contrapuntal technique is as masterful as in the works of a decade
or two earlier, there is a happier choice of rhythmic and melodic
materials. Example 19 shows the kind of melody to which Handel has

Example 19   Handel, Trio Sonatas

turned in this set of trio sonatas. The period 1735–40 marked the
emergence of the organ concertos, the *concerti grossi* for strings, and
Handel's shift from opera to oratorio. At the height of his musical
powers, he could not help but impregnate these trio sonatas with the
dramatic power and lyric beauty of which he was now master. Perhaps
such factors as drama and lyricism inevitably bring with them a
lessened use of counterpoint. Thus Handel at this time composes

sonate da camera instead of the more contrapuntal *sonate da chiesa*. But a glance at the fugal movements of these sonatas will assure one that Handel had not lost his contrapuntal skill. He was, in Opus 5, all that he had been earlier, and much more.

One point remains to be made. The fourth sonata of the Opus 5 set contains an optional part for the viola. In the edition of the Händelgesellschaft this part is printed in smaller notes than the other parts, but the added part is not in Handel's handwriting in one of the autographs,[12] and there seems reasonable doubt of its authenticity. It happens that the first movement and parts of the fourth of this sonata are used in the overtures to *Athalia* and *Parnasso in festa*, two of Handel's choral works from 1733 and 1734, respectively. In these two orchestral overtures there is, of course, a viola part; the latter agrees, note for note, with the added viola part in the corresponding sections of the trio sonata. It seems likely that some enterprising musician who knew all three works abstracted the viola part from the overtures and added it to the trio sonata, thus making the latter, in effect, a string quartet. While speculation is unfruitful, since we know neither the name of the innovator nor the date of the innovation, it will be well to keep this point in mind in later chapters, when the origin of the string quartet is discussed.

BACH

In this account of chamber music the works of Johann Sebastian Bach (1685–1750) must seemingly occupy a place of secondary importance. This may be considered strange, for in most other fields of music Bach represents the pinnacle of achievement. In fugal writing, for example, his works summarize and bring to glorious completion a long line of development extending back for more than two centuries; in the field of choral music the *Passion According to St. Matthew* and the *B minor Mass* mark the highest point ever attained in sustained intensity, religious fervor, and musical sublimity. In his cantatas, his keyboard works, and his orchestral suites and concertos,

[12] According to Frank Walker, in *Cobbett's Cyclopedic Survey of Chamber Music,* I, 508.

likewise, one encounters a breadth of imagination, a logical power, and a degree of poignancy not found in any other composer. And the many chorales exhibit a depth of feeling that epitomizes the entire Protestant religious impulse. Bach's chamber music must be considered in a category both separate and different from any of the above for two reasons: first, it is small in quantity; second, because of the restricted definition of chamber music we have chosen to adopt for this book, much of even that small quantity cannot be included for discussion here.

There are first the three suites and three sonatas for violin alone. These works, magnificent and musically important though they may be, are not ensemble music, hence cannot be examined in this account of chamber music. It must suffice to point out that they exhibit the forms and characteristics of the *sonata da camera* and the *sonata da chiesa*, respectively. With them must be placed the six suites for cello alone; they, too, are in effect *sonate da camera*, with, of course, notable deviations from the form as we have seen it thus far. The four orchestral suites, or *Overtures*, as Bach called them, and the six Brandenburg concertos likewise, cannot be discussed here. While they are sometimes considered chamber music and are often performed by "chamber orchestras," they are orchestral rather than chamber music: more than one player is needed on each string part to insure proper tonal balance. There remain, then, the following groups of works: eighteen sonatas for one instrument and harpsichord, half of them including figured bass and the other half not; two trio sonatas in C major and G major, respectively; *Musikalisches Opfer* ("Musical Offering"), written after Bach's last visit to the court of Frederick the Great at Potsdam in 1747; and Bach's last work, *Die Kunst der Fuge* (*The Art of the Fugue*), 1749–50.[13] A few other chamber-music works are attributed to Bach, but they are of either doubtful or uncertain authorship.

The Sonatas. The eighteen sonatas are divided as follows: nine for

[13] The sonatas are found in Bach's *Werke,* ed. Hauptmann and others, Vols. IX and XLIII[1], *Musikalisches Opfer* in Vol. XXXI[2], and *Die Kunst der Fuge* in Vol. XXV[1].

violin, S.1014–19 and 1021–23; three for viol da gamba, S.1027–29; and six for flute, S.1030–35.[14] The type of support given the solo instrument—either figured bass or written-out keyboard part—greatly influences the texture of the whole. In sonatas with figured bass (S.1014–19 in part, S.1021, S.1023, and S.1033–35), the solo instrument dominates, and the harmonic aspect of the accompaniment is its most striking feature. In the works with written-out keyboard parts, on the other hand (most of S.1014–19, S.1022, S.1027–29, and S.1030–32), a three-voice polyphonic texture is most usual. In these sonatas the harpsichord engages in strict two-part writing; there are thus three instrumental lines—solo instrument (violin, flute, or viol da gamba), harpsichordist's right and left hands, respectively. So obvious is this three-part writing that a number of arrangements of these sonatas for string trio have been made, and the results are eminently satisfactory in sonority and tonal balance.[15]

The two trio sonatas are much alike, except that the first, S.1037, in C major (attributed to Bach's pupil, Johann Goldberg, by some writers), is for two violins and *continuo*, while the second, S.1038, in G major, substitutes a flute for the second violin. Each sonata contains four movements in the usual sequence, and in each sonata the third movement is in the relative minor key. All of the eight movements are in contrapuntal style, with the second movement of the C major sonata and the last movement of the G major appearing as complete fugues. The third movement of the C major is in the form of a strict two-voice canon accompanied by a moving bass line. Here is the greatest difference between these sonatas and corresponding ones of Handel. The latter often abandoned contrapuntal style in the interest of melodic writing; most of Handel's lyric slow movements are in homophonic style. Bach finds this unnecessary; within the

[14] The S. references are item numbers in Schmieder, *Thematisch-systematisches Verzeichnis der Werke von J. S. Bach*.

[15] Arnold Trowell selected movements from the first and second sonatas for violin and harpsichord and arranged them for two violins and cello as Trio II and I, respectively (published by Augener, London, n.d.). As Trio III, for violin, viola, and cello, he chose movements from the three sonatas for viol da gamba and harpsichord.

framework of the strictest and usually most austere of forms, the canon, he writes a melody as lyric, as expressive, as any. Example 20 shows the first few measures.

Example 20   Bach, Trio Sonata, C major

bass omitted

In both sonatas the bass is of equal importance with the upper voices: it takes part in the imitative writing, contains melodic bits, and has very little connection with the old *basso continuo.* Harmonically the result is that the three voices are complete in themselves and scarcely require the harpsichord to fill out the chords, as had been the practice up to this time. The growing independence and musical integrity of the bass line in Bach's music, seen copiously in the solo sonatas, are here evident again.

Musikalisches Opfer. Of completely different quality and stature is the magnificently organized work, *Musikalisches Opfer,*[16] S.1079. When Bach visited Frederick the Great at Potsdam, in 1747, he was given a "royal theme" upon which to improvise. He must have performed to the king's liking, for the visit was completed by the latter's expressions and token of esteem. Upon Bach's return home he employed the royal theme in a series of twelve canons and fugues and one trio sonata, for various combinations of instruments (from two to six) and presented the work to Frederick as a musical offering (*musikalisches Opfer*).

[16] In modern edition by Hans T. David (G. Schirmer).

The work is unique in the symmetry and proportion it exhibits, unique even for Bach, whose musical forms in general show strict adherence to a well-laid formal plan. In *Musikalisches Opfer* the plan is as follows:

I. *Ricercare,* two instruments and bass

II. Five canons, for three instruments

    (*a*) Canon at the double octave

    (*b*) Canon at the unison

    (*c*) Canon in contrary motion

    (*d*) Canon by augmentation and contrary motion

    (*e*) Modulating canon (C, D, E, F sharp, G sharp, B flat, C minor)

> *In these canons the "royal theme" is carried by one instrument, while the other two engage in canonic imitation, in the manner indicated, of original counterthemes.*

III. Trio sonata, two instruments and figured bass
      Largo, allegro, andante, allegro

IV. Five canonic elaborations of the theme, for two to four instruments

    (*a*) Mirror canon, two instruments and figured bass

    (*b*) Crab canon (in retrograde motion) and its retrograde form, two instruments

    (*c*) Contrary motion canon and its inversion, two instruments

    (*d*) Canon in quadruple counterpoint, four instruments

    (*e*) Canonic fugue at the fifth above, three instruments

> *In these canons the "royal theme" itself is made the subject of the canons, while the other instrument or instruments carry the countermelodies.*

V. *Ricercare,* six instruments

Thus there is symmetry in large and small aspects: the work begins and ends with a *ricercare;* the five canons in the second part are balanced by the five in the fourth part. But there is also a gradual increase in size of the canons: those in the second part, for three instruments, are rather short (nine to forty-nine measures, respectively), while those in the fourth part are considerably longer (thirty-six to seventy-eight measures), thus effecting, through sheer size, a greater emotional intensity. Furthermore, in the treatment of the "royal theme" there is a growth of interest: in the five canons of the second part the theme is announced by one instrument, while the other two carry on the two-voice canonic writing around it; in the canons of the fourth part the "royal theme" itself is made the subject of the various canonic devices, while the other voices carry the counter-melodies. Finally, the six-voice fugue that is the last *ricercare* is considerably more intense, longer, and rises to a greater climax than the three-voice fugue with which the work opens.

The royal theme itself, as presented to Bach by Frederick (see Example 21), is well adapted to the contrapuntal treatment it receives.

Example 21   Bach, *Musikalisches Opfer,* Ricercare I

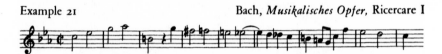

Well-defined tonality, the characteristic leap of a diminished seventh, and a long chromatic line—these elements testify to the good musical judgment of the king in presenting a fugue theme upon which Bach was to improvise. But Frederick could not have foreseen the wealth of technical invention, musical profundity, and organizing genius Bach eventually disclosed in this "musical offering." Obsolete contrapuntal practices were revived and contributed to the greatness of this work. Symmetry, balance between parts, well-proportioned climaxes, and a gradual ascent in emotional intensity—all these, plus a unique plan that is in itself a stroke of genius, are found here. The work as a whole, particularly the charming trio sonata (Part III), is well worth any amount of study one can give it. As a technical *tour de force,* as a monument to Bach's contrapuntal genius, and as a piece of pure music, *Musikalisches Opfer* is unique in the chamber-music literature.

Die Kunst der Fuge. In speaking of the differences between German and Italian instrumental music, Lang calls attention to the Germans' "tone and their fantastic world, ranging far and wide in the metaphysical beyond. . . . It is still this same unfathomable and mysterious musical world which is conjured up in Bach's *The Art of the Fugue* and in the last string quartets of Beethoven. The scholar's work ends here, for while the ear still continues to hear, the intellect ceases to function. We feel everything and we know exactly where we are, but the light that burns in our hearts flickers when we attempt to force the intellect to translate into concrete formulae what we are beholding. It is impossible to explain this music in terms of technical, formal analyses, for it is lost in the sea of the irrational; any formal elements are merely particles washed ashore." [17]

The honesty implicit in the above quotation emboldens the present writer to give primarily a description of Bach's *Die Kunst der Fuge*. Any "explanation" of this great work would, through sheer language inadequacy, become either ponderous, trite, or hysterical, and nothing at all would be gained thereby. *Die Kunst der Fuge*, like *Musikalisches Opfer*, is a unique phenomenon in music; it, more than almost any work in the Baroque period, must be heard, lived with, and experienced fully in order that its scope may be understood and its purpose revered.

Die Kunst der Fuge, written in 1749 and published posthumously, is Bach's last work. Early editions, including the original and six subsequent ones,[18] dealt freely with the order of the various sections of the work, omitting some and in general giving a distorted view of the total plan. A version edited by Wolfgang Graeser[19] was performed in Leipzig in 1927, attracted the attention of the musical world, and was the first that allowed the colossal structure of the work to be seen fully. Erich Schwebsch, in an exhaustive and highly stimulating account of the work,[20] finds that Graeser's ordering of the sections is correct.

In the simplest terms, the work consists of nineteen fugues, the last of which is unfinished. Although it is designed for instruments, as evidenced by the fact that its parts are written on separate staves, the desired instruments are not indicated by name, nor are there any tempo indications. The separate fugues are called "counterpoints" and are numbered from i to xix. Six groups are discernible: Group A, counterpoints i–iv; Group B, counterpoints v–vii; Group C, counter-

---

[17] *Music in Western Civilization*, pp. 488–89.

[18] By Hauptmann, Rust, Riemann, Tovey, etc. The edition in the *Werke*, ed. Hauptmann and others, Vol. XXV[1], is one of them.

[19] *Bachs Werke*, Der neuen Bachgesellschaft, Vol. XXVIII [1].

[20] *Johann Sebastian Bach und Die Kunst der Fuge*, pp. 61 ff.

points VIII–XI; Group D, counterpoints XII–XV; Group E, counterpoints XVI–XVIII; Group F, counterpoints XIX (a,b,c). Running
through the entire cycle as a basic subject, but altered considerably
on each successive appearance, is the theme given in Example 22.

Example 22   Bach, *Die Kunst der Fuge*

Group A, counterpoints I–IV, contains two fugues with the subject
in normal position, two with the subject inverted, all containing some
small but significant rhythmic changes.

Group B, counterpoints V–VII, consists of one fugue with the subject in normal and inverted positions simultaneously, one with both
positions in regular and halved note values (that is, twice as fast),
one with both positions in regular, doubled (half as fast), and halved
note values.

Group C, counterpoints VIII–XI, includes four fugues, but of
greater size and complexity, for here double and triple fugues appear.
It should be remembered that in a double fugue there is an essentially complete fugue on the first subject, a similarly complete fugue
on the second, followed by a section in which both subjects are heard
together. In a triple fugue three subjects are used, and all three appear together in the final section. Of such nature are the four fugues
of Group C. Counterpoints IX and X are double fugues; counterpoints
VIII and XI are triple. The first subject of counterpoint VIII introduces
an element of chromaticism into the cycle; as seen in Example 23a,
it is an undulating (Schwebsch calls it "snake-like" [21]) phrase out of
whose chromatic line the third subject of counterpoint XI will evolve
(Example 23b). The second subject (of counterpoint VIII) is derived
from figurations found in the first section. At this point, when the
fugue's cyclical unity with the first seven fugues is threatened, Bach
introduces a third subject that restores the unity; for the third subject
is yet another version of the cycle's basic subject. Counterpoint XI,
again a triple fugue, contains two transformed versions of subjects

heard earlier in the cycle and a third subject, based on the notes B
flat, A, C, and B natural (Example 23b), which in German terminol-
ogy becomes B-A-C-H.

Example 23   Bach, *Die Kunst der Fuge*

Group D, counterpoints xii–xvi, contains four two-voice canonic
fugues whose apparent innocence conceals a wealth of relationships
to earlier fugues of the cycle. The basic subject is present in all four
fugues of this group, yet it is considerably transformed in contour,
rhythm, and style. Devices of augmentation and diminution of note
values in conjunction with normal and inverted position of the subjects appear together. And the B-A-C-H theme tends to be reabsorbed
into the chromatic line in counterpoint xii.

Group E includes counterpoints xvi-a and b, xvii-a and b, and
xviii-a and b. These are single fugues in contrast to the double and
triple fugues of Group C, but they are also mirror fugues. A fugue
of this type is actually two fugues in one, for in addition to the normal
fugue there is its exact inversion. Every interval of every voice and
each voice itself is inverted throughout the whole course of the movement—it is "mirrored" from below, so to speak. Thus in Group E,
counterpoint xvi-a is followed by its inverted form, xvi-b; xvii-a is
followed by xvii-b; xviii-a is followed by xviii-b.

Group F consists of the uncompleted counterpoint xix-a, b, and c.
Containing a first subject (xix-a) derived from the basic subject of
the cycle, a second subject (xix-b) apparently unrelated to other
themes in the cycle, and a third subject (xix-c) on the B-A-C-H
theme (Example 23c), this gigantic movement is a triple fugue of

²¹ Ibid., p. 241.

the most profound type. But Schwebsch, on the basis of the plan of the whole cycle, on internal evidence, and on his own keen insight into Bach's intention, declares this to be an unfinished quadruple fugue of which a bit more than half was completed. For a fourth subject (xix-d) Bach had planned the original form of the basic theme, thus completing the unity of the cycle, establishing a symmetry of the most subtle kind, and presenting in a complex musical form a symbol of deep significance.

Seen in its entirety, *Die Kunst der Fuge* is a work with a plan of thematic transformation unequaled in the history of music. A tabular view of the entire cycle, adapted from Schwebsch,[22] follows.

Schwebsch sees the cycle as an esoteric work symbolizing the

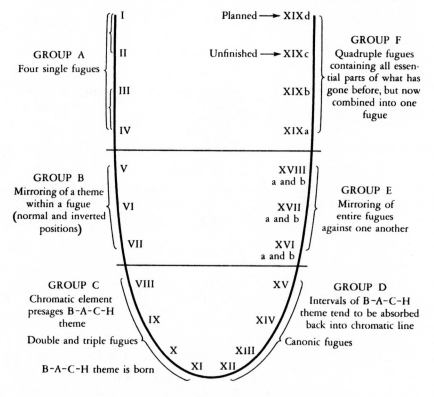

FORMAL PLAN IN BACH, *Die Kunst der Fuge*

[22] Ibid., p. 123.

gradual materialization of the human being's spiritual essence descending out of higher regions (counterpoints i–xi), the entry of the human ego (B-A-C-H theme in counterpoint xi, the midpoint of the cycle), and the gradual return ascent of the transformed human spirit into its spiritual home (counterpoints xii–xix-d). Such an interpretation can come only out of a knowledge of the philosophical and esoteric works of Rudolf Steiner (1861–1925) and a *Weltanschauung* based on these works.[23] As to Bach's participation in esoteric wisdom, Schwebsch points out that Bach was well acquainted with the sermons of the mystic Johannes Tauler (1300–61)[24] and that the connections between the divine and the human were ever present in his mind. As his last work he chose to symbolize the incarnation of the human spirit on earth and its subsequent ascent to a higher existence. Bach's use of his own name as a symbol of the human ego is not to be taken as a light-hearted gesture but as evidence of his knowledge of his own worth. Only a Bach could have carried out so profound a plan, and probably in no other work in western music is such a plan to be looked for.

OTHER COMPOSERS

Three of the great composers spoken of up to this point, namely, Buxtehude, Dall' Abaco, and Handel, are representative of the dozens of composers, great and small, writing sonatas and trio sonatas in Italy, France, Germany, and England. In the works of these men one sees an emphasis on virtuosity, lightness, and humor (Buxtehude), lyric melody and excellence of form (Dall' Abaco), and contrapuntal mastery and a noble singing style (Handel)—although all these elements are found, obviously, in all three composers to a greater or lesser degree. In the many other composers writing in the period roughly from 1700 to 1740 one finds a similar preoccupation with this or that element. Though all of them could write melodies, though all were skilled contrapuntists, and though all were virtuosos at heart,

[23] Published in German by Philosophischer-Anthroposophischer Verlag (Dornach, Switzerland), in English by The Anthroposophic Press (New York).

[24] *Johann Sebastian Bach und Die Kunst der Fuge*, pp. 137 ff.

one or another of these elements shines through their works to the temporary eclipse of the others.

Thus among the adherents of the noble, singing style best represented by Handel, we must include the Frenchmen François Couperin (1668–1733) and Jean Leclair (1697–1764) and the Italians Benedetto Marcello (1686–1739) and Francesco Veracini (1690–c. 1768). While lyric melodies and fugal movements are present in the works of Giuseppe Tartini (1692–1770), Francesco Geminiani (1687–1762), and Johann Birkenstock (1687–1733), the main interest of these composers lies in technical brilliance and display. Tartini is remembered especially for highly ornamented violin sonatas, which, while they are lyric and full of noble expression, opened the way for nineteenth-century virtuosity. Among the lesser masters of counterpoint, whose music is typically Italian in its gayety and charm, are Carlo Tessarini (c. 1690–c. 1765) and Pietro Locatelli (1695–1764). The mention of these names by no means exhausts the list of chamber-music composers writing in the period from 1700 to 1740. To be complete such a list would have to include practically every composer of consequence living at that time. Composers of opera and church music, organists, and harpsichord composers—all would have to be included, for all were interested in chamber-music forms, and all contributed at least a few works to the literature.

Having reached this point, with true sonata-form just a step beyond, we have come to the limits of Baroque form. The essentials of that form, let us recall, were adherence to one mood and one melodic idea per movement, in keeping with the doctrine of the affections. Many composers of the period from 1730 to 1750 were on the edge of violating that doctrine by tending toward a contrasting second theme; in so doing they closely approached the Classical forms of the mid-eighteenth century. Half a dozen important composers after the 1740s still continued to write trio sonatas, but each one came closer to the style and forms associated with the Vienna of Haydn and Mozart. Among these composers Giovanni Pergolesi, Johann Gottlieb Graun, Karl Philipp Emanuel Bach, and Christoph

Willibald von Gluck will be discussed in the following chapter, along with their eminent contemporaries in Vienna and Mannheim.

Thus we close the account of the chamber music of the period from Viadana to Bach, roughly from 1600 to 1750. Each of the composers in the line from Viadana through Marini, Vitali, Corelli, Purcell, Buxtehude, Dall' Abaco, Handel, and Bach wrote music in the style of his times, clothed musical truth and beauty in the aesthetic apparel of his generation. We have substituted another style for the style of these composers, but this in itself is no guarantee that ours is superior to theirs. Styles change, inevitably, as the economic, material, and psychological factors of human life change. Anyone who will take the trouble to assume the aesthetic outlook and adopt the psychology of the Baroque man will find in Baroque music a source of great satisfaction. In clarity, freedom from sentimentality, and forthrightness it stands on a level with the best music of the Classical period. In choice of melodic materials it approaches the nobility and the charm of the great Italian vocal tradition. With these elements as characteristics, the music cannot fail to serve the same purpose as music of every other age: to move human emotions and to inspire us toward a richer life.

5. The Emergence of Classical Style

THE WAYS in which musical style changes gradually come about have been mentioned earlier in this book. During most of music's history several decades have been required to alter the sound and the appearance of the music, decades during which the new style begins to become noticeable in the midst of the old style characteristics, decades in which the latter eventually become submerged in the body of the new style elements. It has been the custom of historians to seize upon a date midway in this transition period, a date at which both styles are clearly defined, and refer to it as a style boundary. We are now confronted with a major change—that from the Baroque style to the Classical. For convenience we can take a date near 1755 to mark the beginning of the latter style. As we shall see below, that date marks the appearance of Haydn's first string quartets.

PRE-CLASSICAL STYLE

But the Baroque did not fade smoothly into the Classical; Baroque characteristics did not, in general, persist up to and past 1755. A large quantity of music written from about 1725 to 1760, and many art, architectural, and literary works of the same period show characteristics which, while derived from Baroque elements, are not based on the same aesthetic principles. In France, under Louis XV, a new style of architectural ornamentation arose, based on the use of artificial rock work, decorated and sculptured shell work, and extravagance of detail in general. Enthusiastically imitated in Italy and Germany, the new style soon left its mark on other art forms, particularly music and literature, in the shape of delicacy of structure, elaborate attention to insignificant details, and choice of some frivolous subject matter. The new style was called *rococo* (derived from the French *rocaille,* rock work); we can refer to the Rococo period in discussing the pre-Classical chamber music of the decades between 1725 and 1760.

As one of the accompanying phenomena of the Rococo (probably the sociologist would put the horse before the cart), the long fight against absolute monarchy, against the domination of one individual by another, flared up afresh. Liberty became a new watchword; enlightenment and reason became ideals. And liberty soon became synonymous with freedom from rules, conventions, and forms. Inevitably, Baroque music, with its strict rules, its conventional affections, and its monumental forms, became one of the first victims of the new urge. "Back to nature" was the popular cry in theater and opera; capriciousness and entertainment were demanded in instrumental music. Inevitably, lowered standards of taste became general. Music was faced with one measuring stick—entertainment value. Much of the music measured up (or really down) to the new taste level.

The emancipation from rules brought with it a search for new effects. Dignity gave way to frivolity, and a new type of melodic line came into being. The Baroque principle of one mood per movement gave way to the practice of contrasting moods within a movement, and musical forms suited to this different content emerged. Dilettantism flourished; every gentleman played the violin, and every lady the flute. This invasion of music by the amateur in search of diversion required a type of music that was within the technical and intellectual limits of the dilettante and made necessary more detailed directions for playing the music itself. Thus, as more or less immediate results of the Rococo social outlook and trend of thought, the sonata-form and the serenade, or divertimento, came into being, along with a new type of expressiveness in the melody, a new type of accompaniment, and the careful marking of dynamic changes in the music. Composers of the Rococo period experimented with these new devices, improved upon them, and in due time passed them on to the great Viennese masters whom we associate with the full flowering of the Classical period.

First-Movement Form. Among the most obvious of the changes brought about during the decades of the Rococo subperiod were those that had to do with form. Late Baroque music had been characterized by the considerable use of short melodic motives. These motives were spun out, employed in sequence, undergirt with fast-changing harmonies, used in polyphonic textures—to such an extent that the typical Baroque form was monothematic, open (that is, recapitulation played little part in it), and based upon a single mood. Whether in slow tempo or in fast, the movement developed considerable harmonic and rhythmic momentum, in the sense that the harmony pressed forward from a tonic chord through contrasting harmonic sections to its cadence; and the rhythmic motion was seldom interrupted in its course. Such Baroque characteristics may be observed in music written until about 1750 and beyond.

Parallel to these style traits distinguishing the late Baroque period were others that are equally representative of the Rococo. Since the latter merged almost imperceptibly with still-later traits that came to their fullest development in the Classical period, they are often described as marking a "pre-Classical" phase; indeed, the Rococo may be said to represent one aspect of pre-Classical style.

The style elements that may be ascribed to this aspect differed considerably from those of the Baroque. First was a gradual decline in the use of the spinning-out technique based on melodic motives. In its place came the use of longer bits of melodic material cast in analogy to sentence structures. Musical phrases complete in themselves and with their own harmonic and cadential schemes were set opposite, or made to contrast with, other such phrases. The melodic material thus formed dominated the musical structure; there was little need for polyphonic treatment in the style, hence the use of counterpoint declined. Balanced pairs of phrases represented one desirable ideal, hence a regularization of period structures—often multiples of four measures in length—became typical. Cadences were spaced with a certain regularity, and sectional structures resulted.

This manner of organizing the melodic material was carried out principally in the two-part form that had been inherited from late Baroque composers. It will be recalled that insofar as chamber music is concerned we have had to do largely with only three formal types. Virtually all the single movements in solo and trio sonatas—whether *sonate da camera, sonate da chiesa,* or their successors—have been representatives of those types. One type, a toccatalike movement containing rhapsodic elements, was found most often as first movement (*praeludium, introduzione,* etc.) in certain works by Corelli, Vivaldi, and others. A second type, found most often in *sonate da chiesa,* was related to the fugal form that resulted from the solidification of the *canzone* elements into a single movement. And the third type, with which we are primarily concerned here, was derived from the dance form found in dance suites as early as the 1650s and in *sonate da camera* after the 1670s.

The dance-derived type consisted of two parts separated by a double bar, with each part designed to be repeated. The first part, beginning in the tonic key, had ended in the dominant, whereas the second part, continuing in the dominant, had modulated back to the tonic. The form may be diagramed as follows:

$$\|: \ I\!\!-\!\!V \ :\|: \ V\!\!-\!\!I \ :\|$$

It was largely within this form that the new organization of melodic materials was carried out, although slow movements, rondos, and minuets were not immune to the new treatment.

While the melodic material arranged within this common form consisted of balanced and often contrasting phrases that usually moved from tonic to dominant and back, the phrases themselves did not necessarily possess distinctive contour or noteworthy melodic shape. During the course of a movement several such phrases would be presented, would move toward the mid-point of the movement, and would end in the key of the dominant. After the mid-point, similar phrases would occur, and the movement would move back to the tonic key. Nowhere could one speak of a theme (defined as the vehicle for a musical thought), and only rarely was a phrase first heard at the beginning of the movement encountered again elsewhere. Thus, any symmetry in the form was confined to the harmony, with the ||: I—V :||: V—I :|| pattern by far the most common.[1]

The keyboard sonatas of Domenico Scarlatti (1685–1757) reveal a consistent step toward a solidification of the form from a melodic standpoint. In the great majority of his more than five hundred keyboard sonata movements—some single and others arranged in sets— the harmonic scheme we have described above applies. But in these works a second scheme appears, this time based on balance of figurations. Scarlatti's practice is to begin with a musical phrase containing some degree of melodic appeal, carry the phrase toward the dominant, and let it dissolve in brilliant figurations in that dominant key; the second part begins with the melodic phrase of the first part, but now in the dominant key, moves toward the tonic key, and ends with figurations similar to those with which the first part ended. There emerges a balance best shown as A—B :||: A—B, contained within the harmonic symmetry of I—V :||: V—I; it will be seen that in the second part the melody and figurations appear with the harmonies reversed. Each section is in effect transposed to the key of the other.

Now, the contour or melody of the A section is in general distinctive enough to be remembered and recognized when it returns at the beginning of the second part; hence it can be called a theme. But the material of the B section is usually not distinctive enough to be remembered and recognized; often it consists of figurations, broken chords, and similar virtuosic devices; it rarely shows signs of melodic shape or phrase structure and cannot be called a theme. It remained for other composers to invest the phrases of the B section with melodic integrity sufficient to call them thematic and thus to prepare the way for the appearance of true first and second themes. When that point had been reached, the diagram given above could be appropriately modified, thus:

Theme	||:	1st	2d	:||:	1st	2d	:||
Harmony		I	V		V	I	

---

[1] ||: I—III :||: III—I :|| usually appeared in movements in a minor key.

Two further variants among the formal plans found in pre-Classical first movements may be noted. In many cases—but by no means in all, as will appear below—the first theme section on the dominant after the double bar was replaced by a section in which a degree of fantasy prevailed. Portions only of the first theme, or melodic figurations, or even phrases of new material were often introduced here; the result was that the section consisted of a working-over of melodic material rather than a thematic statement. And the demands of symmetry, or the felt necessity of "returning" after a thematic departure, made it desirable to reintroduce the first theme, but now on the tonic again. Thus in many cases a true recapitulation is at hand, and the diagram may be further modified as follows:

Theme		1st	2d		transition	1st	2d	
Harmony	:	I	V	: :	V, II, etc.	I	I	:

It must be emphasized that no single diagram can serve to illustrate the practices of hundreds of composers writing dozens of works each. The above diagram represents no more than a generalization that is valid in some compositions by some composers. Yet the plan represented here was largely adopted later by the major composers in the Classical period, and it carries within it the seed of fully developed sonata-form. Other versions of the diagram could be brought forward, of course; for example those in which recapitulation of both themes on the tonic is partially or completely missing.

The Sonata as a Whole. Toward the middle of the eighteenth century the commanding position enjoyed by the four-movement scheme (slow-fast-slow-fast) in the sonata began to weaken. Whether written for solo or trio, sonatas with fewer than four movements are met with increasing frequency—even in works written in late-Baroque style. With the emergence of pre-Classical style elements, the tendency to depart from the four-movement form became stronger, and for several decades a three-movement form was the most usual. Some composers, especially in Italy, favored a two-movement form, but such works are probably in the minority; the two-movement form seems to have been adopted primarily in works intended for amateur or pedagogical use.

Influenced perhaps by the concerto, which had long since developed in the direction of a fast-slow-fast scheme, composers of the new solo and ensemble sonatas adopted a similar scheme. But the model of the pre-Classical opera overture, with its three sections arranged in a fast-slow-fast pattern, may have been of influence also; the *sinfonia* of the time, which eventually developed into the Classical symphony, was essentially an expansion of the opera overture. In any case, the three-movement form in either a fast-slow-fast or fast-moderate-fast scheme became the favored plan in pre-Classical chamber music. The middle movement, most usually an adagio or andante and sometimes cast in variation form, often gave way to a minuet; and in a few works a slow-fast-fast scheme is found. Final movements occur in a variety of forms, with rondos most common.

The two-movement plan was not standardized, virtually all possible combinations of movement being employed. Slow-fast, moderate-fast, fast-rondo, fast-minuet, and other combinations were used, but more frequently in solo sonatas than in trios. With the growing concern for variety of expression and depth of feeling in chamber music toward the last third of the century, two-movement patterns lost ground; but they were retained in keyboard sonatas to the end of the century and beyond.

Texture. In the previous chapter the fact was mentioned that in certain works the *basso continuo* was omitted and the keyboard part was written out in full. The *continuo* had dominated virtually all composition since the early 1600s. It had required the services of a keyboard performer to realize the figured bass. It had left the inner voices of the instrumental group relatively free to take part in imitations, to engage in thematic work, and at times to develop a degree of musical independence. And it had provided a solid harmonic foundation to which the lowest voice was securely bound. Now, in the years between approximately 1735 and 1750, a new musical idea was born—an idea that grew out of the Rococo desire for display, that led to the speedy decay of the *continuo* principle, and that made possible the transfer of the prima donna role to the first violinist.

Now, as one of the characteristics of the *style galant,* came the idea that one instrument was to dominate the musical structure, that the others were to be completely subordinate, both in musical significance and in style. We can best see the nature of this departure by recalling the typical trio sonata of the late Baroque period. Two more-or-less coequal melodies in the two violins, the alternation of melodic importance between the violins, made unavoidable when the factor of imitative writing was so prevalent, and the parallel motion of the violins in thirds and sixths—these had all been present in the trio sonatas of the early eighteenth century.

In the new style musical significance was confined largely to the solo violin; melodic interest was found only in the uppermost part of the ensemble. The bass line and the inner voices became vehicles for indicating merely the harmonic scheme of the piece; and possibly because the composers distrusted the ability of amateurs to realize their intentions as expressed in figured-bass symbols, all the parts were written out in full. Chords below the dominating melody became complete, and all harmonic changes were adequately indicated in the parts for the lower instruments. As a consequence the erstwhile *continuo* part, traditionally realized on a keyboard instrument, became unnecessary, and the practice of writing figured basses became obsolete. At first in orchestra music, later in chamber music, and last of all in opera, figured basses and the *continuo* principle disappeared.

NEW FORMS AND MEDIA

It has been pointed out that in the course of the late Baroque period the solo sonata, for one instrument (violin, flute, cello, etc.) and figured bass, gained in popularity even as the trio sonata took a somewhat less-favored position. We have also seen that at about the same time, but representative of pre-Classical style, there appeared modifications in the two-part movement derived from the dance form, and we have indicated that these modifications eventually led to Classical sonata-form. Additional changes in form and media likewise occurred; they represent still other manifestations of the new style. Among them, the appearance of the divertimento and the evolution of several new performing media with and without keyboard instruments are especially significant.

The Divertimento. Toward the middle of the eighteenth century a practice long known to suitors and lovers in every land became extremely popular, was seized upon by composers, and gave rise to a new musical literature. It became customary to honor one's friends by engaging a number of musicians to play appropriate music under their windows. This practice flourished especially in Vienna, and another step in the evolution of sonata-form is seen in the music composed for that purpose. *Serenade, nocturne, divertimento,* and *cassation* were the terms used to identify this new music; and the terms at once give clues to its nature. Generally it was performed after nightfall (*sera* = evening) in the streets (*Gasse* = lane; *gassatim* = streetlike), and it was light and diverting in character. A few string and/or wind instruments sufficed for the purposes at hand, and generally one player, or at most two, performed each part. Toward 1770 Charles Burney reports that a singer returning to Brescia after a long absence in Russia was serenaded by a band of two violins, mandolin, French horn, trumpet, and cello, "and though in the dark [they] played long concertos, with solo parts for the mandoline." [2]

Various versions of the divertimento[3] differed widely in the number of movements, but all had two features in common: their light, cheerful content and their derivation from the three-movement *sinfonia.* Conservative north German composers adhered to the three-movement form in writing their divertimentos. Many Italian works of this type, on the other hand, contain two movements, one fast and one slow; and the north Germans protested vigorously this "sin against the spirit of the *sinfonia.*" [4] South German and Austrian composers added one or more movements taken from the suite, usually the minuet. And it is this four-movement version of the divertimento that had the greatest influence on the future symphony and string quartet. The sequence

[2] *The Present State of Music in France and Italy,* p. 115.

[3] Let us include in this term all the music of this type, even though there were minor technical distinctions and some differences in instrumentation between serenade, divertimento, nocturne, and cassation.

[4] Adler, *Handbuch,* II, 802.

allegro-andante-minuet-finale is known to everyone as the most usual form for the Classical symphony and quartet of the late eighteenth century. There it was deepened in content and expanded in form, without a doubt; but its kinship to the unassuming, light divertimento of the period from about 1740 to 1755 is seen in its adoption of the latter's essential framework. And the divertimento to a considerable degree bridged the gap between the old trio sonata and the soon-to-be string quartet, both in structural details and in instrumentation.

Many divertimentos were just as suited to performance by small orchestras as by quartets and quintets; often, when the resources of the serenader permitted, they were performed by orchestras of fifteen to twenty-five players. It was characteristic of the divertimento type to be considered both chamber and orchestra music. The distinction between the two fields, never too carefully drawn in the early history of instrumental music, threatened to disappear entirely in the period from 1740 to 1760. We shall see in the following chapter that among Haydn's early string quartets, many of which are divertimentos, is one that is reputed to be his first symphony.

Two divertimentos by Joseph Starzer (1726–87) may be taken as typical of the chamber music of Vienna at that time.[5] Each contains four movements: allegro, minuet and trio, larghetto or adagio, and allegro. Each is for two violins, viola, and bass, without the usual *continuo*. Adler points out that these may be among the first works that omit the harpsichord and its function of realizing the figured bass.[6] The style is ingratiating, noticeably homophonic, and altogether enjoyable. Sonata-form is present in a rudimentary fashion; Starzer does not go beyond the harmonic scheme of Scarlatti, and there is scarcely a trace of a contrasting second theme.

But the works are unique in the responsibility given to the lower instruments of the quartet. The first violin dominates, true enough, in keeping with the *style galant,* of which these divertimentos are good examples. But second violin, viola, and bass all take part in thematic developments and in transitional passages, and all three are far removed

---

[5] Reprinted in *DTÖ,* Vol. XV².
[6] Foreword, ibid., p. xi.

from the function of merely supporting the first violin. In the minuet of the first divertimento the viola is actually the leading voice. Throughout the two works the bass engages in figurations much more worthy of a cello than a bass viol; indeed, if Baroque practice were followed here and the bass part were to be read "for bass or cello," we would have two string quartets in the contemporary sense. Unfortunately there is little possibility of dating these works accurately; a comparison of them with Haydn's first quartets of 1755 with a view to establishing priority would lead nowhere.

It is during these decades of divertimento composition that Germany and Austria assumed their dominant place in the history of instrumental music. From about 1750 the great composers and the great accomplishments in music are identified with these two countries. Operas continued to be written in Italy and were still performed in France. Italians were still active in London, and for that matter in Vienna and some German cities. But the new accomplishments in the field of keyboard, orchestral, and chamber music are henceforth to be looked for north of the Alps. The long domination of the Italians was over; a century and a half of German supremacy was at hand.

The String Quartet. Viennese composers of the period around 1740 were possibly among the first consistently to abandon the use of the *continuo* principle; the divertimentos by Starzer may be counted as two early examples of that practice in larger ensemble works. Soon the new style became a factor in composing at Berlin, Mannheim, and elsewhere. The orchestra, the string section of which had long since included first and second violins, violas, cellos, and basses, found it expedient to add new wind instruments to the few oboes and trumpets already present and to employ the entire wind choir to sustain harmonies. As a consequence the violas and cellos were freed from their task of holding long tones and otherwise providing a chordal background for the melody instruments. They were able to take part in a more lively accompaniment for the dominating first violins, and they achieved a certain amount of melodic self-sufficiency.

In chamber music, where the trio sonata was still the most frequently used instrumental combination, the harpsichord was discarded. Since the remaining two violins and bass were not able to supply a melody plus three complete harmony parts, the addition of a fourth instrument was made necessary. The choice logically fell on the viola. About 1745 that instrument made its appearance in chamber music, along with the two violins and the bass. Shortly thereafter, with the emergence of thematic work in all four instruments, the cello was deemed better suited to the combination than the bass, and the latter largely disappeared from the field of chamber music. So the contemporary string quartet, composed of two violins, viola, and cello, was born about 1745.

Periodically attempts are made to ascribe a somewhat earlier date to the founding of the string quartet. For example, several *sonate a quattro* by Alessandro Scarlatti (1660–1725) are often referred to as the earliest string quartets; they were written between 1715 and 1725 and are for *due violini, violetta e violoncello senza cembalo* (see Example 24).[7] In Chapter 4 we ourselves called attention to a quasi quartet

Example 24   Alessandro Scarlatti, Sonata a quattro

among the trio sonatas of Handel's Opus 5 (1738), a work in which a viola part had been added to the two violins and bass, thus making the *continuo* unnecessary. Other works from the early years of the eighteenth century will probably be unearthed from time to time in which the four string instruments are used without *continuo*, and the

[7] One in modern reprint ed. by Hans T. David (Music Press).

founding date of the quartet will presumably be pushed back again. But we can be sure that such works will be derived from the old *sonata da chiesa* or *da camera* and will have no connection with the innovations in form, style, and general mood that the Rococo period brought about. In short, they will be Baroque works that happen to be written for four string instruments. The Scarlatti and Handel compositions mentioned above fall into that style category. As such, they will not be the direct ancestors of the quartet as Haydn first knew it, nor will they contain the formal elements and aesthetic qualities upon which Haydn built so magnificently.

We may mention in passing the six string quartets of Georg Matthias Monn (1717–50), an important Viennese composer in the generation just preceding Haydn's. Monn's significance lies mainly in the field of orchestral music, however, for in a work of his dated 1740 the minuet makes its first appearance in the symphony. Comparatively few of his works have been preserved; among them are seventeen symphonies of various types, several suites and sonatas, and six string quartets. Each of the quartets contains but two movements—slow-fast, in a style reminiscent of the old *sonata da chiesa*. But the fourth quartet of the series is simply a transcription of the first two movements of Monn's first *sinfonia da chiesa* for string orchestra, and the sixth quartet is similarly derived from the second symphony. Wilhelm Fischer[8] assumes that the other four quartets are likewise fragments of similar symphonies that no longer exist. He points out that such fragments of orchestral *sonate da chiesa* played an important role in the Imperial Chapel at Vienna well into Mozart's time (c. 1785) and that two other examples of this treatment exist among Monn's orchestral suites. Thus, while these works of Monn are quartets insofar as the performing medium is concerned, they are not to be included in the chamber-music literature.

Other New Media. And what of the keyboard instruments in the years after they were forcibly dropped from the field of chamber music? They immediately forced their way back into the field and became more dominating than ever before. The harpsichord (and

---

[8] Preface to Vol. XIX² of *DTÖ*, in which all these works of Monn are reprinted.

later the newly developing pianoforte), being freed from the duty of improvising accompaniments for orchestral and chamber-music ensembles, went its own ways. On the one hand, it reached new dignity and usefulness in three-movement, completely written-out sonatas for keyboard instrument alone—especially in the works of Karl Philipp Emanuel Bach (1714–88), the eldest son of the great Johann Sebastian Bach. The younger Bach was long active at the court of Frederick the Great at Berlin; his keyboard sonatas, similar to the trio sonatas of pseudo Pergolesi (see p. 136), but exceeding them in quality of invention and refinement, were destined to be of great influence on the long line of Classical composers who succeeded him. On the other hand, the keyboard instrument (and from about the 1760s we can speak only of the pianoforte in this connection, for the harpsichord was soon made obsolete) established a new connection with string instruments, in which it now provided the main musical interest; the strings accompanied. Thus sonatas for piano solo accompanied by violin and cello came into being. In many such cases the violin doubled the upper voice of the keyboard part, and the cello the lower; the subordinate role of the strings was assured, and at times the string instruments could be omitted entirely.

In other cases the violin and cello parts differed to some extent from the outer voices of the piano part; hence their presence was obligatory. Such works were called sonatas with violin and cello obbligato. In still other cases the keyboard was provided with violin or cello obbligato or with obbligato parts for violin, viola, and cello. In all these cases the predominant place of the keyboard instrument was clearly maintained. And in these three cases we see the pre-Classical forerunners of piano trio, violin or cello sonata, and piano quartet, respectively. This practice of so qualifying the function of string instruments remained in fashion long after the separation into solo and accompaniment roles had been resolved in chamber music. As late as 1797 Beethoven's cello sonatas, Opus 5, appeared with the legend "For piano with obbligato cello."

From a formal point of view, also, those movements of the composition that were in sonata-form were changed, enlarged, and deepened.

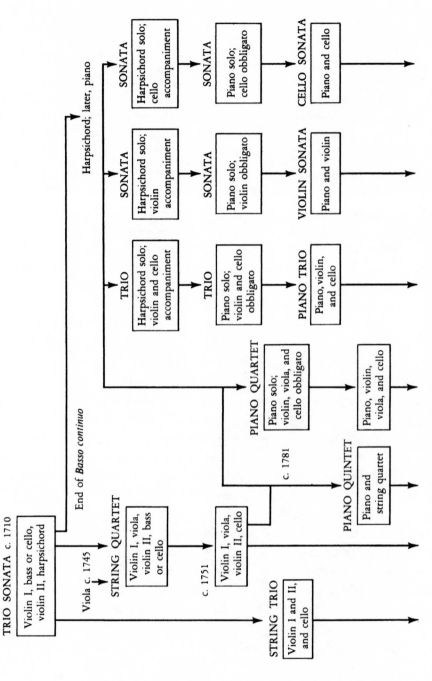

EVOLUTION OF CHAMBER-MUSIC COMBINATIONS

TRIO SONATA c. 1710
Violin I, bass or cello, violin II, harpsichord

End of *Basso continuo*

Harpsichord; later, piano

SONATA
Harpsichord solo; cello accompaniment

SONATA
Piano solo; cello obbligato

CELLO SONATA
Piano and cello

SONATA
Harpsichord solo; violin accompaniment

SONATA
Piano solo; violin obbligato

VIOLIN SONATA
Piano and violin

TRIO
Harpsichord solo; violin and cello accompaniment

TRIO
Piano solo; violin and cello obbligato

PIANO TRIO
Piano, violin, and cello

PIANO QUARTET
Piano solo; violin, viola, and cello obbligato

Piano, violin, viola, and cello

c. 1781

PIANO QUINTET
Piano and string quartet

Viola c. 1745

STRING QUARTET
Violin I, viola, violin II, bass or cello

Violin I, viola, violin II, cello

c. 1751

STRING TRIO
Violin I and II, and cello

The innovations in melodic construction introduced by many composers in the 1730s and later were the starting points for experiments to heighten the contrast between first and second theme groups, to construct themes out of melodies cast in regular period forms (as opposed to melodies growing out of short motives through repetition and imitation), and to construct transitions between themes out of thematic fragments. The end result of these successful experiments was a lengthened exposition section consisting of (a) first theme group of phrases, (b) transition, (c) second theme group, (d) coda—the total often reaching the respectable number of seventy-five to a hundred measures. The development section, too, was broadened to some degree by the use of thematic fragments, characteristic portions of melodies heard earlier in the exposition, and sequence modulation. But its ultimate destiny did not develop for thirty years or more, until the appearance, in 1782, of Haydn's quartets, "composed in an entirely new manner."

This survey of some of the elements responsible for the shape and content of pre-Classical chamber music is necessarily sketchy and general in tone. Many exceptions to the observations made here exist, of course. Indeed, a major characteristic of the time was stylistic and formal multiplicity. But this survey will perhaps serve as background for a discussion of the principal composers and works of the middle third of the century. Exceptions will be noted wherever appropriate.

TRANSITIONAL COMPOSERS

In one group of composers active at the time, Baroque formal and aesthetic practices were still very much in evidence. One such composer is Johann Fasch (1688–1758), resident in central Germany. Among his quantities of excellent instrumental and church music are five trio sonatas and one sonata for four instruments.[9] The first trio sonata is for violin, viola, and bass; the others are for two violins and bass. All five are compounded of the old polyphonic and new homophonic styles. Sonatas 1 and 2 are in four and three movements, respectively; each movement is a two-voice canon accompanied by the

[9] Reprinted in Riemann, ed. *Collegium musicum,* Nos. 8–13.

bass. Canonic devices and less strict imitations are present in sonatas 3 and 4, both of which contain three movements in slow-fast-slow sequence. Sonata 5, in four movements, again shows considerable contrapuntal treatment, extending as far as a complete fugue (second movement) in fast tempo, in the general style of the period.

But there is an equal amount of evidence that Fasch was sympathetic to new style tendencies. Several of the fast movements are in rudimentary sonata-form, whereas others, notably the final movement of sonata 3, are complete with elaborate developments and regular recapitulations. Even in these sonata-form movements, however, Fasch inclines toward the old way of building melodies; he bases his melodic extensions on repetition or sequence of motives rather than on the introduction of new melodic phrases.

The sixth Fasch work, the sonata for four instruments, is for two violins, viola, and bass without *basso continuo*. While it is impossible to date this work accurately, there is internal evidence that it was influenced by the Mannheim composers of about 1755; hence Fasch's omission of the *continuo* is not among the early examples of this practice. The two divertimentos of the Viennese Joseph Starzer (see p. 123) probably antedate Fasch's work with regard to this innovation. The sonata contains four movements in slow-fast-slow-fast sequence. There is the same mixture of old and new elements; homophonic melodies give way to contrapuntal imitations, and fugal sections contain homophonic episodes. Fasch is conservative in his use of the instruments. Much of the time the viola simply proceeds in octaves with the bass or supplies missing chord notes. The two violins are of equal importance in presentation and development of the musical ideas; thus the predominant solo violin is not in evidence. Fasch stands squarely at the crossroads and gives evidence that as late as 1755 certain Baroque practices and factors of musical expression were still very much alive.

Telemann. Another composer with the transitional outlook was George Philipp Telemann (1681–1767). Telemann, director and producer of opera at Hamburg, was a colleague and friend of Handel's and was a prolific composer of operatic, instrumental, and religious music. Among his works are about two hundred French suites for combinations of strings and wind instruments and a series of works called *Tafelmusik,* literally table music or banquet music, written about 1733. Each *Tafelmusik* as a whole contains five sets of movements for various groups of instruments; the sets are always arranged in the order of suite, quartet, concerto, trio, and solo, plus an orchestral conclusion. While the suite, concerto, and conclusion are orchestral, the quartet, trio, and solo are chamber music and deserve to be discussed here. The second *Tafelmusik*[10] is typical and may be examined in detail.

The work begins with an *ouverture,* or suite, for oboe, trumpet, and strings; a French overture (slow-fast) is followed by four airs, each one fast and diverting and in a different meter (vivace 4/4, vivace 3/8, presto 4/4, and allegro 12/8, respectively). Next is a quartet for three flutes and *basso continuo,* similar to works by Dall' Abaco and Handel, for it contains the usual four movements in slow-fast-slow-fast sequence, and the same half imitative and half homophonic style. The third piece is a concerto for three solo violins and string orchestra; it is in the three-movement form (fast-slow-fast) often found in other concertos of the period. Fourth is a trio sonata for flute, oboe, cello, and *basso continuo;* it, like the quartet, is in the traditional four-movement form, with a slow first movement, and is characterized by the same texture and style. Then comes a four-movement solo sonata for violin and *basso continuo;* the same formal structure we found in the trio and quartet, and the same style characteristics, are found here also. The work ends with a conclusion, a one-movement allegro in which the whole orchestra—oboe, trumpet, and strings—comes together again.

There is obviously nothing new in the purpose to which this *Tafelmusik* set is dedicated. Dinner music had existed throughout the previous century, for example, in Schein's *Banchetto musicale* of 1617. Nor is there anything remotely suggesting the formal and stylistic innovations of pre-Classical works. Two other main characteristics may be singled out, however, as pointing toward the future. First are

[10] Three of the *Tafelmusik* sets are found in DDT, Vols. LXI–LXII.

the variety of instrumentation employed in this work and the placing of large and small ensembles within the framework of one musical composition. It will be recalled that throughout a great part of the seventeenth century specific instrumentation for this or that composition was not called for. *Continuo* parts could be played by cello or bassoon or bass—whichever was available. As late as Handel's trio sonatas, Opera 1–5 (1724–40), the phrase "for violins or flutes or oboes" gives a clue to the flexible concept of instrumentation the Baroque composer employed. During the Classical period, well into the time of Mozart, the instrumentation of the symphony and chamber music became standardized, and a more rigid regard for instrumental color became the rule. In these compositions of Telemann we see a step in that direction. A quartet had a function different from that of a trio or a solo sonata or even a full orchestra. In the *Tafelmusik* Telemann combines the existing instrumental groupings, realizing full well that each combination of instruments will carry its own unique message.

The second characteristic is found in the general mood of the music itself. There are slow and fast movements, as there were in older music also. But the slow movements here are not designed to be profoundly moving, as were those of Corelli, Dall' Abaco, and Handel; nor are the fast movements cast in precise formal or fugal patterns, as was the older custom. Both the slow and fast movements of Telemann have a common characteristic: they are meant to be enjoyed and enjoyable. The Rococo spirit of diversion is alive in these works; there is no attempt at serious utterance, no attempt to move the listener. Insofar as the music serves that ideal, it is in the spirit of Telemann's age (it should be remembered that Telemann was typical of his time and that his great contemporary, Bach, was considered old-fashioned even in his day) and is a forerunner, in mood at least, of the serenades, nocturnes, and divertimentos mentioned above.

Gluck. The strength of Baroque tradition continued to make itself manifest even in the works of composers who in all respects are representatives of the newer style tendencies. The three-movement form, now well established in chamber music, often appeared with the first movement in slow tempo, as it had normally been in the Baroque period. The fast movement in turn often contained either thematic contrast or recapitulation, but seldom both. These points may be illustrated by reference to the trio sonatas of Christoph Willibald Gluck (1714–87), a composer more famous for his operas and operatic reforms than for his chamber music.

Seven of Gluck's trio sonatas are available in modern reprints.[11] The first six, originally published in London in 1746, are much alike in that all have three movements, all the first movements are in slow tempo, all the second movements are fast, and all but one of the last movements are minuets (the exception being the first trio in C major, in which the movement is in the form of a fast two-voice canon). The majority of the eighteen movements of these six sonatas follow the formal practices of the time. Usually there are two contrasting sections (A and B) in the first part, on tonic and dominant, respectively. Usually there is a double bar, after which the second part begins on the dominant. But there the similarity ends. For while it is Gluck's practice to begin the second part with motives derived from the first part, there is no consistent attempt to recapitulate the entire first part on the tonic. A tabular view of selected movements will make his procedure clear (see Table V). Once in the seven trio sonatas, however, Gluck employed the pattern that was to reach its fullest development

TABLE V

SONATA-FORM MOVEMENTS IN GLUCK

A—A devel.—	Coda	Devel.—	A—	Coda	No. 1, C major
I V	V	V	I	I	2d movement
A—B—	Coda	A devel.—	B (quasi)—	Coda	No. 2, G minor
I III	V	III	III	I	2d movement
A—B—	Coda	A devel.—	B and	Coda	No. 3, A major
I V	V	V, VI, etc.	I	I	1st movement
A—B—	Coda	A devel.—	A—	Coda	No. 4, B flat
I V	V	V	I	I	1st and 2d movements

[11] In Riemann, ed. *Collegium musicum*, Nos. 32–38.

in the works of the Classical masters. The last movement of the seventh sonata contains well-contrasted themes in the first part (before the double bar) and a quasi-development with complete recapitulation on the tonic in the second part. This form, found occasionally in the works of other composers mentioned above, contains in miniature all the structural elements found in later fully developed sonata-forms by the great masters from Haydn to Brahms and beyond. Much of the finest music composed since 1759 has been written in this form; as such it deserves more than passing reference.

PRE-CLASSICAL COMPOSERS

In the works of other composers contemporary with those discussed above, the presence of pre-Classical style elements is so self-evident that the works must be considered truly representative of the newer trends —even though a Baroque stylistic device or mannerism appears occasionally. The chamber-music works of G. B. Sammartini, Boccherini, J. C. Bach, and those attributed to Pergolesi may be taken as typical examples.

Sammartini. Giovanni Battista Sammartini (c. 1700–1775) was first active principally at Milan as a church organist and composer, but he turned to the field of instrumental music in the 1730s. He became successful as a teacher, Gluck being his most famous pupil, and Mozart, J. C. Bach, and others were influenced by his style of composition. An exact list of Sammartini's chamber-music works cannot yet be given, for many items attributed to him are by other composers,[12] and, conversely, some of his own compositions first appeared under the name of his brother, Giuseppe. However, over fifty trios, five quartets, and almost two dozen solo sonatas may be safely credited to him.

Taken as a whole, Sammartini's chamber music follows the course described above, from Baroque to pre-Classical style. Some works, notably certain trio sonatas of Opus 1 and Opus 2 (c. 1740–1745), exhibit the directness, inexorable rhythmic drive, fast harmonic rhythm, and motive-derived melodies that characterize the works of

---

[12] Notably the well-known G major sonata for cello and keyboard—actually written by Giuseppe Dall' Abaco.

Vivaldi. Such elements are not far removed from Baroque practice. In later works, dating from about 1760, a florid, ornamented melody cast in phrases and periods and set in slow harmonic rhythm became typical. In these works the rhythmic momentum has been abolished in favor of greater rhythmic variety, pauses at phrase ends, and well-marked cadences.

In keeping with their pre-Classical style, counterpoint plays little part in Sammartini's later chamber music. Occasional bits of imitation between the two violins in the trio sonatas remind one that Sammartini was an experienced church-music composer and that strict polyphonic writing was among his accomplishments. But in general the first violin dominates in the trio and quartet settings, the other voice or voices then being confined to harmonic parts. As far as can be ascertained here, the majority of the bass parts in these works are all figured; thus a realization of the harmonies by a keyboard instrument is essential.

One of Sammartini's last sets, published in 1766, is of the type described above as the accompanied sonata. Here the main weight—almost the entire weight—is on the written-out harpsichord part, and the latter is accompanied by the violin. This, of course, marks a complete reversal from the practice of the Baroque period, in which the keyboard instrument did little more than provide a harmonic support for the melody instruments.

In his manipulation of thematic material Sammartini was a man of his time. Sharply defined thematic contrast, which often became a major characteristic of Classical music, is seldom found, although harmonic contrast between adjacent sections is clear and present. Sammartini's themes, being based on conventional materials (triadic forms, scale passages, and the like), do not usually possess the distinctive contours necessary to establish contrasting moods. Recapitulations, too, played a relatively minor role in the structures, the main element of recapitulation being simply a return to the tonic key after the centrally placed transition.

As far as the number of movements is concerned, the three-movement pattern is most common in the earlier sets, but gives way to two-movement sets in the later works. Virtually all the usual sequences of tempo (fast-slow-minuet, slow-fast-fast, fast-minuet-fast, etc.) are found, except that a minuet is most often employed as a last movement. Contrary to the usual practice, however, Sammartini's minuets are not often set in pairs (in the form minuet I—minuet II—minuet I *da capo*) but are composed as single movements with a harmonically contrasting middle section.

Pergolesi. Giovanni Battista Pergolesi (1710–36), born near Naples, concerned himself primarily with church music and operas. His comic gem, *La Serva padrona* ("Maid as Mistress"), is his best-known work and is the composition upon which much of his later enviable reputation was founded. Twelve trio sonatas long attributed to Pergolesi are now generally considered not to be by him. The sonatas, presumably written about 1732, were not published until about 1770. The experts in the field base their views (about the false attribution of the trios to Pergolesi) on the fact that the sonatas in question are not in the known Pergolesi style, that certain elements in them could not have occurred as early as about 1732, that few other instrumental works by Pergolesi are known, and so on.[13] But since no more likely candidate for authorship has been put forward, we shall call the composer "pseudo Pergolesi" here, with the hope that the question of authorship will be solved eventually.

In these twelve trio sonatas there is a successful attempt to build up long singing melodies in fast tempo; and if the date of 1732 proves to be correct, this may represent one of the earliest such attempts in instrumental music. The old late-Baroque manner of extending a melody by means of a short motive or phrase manipulated contrapuntally is here discarded. The new process is best seen in the first movement of the first trio sonata, in G major (see Example 25).[14]

A two-measure phrase (A in Example 25) ending on the tonic is

[13] Charles Cudworth, "Notes on the Instrumental Works Attributed to Pergolesi," *Music and Letters,* XXX, No. 4 (Oct., 1949), 321–28; Frank Walker, "Two Centuries of Pergolesi Forgeries and Misattributions," ibid., 297–320.

[14] The first two of pseudo Pergolesi's trio sonatas are reprinted in Riemann, ed. *Collegium musicum,* Nos. 29 and 30. The complete set of twelve, published by Bremner (London, n.d.) is in the Library of Congress, Washington, D.C.

Example 25   Pergolesi, Trio Sonata No. 1

heard and is immediately repeated with a cadence on the dominant; another two-measure phrase on the dominant follows, which in turn leads to a transitional phrase of three measures ending on the dominant of D major. At this point a new, somewhat contrasting phrase in D major appears (B in the example); this phrase is repeated and provided with a coda (literally, tail), much as the first phrase (A) had been. The facts that all three instruments are essential in the presentation of these themes and that a closely-knit period structure results are noteworthy.

And of great significance for the future development of sonata-form is the fact that the second half of the first section (phrase B in the example) now begins to assume melodic integrity, begins to have a recognizable melodic shape, and is no longer merely a broken chord or running scale pattern. The way to an independent second theme, contrasting in contour, style, and key, is now open. Though pseudo Pergolesi did not progress as far as an independent second theme, he was consistent, in the majority of his trio sonatas, in giving the section under discussion a definite melody, an advance over the form as Scarlatti left it.

As a consequence of that achievement, other advances are to be noted also. The most immediate one can best be described by recalling

(a) that earlier composers of the form had contented themselves with achieving a harmonic symmetry of $||$: I—V :$||$: V—I :$||$, no noticeable formal scheme having been apparent in the choice of melodic materials; (b) that in those composers' hands the form achieved a kind of balance based on similarity of melodies in the first section of each part and a similarity of figurations in the second section of each, depicted by the diagram A—B :$||$: A—B; (c) that now, in the present works and with a melodic section at the end of each part, a true melodic balance of $||$: A—B :$||$: A—B :$||$ over the harmonic symmetry of $||$: I—V :$||$: V—I :$||$ became possible. This new departure in form is obviously a direct result of transposing the melodies of the first part to the keys of the second, but that it was of great significance in the future development of the sonata's first movement may not be clear at the moment. Its full importance can be realized best in retrospect, when we examine the sonata-form of the late eighteenth century in the following chapter.

A third innovation tending toward the fully-developed Classical form is also to be encountered in these trio sonatas; we now turn our attention to the second part of the first movement. When once the dominant key had been established and the second part had begun (in that key) with the melody of the A section, the composer showed great skill in hinting at the forthcoming B section in the tonic key, while still concerned with the phrases of the A section. In several cases in the twelve sonatas, shortly before the B section is recapitulated in the tonic key, bits of the A, also in the tonic key, appear. The end result is that finally the whole of the A section, now entirely in the tonic key, appears between the A (dominant) and B (tonic) sections of the second part. Thus, the following form appears:

Melodic section: $||$: A—B :$||$: A—A—B :$||$
Harmonic scheme: $||$: I—V :$||$: V—I —I :$||$

And so it is found in eight of the twelve first movements. It may be remarked that three of the first movements (numbers 6, 9, and 12) are fugal; thus actually eight out of nine movements contain the form described above. Only in the seventh sonata is a different scheme to be observed: the movement is in G minor, and the harmonic sections are ||: I—III :||: I—VI—I :||. The second sonata, in B flat, illustrates the new procedure in detail. The A theme gives way, after eight measures, to a B theme, of which the two halves total eleven measures. In the second part of the movement the A theme, in the expected dominant key, is developed in the direction of the tonic for thirteen measures. Now a complete recapitulation of the A theme with a five-measure extension occurs, after which there is an equally complete recapitulation of the B theme, transposed note for note to the tonic key. We shall look back upon this movement in the chapters that follow and see it as a beautiful example of sonata-form in miniature, with all the essential details—contrasting themes, quasi-development, and recapitulation—in place.

Second and third movements of these trio sonatas do not bring such important innovations with them. In the G major sonata, for example, the second movement is slow, in triple meter, and in E minor. It is largely in note-against-note style, with a lyric melody, very much in the manner of Corelli's slow movements. In the third movement the composer reverts to the old *sonata da chiesa* practice by writing a fugue, but unlike the *da chiesa*, in fast tempo. Likewise in the B flat sonata: the second movement is slow, in triple meter, and in E flat major; the third is a presto in triple meter and is similar to the first movement in having an ||: A—B :||: A—B :|| melodic form over a ||: I—V :||: V—I :|| harmony. In these works, as well as in most of the symphonies, sonatas, and quartets later in the century, the main emphasis is on the first movements. It is here that the composer was most ingenious, took greatest pains, and provided the greatest amount of innovation.

Boccherini. The nearly five hundred instrumental compositions of Luigi Boccherini (1743–1805), ranging from sonatas to quintets, are among the many groups of pre-Classical works that have not yet been thoroughly examined. Boccherini was well known in his day, enjoyed great success as a cellist, and much of his music was published during his lifetime. But changing patterns of taste and the advent of the Classical style may have contributed to a decline in his fortunes. After an

active career as performer and composer in Italy and France, Boccherini settled in Madrid, which became his home except for tours and
long visits to other cities.

The exact number of Boccherini's works cannot be given accurately,
but over a hundred quintets (two violins, viola, and two cellos), about
a hundred string quartets, almost fifty string trios (two violins and
cello), and twelve quintets for strings and keyboard are known, along
with numerous sonatas and other works. His opus numbers are confusing, for often a separate set of numbers is assigned to each genre,
and many works counted among the manuscripts are counted again in
publications. More thorough bibliographical work will be needed before a complete evaluation of this prolific composer can be attempted.

The available works of Boccherini show him to have been a resource-
ful and imaginative composer not given to standardizing forms. In one
or another of his compositions virtually every musical pattern known
to the pre-Classical period appears. Many of the sets are cast in four
movements, the most usual pattern then being fast-slow-minuet-fast or
fast-minuet-slow-fast. Three-movement forms appear with great frequency, in the order fast-slow-fast, slow-fast-fast, or fast-slow-minuet.
Two-movement forms also are common; moderate-fast, slow-fast, or
slow-minuet are the most usual combinations. The single movements
themselves range from simple two-part forms with no thematic distinction to complex forms containing all the ingredients of sonata-form.
Rondos, minuets with or without trios, sets of variations, and even
fugues in fast tempo are also found.

One element of Boccherini's style is consistently employed, however
—a melodic type that embodies all the charm and grace of the *galant*
decades. Phrases and longer sections are often based on the elaborations of a single motive, to be followed in succeeding phrases by other
motives (see Example 26). In other cases a melody is formed out of
highly embellished and rhythmically varied undulating scale fragments, with songful and charming effect (Example 27).

Although the first violin dominates in the majority of Boccherini's
chamber-music works, the cello comes to the fore on many occasions.
Thematic statements first presented by the violin are later given to

Example 26   Boccherini, Trio, Opus 35, No. 6

Example 27   Boccherini, Cello Sonata No. 6

the cello. Rapid string crossings and other virtuosic devices are also common in the cello parts. A minuet in the string trio, Opus 35, No. 2, is based on a texture in which the cello has all the thematic material while the two violins accompany; the same is true in many of the string quintets. A cellist himself, Boccherini was among the first composers fully to realize the potentialities of that instrument. Broad, singing, and expressive melodies in the high register of the cello contribute a new tone of lyricism to chamber music. Without often resorting to true polyphonic writing, Boccherini displayed a sensitivity to good voice-leading in the inner parts. Discreet imitations, bits of counter-melody, and imaginative accompanying figures did much to establish models for the "quartet style" that emerged in the works of his great Classical contemporaries, Haydn and Mozart (see Example 28).

Eleven years younger than Haydn, Boccherini yet remained outside

Example 28   Boccherini, Opus 27, No. 2

the mainstream of developments that led to Classicism. To the end of his life he remained true to his own style, which was graceful, ornamental, melodious, occasionally brilliant, seldom dramatic, but always refined. The variety of his forms testifies to his unwillingness to be bound by a formula and to his awareness that his musical ideas created or suggested their own forms. His music revealed some of the possibilities inherent in the slowly emerging Classical style. It remained for other and greater composers to carry those possibilities forward.

THE MANNHEIM SCHOOL

The aesthetic content of sonata-form continued to be altered as the eighteenth century passed its midpoint. Subjectivity made its appearance, and dynamic changes introduced purely as expressive devices became new factors in musical composition. Since the early decades of the century many composers had taken steps away from the single-mood movement of the Baroque and steps toward the contrasting-mood movement (brought about through the use of contrasting first and second themes) of the Classical period. By 1745 such contrasts were well established, but in a diffident and refined manner. In the works of composers at Mannheim, of whom Johann Stamitz is the foremost representative, we have an orchestral and chamber-music literature that is largely subjective, contains extreme contrasts between thematic groups—hence is in keeping with the new aesthetic practices —and makes use of all the important changes and innovations in sonata-form that had been accumulating during the previous twenty-five or more years.

Stamitz. In the years from 1720 to about 1750 Mannheim, in central western Germany, rose from a modest existence as a provincial town to a place in the musical sun. The transfer of the courts of Düsseldorf and Heidelberg to Mannheim and the presence of the music-loving Elector Karl Theodore at the head of the court were the external stimuli that led to the establishment of an orchestra renowned in all parts of Europe, to the assembling of a group of capable composers with Johann Stamitz (1717–57) at their head, and to a new style of performance. The discoverer of the Mannheim school, Hugo Riemann, evaluated its contributions to the rise of the Viennese Classical school [15] in terms so enthusiastic that a lively controversy arose between him and the spokesman for the early Viennese composers, Guido Adler. Riemann credited the Mannheimers with creating all the musical factors for which they were famous in their day, namely, abruptly contrasting dynamics in sharply contrasting melodic fragments, expressive crescendos and diminuendos, and the form of the symphony itself. Adler points to Monn, Starzer, Wagenseil, and others of the Viennese generation from c. 1740–1760, emphasizes their inclusion of the minuet in the symphony, their abandonment of the *basso continuo*, their reseparation of orchestral and chamber music,

---

[15] Forewords to Vols. III[1], VII[2], VIII[2], XV, and XVI of *DTB*.

and considers them the true forerunners of Haydn, Mozart, and the early Beethoven.[16] Opinion is still divided as to the exact place of the Mannheimers in music history.

Johann Stamitz had secured his positions as Karl Theodore's concertmaster (1743) and director of instrumental music (1745) by virtue of his excellent violin playing. His principal works are six orchestral trios, Opus 1, and a number of symphonies. The orchestral trios, which Riemann considers the starting point of the new style, may be taken as typical of Stamitz' works.[17] Dating from about 1751, each of these works contains four movements, in the sequence we have seen in a few Viennese compositions a decade earlier: fast, slow, minuet, fast. They are for two violins and bass with *basso continuo* and thus are typical of earlier eighteenth-century practice. But several other features set these trios apart from contemporary compositions.

There is first the use of extreme differences of texture that provide for musical as well as psychological contrasts, to a degree unknown before. Example 29, drawn from Stamitz' Trio, Opus 1, No. 4, is seen to begin with a loud, forceful unison passage; this is immediately followed by a restrained, thin-textured section that contrasts with the first in style, tonality, texture, and mood. The forceful passage returns, and the restrained one likewise—all within a space of twenty-two measures. Such treatment of contrasting moods naturally brought with it a new use of dynamic changes. Let us review briefly the status of dynamics up to this point so that we may properly appreciate the extent of Stamitz' innovation.

Dynamics in instrumental ensemble music up to about 1750 had been confined largely to alternations of loud and soft. Based on echo effects centuries old, used consistently in antiphonal choral works before 1600 (cf. the two Gabrielis), and forming an important expressive element in all seventeenth-century trio sonatas, this tradition of

---

[16] *Handbuch,* II, 774 ff.

[17] Reprinted in Riemann, ed. *Collegium musicum,* along with a trio in E major, Opus 5, No. 3, as Nos. 1–7. The opus number by no means indicates that the orchestral trios were Stamitz' first works; publishers were prone to assign opus numbers in the order in which the works reached their publishing houses, not in the order of composition.

Example 29   Johann Stamitz, Opus 1, No. 4

loud-soft (the so-called terrace dynamics) was characteristic of practically all Baroque music. Numerous works based on this tradition are
well known: the sonata *Pian e forte* of Giovanni Gabrieli, the *Echo
Song* of Lasso, the chorus "In Our Deep Vaulted Cell" from Purcell's
Dido and Aeneas, and the closing chorus of Bach's *St. Matthew Passion* are some of the most famous. But in all these cases the softer
phrase was simply a repetition of one heard previously; the alternate
dynamic level had done nothing to change the form or style of the
music. Indeed, in the Baroque period it could not have been otherwise. By the doctrine of affections, only one mood per movement was
permitted in music; and a Baroque musical phrase, whether played
loudly or softly, was tied to the phrases that surrounded it by the
requirements of the single affection being exploited, and was indifferent to dynamic levels.

In the music of Stamitz, on the other hand, the alternate dynamic
level was not used to bring about a modified repetition of a previously
heard phrase. Rather, the musical contrast, embracing style, texture,

and mood, was so complete that it inevitably required a different dynamic level as well. And so it appears in Example 29. The contrasting phrases (beginning in measures 9 and 17) by their very nature must be played softly. Their unassuming and intimate appeal, the fact that they carry on after virtually all the bombastic thematic motion has ceased for the moment are characteristics assuring the musician that a lower dynamic level is made necessary. In this and countless other cases Stamitz at once gave dynamics a new function by making them organic parts of musical composition. With this one set of six orchestral trios he showed for all time that a new music was at hand, a music in which emotional contrasts were achieved by dynamics as well as by tones.

The restriction of "terrace dynamics" was applied, in the Baroque period, primarily to instrumental groups. Such groups, always under the thumb of the keyboard performer realizing the *basso continuo,* knew of no other way of performing music than to engage in alternations of loud and soft; intermediate nuances were unknown in their activity. But not so with singers and violin soloists. They, in distinction to instrumental groups, had long since employed dynamic levels between loud and soft, had employed gradually increasing and decreasing volumes of tone in moving from one tonal level to another and had made full use of the conventional signs for a swelling tone ($<$ $>$). It remained for Stamitz, and to an even greater degree to later adherents of his style, to make use of the terms *cresc.* and *decres.*[18] and to develop an orchestral discipline that made this refinement possible in performance. So simple an effect as that seen in Example 30 (measures 8–10) was a great innovation in his day, and the Mannheim crescendo became famous throughout Europe.

The stylistic devices found in Stamitz' music were considered by Hugo Riemann (writing in the years about 1902–6) to have been innovations and even "inventions" of the Mannheim leader. Later research has shown, however, that "Mannheim rockets" (short melodies based on chord tones and ascending at high speed), "Mannheim sighs" (accented suspensions or appoggiaturas), and similar devices

[18] Riemann, *Handbuch*, II³, 146.

Example 30   Johann Stamitz, Opus 1, No. 2

can be found in the music of Stamitz' contemporaries far removed from Mannheim. The conclusion must be drawn that a universal style was coming into being toward the middle of the century and that Stamitz seized upon the idioms and elements of that style and incorporated them into his music. It is likely that the superiority of Stamitz' orchestra and the generally rich musical life (except for keyboard music) at Mannheim attracted the attention of the musical world of the time and brought the so-called Mannheim style to an influential position. Countless examples of the use of sighs, rockets, and all the other devices in the music of Mozart and Beethoven give evidence of the influence of that style on the great works of the Classical period.

Returning now to the orchestra trios of Stamitz' Opus 1, we must recognize that they are not true chamber-music works, even though only three voices (plus *continuo*) are indicated. On most occasions they were undoubtedly played by string orchestra and harpsichord; on others, wind instruments were added to reinforce the strings in the loud passage. Indeed, the earliest preserved edition of these Opus 1 trios, one published in Paris, includes in its title *ou à trois ou avec toutes l'orchestre*.[19] For true chamber music we must turn to other Mannheim composers and to non-Mannheimers influenced by the style of Stamitz. Vol. XVI of the *Denkmäler der Tonkunst in Bayern* contains a bibliography and thematic index of forty-seven Mannheim composers, many of whom were prolific in the field of chamber music. None attained to the level of Johann Stamitz' musical ideas nor to his degree of originality. Several, however, stand head and shoulders above their colleagues, and their music may profitably by examined. Among them are Franz Xaver Richter (1709–89), Ignaz Holzbauer (1711–83), Johann Baptist Wendling (c. 1720–1797), Giuseppe Toëschi (c. 1724–c. 1800), Ernst Eichner (1740–77), Wilhelm Cramer (1745–99), Karl Stamitz (1745–1801), Anton Filtz (c. 1730–1760), and Christian Cannabich (1731–98). We shall confine ourselves largely to a discussion of Franz Richter, the oldest of the group and in a sense the best musician among them.

Richter. Franz Richter seems by nature to have been more conservative than some of his younger associates. There is first of all, throughout most of his works, a contrapuntal element that one seeks vainly in Stamitz and in the majority of the other Mannheim composers. Richter's contrasts are achieved by changes in melodic contour, by changes in key, and to some extent by changes in texture. Almost never does he employ the abrupt changes of style, psychological as well as musical, that are so characteristic of Stamitz. In dynamic contrasts, too, Richter is more conservative than the latter. Sudden fortes or pianos and overwhelming crescendos are both foreign to his manner of writing, even though on a few occasions such dynamic contrasts do appear.

In formal scheme, also, Richter leans on past decades. Of the more

---

[19] Riemann, *Handbuch*, II[3], 133–34.

than forty of his chamber-music compositions listed in the *DTB* thematic index the six string quartets of Opus 5 may be singled out.[20] Each of the six quartets contains three movements, and only two of the movements (the finales of Nos. 3 and 4) are minuets. It will be recalled that all six of Stamitz' orchestra trios had contained minuets as the third of four movements and that the inclusion of a minuet was a decided innovation in the decade from 1750 to 1760. Thus in his choice of forms Richter was conservative.

In another characteristic, however, Richter was well in advance of his contemporaries, for he gave great responsibilities to the viola and cello. Only rarely does the first violin dominate in the six string quartets of Opus 5. The lower instruments are equal in importance to the upper, and the cello in particular is entrusted with running passages and figurations not seen in chamber music—except in the Starzer divertimentos mentioned above—since the trio sonatas of Buxtehude. Example 31, drawn from the first movement of Opus 5, No. 3, will serve to show how the parts are divided among the four instruments and how this type of writing, which the Germans call *durchbrochene Arbeit,* leads directly to the genuine quartet style of the later Classical period.

Other Mannheim Composers. Anton Filtz (c. 1730–1760) was another of the enthusiastic but uninspired disciples of Stamitz. In none of his numerous works (Eitner's *Quellen-Lexikon* lists about thirty) did he rise above the level of youthful apprenticeship.[21] But in one respect he deserves mention here: he was one of the earliest composers to write string trios for two violins and cello without *continuo,* a combination that became one of the standard groupings of the Classical period (the string trios of Boccherini mentioned above are later in date of origin than Filtz's). A trio of Filtz's, Opus 3, No. 6, reprinted in *DTB,* Vol. XV, is one of the relatively few four-movement chamber-music works to be found in the entire Mannheim stock and is perhaps one of the first works in which three string instru-

---

[20] Reprinted in Vol. XV of *DTB;* originally published in 1767, according to Riemann; in 1765, according to Eitner, *Quellen-Lexikon;* but quite possibly written much earlier.

[21] Riemann, *DTB,* XV, xii.

Example 31   Richter, Opus 5, No. 3

ments, unaccompanied by *continuo* and with a degree of equality
among themselves, are employed.

In general, regularity of form seems not to have been a characteristic
of chamber music written by the minor Mannheim composers. Of the
twenty-nine trios, quartets, and quintets by various members of the
school published in Vols. XV and XVI of *DTB,* eleven have two
movements, sixteen have three, and only two contain four movements. Still more noteworthy, only one of these last two—a wind
quartet, Opus 56, No. 2, by Franz Danzi (1763–1826)—contains
movements in the order fast-slow-minuet-fast. The two-movement
works are evenly divided between slow-fast and fast-slow, and twelve

of the three-movement works are fast-slow-fast, the last movement often being a fast minuet. Thus only in the very first works of the Mannheim school is the model for the four-movement form of the emerging Classical period to be seen consistently: the six orchestra trios of Stamitz' Opus 1, all of which are in the order fast-slow-minuet-fast. We shall see in the following chapter that Haydn, whose first quartets are roughly contemporary with Stamitz' trios, adopted a similar form.

Schobert. We now leave the Mannheimers at Mannheim and come to a composer whose music shows many characteristics of the Mannheim style even though he apparently had little contact with that center. Johann Schobert (c. 1730–1767) was a contemporary of Haydn's and a composer whose chamber music with piano opened up new paths that led directly to the giants of the Classical period: Little is known of Schobert's life except that he was either Austrian or Silesian by birth, that he was engaged as chamber musician to the Prince of Conti at Paris, and that he—with his entire family—died of mushroom poisoning. A selection of his works is reprinted in *DDT,* Vol. XXXIX; the chamber-music compositions found there include five sonatas for piano and violin, two piano trios, and two quartets for piano, two violins, and cello.

In Schobert's music we find, possibly for the first time ١e Mannheim style transferred to the piano. Here are the same type of melodic line, the same Mannheimer "rockets" and "sighs." But along with Mannheim characteristics are an impulsiveness, a power, and a degree of force that even Stamitz' music lacks. Schobert makes considerable use of thunderous tremolos, of rapidly moving figures in the left hand, of unexpected melodic turns—all of which combine to give his music an air of virtuosic brilliance. He must be reckoned as one of the founders of modern piano music; many devices we associate with the mature Beethoven are first found in Schobert.

But the string parts of the sonatas, trios, and quartets do not bear out the promise given by the piano parts. In the truest sense of the word, the strings accompany. In the trios and the quartets, for example, the cello doubles the bass notes of the piano part; in those works, as well as in the sonatas, the violin part contains a few small counter-melodies, progresses in thirds with the piano melody, or adds a bit of rhythmic vitality to the harmony notes. Occasionally the violin is entrusted with the theme for a few measures, but then lapses into its accompanying role again. Two exceptions to this practice may be seen in four minuets: in the trios, Opus 16, Nos. 1 and 4, and in the quartets, Opus 7, No. 1, and Opus 14, No. 1. In the first two cases the violin and the cello progress in thirds and sixths and alone provide melodic interest. In the two latter cases the two violins are similarly employed; here the cello is again relegated to a bass role. In all four cases the piano engages in a modest figured accompaniment that shows admirable restraint. The conclusion can be drawn that minuets were still newcomers in the sonata's framework and hence deserved to be treated somewhat as they were treated in the dance suite of the Rococo period. At any rate, these four minuet movements give the only available evidence that Schobert was ever diffident in writing his piano parts.

Schobert's piano trios and quartets testify to the new place of the piano in chamber music. Its old place as realizer of the *basso continuo* now gone, that instrument assumed the dominant role in one branch of chamber-music literature. As we have seen in these works, the strings either accompanied or were obligatory. Indeed, Schobert sometimes designated his string parts as "ad libitum," and his publisher often furnished a second keyboard part in place of the strings.[22] But in spite of this characteristic, Schobert must be credited with systematically establishing a chamber-music literature in which the piano part is fully written out and with laying the groundwork for the important contemporary media of piano quartet and piano quintet.

Johann Christian Bach. A number of composers still remain essentially undiscussed, notably two sons of Bach—Karl Philipp Emanuel (1714–88) and Johann Christian (1735–82). The first, who was briefly mentioned above in connection with the development of the keyboard sonata, must take a minor role in chamber music. String trios (from 1756) and string quartets (1773) bearing his name remain

---

[22] Moser, *Geschichte der deutschen Musik,* II[1], 344.

cool, conservative north German works distinguished only by their grace and their use of well-contrasting second theme groups. Johann Christian, on the other hand, was in all essentials a follower of the Mannheim composers. Among his most important works are the six quintets of Opus 11, published about 1776;[23] these quintets are even dedicated to Karl Theodore, the Elector Palatine, head of the court of Mannheim. They are for flute, oboe, violin, viola, and cello; the second, third, and fifth quintets contain two movements, the others three—again a Mannheim characteristic. Much of the time the quintets are in the form of dialogues between two pairs of instruments: flute and oboe opposite violin and viola, with the cello providing an old-fashioned bass, figured to some extent. The figuring indicates that Bach desired a *continuo* accompaniment in these works; but such accompaniment is by no means necessary. The harmonies are complete even without the realized bass; there are ample motion and rhythmic vitality in the string and wind parts to insure a satisfactory performance even without the keyboard accompaniment.

[23] Reprinted in *Das Erbe deutscher Musik,* Vol. III. A trio in D major is found in Riemann, ed. *Collegium musicum,* No. 19.

6. Franz Joseph Haydn

An APPROACH to Haydn's chamber music may be prefaced by the observation that up to about his thirtieth year his music was in virtually every stylistic respect similar to that of the pre-Classical composers discussed in the previous chapter. Indeed, one may speculate that had Haydn lived no longer than Mozart, who died at the age of thirty-five, his place in music history would be a small one. He began to reveal himself as a major figure only in the late 1760s, and he did not attain his full stature for a decade or more after that time. Having become one of the musical giants, he did not regress. His compositions up to the turn of the century and beyond display all the freshness and charm of a younger composer, along with a depth and expressiveness that few can equal.

LIFE

Franz Joseph Haydn was born in 1732 at Rohrau, a little Austrian village near the Hungarian border, the second of twelve children, six of whom died in infancy. His parents—industrious, honorable people in humble circumstances—came from a line of artisans and farmers. Franz Joseph's father was a wagon maker and his mother had been a cook. Although neither parent was trained in music, the elder Haydn was fond of singing and music-making of all sorts.

In his early years Franz Joseph was consigned to the care of his relative Matthias Franck, in a neighboring village. There he attracted the attention of the choirmaster of St. Stephen's Cathedral at Vienna and was promptly engaged for the choir of that church. At the age of eight he set out for Vienna. He remained in the choir until his voice broke, and at the age of seventeen, in 1749, he was cast adrift.

His musical instruction had been perfunctory—a few lessons on the violin and harpsichord and a few voice lessons—and he had received only rudimentary instruction in Latin and other subjects. But Haydn's interest and keen observation had enabled him to go far beyond the bounds of formal teaching. The experience at St. Stephen's gave him a practical insight into the problems of music and a knowledge of choral repertoire. What more he needed to know he found out for himself. To the end of his life he was his own teacher.

At the time Haydn was thrown upon his own resources Vienna was probably the most musical city of Europe. No festivity was complete without music, serenaders roamed the streets, and everyone composed. Haydn's cheerful, equable disposition found some satisfaction and a meager livelihood in joining groups of serenaders; he played with them and wrote for them. But such an existence was not to be endured forever. Good fortune placed Haydn in the path of several influential friends, among them Metastasio, the court poet, and Porpora, renowned composer and teacher. Through them he met his first employer, Von Fürnberg, about 1755.

This Austrian nobleman, as fond of music as most of the aristocracy, engaged Haydn as violinist to assist in his chamber-music evenings, to which cultivated amateurs and professionals alike were invited. Haydn remained with Von Fürnberg less than a year, for in 1756 he was again without regular employment. About 1759 he was engaged by Count Morzin and given the title of composer and director of music. Morzin's musical resources were somewhat greater than Von Fürnberg's had been, for at the former's estate Haydn found himself in charge of twelve or more musicians. Two years later Morzin was obliged to cut expenses (the rumor is that his impending marriage made the step necessary), and the small orchestra was disbanded. But Haydn was immediately engaged by Prince Paul Anton Eszterházy in the employment of whose family he remained until death. Thus in 1761 began the long association with the wealthy and sympathetic Eszterházys, who provided the external means to make Haydn's enormous musical output possible.

Prince Paul's main residence was the huge old moated castle of Eisenstadt, some thirty miles from Vienna. There the prince maintained an elaborate establishment that included some fifteen or twenty musicians, instrumentalists as well as singers. Haydn was placed second in command of these musical forces, for Joseph Werner, appointed musical director in 1728, was still active in 1761. Little less than a year after Haydn's appointment Prince Paul died and his brother Nicholas became heir to all the extensive Eszterházy estates. Nicholas, familiar with the palace of Versailles, immediately made plans to build a comparable residence on the Hungarian plains. Still farther from Vienna than Eisenstadt had been, the new palace, which Nicholas called "Eszterháza," was completed in 1766. Shortly before the household moved to the magnificent new estate Werner died; Haydn succeeded him as musical director and composer to Prince Nicholas.

At Eszterháza, Haydn lived and worked for twenty-four years, until the death of Nicholas in 1790. Encumbered by a shrewish, unsympathetic, and selfish wife, far removed from the stimulation regular contact with other composers and other music might have given him (his friendship with Mozart did not begin until 1781), isolated, except for winter visits to Vienna, burdened by a mass of administrative and disciplinary detail, Haydn nevertheless remained serene, joyful, and good-natured. His creative activity during these years was enormous; we shall give an account of its scope below.

Nicholas' heir, in 1790, was another Paul Anton Eszterházy. The latter, however, had little interest in music. Immediately upon taking possession of the estates Paul disbanded the orchestra and retired Haydn, after increasing the handsome pension Nicholas had willed to his faithful friend and composer. Haydn, free for the first time in three decades and well provided for, returned to Vienna. Almost immediately an enterprising concert manager from London, Johann Salomon, prevailed upon him to go to that city, to compose an opera, six symphonies, and a number of other works, for a handsome fee. Late in 1790, at the age of fifty-eight, never having been more than

a short distance from Vienna, Haydn embarked upon his first visit
to England.

It is interesting to note that Haydn had become much better
known and was much more highly respected abroad than in Austria
and Germany. As early as 1764 a Parisian publisher named Venier
had issued a number of Haydn's early quartets, together with works of
other composers (Beck, Pfeiffer, and Schetky, among them), with
the legend, "Unknown names which it is well to know." [1] By 1785
Haydn had received a commission to compose for the cathedral at
Cadiz, and his works were regularly performed in Paris and London.
Yet as late as 1793, after Haydn's enormously successful London
visit, the Bonn correspondent of a Berlin paper wrote that "one begins to allow Haydn to be grouped with Cannabich, K. Stamitz, and
their consorts." [2]

Haydn's visit to London lasted almost two years and was eminently
successful in every respect. His musical fame secure, his compositions
universally admired, Haydn returned to Vienna with the applause
of all London ringing in his ears and the degree of Doctor of Music,
conferred by Oxford, in his pocket. After some eighteen months of
resting in Vienna Haydn returned to London for a second time, again
through the urging—and financial guarantees—of Salomon. The second visit, lasting from February, 1794, to August, 1795, was as successful as the first.

But Haydn had aged during the London visits. The hundreds of
pages of music, the dozens of large and small works, the strain of constant activity had begun to wear down the industrious composer.
From 1795 composition became more difficult for him, although
songs, quartets, and the two great oratorios, *The Creation* and *The
Seasons*, were written. In his last years he found refuge in his friends
and his memories. Increasing weakness made public appearances
impossible; increasing age dried up the stream of compositions that

[1] Oliver Strunk, "Haydn's Divertimenti for Baryton, Viola, and Bass," *The Musical Quarterly*, XVIII, No. 2 (April, 1932), p. 227.

[2] Riemann, *Handbuch*, II², 151.

had flowed so copiously for almost sixty years. In 1809, at the age of seventy-seven, with Napoleon's armies beginning the bombardment of Vienna, Haydn died.

Social Conditions. One can best understand some aspects of Haydn's style after realizing the conditions under which he worked. Haydn's position with the Eszterházy family was typical of scores of similar positions in great and small aristocratic households throughout Europe. Musicians placed at the heads of such private establishments were conductors, composers, disciplinarians, administrators, and musical men-of-all-work. They wore livery, dined with the servants, waited upon their noble employers for detailed instructions concerning this or that assignment, and in general were upper-class menials.

On the positive side, one can point out that such musicians had relative security, were sure of having their works performed, and were given ample opportunity to compose—even though they did compose to order. At a time when public concerts were rare, when performance royalties were unthought of, when plagiarism was the order of the day, when a livelihood for the independent composer did not exist, the relationship of musician to patron was a wholesome one. Many of the aristocrats able to maintain private orchestras were themselves cultivated and sincere music lovers.

The twenty-nine years of active association between Haydn and the Eszterházys were on the whole pleasant ones. Haydn worked early and late at his various duties: composing and rehearsing operas in preparation for some noble guest's visit, writing new symphonies as they were called for, producing new Masses for festivals and holy days, having available new quartets for regular and special occasions. That Nicholas Eszterházy was for so long pleased with these new works speaks well for his musical taste.

But Haydn suffered greatly from the enforced isolation that residence at Eszterháza brought with it. Again, as in his teens, he was thrown upon his own resources. He was compelled to develop his own style in solitude, to experiment, to invent. His own self-criticism, his innate sense of what was right in music, kept him from deteriorating into just another craftsman. What in another situation would have acted as a stimulant and corrective—namely, contact with other music and other musicians—was, in his early years at Eszterháza, almost entirely missing. He knew the works of Karl Philipp Emanuel Bach and other contemporary composers; later he was to know and admire and learn from Mozart. But live association with the great world of music, with performances of old and new works, with professional shop talk, was denied him to a great extent in the first twenty years at Eszterháza, in the years when his style was developing its personal characteristics.

SURVEY OF HAYDN'S WORKS

It is not surprising, in the light of the above, to find that much of Haydn's work is uneven. In the stress of constant composition, usually against a deadline, many pieces issued from his pen that were unworthy of him. But having once erred, he seldom repeated the bad judgment. The works show a gradual improvement up to the point where he felt his style had reached its full development. When that point had been reached Haydn did not regress. One has only to listen to his London symphonies, to his last quartets, to *The Creation*, all written in his sixties, to realize how firmly Haydn retained control of his musical faculties.

The conditions under which he wrote did not lend themselves to an orderly indexing of his works. Some pieces were written to be performed once; many were designed for publication, and were better cared for; most of them found their way into the private library of the Eszterházys, and were brought out as the occasion demanded. Other factors, too, contribute to the confusion that faces the Haydn scholar. For example, the sheer bulk of his compositions and the many spurious works bearing his name make an exact tabulation uncertain. Many manuscripts have disappeared and others are widely dispersed in various parts of Europe. Early editions of his music dealt freely with opus numbers, genres, titles, and even sequence of compositions within sets. As a consequence an accurate Haydn chronology is difficult to establish, and the tracing of influences and style development is precarious at best. As one result of these conditions, fewer works of Haydn have reached the general public than of any other major composer.

These conditions, too, are reflected in the state of Haydn publication. A complete edition of his works, begun by Breitkopf & Härtel in 1907, was planned to embrace some eighty volumes; after some twenty-five years, when the work came to a halt, less than a dozen volumes had been issued. A continuation, by the Haydn Society of Boston, resulted in the publication of four additional volumes between 1949 and 1952. A third attempt to complete the publication of Haydn's works, begun by the Haydn Institute of Cologne in 1954, is now under way.

The scope of all three projects gives an insight into the enormous quantity of Haydn's compositions. A vast amount of his music was composed for and with voices: about thirty works for the stage, including operas, operettas, and pieces for marionettes; twelve or more Masses; three oratorios; almost two hundred songs, airs, catches, and vocal canons; and a number of motets and fragments of other sacred music. Among the instrumental works are found between one hundred four and one hundred forty symphonies;[3] five or six dozen pieces for groups of wind and string instruments, including serenades, divertimentos, and related forms; fifty or more concertos for various instruments; almost two hundred pieces for the baryton;[4] and more than fifty sonatas for keyboard. And finally, within what we have defined as chamber music, are eight violin sonatas (most of them arrangements), sixty-six string trios, more than thirty piano trios, and eighty-three string quartets.

A fearful list! One does not envy the editors of the various "complete" editions their task of preparing it for publication, discarding spurious works, removing duplicates, and tracing relationships in this vast accumulation. That many of these works have been lost goes with-

---

[3] The presence of some spurious works and some doubtful ones makes the exact count uncertain. Not even the most thorough recent research, such as that represented by Hoboken, *Joseph Haydn, thematisch-bibliographisches Werkverzeichnis* (1957), has been able to clear up all the problems in this field.

[4] The *viola bordone*, an eighteenth-century string instrument upon which Nicholas Eszterházy was proficient.

out saying, and that many are mediocre or worse is equally plausible. No composer has yet succeeded in writing only masterpieces; even the greatest geniuses slip from their lofty perches at times. This is gratifying in a way, for it serves to remind us that they, too, are human. And Haydn was human indeed.

The cold statistical listing above can perform only one service here: to show us weaker mortals what a lifetime of industry can bring forth. The curious reader may estimate the number of separate movements contained within the total works of Haydn. He will find some twenty-five hundred. Apportioning these to the fifty years of Haydn's creative activity, roughly from 1750 to 1800, he will arrive at an average of one movement a week for half a century—the equivalent of one symphony a month for two generations, of a quartet every four weeks, of a sonata per fortnight—sustained throughout a lifetime! And composing was only one part, almost a minor part, of Haydn's work; rehearsing, performing, and administering took up equally large segments of his time. One never ceases to marvel that so large a proportion of Haydn's available compositions are of masterful quality, that he so seldom repeated himself, that he was never at a loss for worthwhile, characteristic musical ideas.

The vocal portions of this mass of music lie outside our interest here, as do the concertos and smaller pieces. The symphonies will engage our attention only as they demonstrate a point not made in the chamber music. And even in the latter field we will restrict ourselves. The trio sonatas probably would offer nothing that we have not already seen in earlier examples by other composers. Two or three of Haydn's trio sonatas are available at present writing; if they may be taken as typical of the larger bulk, one may draw parallels between Haydn's trio sonatas and those of Gluck, Sammartini, and other mid-century composers. Likewise the piano trios; here again little would be gained by a detailed discussion of those works. While many of them are excellent, and some contain Haydn's finest musical inspirations, they are essentially piano sonatas with violin and cello accompaniment. No harm is done if the string instruments are omitted in performance.

THE QUARTETS

But the eighty-three string quartets are another story. These works loom so large in a survey of Haydn's compositions that a detailed account of them alone would give a true picture of that composer's total style, development, and importance in music history. Haydn and the string quartet are so closely linked together in the chamber musician's mind that concepts of Haydn and the piano trio or Haydn and the trio sonata cause something of a jolt. Finally, some twenty or thirty of the quartets are among the most important part of the string quartet's repertoire; they can best be evaluated and appreciated if their relationships to the remaining quartets are seen in detail. For these reasons the balance of this chapter will be concerned only with the eighty-three string quartets of Haydn.

Several points must be kept in mind in reading this account of Haydn's early quartets. First, no real distinction was made between orchestral and chamber music in the middle of the eighteenth century. The terms *symphony, divertimento,* and *trio* were rather freely bandied about; one has only to recall the Stamitz "trios" for orchestra, the many "simphonies" for three to five instruments, and the indiscriminate instrumentation of compositions of the divertimento class. Titles can serve no purpose here; one must look to the content of the works themselves. Second, divertimentos usually contained minuets; symphonies in general did not. Often one's only clue to the genre of a work is the number of its movements—at least in the early decades of the Classical period. And third, the real test of whether a work is modern—in the sense of 1750 or thereabouts—is whether or not it includes a *basso continuo.*

Opus 1 and Opus 2. During the course of Haydn's first employment, as violinist and chamber musician to Von Fürnberg in 1755–56, he wrote twelve works; we know them today as the two sets of string quartets, six in each, labeled Opus 1 and Opus 2. But these twelve works were not all quartets in their original versions. Opus 1, No. 5, is Haydn's first symphony, and was not at first included in the quartets. Opus 2, Nos. 3 and 5, were originally sextets with two horns.

Both sets were at first known as divertimentos and appeared in the early catalogues as written for two violins, viola, and *basso*. To complete the list of characteristics that sets these works apart from later ones, we may mention that all but Opus 1, No. 4, contain five movements; a minuet appears both preceding and following the central slow movement. The one feature that establishes these works as belonging to the future is that there is no trace of a *continuo* part or need of a *continuo* performer. The evidence is strong that as late as the London visits, 1790 and 1794, Haydn accompanied his symphonies at the keyboard, amplifying the harmonies and strengthening the bass in the good old traditional manner. But this was not the case in the chamber music; even in the earliest works that practice has no place.

The texture of these quartets is homophonic in the extreme. Thematic material is based largely on broken-chord patterns whose repetitions and naïve elaborations are confined to the first and second violins. Indeed, in distribution of melodic materials the two violins come off as well as they did in the old trio sonatas. Viola and cello (we may read the *basso* as "cello or bass," with the certainty that the cello was employed more frequently than the bass) are confined to harmony notes and to animated pedal points.

In Chapter 5 we discussed the preliminary steps leading toward sonata-form. Our discussion may have left the impression that with Haydn all stumbling toward that form ceased and that from 1755 we have the real thing. Far from it! The quartets of Opus 1 and Opus 2 exhibit hardly any advance over the simple two-part forms we found in the late Baroque and Rococo periods. A typical first movement begins and ends in the tonic key; its middle part gravitates to the dominant and ascends again toward the tonic. But there is still little trace of growth in the themes, of comment upon them, of subtle contrasting of their component parts—elements that characterize the form as it appears from 1781 onward.

But three features that marked Haydn's music throughout his lifetime are present even in these youthful works: dramatic utterance in a compact and harmonically simple form; a masterful handling of phrase lengths, resulting in typical phrases five, seven, or any other number of measures long; an ingenuity and boundless inspiration in minuets. And wherever the mood of the music permits—notably in the last movements—an effervescent humor, a light-hearted play with comic elements, is the rule. If music is a reflection of a composer's temperament, Haydn must have been a delightful person to know—never stodgy, never conventional for the sake of convention, never trite. Even these early works give us the picture of a man to whom morbid gloom was virtually unknown.

We might ask what significance may be attached to the fact that eleven of these twelve works contain five movements instead of the four movements of the old trio sonata. A brief review of the content of the latter may clarify the picture. The trio sonata's four movements, it will be remembered, were slow-fast-slow-fast; we have traced their origin back to the contrasting slow and fast sections of the sonata of the 1620s. The innovations of the period 1735–50, however, had taken place not in the four-movement form thus achieved but in the three-movement form indirectly derived from the pre-Classical opera overture, even though many works of the time were also called trio sonatas. And the sequence of tempos in those works was most usually fast-slow-fast. One does well to keep in mind this duality of trio-sonata types. We have seen that toward the mid-century the Viennese divertimento composers had chosen the three-movement version for their vehicle and had built upon it by adding additional movements. There was no limit to the number of movements that might be so added. Entrance and exit marches appeared at either end of the set of three, and minuets were interspersed between other movements. Haydn, in adhering to the tradition of the time, wrote his first works in the divertimento manner, both as to content and as to exterior framework: two minuets seemed appropriate, and two minuets were written.

Opus 3. Not until the six quartets of Opus 3 appeared—and the dates are variously reported from 1755 to 1765—did the *modern* four-movement form achieve some degree of regular employment.

These quartets, along with those of Opus 1 and Opus 2, seem to have filled a great need, for they were published in many parts of Europe: all eighteen quartets were published in Leipzig in 1760 and in Paris in 1764–69; Opus 1 was published in Amsterdam in 1765.[5] And with Opus 3 the quartets of Haydn begin to find a place in the modern repertoire. Here we come in contact with music that may be heard on the concert stage today.

Almost every major composer has written at least one piece that touches the popular heart. Brahms's "Lullaby," Beethoven's "Minuet in G," and Rachmaninoff's "Prelude in C sharp minor" are typical examples. For Haydn the piece is the famous "Serenade"; and that piece is the slow movement of Opus 3, No. 5, a good example of the songlike style of Haydn's early slow movements. Two characteristic elements are found in at least nine of the first eighteen slow movements: a lyric or dramatic melody played by the first violin, surrounded by a large or small amount of embroidery and other ornamentation and a discreet and subdued accompaniment of pulsating repeated notes or (as in the case of the "Serenade") pizzicato chord tones. Dramatic moments are present in abundance, and the change of pace upon which drama depends likewise. But a distribution of the more important (or at least the more obvious) musical details among all the instruments is lacking in these early works.

Opus 9. The six quartets of Opus 9, probably written about 1769, mark another step forward in Haydn's musical development. That they were musically superior to the first eighteen quartets was known to Haydn himself. August Artaria, a son of the Artaria who published most of Haydn's works from 1780 on, often heard his father say that in later years Haydn wished his early quartets to be ignored and to have the numbering begin with the nineteenth quartet (the work we know as Opus 9, No. 1). The elder Artaria complied with the composer's wish and drew up a thematic catalogue of the quartets, omitting the first eighteen.[6] Still later, when the early works of Haydn

[5] Pohl, *Joseph Haydn*, I, 333–34.
[6] Artaria and Botstiber, *Joseph Haydn und das Verlagshaus Artaria*, p. 87.

were reprinted by Artaria, the quartets we know as Opus 9 and Opus 17 were reprinted as Opus 1 and Opus 2.[7]

It is difficult to call attention to certain details and demonstrate that one quartet is superior to another. We shall have to be content with pointing out that the themes of Opus 9 are no longer so firmly tied to the tonic triad but are full of imaginative little melodic bits, that they are, in general, shorter and more amenable to working over, and that the quartets are more perfectly formed, more appealing— in a word, better. One must hear these quartets and immediately thereafter the earlier ones; then and only then is the superiority of Opus 9 revealed.

A parenthetical remark is in order here. The work of the musical historian and analyst resembles the function of milestones and road markers. The analyst, having gone before, is in the position of pointing out details, of directing the reader's attention to this or that musical fact. But everyone must do his own traveling; he must arrive at his destination under his own power. To depend upon analysis or historical description to the exclusion of personal acquaintance with the musical works themselves is to negate the purposes of both music and musicology. There is no substitute for hearing the music; and in these days of inexpensive editions, innumerable recordings, and inexhaustible musical enthusiasm there is no excuse for not hearing it.

Opus 17. Haydn's next set of quartets, Opus 17, written in 1771, presents several new features. First, it is as though the violinist for whom Haydn was writing had suddenly achieved a virtuosic brilliance. During his many years at Eszterháza Haydn enjoyed the friendship and the sterling musical qualities of Luigi Tomasini, the prince's first violinist. There can be no question but that the excellence of Tomasini's playing influenced Haydn in his quartet writing;[8] it seems likely that the latter wrote with the violinist actually in mind. The first violin had always dominated in Haydn's quartet writing; now he begins to dazzle even his colleagues. Double stops, arpeggios,

[7] Ibid., p. 99.
[8] Pohl, *Joseph Haydn,* I, 262.

string crossings, passages that ascend to the violin's stratosphere—in short, all the traditional virtuosic devices are there in abundance. Along with this increased brilliance in the fast movements is an increased thoughtfulness—perhaps *expressiveness* is a better word—in the slow ones. Dramatic tension is temporarily lost sight of in the interests of greater melodic beauty and more equable distribution of melodies among all four instruments. Haydn seems to have become aware of viola and cello as musical individuals in the quartets of Opus 17. Their long apprenticeship as supporters of the melody, as providers of the harmonic foundation, now over, the lower instruments are entrusted with running passages, discreet tunes, and occasionally with the principal melody, to a degree unknown in the early quartets. Viola and cello must now begin to practice, to prove themselves worthy of being in the company of the brilliant first violin and the competent second.

We also note in these quartets an unevenness that is surprising when we look back upon the quartets of Opus 3 and Opus 9. Movements of outstanding beauty, charm, and wit are interspersed with others that are dull and stodgy. We have come to expect more of Haydn than the minuet of Opus 17, No. 1, gives us. The movement is adequate, but nothing more; one waits for something striking to happen, and nothing does. The same is true of the finale of Opus 17, No. 2; the theme is abrupt and angular and is paced neither to provide a sense of inexorable motion toward a climax nor to elevate one through sheer joy at the rapid movement. Several times Haydn threatens to break out into an accompanied fugue—which would have been a decided novelty in this set—but fails to do so. Similarly, two or three other movements are disappointing and below the standard Haydn has set for himself thus far. But, on the whole, unevenness of quality should not condemn the whole set; Opus 17, in its brilliance, marks a considerable advance over the quartets of Opera 1, 2, 3, and 9.

Opus 20. The six quartets of Opus 20, although written only a year after the Opus 17 set, namely, in 1772, mark a real milestone in Haydn's path of development. The two sets are roughly contemporary, but Haydn made giant strides in his progress toward complete mastery between the writing of the two series. Having achieved the brilliance typical of the earlier set, Haydn now moves in other directions. Beginning with Opus 20 it is no longer feasible to treat a whole set of quartets together (but we shall probably continue that type of treatment occasionally if only for reasons of convenience); no one quartet is typical of a set, and individual differences are greater than formal similarities. Each of the twenty-four movements of Opus 20 bears some mark of Haydn's genius, whether in the direction of melodic contour, of formal innovation, or of technical competence, and in almost every case the mark is a different one. From the very first quartet of this set Haydn shows a new regard for tone color, for the melodic possibilities of the cello. Quartet style, one factor of which is musical equality of all four instruments, is well on the way to completion through this new use of the cello.

The best evidence of the newest development is seen in the first few measures of Opus 20, No. 2. The cello announces the theme while the first violin actually has six measures rest. This simple fact is striking when one realizes how completely the first violin had dominated in the first thirty quartets. In the one hundred twenty-seven movements of those quartets there are only three that do not begin with the first violin's announcement of the theme at the very outset of the movement; and in all three of the exceptions the second violin, which is in a sense the first playing in a lower octave, temporarily takes over the dominating role. Now, suddenly, the picture changes. In Opus 20, No. 2, the cello sings out the theme, the second violin ambles along in thirds below the cello, and the viola provides the bass. Later in the same movement the viola announces the theme for a single measure, the first violin accompanies, and the second provides the bass.

These are small beginnings, it is true, but the ice has been broken. Haydn seems a bit uncertain of the new technique at first, for the following quartet begins with viola and first violin announcing the theme in octaves. Does he not trust the new method? His confidence, however, seems to be quickly restored, for in the last movement of the same quartet the second violin, bravely and alone, presents the melody upon which the movement is based. And in the trio of the following quartet's minuet the cello is given the theme. So it goes: at first tentatively and with some doubts, later definitely and in full confidence. A true four-voice texture gradually appears, a texture in which each instrument has something to say, after which it is relegated to the background. It must be said that even so, the first violin's background is considerably in front of the other instruments' foreground. The former's domination, while more discreet and less consistent, is not canceled quite so easily.

Meanwhile, consequences of the new method, consequences of great import, are being realized by Haydn. Having once broken away from the *galant* characteristic of a single melody always in the uppermost instrument, Haydn is in a position to carry the new freedom to its logical conclusion. He is faced with a medium employing four equal instruments, a medium in which concepts of solo melody and group accompaniment may at times be disregarded. And the logical consequence of this freedom is counterpoint. At this moment Haydn returns to a device virtually ignored by a generation of pre-Classical composers and writes contrapuntally. The final movements of three of the quartets (Opus 20, Nos. 2, 5, and 6) are four-voice fugues. Haydn labels them with four subjects, two subjects, and three subjects, respectively, depending upon how many countermelodies accompany the principal subject throughout the fugue.

The fugues are treated with considerable formal freedom in respect to number of expositions, length and content of episodes, and the like; and in this fact lies a clue to their importance to Haydn's total style development. They support the view that a fugue is a style of treatment rather than an established form, that the fugue's use of polyphonic texture within a logically conceived harmonic structure is its most significant feature. In essence it is the polyphony that is important, not the fugal vehicle. Seen in conjunction with a backward glance over the earlier quartets, the fugues of Opus 20 represent the logical fulfillment of Haydn's desire to develop a texture made out of four equally important instrumental lines. Seen as fugues per se, they mark a return of the contrapuntal element to instrumental music, a return seldom apparent since the Baroque gave way to the early Rococo (c. 1730). But seen with a look into the future, they enable Haydn to employ all the contrapuntal devices of the past in combination with the melodic and formal developments of his own time. The use he makes of them will prove to be of great importance to the evolution of quartet style and to sonata-form itself.

Melody has been defined as a succession of musical tones that together convey a musical thought. In the thirty-six quartets from Opus 1 to Opus 20 Haydn has written hundreds of melodies. The typical melody up to this point has a beginning, a middle, and an end; it has a contour and a rhythmic shape, so that it may be perceived as a unit; and it generally appeals to our sense of either lyric beauty or dramatic tension. In almost every case it is accompanied by a more or less elaborate harmonic substructure. Thus melody and accompaniment, being composed of different musical materials, are on different planes of musical thought; their interaction has produced a texture quite similar to that of the *style galant* of the Rococo period.

Now, fugues contain melodies too. But fugues differ from other musical styles in that there is no separation into melody and accompaniment; all voices are engaged in simultaneous melodic utterance, and all voices are on the same musical plane. Hence the term *polyphony* is applied to fugal style, for polyphony is the art of employing two or more melodies simultaneously. One further characteristic of fugal style may be noted: usually the first or principal melody is heard together with another melody differing from the first in contour, rhythm, and place within the metrical group (or measure).

Opus 33. Does Haydn write only fugues from this point on? Scarcely, for this would have meant reverting to late Baroque style. He does something much better and vastly more important for the future of music. He finds a way of combining homophonic melodies and polyphonic textures; or, better, he employs a polyphonic texture in forms whose content had been largely that of the homophonic Rococo period. That he was fully aware of his innovation is proved by his propaganda for the next set of six quartets, Opus 33, written about ten years after the Opus 20 set. In his announcement of the Opus 33 quartets, first published early in 1782,[9] he proclaims quartets "written in an entirely new manner." The new manner contains two features.

First, the melodies contain a greater variety of distinctive intervals and a more elaborate rhythmic scheme. They are more loosely held together and are in fact composed of a number of short contrasting motives. Example 32 gives phrases of both old and new types; the new are, of course, those found in Opus 33 and later.

Example 32   Haydn, Opus 17, No. 2

Second, when Haydn begins to construct a musical piece out of a melody of the new type he proceeds to dissect it, to break it down into its motives, and to reassemble the fragments with all the contrapuntal arts of which he is now master but of which he had given virtually no hint before the fugues of Opus 20. The best example of the new manner is seen in the first movement of Opus 33, No. 2, the principal theme of which has been quoted in Example 32. A fragment of the development section of that movement is given in Example 33. To make the point still clearer, it will be well to compare it with the old style. Example 34 is drawn from Opus 17, No. 2, whose theme was quoted in Example 32a.

At this late date, when music of the Classical period is spread before us in wholesale lots, when generations of composers after Haydn have appropriated his "new manner" and have made us thoroughly familiar with applications of it, one can realize the importance of the innovation only with difficulty. At the moment when Haydn realized the implications of the new manner and made it an element of his

---

[9] Artaria and Botstiber, *Joseph Haydn und das Verlagshaus Artaria,* pp. 21, 93.

Example 33   Haydn, Opus 33, No. 2

mature way of life the quartet was completed and quartet style was an accomplished fact. A new principle had been given to the art of music—the principle of thematic development based upon contrapuntal devices and employed in a homophonic context. From this point on the quartets of Haydn become deeper or lighter or more lyric or more comic—in a word, they become individual works of art, bound together by adherence to a common style but bound no longer by type characteristics.

At first the new manner is used tentatively. A few measures here, a few there, suffice. Large sections of these works are still in the style of Opus 20, with one notable exception: the minuet movement becomes faster and receives the name *scherzo*. This Italian word implies playfulness or a jokelike character and gives a clue to the changed content. The fifty or so minuets Haydn has written up to this point

Example 34   Haydn, Opus 17, No. 2

meas. 64-71

are astonishing in their great variety of mood. Some are full-bodied
and severe, others light and flowing; many are gleeful, others merely
gay. But almost all have some semblance of dignity reminiscent of
the courtly dance out of which they came. The scherzos of Opus 33
have lost some of their dignity and gained a great deal of humor.
But it would be a mistake to place them in the same category with the
enormous movements to which Beethoven gave the same name a few
decades later. The latter, as we shall see in due course, transferred
the principle of thematic development to the scherzo and confided
to it some of his most dramatic ideas. Complete sonata-form movements are found among Beethoven's later scherzos—a phenomenon
we do not find among Haydn's. We must be satisfied that Haydn
invested the minuet with a new content, accelerated its tempo, and
provided moments of real humor in 3/4 meter. It is noteworthy that
Haydn did not use the word *scherzo* after the Opus 33 movements,

even though several "minuets" among his last quartets are marked
presto and are very similar to the movements now under discussion.

Location of Minuet. Here is an appropriate place to mention a
point that, as far as the author knows, has never been adequately
examined: the location of the minuet-scherzo type within the quartet's
four-movement structure. If we omit for a moment any consideration
of the quartets of Opus 1 and Opus 2 (for there we have to do with
a five-movement form in which a minuet is placed before and after
the middle movement, probably with no more significant purpose
than symmetry) we find a rather regular placement of the minuet as
second movement in the early quartets but as third movement in the
later ones. The table of Haydn's eighty-three quartets on page 176
shows both the regular location and the exceptions.

It is far too easy to assert that the minuet's location doesn't matter,
that it happens to be where it is because of accident, coincidence, or
even willfulness. A great artist does not give way to willfulness, nor
is he subject to such neat coincidences. He is conscious of what he is
doing, and he does his work with full realization of its aesthetic effect. Nor may one say that the balance of a quartet, or its drive
toward its end, is not altered if the sequence of movements is altered.
Even superficial reflection will convince one that a dramatic slow
movement provides more effective contrast when placed just before a
fiery or humorous presto finale than it does when placed before an
ambling, moderately paced minuet, or that a first movement of a
certain type may better set the stage for a minuet than it does for an
adagio. The sensitive listener will have heard too many examples of
cumulative pace in sonatas, symphonies, or quartets to have any doubts
on that score.

We begin to ask, then, what kind of music surrounds the minuet
when it is placed second in the series of four movements? What
kind when it is placed third? The answers are disappointing, for in
both cases fast, moderate, and slow movements precede, and fast,
moderate, and slow movements succeed the minuet. We look for
differences in texture, and we are again disappointed; all kinds are
found, irrespective of the minuet's location. We try once more, this

time from the standpoint of enjoyment; both arrangements are equally enjoyable. There remains an examination of the harmonic content of movements. Let us try that approach.

One principle that every composer of Haydn's day kept in mind was over-all unity of tonality. No piece dared wander too far from its tonic key, and no piece in a four-movement form dared to present a tonality not closely related to the key of the whole series. A study of the key relationships existing among the movements of these quartets will give ample evidence that Haydn adhered very closely to the second half of that principle. With the exception of the so-called quartets of Opus 51, which will be discussed below, only one quartet exhibits an unorthodox key relationship among its several movements: Opus 76, No. 6, in E flat, contains a slow movement in B minor and major, but that movement is labeled "fantasia." No other movement goes further than to subdominant or dominant, to relative major or minor, to tonic major or minor, or to mediant or submediant. The great majority progress to the most closely related keys of all, namely, subdominant or dominant. And it is always the slow movement, regardless of its place in the series, that presents a contrasting key; the minuet, like the first and last movements, is always in the tonic key. Thus we have in the minuet a stabilizing force, a movement that, through its clarity and unpretentiousness, is well suited to recalling a quartet to its harmonic senses should it threaten to depart too far from its tonal center.

One possibility of discovering the reason that the minuet wanders around within the framework remains. A hypothesis may be established: when Haydn feels that he has violated the principle of harmonic unity in his first movement, he places the minuet second, to reestablish the tonality firmly before departing on his second excursion into the tonality of the slow movement. And when he feels that the first movement is normal harmonically, and the second is merely a dip into a closely related key, he is happy to put the minuet in third place in order to develop sufficient momentum toward the rapid last movement. It may be suggested that as Haydn achieved full maturity during the writing of the Opus 33 set and became less fear-

TABLE VI
HAYDN'S STRING QUARTETS

m minuet   s scherzo   * instances of chromatic usage (see pp. 183–184)
Blank spaces represent the normal arrangement of fast first and last movements and
slow middle movement; the exceptions are marked.

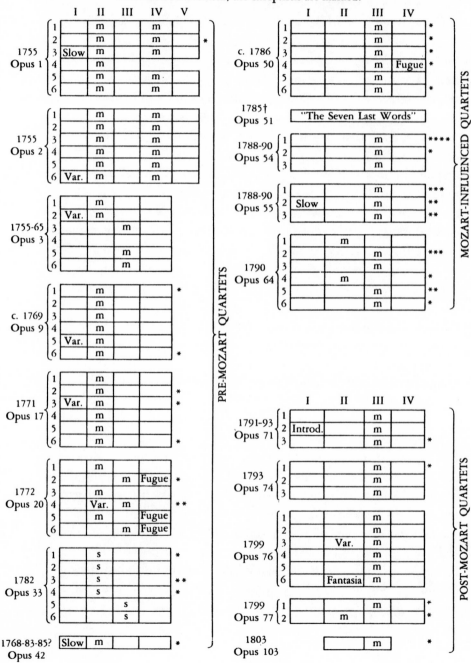

†arranged 1787–1794?

ful of violating harmonic unity, he tended more and more toward favoring the climax of tempos achieved by placing the moderate minuet between the slow second and fast final movements. The table on page 176 shows that with only two or three exceptions the last thirty-six quartets contain the minuet in third place. But this hypothesis and suggestion are not completely satisfactory. Only a careful analysis of all the harmonic vagaries of all the movements will throw final light upon this problem. And that study has not yet been undertaken.

Opus 42. The single quartet of Opus 42, in D minor, seems to have puzzled commentators more than any similar work. Pohl, Haydn's best-known biographer, feels it to be one of the composer's early works, contemporary with Opus 9—that is, dated about 1768.[10] Altmann, in his edition of the eighty-three quartets published by Eulenberg, gives the date as 1768, thus agreeing with Pohl. Tovey points out with considerable conviction[11] that it could not have been written earlier than its place in the opus numbers indicates, namely, a year or so after 1782, which marks the publication of Opus 33. Karl Geiringer refers to the original manuscript as bearing the date 1785.[12] Thus we have a typical musicological problem: 1768, about 1783, or 1785? And the question is not an academic one (in the worst sense of that phrase), for this quartet of Opus 42 contains features that are still noteworthy in 1785 and would decidedly be innovations in 1768. The slow movement is a lyric gem, with a long, singing melody such as is virtually unknown in the early quartets. The finale is in imitative, almost fugal style, reminiscent of Haydn's Opus 20 (1772) and certainly not found earlier. And yet the work as a whole is unassuming and does not have the air of brilliance one finds in almost all the quartets from Opus 33 onward.

Opus 50. About 1786 or 1787 Haydn wrote the set of six quartets in Opus 50; they were published in 1787 with a dedication to Frederick William II (1744–97), king of Prussia from 1786 to 1797. The dedication becomes significant when one glances at the cello parts of

---

[10] *Joseph Haydn,* II, 43. Here he labels it Opus 8.
[11] In *Cobbett's Cyclopedic Survey of Chamber Music,* I, 540.   [12] *Haydn,* p. 253.

these quartets. Frederick William, a nephew of Frederick the Great, was a capable cellist and took delight in playing chamber music. Haydn, to please his noble patron, took full advantage of the cello's lyric, dramatic, and technical possibilities and wrote cello parts far richer (and more interesting to the cellist, one might add) than any had been previously. We shall see later that Mozart's procedure was identical in his "Frederick William" quartets; he, too, provided the king with ample material.[13] Returning to Haydn, we find that the cello had paved the way to a more brilliant utterance, and therefore the other parts are increasingly filled with sparkle, with touches of deft humor, or with romantic melancholy. A much greater variety of material is found in the Opus 50 quartets; they range from extreme delicacy, as in Opus 50, No. 1, to the great forcefulness of No. 6, and they include one of the finest quartets of all: No. 4, with a masterful fugal finale.

It is necessary to cast a backward glance over the forty-three quartets we have discussed in the preceding pages, for in one respect Opus 50 exhibits formal characteristics not found in the previous quartets. We must even, for a moment, exhume the musical form of many pre-Classical composers. In that form we saw three sections on tonic, dominant, and tonic, respectively, but confined within a two-part form.

$$
\begin{array}{lll}
\textit{Exposition} & \textit{Development} & \textit{Recapitulation} \\
\text{A} - \text{B} : \| : \text{A} - & \text{A} - \text{B} \\
\text{I} - \text{V} : \| : \text{V} - & \text{I} -
\end{array}
$$

The factors labeled A and B, we had indicated, differed in contour and rhythm; they were not sufficiently contrasted, however, to justify calling them first theme and second theme, nor did their interaction contribute essentially to the development section. That lack of real contrast in style, as we noted in Chapter 5, was typical of the many divertimento composers in the generation before Haydn. And that same lack of contrast, we may now point out, was typical of Haydn himself, in the quartets of Opera 1, 2, 3, 9, 17, and 20. A group of

[13] Beethoven likewise, in his two cello sonatas of Opus 5.

phrases in the tonic key sufficed for the A part; a different group for the B, but, of course, in the dominant. Development consisted largely of sequential modulations, derived phrases, figurations, and other embroidery—all of which led back more or less regularly to the recapitulation, in which both A and B parts were in the tonic key.

From Opus 33, then, comes the great innovation: the use of thematic development, the fragmentation of the phrases, and contrapuntal development of those fragments. The extent of the innovation and the results directly traceable to it have been described. But even in the quartets of Opus 33 the symmetrical form had not been altered appreciably. The three large parts—exposition, development, and recapitulation—were still in the same relationship to each other that they had been previously.

From Opus 50 onward, the picture changes. Donald Tovey has made a generalization about the new procedure that is well borne out by the facts. He points out that in the works of Haydn it is difficult to speak of first and second "subjects" (we would have called them themes); rather must one speak of first and second theme-groups: collections of phrases in tonic and dominant keys, respectively. The generalization, with detailed examples to demonstrate its correctness, follows: "Haydn invented a brilliant type of coda à la Beethoven, and used fully developed codas instead of recapitulations. . . . From Opus 50 on, there is no dealing with Haydn's first movements except by individual analysis." [14]

By this Tovey indicates that the principle of thematic development, which in Opus 33 had been confined largely to the development section, had in Opus 50 and thereafter also become active in the recapitulations. Key relationships in the recapitulation had remained; indeed, the symmetry of tonality was a reality from which Haydn almost never broke away. But exact return of first and second theme-groups was now a thing of the past. To what extent Haydn differed from Mozart in this respect, and anticipated Beethoven, will be seen in Chapters 7 and 8.

Opus 51. Haydn's Opus 51 is a strange work, with an unusual

[14] In *Cobbett's Cyclopedic Survey of Chamber Music,* I, 541.

history. Discussion of the work is in order here for two reasons: it
appears in the authoritative Peters edition of Haydn's complete
quartets, and it is included in the numbering whenever Haydn's
"eighty-three" quartets are mentioned. We have included it thus far
in the interest of conforming to general practice.

About 1785 Haydn accepted a commission from the cathedral of
Cadiz to compose appropriate music for a Good Friday service com-
memorating the seven last words of Christ. The result was a series of
seven slow movements: largo, grave, grave, largo, adagio, lento, and
largo, respectively; the whole is preceded by an adagio introduction
and followed by a presto "Earthquake." It is an orchestral piece, and
its instrumentation is that of the symphony of the time. Because of
its "singularly expressive character" and its suitability as a "vocal
Passion piece," [15] Joseph Friebert, an obscure church musician in
Passau, added, in 1792, a set of vocal parts and a sacred text and
performed the work on many occasions. Haydn heard such a performance in Passau on his second trip to England (in 1794) and was
pleased with the result but felt that "he could have done the vocal
parts better." Subsequently he did make alterations, but he retained
considerable portions of Friebert's vocal additions as well as short
recitatives the latter had seen fit to add at the beginning of each
movement. Some years earlier Haydn had arranged the orchestral
version of the work and published the seven slow movements for
string quartet, allowing them to be included in his series of quartets
as Opus 51.[16]

The work is undoubtedly effective in its orchestral version, and
there is evidence that Haydn was greatly pleased with the arrangement for chorus and orchestra. But the quartet version leaves much
to be desired. The several movements are stripped down to bare essen-

[15] Geiringer, *Haydn*, p. 305.

[16] According to Artaria and Botstiber (*Joseph Haydn und das Verlagshaus Artaria*,
pp. 35 and 94) the quartet version was published in 1787, almost simultaneously
with the original orchestral version. Geiringer (*Haydn*, p. 270) agrees with them.
Thus the latest authority differs from Adolf Sandberger ("Zur Entstehungsgeschichte
von Haydns sieben Worte des Erlösers am Kreuze," in his *Ausgewählte Aufsätze
zur Musikgeschichte*, pp. 266 ff.), who asserted that the quartet version was made
after the vocal version of about 1795.

tials. Contrapuntal treatment, which had become so essential a factor in Haydn's style from Opus 33 on, is noticeably absent. What remains is a series of dramatic, passionate, and exquisitely beautiful melodies, with an adequate accompaniment in the lower instruments. The final "Earthquake," when heard in quartet guise, verges on the comic— so inadequate are the tremolos and the *tutti forzi* for carrying Haydn's great programmatic intentions. One remains puzzled by his questionable judgment in including these seven works among his quartets, and it is well to attribute to him not eighty-three, but seventy-six.

Opera 54–74. Returning to the line of true quartets, we encounter three in Opus 54 and three in Opus 55; both sets were written about 1788 or 1790. Having spoken of earlier quartets as great works, as dramatic or light-hearted or profound, we find that none but the same phrases will do for the later ones. The quartets of Opus 54 and Opus 55 are all that the earlier ones were; they are also written with contrapuntal development, with freer forms, and with greater melodic charm. Moreover, where the earlier quartets sparkle, the later ones glisten. Where the earlier are moving, the later are poignant. Where the earlier make much of a new device or a new treatment, the later are so closely identified with the new device or new treatment that they are unthinkable with a single detail changed. In a word, they are musically greater in every respect. It is a continual source of amazement to see (or to hear) in how many ways Haydn can be humorous, or how many gradations of humor are possible. One never ceases to marvel at the number of ways a lyric phrase can be turned in order to lead to a mood of resignation or to a mood of dramatic abandon or even to a continuation, across a long period, of the lyric mood. And it is precisely this enormous variety that gives the quartets of Haydn their eternal freshness, their spontaneity, and their everlasting charm.

Formal descriptions of the quartets beyond Opus 55 would lead nowhere. Each one is unique in the way it disposes of its musical materials, to the great enrichment of musical literature. Each one gives us the composer in a new light and fills us with gratitude for the creative power of a genius. Each one provides a new experience in the field of emotionally moving and aesthetically stimulating music. There is no substitute for hearing, playing, and living with these works. A bare catalogue of them must suffice here.

Six quartets, Opus 64, written about 1790, follow upon the Opus 55 set. One of the former, Opus 64, No. 5, has become famous under the nickname "The Lark"; it, along with the two quartets that surround it, are among Haydn's most popular works. Three quartets in Opus 71, presumably written in London about 1791, but published in 1795, are next in order. Opus 71, No. 2, contains the only slow introduction to a fast first movement in all of Haydn's quartets. Slow introductions were characteristic of his symphonies; their noteworthy omission in the quartets points to Haydn's feeling that a quartet is not a miniature symphony and does not require a pretentious introduction. Indeed, such introductions would stand in the way of the intimate, essentially cheerful mood he takes great pains to establish. Three quartets of Opus 74, written about 1793 and published in 1796, include the favorite G minor (No. 3), nicknamed "The Rider" because of its prancing first theme.

Opus 76 and Opus 77. If words fail us in approaching the previous works, what are we to do when the six quartets of Opus 76 (written about 1799) are reached? Even the most fragmentary analysis will not be attempted here; it must suffice to point out that Opus 76, No. 2, is "The Quinten": its descending fifths in the first movement give a clue to the origin of the nickname. Number 3, "The Emperor," contains the famous variations on the hymn, "Gott erhalte Franz den Kaiser," a tune that Haydn had composed a short time before and that remained one of his favorites even on his deathbed. Number 4 is "The Sunrise"; the aptness of the nickname can be appreciated only by those who know the quartet. Number 5 contains the marvelous largo in F sharp major, possibly one of the most sublime creations of this composer. Finally, No. 6, with the slow movement marked fantasia, is a unique piece in B major modulating to B flat, A flat, and back to B major (in a quartet whose other movements are in E flat), and one that presents the only movement so remotely related in all the seventy-six quartets.

About 1799, after the two London visits, when Haydn had withdrawn into semiretirement, the two works of Opus 77 were written. At first composed for flute and piano, they were later transcribed by Haydn for string quartet and were published in 1802. In these quartets the highest point of Haydn's creative activity is reached. Hearing the works and knowing them is all that is needed; talking about them would be futile. Finally, in 1803, Haydn wrote a slow movement and minuet, Opus 103, for what was evidently designed to be a quartet in D minor. The slow movement is in B flat, the minuet in D minor; consequently the quartet is referred to (in *Cobbett's* and elsewhere) as in B flat. But it was Haydn's consistent practice to place the minuet in the key of the first and last movements. Hence if there had been two more movements they would undoubtedly have been in D minor.

Chromaticism. Two final points must be mentioned here before bringing this survey of Haydn's quartets to a close. The full significance of the first will not be seen until Mozart's chamber-music works have been discussed. A glance through the many pages comprising Haydn's quartets up to Opus 42 reveals an astonishing lack of passages made out of chromatic scale fragments. The diatonic scale, with its neighboring tones, provides the material from which almost all the melodies and figurations are constructed. But a similar inspection of the quartets from Opus 50 through Opus 64 discloses, suddenly, a marked use of the chromatic line. Finally, the group from Opus 71 to Opus 103 contains very few such passages.

The statistics may prove interesting to those for whom no detail is unimportant. In the group from Opus 1 to Opus 42—forty-three quartets in all—there are actually fourteen instances of the use of chromatic melodies four or more tones in length.[17] In the eighteen quartets from Opus 50 through Opus 64 twenty-four instances are to be found; and in the fifteen quartets from Opus 71 to Opus 103, five instances. In the first group there is, on the average, one chromatic

[17] A chromatic line of less than four tones indicates merely the filling-in of two neighboring diatonic scale tones; as such, it is of little emotional interest. When the line persists for four or more tones in the same direction, the peculiar richness and pathetic appeal of the chromatic scale are made evident.

instance in every three quartets; in the second group, four instances in every three quartets; in the last, one in every three again.

Now what is the significance of this? It happens that Haydn and Mozart met about 1781 and their mutually fruitful influence became apparent shortly thereafter. In 1785 Mozart dedicated his six great quartets (written about 1783) to Haydn. And it was after hearing these works that Haydn made his famous remark to Mozart's father about Wolfgang's being the greatest composer of whom he had any knowledge.[18] From about 1785 on, Haydn was strongly influenced by Mozart; we shall see in Chapter 7 what form that influence took. Of importance here is the fact that before 1785 (that is, up through Opus 42) the quartets show no appreciable use of chromatic lines, that during the rest of Mozart's lifetime, up to 1791, the chromatic line is much in evidence in Haydn (the quartets from Opus 50 through Opus 64 fall in the years 1785 to 1790), and that after Mozart's death Haydn reverted to the diatonic scale formulas (in the quartets Opus 71 to Opus 103, between 1791 and 1803) as consistently as he had in the pre-Mozart quartets. The chromatic scale in Mozart's work forms an important aspect of his style, as we shall see below.

Other Quartets. The last point has to do with the incompleteness of the available Haydn quartet repertoire. Throughout the Haydn literature one finds references to quartets that are not included in the generally accepted list of seventy-six (or eighty-three, if one includes *The Seven Last Words*) or in the thematic indexes of his works made by various publishers. A few such items may be noted here.

A divertimento appearing as a string quartet about 1765 is mentioned by Pohl.[19] This work was not included in Haydn's own thematic catalogue, nor, according to Haydn himself, was it ever published. Two similar quartets appeared in Breitkopf's catalogue about the same time, but Haydn ignored these works. Yet when the six quartets of Opus 9 first appeared, about 1769, they were numbered,

---

[18] Jahn, *W. A. Mozart*, 4th ed. (Leipzig: Breitkopf & Härtel, 1905–7), II, 11.
[19] Pohl, *Joseph Haydn*, I, 258.

presumably by Haydn, as quartets 21–26.[20] We know of eighteen quartets in Opera 1, 2, and 3; Opus 9 should, accordingly, have been 19–24, not 21–26. Where are the others? Possibly the quartet we know as Opus 42 (which Pohl called Opus 8) is one of them; possibly not. And in connection with the two quartets of Opus 77, published in 1802, Botstiber mentions a "third and last quartet in B flat" dedicated to Count Fries and published by Artaria in May, 1807.[21]

In recent years a quartet in E flat major, called "No. 0," has been found. Originally included in Haydn's Opus 1, it disappeared from later editions and was replaced by the "symphony," Opus 1, No. 5. Haydn himself listed the quartet among his divertimentos, where it was discovered independently by Karl Geiringer and Marion Scott about 1932.[22]

The Haydn authorities throughout the world assure us that all of the seventy-six quartets are authentic. They imply that certain other quartets that circulated under Haydn's name, even during his lifetime, may be spurious.[23] And they hold out the hope that if and when a publication of the works of Haydn is completed, some of these questions will be answered and the world may have even more Haydn masterpieces to enjoy. Let us hope that a few choice works will be added to the quartet literature from the pen of this sincere, profound, and human genius.

[20] Ibid., II, 43.
[21] Artaria and Botstiber, *Joseph Haydn und das Verlagshaus Artaria*, p. 100.
[22] Geiringer, *Haydn*, pp. 194–95.
[23] See Geiringer's remarks (ibid., p. 208*n*) about the E major quartet attributed to Haydn.

7. Wolfgang Amadeus Mozart

WHAT IS the source of Mozart's style? Whom can one single out as having provided him with his musical models? Concise answers to these and similar questions are difficult to give, for the whole world of music lay open to Mozart, and the mainspring of his style is that world itself. For any given period the teacher or the model was a different one; yet Mozart is more than the sum of such teachings. Throughout his lifetime he was extremely sensitive to musical impressions. Each new work, each new style, left its mark upon his mind. And during his extensive travels he had ample opportunity to hear new works, possibly the greatest opportunity that any composer has ever had. Mozart's style is so largely the result of his many journeys that the style cannot be considered without the journeys.

LIFE

Joannes Chrysostomus Wolfgangus Theophilus[1] Sigismundus Mozart was born at Salzburg in 1756. Of his parents' seven children only he and his sister Maria Anna ("Nannerl") survived infancy. It need hardly be mentioned that both were child prodigies, so well known are the many anecdotes concerning the concert tours of the young Mozarts. At the age of three Wolfgang began serious and organized musical studies with his father, a competent musician in his own right.

The older Mozart (1719–87) was employed from 1743 at the court of successive archbishops of Salzburg as composer, court violinist, and,

---

[1] Sometimes Amadeus, sometimes Gottlieb. See Jahn, *W. A. Mozart* (4th ed.), I, 19*n*.

later, as vice-chapelmaster. His famous work, *Versuch einer gründlichen Violinschule*, published in the year of Wolfgang's birth, was highly regarded by contemporary musicians, was issued in many editions and several translations, and was for some years the only fundamental violin method in use. Thus Wolfgang at once fell into the hands of an experienced musician and teacher, well qualified to foster and develop his young son's enormous talent.

In his earliest years at Salzburg Mozart's father supplied him with music of all sorts: works of his own, music by great and small contemporaries, and music of past generations. The young student heard contrapuntal pieces (old-fashioned even then) and pieces in the new *galant* style. And from his sixth year on, when the long series of concert journeys began, he heard remote and foreign music as well.

The first tour was modest enough—a one-year visit to Munich and Vienna. But the scope of the journeys soon widened; a three-and-a-half-year visit to Paris, London, and Paris again, 1763–66, was the most extensive of all. There Mozart learned to know the music of Johann Schobert and Johann Christian Bach, echoes of which appeared in his own music as much as twenty years later. On his return to Salzburg he studied the *Gradus ad Parnassum* of Fux, one of the great contrapuntalists of the Baroque period. Then came one and a half years in Vienna, 1767–69, and three separate trips to Italy between 1770 and 1773.

At first the tours followed a uniformly successful pattern. Extended stops were made at each city on the route. Public concerts and private performances for the nobility were quickly arranged. Wolfgang played the violin, the harpsichord, and the organ, read the most difficult compositions at sight, and presented programs of his own new works. Maria Anna carried her share of the musical burden as well. Both children delighted their hearers by their charm and unspoiled natures, and many valuable gifts were showered upon them. The receipts at the public concerts more than covered the family's expenses, and each stop was a financial as well as a musical success. The reputation of the famous prodigies often preceded them and made their next appearance eagerly expected. Each stop brought with it opportunities

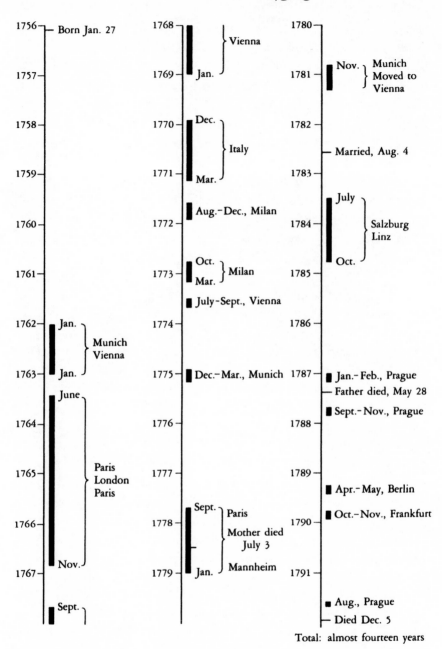

1756 — Born Jan. 27

1757 —

1758 —

1759 —

1760 —

1761 —

1762 — Jan. ⎫
              ⎬ Munich
1763 — Jan. ⎭ Vienna

         June ⎫
1764 —   │
              │ Paris
1765 —   │ London
              │ Paris
1766 —   │
         Nov. ⎭

1767 —

         Sept. ⎫
                ⎭

1768 —
              ⎫ Vienna
1769 — Jan. ⎭

1770 — Dec. ⎫
              ⎬ Italy
1771 — Mar. ⎭

         Aug.-Dec., Milan
1772 —

         Oct. ⎫
1773 — Mar. ⎬ Milan
         July-Sept., Vienna

1774 —

1775 — Dec.-Mar., Munich

1776 —

1777 —

         Sept. ⎫ Paris
1778 —   │ Mother died
              │ July 3
1779 — Jan. ⎭ Mannheim

1780 —

         Nov. ⎫ Munich
1781 —   ⎬ Moved to
              ⎭ Vienna

1782 —

         — Married, Aug. 4

1783 —
         July ⎫
1784 —   ⎬ Salzburg
         Oct. ⎭ Linz

1785 —

1786 —

1787 — Jan.-Feb., Prague
         — Father died, May 28
         Sept.-Nov., Prague

1788 —

1789 —
         Apr.-May, Berlin
         Oct.-Nov., Frankfurt
1790 —

1791 —

         Aug., Prague
         — Died Dec. 5

Total: almost fourteen years

MOZART'S TRAVELS

to hear the music of local and regional composers. And for Mozart, to hear was to remember. All the mannerisms of good and bad composers, all the formulas and clichés of the *galant* style, became material for Mozart to use, to transform in the light of his own taste, or to discard. In Italy he became familiar with the operatic music and spirit of that country; in Germany and Austria, with the solid counterpoint of the serious composers and the diverting melodies of the Rococo. His style is thus a synthesis of all that Europe had to offer.

But even dazzling reputations, even unique accomplishments, could not forever attract audiences and win patrons. As Wolfgang grew older and became less of a child prodigy, interest in his talents and accomplishments waned. His father persisted in his sincere desire to let the world share in his son's great musical abilities and, incidentally, to procure a court appointment for him; he did not become discouraged. His employer, the Archbishop of Salzburg, had finally grown weary of repeated requests for leaves of absence, and in 1777 he forbade the elder Mozart to take another journey. The latter pressed his wife into the role of traveling companion to her son, and the journeys began again. In 1778, while on a two-year visit to Paris and Mannheim (1777–79), Mozart's mother died. In his twenty-second year Mozart was on his own, for the first time in his life.

The countless musical experiences Mozart had had during his adolescence had done much to influence his own style. But in many cases the influences appeared decades after the impression was made. The dark colors, the passionate fire of Schobert's music deeply impressed Mozart as a child of eight, but not until the middle 1780s, when he was almost thirty years old, did these characteristics become a part of his style. On the other hand, the gracefulness of Johann Christian Bach and the lyric flow of Italian music, to both of which he was exposed between his ninth and his fifteenth years, were more immediately apparent. It could hardly have been otherwise. A boy in his adolescent years, even if he is a prodigy, cannot be expected to feel dark thoughts, to paint in dark colors; but even a boy can sing, and sing gracefully. Thus we find that Mozart's early works are full of *galanterie* and charming melody, carried on the surface of the music, much in the style of the "London" Bach and his spiritual relatives, the Mannheim and Italian composers.

Mozart was now twenty-two. His childhood accomplishments had long since been forgotten by the world at large. There remained only his prestige as a performer and his solid achievements as a composer. Commissions for operas and other works had always come his way, but successful as the results usually were, they never endured. The one thing both father and son longed for, a permanent appointment as court or opera composer, was still denied Mozart, as it was denied him throughout his lifetime. The best he was able to achieve was the post as concertmaster and organist to the Archbishop of Salzburg, a post that was offered and regretfully accepted in 1779. And from that position he was forcibly separated two years later in Vienna. His marriage to Constanza Weber took place during the summer of the following year (1782) and resulted in the Mozarts' making Vienna their permanent home.

Innumerable engagements came to him during the next few years, and Mozart presented many concerts of his own works. But income was uncertain, and his wife was, if possible, even less capable in financial matters than her husband. Always in debt, always pressed for money, always living in the vain hope of receiving a regular position, Mozart's life from 1782 to his death was full of great discouragement and grinding poverty.

The successes of *The Marriage of Figaro* (1786) and *Don Giovanni* (1787) did much to add to Mozart's prestige, but did little to alleviate his financial troubles. Debts continued to mount, and it was in the hope of bettering his financial condition that he paid a visit, in 1789, to the court of Frederick William II, at Berlin. And when finally a worthwhile offer was made to him there—the post of chapelmaster to that Prussian king—Mozart refused it out of misguided loyalty to his emperor, the man who had so deliberately neglected him. One tangible result of the visit was a commission to compose some quartets, of which we shall speak again.

In the last year of his life several commissions came his way, notably those that gave rise to *La Clemenza di Tito, Die Zauberflöte,* and the unfinished *Requiem*. The first, composed for the coronation of Leopold II at Prague, was coldly received. Mozart had traveled to that city for rehearsals and the performance; his disappointment in the reaction of the court was great. The second, composed for a small theater in Vienna, found equal disfavor with its first audience; only later did it grow in popular regard. The disappointment at the "failure" of these two works, plus the constant worry over finances and livelihood, contributed to the complete undermining of Mozart's health. When he died, in December, 1791, a few months after the apparent fiascos, a few friends accompanied the body part way to the cemetery. Mozart lies in an unmarked pauper's grave. He was not quite thirty-six when he died; his journeys had begun at the age of six. In the nearly thirty years from January, 1762, to December, 1791, Mozart had been away from home for a total of fourteen years.

SURVEY OF WORKS

Seen in the light of a normal span of years, Mozart lived only half a lifetime. He had certainly attained the height of his musical powers in 1791; presumably he would have retained or exceeded those powers had longer life been granted him. But Mozart began his creative activity at an age earlier than most composers. Leaving out of account the half-dozen minuets from his fourth year, his first large compositions —six sonatas for violin and piano—were written about 1763, when he was seven. From that day until his death he composed; his activity embraces twenty-nine years. In that sense he was given almost as full a life as many other composers. Thirty-five years elapsed between Beethoven's Opus 1 and his last work; Brahms had had scarcely forty years of composing when he died. And Mozart's activity was continuous during his twenty-nine years of writing.

The quantity of his work, while not as great as Haydn's, is considerable. Among the works are some twenty operas, operettas, and similar works for the stage; fifteen Masses, seventeen sonatas for organ and strings, and numerous other sacred compositions; more than a hundred airs, songs, choruses, and vocal canons. The instrumental works include almost fifty symphonies, more than three dozen serenades, divertimentos, and shorter pieces for orchestral and other ensemble combinations, about fifty concertos (of which more than half are for piano and orchestra), seventeen piano sonatas, a number of short pieces for piano, and many small pieces for violin and piano. The chamber music consists of twenty-six string quartets, eight string quintets (two of them with one wind instrument), over thirty violin-and-piano sonatas, seven piano trios, two piano quartets, and almost a dozen larger or smaller works for various combinations.

A word must be said about the numbering of Mozart's works. Mozart rarely used opus numbers and left few clues about the chronology of his many compositions. About the middle of the nineteenth century Ludwig von Koechel, an Austrian naturalist, musician, and, later, nobleman, began the process of collating the compositions with Mozart's letters, contemporary newspaper accounts, internal evidence supplied by the quality of paper and ink, and similar information. The result was the publication, in 1862, of Koechel's *Chronologisch-systematisches Verzeichnis,* listing all Mozart's works. Better known as K. or K.V., it furnishes chronological data and thematic *incipits* of all Mozart's compositions. Reference to that music customarily includes the K. item numbers. A revision of the *Verzeichnis,* which corrected certain inaccuracies and came closer to completion, was made by Alfred Einstein in 1937. In the interest of presenting a more accurate chronology than the traditional Koechel numbers can give, we shall in this book adopt the Einstein revisions; but in order to be able to make comparisons with older printed editions and reference books we shall also include the old Koechel numbers in parentheses, thus: K.417b (421)

THE STRING QUARTETS

The Early Quartets, 1770–73. Mozart's earliest string quartet, K.73f (80), in G major, was written during the first of three visits to Italy. The manuscript is dated Lodi, March 15, 1770, 7 P.M. In its original form it contained three movements: adagio, allegro, and minuet with trio; a rondo, as fourth movement, was added late in 1773. This quartet is not a distinguished work, nor does it differ greatly from similar works written by Mozart's older Italian contemporaries. The violins move in thirds and sixths much of the time, the lower instruments are confined to an accompanying role, and kinship with the old trio sonata is not remote. While the formal details are well handled and the writing is clear and precise, the general effect is not one of maturity. The quartet is influenced by Italian love of melody; one short tune follows another, transitions between themes are composed of new material, and one is reminded of a potpourri. The prevailing style is homophonic; the few contrapuntal passages serve only to remind one that Mozart was a well-educated young musician, trained in all styles.

After two successful trips to Italy Mozart returned to Salzburg. His stay at home, from December, 1771, to October, 1772, was the longest since his travels had begun, almost ten years earlier. Among the fruits of this stay at home were three quartets or, as they are called on the manuscript, divertimentos, K.125a-c (136–138). But these are not the usual kind of divertimento, for they are three-movement works without minuets; a divertimento of this time almost always contained at least one minuet.

The Italian influence prominent in K.73f (80) is here noticeably absent. In its place one finds the ingratiating qualities and clichés of the Rococo period. Broken chords and scale passages give rise to a feeling of restlessness. Rapid pulsations in eighth notes, usually carried by either the viola or the cello, are characteristic throughout these three quartets and serve to disguise lack of harmonic movement. But even in these early works there are foretastes of the genius Mozart was to show in later life; they are best seen in the sonata-form movements, at the transition from first to second theme in the recapitulation. In that section (the recapitulation) the musical intention is to present both themes in the tonic key, but to approach the second theme as though it were still in the dominant, as it had been in the exposition. The problem of balancing exposition and recapitulation sections, one containing themes on I and V, the other on I and I, was apparently a fascinating one for Mozart. Nowhere did he show his genius so clearly and so often as in these transitions. An early example of that skill is seen in the first movement of the B flat quartet, K.125b (137); a series of chromatic bass sequences leads to the return of the second theme in a highly original way. In other respects these quartets are not noteworthy. Developments are short, and the typical Mozartean device of introducing a new subject in the development is seen, as in K.125c (138). The first violin dominates in these quartets; the second has the dual role of accompanying the first violin in thirds or in imitations and of adding its voice to the purely harmonic accompaniment provided by the viola and the cello.

A few months after these quartets were written the Mozarts were again on the road to Italy, to remain from October, 1772, to March, 1773. On the way to Milan Mozart composed a quartet (Jahn hints at boredom during a stopover at Bozen[2]); before returning home he wrote five more. These six quartets, K.134a, K.134b, K.157–159, K.159a (155–160), although written within a few months of the K.125a-c set, show again with what giant strides Mozart approached artistic maturity. Each of the six contains three movements, but there all similarity with the earlier set ceases.

There is first of all a greater degree of freedom in Mozart's handling of the lower voices. In K.134a the second violin emerges with a charming melody; in K.159 it announces the first theme, while the first violin rests. The cello is given a part in imitative developments in K.157, and in K.158 all three lower instruments share honors with the first violin. Formal details, also, are treated with comparable freedom. Transitions hint at forthcoming themes; a second theme on occasion (K.134a) modulates throughout its entire course; an increasing competence in contrapuntal technique is recognized (K.158).

Mozart has also grown wiser in his choice of themes. First and second themes contrast to a greater degree than they do in the earlier quartets and, for that matter, than they do in many of the Haydn quartets up to Opus 20. The consequences of thematic contrast have not yet been realized by Mozart; the vivid interplay of diverse dramatic and lyric bits, as we find in twenty-five years later in Beethoven, was seldom to become a factor of Mozart's style. Perhaps we do the latter

[2] Jahn, *W. A. Mozart* (4th ed.), I, 355.

an injustice in pointing out the absence of this useful and expressive device in the early compositions. We should be content that Mozart wrote these cheerful works and be glad that they pave the way for the great quartets of the following decade.

There are evidences of growth, of changes leading toward a mature style, in almost every major composer. A late work when compared with an earlier one reveals how the composer has acquired a more sensitive feeling for melody, has found a new use for counterpoint, has changed his rhythmic habits, or has altered his style in general. Such growth is typical of Mozart, too, as we have seen above. But what sets Mozart apart from other composers is the rapidity with which major changes in style take place. Almost a decade was required for Haydn to progress from counterpoint to imitative development; seven years went by before the Classical Beethoven became the Romantic Beethoven. Comparable changes took place in Mozart after a few months had elapsed. He, too, suffered the growing pains that are the lot of every composer, child prodigy or not, but his rate was much faster than anyone else's. His year encompassed another man's decade.

A case in point is provided by the next set of six quartets (K.168–173), written in 1773, the year that also saw the writing of the K.155–160 set. Mozart spent the summer of that year in Vienna, where he became acquainted with Haydn's quartets of Opus 20 (published in 1772), those in which Haydn rediscovered counterpoint and wrote fugues. What was the result? Mozart discovered that counterpoint is admirably suited to quartet writing, and composed fugues: two of the quartets (the first and the sixth) contain fugal last movements, and for the first time he employed the four-movement form, a form found in Haydn ever since his Opus 3, about 1755–60.

Nor does the resemblance end at this point. K.168 begins with a nine-measure period composed of one three-measure phrase and three phrases of two measures—an irregularity typical of Haydn. The second movement begins with the intervals found in Haydn's Opus 20, No. 5. Likewise in the others of this set; the fugal finales, mentioned above, and the first movement of K.170, which is an andante with variations, as in Haydn, give further evidence of direct influence. Einstein, in his account of these quartets,[3] lists several other similarities and points out how directly and unashamedly Mozart leaned on his older contemporary. It could not have been otherwise, Mozart being what he was. Throughout his lifetime he was the perfect assimilator: he borrowed, to discard after one trial or to refine on a higher level, from every composer with whom he had any feeling of kinship. His genius shows most clearly in the uses he made of other men's innovations. Having once seen or heard a new device, a new texture or style, or even a new melody, Mozart was able to estimate its worth accurately, alter it to conform to his needs, and make it an element of his style. Thus his music becomes in a sense the synthesis of all he heard and experienced, but purified and brought into order through his immaculate taste and musical perception.

Mozart left Salzburg only once between the fall of 1773 and September, 1777, for a four-month trip to Munich in the winter of 1774. For the first time since early childhood he stayed at home long enough to taste the real flavor of his native city. He had never liked Salzburg; he found its society dull and his court duties boring. And of especial significance here, he found little interest in string quartets, and he received no commissions to write for that medium. Being a practical musician, he wrote none.

Quartets with Winds. He wrote no string quartets on the almost two-year visit to Mannheim and Paris, September, 1777, to June, 1779, during the course of which his mother died. He did compose four quartets for flute and strings: K.285, K.285a, K.285b, and K.298. The first three were written at Mannheim as the result of a commission, and several facts indicate that Mozart considered these works off the beaten path. The first contains only three movements, the second and third only two; Mozart had adopted the four-movement form for his string quartets several years earlier, in the K.168–173 set. Again, the flute predominates to a large extent, while the strings merely accompany. The first quartet, in D major, is on the whole a charming work, typically Mannheim in its graciousness, melodiousness, and

---

[3] Einstein, *Mozart,* pp. 175–78.

absence of deeply felt sentiment. The second and third, K.285a and K.285b, not being included in the *Sämtliche Werke*,[4] are not available. Einstein reports that "they are in good style and 'tender,' nothing more." [5] The fourth of the flute quartets (K.298), written in Paris in 1778, is, again according to Einstein, a parody. Exuberant, perfunctory, at times almost insipid, it is not among the important works of Mozart.

After the Paris-Mannheim visit Mozart returned home for a year and a half. Salzburg offered no more stimulation than it had earlier, and he felt no compulsion to compose string quartets during that stay. Late in 1780 Mozart went to Munich, and there, early in 1781, the quartet for oboe and strings, K.368b (370), was written. Unlike the flute quartets, this work deserves a high place in the music of that period. It embodies many of the stylistic elements that were later to become so characteristic. The oboe is treated in general as one of four equal instruments; it no longer dominates as the flute had done in the earlier works. And while it too contains only three movements (the minuet is omitted), the quartet provides for great contrasts of expression. A graceful yet sturdy first movement is followed by a moving adagio in which the oboe is given full opportunity to exhibit its possibilities. The final rondo, in 6/8 meter, contains a unique passage in which the oboe proceeds with an embellished melody in 4/4 while the strings continue in 6/8, a device most unusual in Mozart.

In 1781 came the eventful move to Vienna. Mozart, summoned from Munich by his archbishop employer, arrived in a resentful mood, was greatly dissatisfied with the conditions of his employment, and succeeded in breaking away from the disliked archbishop. He was free, without prospects, without funds, and he was twenty-five. Secure in the knowledge of his own gifts, confident of his future, and glad to be rid of Salzburg, Mozart decided to remain in Vienna. From that time on, from June, 1781, his activities were centered in that most musical, therefore most stimulating of cities. But still no string quartets!

The "Haydn" Quartets. At about the same time Haydn was completing his Opus 33 quartets, those written "in an entirely new

[4] Ed. Gustav Nottebohm and others.   [5] Einstein, *Mozart*, p. 178.

manner." In the winter of 1781 Haydn came to Vienna to supervise the performance of the quartets at the Austrian court, and there is a strong likelihood that Mozart met the older man during that winter.[6] Here began the ten years of friendship and mutual esteem, years full of reciprocal influence and stimulation. Mozart modeled his works on those of Haydn, yet Haydn "learned from Mozart how to compose quartets." With the stimulation provided by Vienna, the encouragement and respect offered by Haydn, and the Opus 33 quartets available as models, Mozart returned to the path he had left almost ten years earlier. He began to write quartets again in December, 1782.

It was not Mozart's custom to compose without an external reason. A great number of his works were written to complete his commissions. Many were designed to demonstrate his fitness for a particular position. Others he wrote as material for his own concerts; with some Mozart hoped, through appropriate dedications, to influence prospective employers. Only a few seem to have been composed for inner reasons, to fill some need in Mozart's life. The six quartets written at Vienna between December, 1782, and January, 1785, fall into the latter class. They were not commissioned, Mozart had no professional need for them, they were not directed toward a particular nobleman. They arose solely out of the desire to write for musical Vienna, to demonstrate his prowess in the long-neglected field of quartet writing, and to pay homage to Haydn. The six are: K.387, in G major; K.417b (421), in D minor; K.421b (428), in E flat; K.458, in B flat ("The Hunt"); K.464, in A major; and K.465, in C major. These six, together with four later quartets, which will be discussed below, are usually published together as the "ten famous quartets."

The first three were written within a year of December, 1782; the last three between November, 1784, and January, 1785. Published in September, 1785, they carried a dedication to Haydn in which Mozart spoke of them as being the "fruit of a long and laborious work." But no trace of effort appears in the music; only the autograph gives evidence of how Mozart altered, erased, discarded, and substituted. And the results are models of perfection—not a false gesture, not a

[6] *Grove's Dictionary of Music and Musicians,* IV, 153.

faulty proportion. The six quartets stand as the finest examples of Mozart's genius.

We have seen that Mozart had been greatly influenced by Haydn's quartets of Opus 20 a decade earlier; he had imitated the older man's style, his counterpoint, and even his melodies. He was, perhaps, even more strongly influenced by Haydn's Opus 33, with which he became acquainted in 1782; but this time he was stimulated to go in other directions. With Haydn's Opus 33 the quartet's structure and style were virtually completed; the "new manner" of Haydn had provided the bridge betweeen *galant* melody and "learned" counterpoint, and sonata-form was fully established. Mozart, ever willing to build on another man's achievements, immediately seized upon that new manner and made it his own—with what difficulty the autographs and the dedication give evidence.

If one is to characterize the Mozart of these quartets, one must think in terms of restraint and subtlety. On a fabric that is in turn gloomy, pensive, resigned, and gay the designs, usually in the darker shades, are laid in a variety of patterns that defy description. Mozart does not brood, although he is aware of life's sternness; his gloomier moments are subtly lightened by contrasting passages that restore one's optimism. He does not laugh uproariously, although he is gay by temperament; his humor is always tinged with the knowledge that comedy and tragedy are a short step apart. His sunlight carries with it the promise that it will soon be cloudy, but, miraculously, one is glad to accept whatever weather Mozart ordains. Therein lies one of the great delights of these quartets. We are in the hands of a great guide, seeing through his eyes the components of human emotion. And though we may look into the darker pools, we are not plunged into them—as we will be by Tchaikovsky. Though we may observe the unrestrained humor of peasants, we do not ourselves take part in it—as we did with Haydn. Mozart in an impersonal way shows us what exists, reflects upon it with us, and returns us, moved but unimpaired, to our own worlds. That is the essence of Classical music.

It is one thing to point out the restraint and impersonal nature of these quartets; it is quite another to describe the musical means whereby they are achieved. We could quote this passage and trace the subtle overlapping of phrases; we could quote that passage and compare its effect with a similar one; or we could point to a sequence of chords, to this turn of a melody, to that combination of motives. All this would be true and relevant and yet it would not "prove" anything. A sensitiveness to untheatrical music, an appreciation of musical refinement, and an awareness of the myriad facets of human life and emotion are necessary to evaluate these six quartets properly.

Style Characteristics. One technical detail may be singled out, however—the chromatic scale or, more accurately, the fragment of chromatic melody. Mozart had often used chromatics before 1782; after that date they became characteristic. From the G major quartet (K.387) of that year to the *Requiem* (K.626) of 1791 they are almost constantly in evidence. The half-poignant, half-resigned tone of Mozart's late works is due in no small part to the use of short chromatic lines.

For two centuries before Mozart, composers had turned to chromatic melody to depict intensities of emotion not easily achieved through the diatonic scale. Purcell, in *Dido and Aeneas*, and Bach, in the *B Minor Mass*, surrounded some of their most pathetic utterances with chromatic lines. But Mozart found that intensity need not be restricted to pathos. He arrived at a concentration of emotion in fast-moving passages and in minuets as well. The presence of a series of half steps lends a conciseness, a weight, and a drive to melodic passages that a diatonic series cannot always supply. Mozart uses the chromatic line most often in transitional passages where contrast is needed or where a change of mood is anticipated; the first movement of the G major quartet is an example. The device is used subtly to intensify a moving bass line, as in the minuet of the D minor. And in one of the most masterful of all passages, the introduction of the C major (see Example 35), it brings a mood of despair and resignation unequaled in all of Mozart's works. Chromatics appear numberless times in the six quartets; often they are concealed, but their effect is felt nonetheless. Several themes in the E flat quartet are based upon

Example 35   Mozart, K.465

chromatics; the A major, despite its bright key, is melancholy in part, and chromatic passages are largely responsible.

In Chapter 6 (pp. 183–184) the place of chromatics in Haydn's quartets was touched upon. We find a noticeable lack of chromaticism in the quartets before 1785 and in those after 1791, but the device is used extensively in the period between those dates. And that is precisely the period during which Haydn and Mozart were mutually influential and Haydn learned to know the six quartets of his younger friend. Between 1785 and 1791 Haydn wrote his quartets from Opus 50 through Opus 64; in them he made use of the chromatic elements whose effectiveness Mozart had demonstrated. But Haydn was not by nature as intense or as pensive a man as Mozart; the concentrated style was not natural to him. Small wonder, then, that during his London visits and in his later years, after Mozart's direct personal influence was no longer present, Haydn returned to the direct, expansive and open style that was innate. The element of intensity, introduced by Mozart, was to await further use at the hands of Beethoven.

A second difference between the quartets of Mozart and those that influenced them comes to light when the element of subtlety is examined. Haydn, a simple man, was honest with himself and his listeners. His music is a reflection of a mind that was serene and strong in religious faith. Mozart during the last ten years of his life gave us music in which unrest, a degree of pessimism, and some concern over the prospect of death are reflected, however faintly. Even in the minuet, the form that Haydn had filled with sly wit or outspoken humor, Mozart remained aloof, dignified, and reflective. Haydn's finales are full of boisterousness and unrestrained animal spirits. Mozart's are occasionally gay, as in the B flat quartet, or serene, as in the C major; but the humor and the liveliness are seen as though from a distance.

Finally, a basic difference between the character of the two men is seen when formal aspects of the quartets are examined, notably the recapitulations of the sonata-form movements. Haydn was a master of the unexpected. His themes often recur in an unorthodox fashion, and, occasionally, when their return has been prepared for in the usual way, they do not reappear at all. Mozart was not given to shocking or surprising his listeners. The expected thing takes place, but in ever new and interesting ways—therein lie the surprises in Mozart. The transitions between development and recapitulation and the transitions between main themes best show his genius and marvelous subtlety. It is fair to say that Haydn had his listeners in mind when he composed, that he chuckled at the thought of their reactions to this effect or to that, but that Mozart remained divinely aloof from the world, preferred to write music that expressed what was in his mind and heart, and concerned himself only slightly with the reactions of individual listeners. In that sense Mozart was an aristocrat.

K.499 and K.546. In variety of mood, quality of workmanship, and musical excellence the six quartets of 1785 are among Mozart's great works. The composer had taken all possible pains with them and felt that they were quartets to be proud of. Haydn, as we know, was enthusiastic about them; the playing of the last three occasioned his famous remark about Mozart's being the greatest composer of whom he had any knowledge. But public reaction to them was not satisfactory. They attracted no great attention, nor did they lead to commissions. More than a year elapsed before Mozart again tried his hand at quartet writing: a single quartet in D major (K.499) was the result.

The work was published about 1788 with a dedication to Franz Anton Hoffmeister, publisher and Mozart's friend. Jahn surmises that in this quartet Mozart tried to approach public taste without lowering the standards of quartet style.[7] But there is no trace of such popularizing in the music.

It is first of all a gracious work, clear and direct in its first movement, strong in its minuet, and deeply moving in its adagio. Only in the last movement are there traces of the melancholy tone that pervades so many works of these years. And even there it is concealed under the outward signs of brightness—D major tonality, bustling vitality in the themes, incisive pauses between phrases. Perhaps this general restlessness contributes to the feeling that all was not well with Mozart when he wrote the quartet.

The Adagio and Fugue, for string quartet (or string orchestra), K.546, has an interesting history. In December, 1783, Mozart completed a fugue for two pianos, one of the only two works he wrote for that pair of instruments. About a year earlier Mozart had first become acquainted with the music of Johann Sebastian Bach. Deeply impressed with the grandeur of that music, he had arranged some of Bach's music for string groups, had written other works in the style of that master, and finally, according to his established custom, had made elements of that style his own. The fugue for two pianos (K.426) is one of the results. In June, 1788, he arranged that work for strings and added a prelude. In the latter form it is known as K.546. The prelude, appropriately enough, is somewhat like an old French overture. A slow, stately section with dotted rhythms, in the style of Handel and Bach, alternates with quiet lyric bits typical of the pensive Mozart. The fugue is a masterpiece. The style, in a technical sense, is that of Bach: all the contrapuntal arts of inversion, expansion, and overlapping of phrases are present. Yet the piece is unmistakably by Mozart. Sinuous chromatic lines, characteristic melodic figures, and Mozartian phrase structure provide the trademarks. In all respects the piece is worthy of a high place in Mozart's works.[8]

[7] Jahn, *W. A. Mozart* (4th ed.), II, 217.

[8] The Adagio and Fugue, along with K.155–160, K.168–173, the two flute quar-

K.575, K.589, and K.590. In the spring of 1789 Mozart visited at the court of Frederick William II, king of Prussia, the sovereign to whom Haydn had dedicated his Opus 50 quartets two years earlier. One result of the visit was a commission to compose some quartets— apparently the first time that an actual request for quartets had come to Mozart. The commission seems to have pleased him greatly, for the first quartet was completed and sent to the king during the month following his return to Vienna. Financial worries arising out of dire poverty hindered the completion of the commission: the two remaining quartets were delayed almost a year, until May and June, 1790. Mozart's letters of that year indicate his troubled state of mind and his serious concern for the future, but no traces of that worry and gloom are found in the music. The three quartets are: K.575, in D major; K.589, in B flat; and K.590, in F major. They were published late in 1791, a few weeks after Mozart's death.

Few late works of Mozart are as unburdened and free from doubt as these three quartets. If reserve and pensiveness are characteristic of the six "Haydn" quartets of 1785, then sheer beauty and serenity describe the three of 1789–90. Hardly a single moody passage is found anywhere in the quartets; the few turns into minor and the few excursions into darker keys only serve to emphasize the optimism present everywhere else. One melody flows out of another and gives way to a third—all under an unbroken, cloudless sky. Not that Mozart loses his dignity and becomes merely tuneful. But the inner soul-searching, the reflective moodiness so characteristic of the 1785 set is no longer present.

And a new element appears in these quartets—virtuosity. Frederick William was a competent cellist. As Mozart's patron in this instance, he deserved richer cello parts than the chamber music of that time usually afforded. And Mozart provided them. Themes are about equally divided between first violin and cello, and occasionally the cello is given a solo, as in the trio of the minuet in the D major quartet. Nor is the cello spared in the figurations and passage work

tets, and the one for oboe, are contained in an American edition published by Kalmus (New York) as Vol. II of Mozart's Quartets.

with which these quartets are replete. Brilliant scale passages, rapid string crossings, and a full share of development episodes fall to that instrument—all without destroying the balance of the four instruments. Mozart achieves this quite simply by first raising the cello to a dominating position and providing it with glorious melodies, then lifting the other instruments proportionately high and restoring the balance. As a consequence, the whole level is raised, and new standards of brilliance are set. Only in one or two movements, notably in the minuet of the F major quartet, does Mozart forget that his cello part is for a king of Prussia. There he writes in the accustomed simpler vein.

The line of string quartets that began in 1770 with K.73f (80) breaks off with the F major quartet (K.590) of 1790. We have in these twenty-six works a complete record of changes in Mozart's style. Italian characteristics, the warm sentiment of Johann Christian Bach, the mannerisms of the Mannheimers, and the benign influence of Haydn—all appear in turn. Changes in Mozart's temperament, or rather in his outlook, are observed, and the development of his genius is laid down for all to see. The other series of chamber-music works, notably the string quintets and the piano trios, are not nearly as complete; they illustrate now one, now another aspect of Mozart's style. Only in the quartets has he left a complete record of his growth as a chamber-music composer.

THE STRING QUINTETS

K.174. The majority of string quintets contain a part for second viola added to the usual string quartet.[9] Exactly who first contrived this instrumentation is not known. There are several quintets among the works of the Mannheim composers, but most of these include two or three wind instruments. Some of Mozart's early symphonies contain parts for two violas; perhaps the idea of string quintet originated there. The quintets of Luigi Boccherini (1743–1805) were known

---

[9] Einstein, *Mozart*, p. 189, believes that Boccherini's one hundred thirteen quintets with two cellos are actually for two violins, two violas, and one cello; the "alto violoncello" part is written in viola clef throughout. This belief is not shared by other scholars, however.

to Mozart in the 1770s; Michael Haydn (1737–1806), Mozart's fellow townsman and friend, wrote several quintets during those years. But no composer before Mozart had invested the medium with such a wealth of musical ideas, profundity, and charm. The obvious rejoinder is that Mozart was the first major composer to be interested in that medium. Only one or two of Mozart's eight quintets are believed to have been ordered; various other reasons contributed to his choice of the quintet medium. The first, in B flat (K.174), written late in 1773 at Salzburg, may have been modeled upon the quintets of Michael Haydn.[10]

The year 1773 had seen the writing of the six string quartets K.155–160, those in which Mozart progressed far beyond Rococo mannerisms; it had seen also the emergence of the K.168–173 set, in which Mozart made use of Haydn's rediscovery of counterpoint. And the very next work was the quintet. But the contrapuntal treatment, which Mozart had so wholeheartedly appropriated a short time before, is noticeably absent in the quintet. Except for a few bits of imitation in development sections, the music goes on for page after page in a melodious, homophonic style. Only in the finale, a long, fast, sonata-form movement, does Mozart allow himself to write contrapuntally; yet even there extended passages based on busywork in the middle voices tend to remove the piece from the category of pure counterpoint. On the whole, the quintet is a diverse work, full of episodes of orchestral weight, of others filled with virtuosic brilliance, and still others that are in the tradition of chamber music.

K.515 and K.516. Fourteen years elapsed between the writing of the B flat quintet and the two following ones, in C major (K.515) and G minor (K.516). In the interval Mozart had written the moody "Haydn" quartets and the ingratiating "Hoffmeister" quartet (K.499). The intensity and charm of those works are found again in the quintets of 1787.

The C major quintet begins with a rising arpeggio figure in the

---

[10] Jahn, *W. A. Mozart* (4th ed.), I, 357, states that the work was written following Mozart's return from Vienna in the fall of 1773; Einstein, *Mozart*, p. 188, declares that it was written in the spring of that year (that is, before Mozart became acquainted with Haydn's Opus 20), and was revised in December.

cello, a graceful lyric comment in the first violin, and a light, pulsating accompaniment in the inner voices (see Example 36). These

Example 36   Mozart, K.515

simple elements, plus a scale fragment in broken thirds, are enough to enable Mozart to construct a movement unequaled for strength, dramatic concentration, and excitement. And the stage is set for three other movements equal to the first in quality but expressing contrasting moods. A sturdy minuet is followed by a charming slow movement with beautifully ornamented lyric melodies. The quintet ends with a finale whose deceptive simplicity conceals a wealth of contrapuntal subtleties and imaginative developments.

The following quintet, in G minor, is a direct antithesis of the C major work. Here all is dark and hopeless; the resignation of the "Haydn" quartets has turned to despair. The concentration of mood in the first movement is scarcely duplicated anywhere in the literature. A short phrase with the inevitable chromaticism and a downward inflection (Example 37a), another phrase that rises and falls (Example 37b)—these are the elements out of which this most pathetic of movements is created; both themes appear in G minor, and the piece ends in that key. The minuet gives the impression of one stumbling in the gloom; the adagio is a rich movement in which the stumbling is replaced by groping, but still in the darkness. After three such intense, almost desperate movements, the final rondo is disappointing. It does not measure up to the others in either content or style.

Example 37   Mozart, K.516

The Late Quintets. In September, 1789, a short time after the first
quartet for the king of Prussia was written, Mozart composed a quintet in A major for clarinet and strings (K.581). It was designed for
his friend Anton Stadler, an excellent Viennese clarinetist. The combination of wind and string instruments in chamber music was not
new. We have seen dozens of trio sonatas for flute and violin; we
have mentioned Mozart's own quartets in which flute and oboe, respectively, are used; we shall shortly hear about his trio, quintet,
and sextet for combinations of winds and strings. What is new in the
K.581 quintet is the way in which the five instruments are combined.
Mozart was faced with the possibilities of treating the clarinet as a
solo instrument, thus writing nonchamber music, or of ignoring its
special characteristics and treating it as just another voice in a five-
voice texture, thus writing dull chamber music. He made neither
mistake, but evolved a texture in which the beauties of the wind instrument shine through, in which no instrument is slighted, and in
which tonal balance is achieved perfectly. First violin and clarinet

alternate in the first announcement of the themes, but lest that practice seem too ordinary, Mozart writes so that all the instruments share in subsequent thematic statements. The result is a piece of music whose charm and delicacy are difficult to duplicate in the literature for strings and winds.

Two more string quintets were written during the last year of Mozart's life: the D major (K.593) in December, 1790, and the E flat (K.614) in April, 1791. The feeling of oppression, so characteristic of the G minor quintet and the six "Haydn" quartets, is completely missing in both the D major and the E flat quintets. Such darker moments as exist are full of noble sentiment and great feeling rather than pensiveness or gloom. The fast movements incline toward Haydn's type of humor. Light, bustling figures are characteristic, and an air of openness and naïveté takes the place of subtle turns toward dark moods. Both quintets are alive and sparkling, in a manner reminiscent of the Prussian quartets of 1789, and are on the same level of brilliance and virtuosity.

There remain for discussion four works in different categories and in different styles. About 1782 Mozart wrote an octet for wind instruments, K.384a (388)—two each of oboes, clarinets, horns, and bassoons—and in that form it is one of his finest works. The title "Serenade" is misleading, for this is no occasional piece to be performed out of doors, even though it was commissioned for such a purpose. The work contains the four movements usually found only in the more serious quartets and symphonies. Its dark color, its many gloomy moments, the contrapuntal genius shown especially in the minuet, the flares of passion, are all inappropriate for a serenade. Why Mozart later arranged the work for string quintet is not known with certainty. Einstein assumes that the four quintets of 1787–91 (K.515, 516, 593, 614) were written with an eye to dedicating a set of six to Frederick William II (hence the prominence of the cello part in several of these works) and that "to hasten the achievement of that goal he even arranged one of his own wind serenades as a quintet—surely against his artistic conscience." [11] The quintet version, known as

[11] Einstein, *Mozart*, p. 190.

K.516b (406), can hold a place with any of the regularly conceived chamber music. The loss of the wind-instrument color found in the original is more than compensated for by the greater expressive flexibility of the string version.

In addition to a string-instrument arrangement of the clarinet quintet K.581 there exists a quintet for horn and strings, K.386b (407). This three-movement work in E flat, written about 1782, is for violin, two violas, horn, and cello. It is an unassuming piece that is part serenade, part concerto for horn, and part chamber music. The overweighting with low-register instruments accounts for a certain lack of sprightliness, to which the general emptiness of melody and figuration contributes.

WORKS WITH KEYBOARD

Before discussing the thirty-two violin sonatas, seven piano trios, and two piano quartets of Mozart, one does well to recall the place of the keyboard instrument in chamber music in the decades before about 1760. The trio sonata was a vehicle dominated by the two violins; the harpsichord (later, the piano) supplied missing chord tones, provided a degree of rhythmic movement, and augmented the musical texture in general. And the bass or cello merely amplified the lowest voice of the keyboard instrument. Thus the piano served only in an accompanying role. With the emergence of the string quartet the piano was thrown out of its relationship with the strings, only to develop its own solo literature in the field of the piano sonata. Then arose the unlikely medium of piano solo accompanied by violin and/or cello. And out of these grew the modern violin sonata, cello sonata, and piano trio.

In the early years of the piano trio's life, notably in the works of Haydn, the idea still prevailed that the piano should dominate. Many of the Haydn trios can dispense with violin and cello without great loss to the performance. And the same is true of almost half of Mozart's violin sonatas and the first of his piano trios.

The Violin Sonatas. Mozart's sonatas for violin and piano represent not only the largest category of his chamber-music works but also the only category that extends from his earliest years to the time of his fullest maturity. His career as a professional composer—albeit a youthful one—began with four sets of violin sonatas: K.6 and 7, K.8 and 9, K.10–15, and K.26–31. The first two sets were published in 1764 in Paris (there called Opus 1 and Opus 2) and the third in London (Opus 3) in the same year. Mozart was then eight years old. The fourth set (called Opus 4), published at The Hague, was delayed until 1766.

The sixteen sonatas taken together testify to the keenness of the young Mozart's musical perceptions, for they reflect the *galant* style of the time and are obviously the result of what he was hearing during his travels. Several movements of the sets were originally written for keyboard instrument alone, the accompanying violin being added later; and in virtually all of them the piano dominates. The violin, most often kept below the right hand of the largely two-voice piano part, fills in chord tones, accompanies in thirds, and is relegated to a minor role.

Another set of six sonatas was composed in 1778—K.293a-d, K.300c, and K.300l (301–306)—during Mozart's long visit to Mannheim and Paris. Here, following other models, Mozart called them "piano duets with violin," and took a long step forward toward true ensemble writing. Violin and piano alternate in the presentation of themes, rich contrapuntal textures appear, and in a few cases brilliant violinistic writing gives a foretaste of what was to become characteristic.

This set in turn was followed by a further set of six composed variously at Mannheim, Munich, and Vienna from 1778 to 1781 and published in Vienna in 1781; the set includes K.296, K.317d (378), K.373a (379), and K.374d-f (376, 377, 380). Finally, four single sonatas, K.454, K.481, K.526, and K.547, were composed between 1784 and 1788. The last of these, a smaller "piano sonata for beginners with a violin," was written in the incredibly fertile summer of 1788, in which Mozart completed his last three great symphonies, two piano trios, and several smaller works as well.

Throughout the course of these thirty-two sonatas one may see a gradual change in the relative positions of the violin and the piano. The first three youthful sets are clearly accompanied piano sonatas, and the fourth set is so in part. Much of the time the violin part can be omitted in performance without loss to the texture. The London set, K.10–15, includes cello parts in some of the early editions; here, too, the cello, which serves only to double the left hand of the piano part, is clearly dispensable. The sets of 1778 and 1781, on the other hand, are at the level of duets; the violin provides an obbligato to the piano, has independent figurations, and carries its share of thematic presentations. And in all but the last of the four single sonatas of 1784–88 true partnership is reached, and the violin emerges in its own right as a concertizing instrument.

In number of movements the violin sonatas reflect the changing patterns of the time. It had been the young Mozart's practice to include at least three movements in each of his solo piano sonatas; the early violin sonatas (that is, piano sonatas accompanied by the violin) had likewise been given three movements each. Later, as the works of Johann Christian Bach came to exert an ever-stronger influence on the younger composer, Mozart followed Bach's example by writing two-movement violin sonatas; five of the six Hague sonatas of 1776 contain two movements, as do four of the six Mannheim sonatas of 1778. Thereafter, however, as Mozart became less susceptible to the influence of other music, he adhered to the three-movement form; the last ten sonatas (six in the 1781 set and the four later ones) all contain three movements each.

The Piano Trios. In the first of Mozart's piano trios, K.254, in B flat, written in the summer of 1776 (when Mozart was twenty), the piano is still the dominant instrument. The violin part in the first of the three movements contains nothing more than a few accompanying figures and a few doublings of the piano's upper voice; the cello is tied to the bass line throughout. In other movements the violin is used more individually. Seen as a balanced trio, the work is at an elementary stage. As a piece of music, on the other hand, it holds its own with other works of that period. The first movement is light and entertaining, the last is graceful. The slow movement contains an arialike, broad melody over a running accompaniment, in Mozart's most romantic vein.

Ten years elapsed before Mozart again turned to the piano trio. (One work, K.442, in D minor, begun about 1783, had remained unfinished.) In 1786 he composed three in quick succession: one in G major, K.496; one in E flat for clarinet, viola, and piano, K.498; one in B flat, K.502. Two years later, in 1788, three more were written: the E major trio, K.542; the C major, K.548; and the G major, K.564. Taking them in order, one feels a rising level of quality when approaching the E major trio and a rather quick falling off afterward. The first G major (K.496) is no longer of the type that K.254 represents. The violin and the cello are responsible individuals; they are no longer confined to accompanying roles, but have important parts to play in the creation of the musical structure. And near the beginning of the first movement one realizes that a new texture is about to be born: a texture composed of two dissimilar tonal bodies. Violin and cello, working together, are opposed by the piano; a duality of intention results. This division of textures becomes important in Beethoven and reaches its peak in Brahms. But without doubt it begins with Mozart.

The G major trio is an excellent and satisfying piece of chamber music in all respects. But it is overshadowed by the unique tone color, peculiar charm, and complete perfection of the E flat trio, K.498. The choice of instruments is unusual: both clarinet and viola are on the dark side, and both are essentially in the alto range. These facts, coupled with the fact that the trio's first movement is an andante, should go far to establish a melancholy mood in the music. But, miraculously enough, a mood of well-being, of melodic serenity, pervades all three movements. The final rondo is a marvelous example of musical sensitivity and takes a place high among Mozart's finest works.

The rising level of quality continues in the B flat trio, K.502, of 1786. That work contains everything that Mozart had achieved up to this point. It has an air of gentle brooding, combined with moments of brilliant display; it reveals perfection of form with daring and unexpected turns of phrase; and it presents sublime melodies with roughly dramatic contrasts. The trio as a whole is a great musical achievement and is perhaps equaled only by the E major trio, K.542, written in the summer of the year (1788) that saw the three great symphonies come to light—the E flat, the G minor, and the "Jupiter." If the E major trio seems more brilliant than the B flat, it is only because of its brighter tonality; if it seems richer, it may be because of remote and colorful modulations. Drama, lyric beauty, charm, repose, fire—everything is there. One cannot choose between these two masterworks; they remain among the great music of the Classical period.

Quite differently placed are the two remaining trios of 1788—the C major, K.548, and the G major, K.564. The C major trio has about it an air of reserve, of seeming unwillingness to be brilliant or dramatic or even lyric. It is "correct" and moves along in expected, traditional fashion. But beyond that it leaves one unenthusiastic, and it provides a good example of the untutored layman's idea of "classical music." The G major trio was, according to Einstein,[12] originally a piano sonata, "obviously intended for beginners." Although it contains charming movements and would undoubtedly rank high among the piano sonatas, the trio version leaves much to be desired. The texture is rather thin; the string instruments add nothing really essential to the structure. If these two trios are disappointing, we must remember that "the yardstick of perfection against which we measure these two works was put into our hands by Mozart himself." [13]

Piano Quartets. Two piano quartets, in G minor, K.478, and in E flat, K.493, were composed in 1785 and 1786, respectively. These are among the first examples of a vehicle that was to become important in the nineteenth century. It may be recalled that Haydn wrote no piano quartets, that when the Mannheim composers (among whom we may include their spiritual brother, Johann Christian Bach) wrote for piano and other instruments they turned out either piano concertos or *galant* pieces in which the piano dominated. The

---

[12] Einstein, *Mozart,* p. 263.   [13] Ibid.

G minor piano quartet is completely different from such earlier works; it is a piece of true chamber music, making virtuosic demands upon the pianist but allowing the strings full responsibility in establishing a real ensemble texture. The E flat quartet is like its companion except for the differences brought about by the tonality. Where the G minor is pensive, dark, or morbid, the E flat is energetic, dramatic, and straightforward. Einstein calls attention to the influence on the latter work of a quartet by Schobert that Mozart had first heard two decades earlier and whose sweeping power "enriches Mozart's fantasy years later." [14] Such other piano quartets as are attributed to Mozart are arrangements: the quintet for piano and winds, K.452, and the string quintets, K.581 and 593.

OTHER WORKS

The last two works to be discussed are completely different from each other. The sextet, K.522, for string quartet and two horns, written in 1787, is a *musikalischer Spass*—a musical joke. Full of wrong notes, structural defects, uncalled-for cadenzas, and the like, the piece represents a playful, practical-joking vein in Mozart of which his biography gives ample evidence but which his music seldom exhibits.

The divertimento in E flat, K.563, for violin, viola, and cello, is a serious and profound work. Again the title is misleading. For while this trio contains six movements in the manner of a divertimento (allegro, adagio, minuetto and trio, andante, minuetto and two trios, allegro), it is not music written to be merely diverting. This is sincere, heart-felt, and deeply moving music, whose variety of effects is astounding. It is a never-ending source of astonishment that Mozart was able to draw so many different textures and so great a variety of colors from three instruments. No feeling that an instrument is missing, no feeling of incompleteness or of hampered resources exists. Rather one receives an impression of intensity and concentrated power; seldom does a work achieve so much with such limited means. The contrasts between the powerful first movement and the beautiful

[14] Ibid., p. 115.

adagio, between the comfortable andante with variations and the happy finale, are only parts of the picture. Moments of concentration and dramatic power and details of counterpoint add to the completeness of the work and make it one of Mozart's most satisfying chamber-music compositions.

8. Ludwig van Beethoven

THE STORY of Beethoven's life has been told so well, so often, and in such detail by so many writers that nothing would be gained by attempting yet another version. It is a fascinating story, if only as an example of how a strong-willed person—and Beethoven was one of the strongest—can master the events that shape the course of his destiny. Seldom does a great composer allow external affairs to influence the content of his music; nor did Beethoven. Yet seldom has a composer so completely transformed his personal difficulties into the difficulties of all humanity and made them in turn the background out of which he writes. There is in that sense a close relationship between Beethoven's biography and his music. Crises in his personal life made their mark upon his musical style; three distinct series of happenings are largely responsible for the three periods into which his music is usually classified. In order that we may be able to relate certain style changes directly to the principal events of Beethoven's life, a condensed biography is appropriate at this point.

LIFE

Ludwig van Beethoven was born at Bonn, on the Rhine, in December, 1770. He was the second child of his parents; the first, also named Ludwig, had died in infancy a year before the composer's birth. His brothers, Karl and Johann, were born in 1774 and 1776; a sister, Maria, was born in 1786 but lived only a year. Ludwig's musical heritage came largely from the paternal side: two generations of Beethovens were employed at the court of the Elector in Bonn. His grandfather held the honored post of chapelmaster until his death in 1773; his father, a lesser person in all ways, sang in the choir. His mother's father had been chief cook at the famous castle of Ehrenbreitstein, known to every Rhine traveler.

Ludwig grew to adolescence amid the musical influences of the ecclesiastical court, whose seat had been removed from Cologne to Bonn in the thirteenth century. Musicians were numerous in Bonn, and his early teachers were his father's professional friends or local church organists. But his studies were desultory, his father's discipline harsh, and home life anything but well ordered or conducive to quiet growth. With the example of the Mozarts so lately before his eyes, the elder Beethoven sought to exploit Ludwig's talent, much as Leopold Mozart had Wolfgang's. But great as Ludwig's talent was, it was not that of a child prodigy, nor had his instruction been as thorough as was Wolfgang Mozart's.

In about 1781 Ludwig came into the hands of Christian Neefe, organist, well-trained musician, and an excellent person. Under Neefe's guidance Beethoven made rapid progress and began to compose. Hardly a year later Ludwig was able to substitute for Neefe at the organ when the latter was away from Bonn. Neefe's influence on Ludwig was strong, and the boy was well aware of its quality. Two years later, about 1784, Ludwig was officially appointed assistant court organist—this in addition to his duties of playing viola and harpsichord in the Elector's orchestra. In both positions he had opportunity to learn new music of all sorts: church music, operas and other theater music, and even dinner music. Through taking part in chamber music at the homes of wealthy amateurs he learned to know that field also.

This existence, in which the teen-age boy successfully discharged a grown man's professional duties, was interrupted in the spring of 1787. Beethoven was enabled to go to Vienna, the lodestone of all musicians of that day. There he met and played for Mozart, who was greatly impressed by Ludwig's achievements and talent. And he received a few lessons from the master whom he had always admired. A few months later he was recalled to Bonn by his mother's serious illness. The long series of deprivations and neglects to which she had been exposed culminated in tuberculosis. She died in July, 1787.

Ludwig was deeply affected by his mother's death. She alone had shown any understanding of her son's talent, any sympathy with his problems. With his mother gone, he was forced to assume full responsibility for his two brothers and his erratic father. Throughout his lifetime he keenly felt his obligations to look after members of his family, most often in spite of violent disagreements and other unpleasantnesses.

Ludwig returned to his position in the Elector's orchestra. His many loyal friends smoothed his pathway wherever possible and provided a substitute for the home life he could not enjoy under his own roof. He faithfully discharged his orchestral duties, composed a great deal—we shall hear more of these compositions of the Bonn period below—and made the most of every opportunity to improve and educate himself.

In 1790, and again in 1792, Haydn passed through Bonn on his way to and from London. The orchestra entertained him on both visits, and Ludwig took advantage of the occasions to become acquainted with the famous composer. Haydn, for his part, was sufficiently impressed with the boy's accomplishments to agree to accept him as a pupil in Vienna. Arrangements were made, Ludwig was granted a leave of absence by the Elector, and the trip was made. In November, 1792, Ludwig bade a last farewell to his Rhenish homeland and set out for the Mecca of all musicians.

Personal troubles, Beethoven's constant companions throughout his lifetime, followed him to Vienna. A few weeks after his arrival his father died in Bonn; money set aside to care for his brothers had been squandered. Remittances from the Elector ceased early in 1793, when the French invasion of Bonn put an end to the court. And political affairs in Vienna itself were confusing. Conditions for launching a new career at that time were anything but propitious.

But Beethoven's quality as a performer and the genius of his improvisations stood him in good stead. He quickly came into demand as a piano virtuoso and teacher. His pupils were drawn mainly from the aristocratic circles of Vienna, circles whose love of music and generous sponsorship of musicians were sincere. Beethoven's ability to move in those circles had been demonstrated in Bonn. In Vienna it grew; he soon numbered among his loyal friends and stanch supporters some of the noblest families of the empire. But he did not cringe before them or cater to their tastes. He accepted them on his own terms, and they respected him for his independence.

Along with the career as a performer and teacher came the lessons with Haydn. But Beethoven proved himself a difficult pupil, and the lessons soon became mutually unsatisfactory. Haydn's second London visit, early in 1794, provided an opportunity to end the arrangement. Beethoven began to study with Albrechtsberger, a famous contrapuntalist, and Salieri, court composer of operas. Within a year or two those lessons, too, had ceased, and Beethoven became his own teacher. Little academic schooling, a succession of minor music teachers, and short terms of study with two excellent teachers and three eminent composers—such is the extent of Beethoven's formal instruction. But education went on; he read, studied, experimented, and became his own severest critic.

The years to the turn of the century passed uneventfully enough. Beethoven was highly esteemed as a pianist and a teacher and earned a fair income from these sources. As a composer he was attracting favorable attention; his first symphony was well known, his dozen or so piano sonatas were accepted, and a number of his chamber-music works were played in wealthy homes. Beethoven's career as a virtuoso performer in the salons of Vienna seemed assured.

In the last year of the century Beethoven became increasingly aware of a deterioration in his hearing. By June, 1801, he realized that his deafness was increasing rapidly, that a cure was unlikely, and that his performing career was over. He saw himself cut off from normal social relationships and living in a world of hideous silence. At first plunged into despondency and contemplating suicide, he forced his enormous strength of will to come to the rescue. He would compose in spite of the deafness, he would "take Fate by the throat" and master it, helped, presumably, by a young countess with whom he had fallen in love. Her marriage, in 1802, to someone else brought back the despondency. Not until the winter of that year was some measure of balance restored.

The next dozen years, from 1803 to about 1815, passed quietly enough. A succession of great works, including the third to the eighth symphonies, a dozen sonatas of various kinds, nine chamber-music compositions, and dozens of larger and smaller masterpieces occupied Beethoven. A series of love affairs, all coming to the same heartbreaking conclusion, raised him to the heights and plunged him to new depths. And always there was the increasing deafness and the never-ending hope for an eventual cure.

In 1815, then, came another crisis. Beethoven's older brother, Karl, died. In his will the latter appointed Ludwig guardian of his nine-year-old son, Karl junior, and specifically mentioned his desire that the son not be taken away from his mother. Beethoven thoroughly despised his sister-in-law, considered her unfit to care for her own son, and immediately took steps to remove her from the scene. Early in 1816 he was awarded sole custody of his nephew. For the next four years Karl was a constant source of worry and anguish; Beethoven was continually torn from his music to look after his ne'er-do-well nephew. Karl's mother made determined efforts to have her son restored to her, Beethoven was equally determined to retain him, and in the end he succeeded. But at what a price to the world! The steady stream of great works all but dried up. Litigation and heartsickness over his nephew, the deafness that had become almost total, the continuing series of fruitless love affairs—these are among the external reasons for the small number of compositions ascribed to the years 1816–18. And when Beethoven began to compose again, about 1818, his style had changed completely.

The following years were devoted mainly to the production of a few works of such grandeur that all mention of external happenings seems trivial. Indeed, one can only report this escapade of Karl's, that disagreement with friend or publisher, a move to Baden or some other suburban town, and a return to Vienna. But two things there are—

the ever-increasing reputation of Beethoven as the greatest living composer and the deterioration of his general health. In 1826 the final blow came: Karl, made aware of his unpleasant position and possibly overcome by the difficulties he had caused his uncle, attempted suicide. The hateful business passed over, but at the cost of much of Beethoven's remaining strength. He aged suddenly and declined rapidly. The winter of 1826–27 was one long illness: pneumonia, dropsy, and cirrhosis of the liver.

In his last months he was haunted by fear of poverty; he had set aside the bulk of his modest resources for Karl and refused to touch it for his own needs. Unable to compose, neglected by his surviving brother, he was maintained only through the help of his loyal friends. Nevertheless he still planned new works and looked forward to renewed health and activity when spring came. But fate decided otherwise. Late in March, 1827, Beethoven died.

SURVEY OF WORKS

Various commentators have noticed that the lives of composers divide themselves into three well-defined periods. There is first a time in which the composer imitates his teachers and the models around him. Then, having acquired full maturity, he gives full sway to his own artistic impulses; his thoughts turn toward the world, and the world becomes mirrored in his works. Finally, having grown old and his passions having cooled, he becomes introspective and interprets his own soul.

Within certain limits Beethoven's life supplies a striking example of this generalization. His earliest works, those written at Bonn as well as those written during the first years at Vienna, disclose a kinship with works of Mozart and Haydn, with Schobert, and with the Mannheimers. But they are not imitations of those works. From the first they have a forthrightness, a degree of originality, and a powerful quality not often encountered in the works of the composers that they resemble most closely. The compositions of Beethoven's second period, falling roughly between the years of the two great crises in his life— 1800, with its first intimation of deafness, and 1816, with the litigation over his nephew—are not subject to a generalization, however wide its terms may be. In that period Beethoven departed from the concise, transparent form and content of the Classical period, true enough, but he did not abandon balanced form nor give way to the other excesses that characterize many newly matured composers. His second-period works exhibit a logical power, a feeling of inevitability, and a discipline that scarcely any other music possesses. Then, beginning about 1816, came the series of legal and emotional disturbances, and with it a break in the steady flow of compositions. About 1818, when he resumed intensive work, Beethoven had again changed his style radically; the third period discloses a reversal of the intents shown in the second. He turned inward and cast off the last traces of interest in external events. His music became stark and severe, expressed the greatest of contrasts in emotion—and consequently in dynamics and tempo—and became filled with a profundity matched nowhere in the literature.

Throughout Beethoven's lifetime chamber music remained one of his major interests. Among his very first works are three piano quartets, and a string-quartet movement was his last completed composition. Leaving out of account a number of fragments and duets, there are sixty-two works in all categories. A summary discloses the following: ten violin sonatas and five for cello, twelve piano trios, three piano quartets, and one work that was issued simultaneously as a piano quartet and as a piano and wind quintet, seven trios (five for strings, one for winds, and one for strings and winds combined), one string quintet, and one fugal fragment for the same combination, a sextet, an octet, and a one-movement rondino (all for wind instruments), a sextet and a septet for strings and winds in combination. Finally, there are seventeen string quartets, which form the backbone of chamber-music literature. Other works are arrangements, some by Beethoven and some not, of certain of the above works.

In previous chapters it has been possible to discuss works in more or less chronological sequence. In the works of both Mozart and Haydn, composition and publication dates have coincided rather well; a methodical account of the style development of those composers emerged when their works were discussed in the order of publication. With Beethoven a similar procedure is impractical. Several works written in his earliest years were not published until decades later and were then supplied with high opus numbers. Other works, finished at one time, were completely rewritten before publication. And it was Beethoven's habit to work on several compositions at once. The end result is that reference of compositions to specific years is in most cases only approximate. Further, in no one category of Beethoven's chamber music are all phases of his style changes to be observed. Piano trios, for example, were among the first works written, but the line of trios ends on the very border of the third period. Conversely, while the string quartets include his last compositions, there are no quartets that reveal his very earliest style (the quartets of Opus 18 represent a late phase of the first period). With these chronological difficulties in mind, the following order will be followed in the present account: the seven compositions of the Bonn period; the nine piano trios from Opus 1 through Opus 121a; the fifteen sonatas for one instrument and piano; the thirteen miscellaneous works from the wind octet, Opus 103, to the C major string quintet, Opus 29; finally, the seventeen string quartets from Opus 18 to Opus 135.

THE CHAMBER MUSIC

Early Works. In 1785 Beethoven was a well-established member of the Electoral orchestra in Bonn. His duties as organist, harpsichordist, and violist could not have been too formidable, for he found time to compose three piano quartets. The works were published posthumously in 1828, in the sequence of E flat, D, and C major. The C major was the first to be written, however, and hence may be recorded as Beethoven's first chamber-music composition. The composer was fifteen at the time; but because of his father's falsification of the son's birth date—he hoped to make the prodigy seem even younger than he was—Beethoven wrote the quartets in the belief that he was thirteen years old.

The question immediately arises, what were Beethoven's models for these works? It will be remembered that Haydn wrote no piano quartets, that works for that combination by the Mannheim composers were essentially piano sonatas with minor string accompaniments, and that Mozart's only two piano quartets were written during the winter of 1785–86, after Beethoven's quartets were composed. It is not likely that Mozart's were modeled upon Beethoven's, for Mozart remained firmly planted in Vienna from October, 1784, to January, 1787. Conversely, Beethoven's quartets in manuscripts could hardly have been circulating in that city. The conviction grows that the two composers, one a boy of fifteen, the other a mature master of thirty, developed the new medium almost simultaneously and quite independently of each other. Mozart's piano quartets were among the first piano and string combinations in which a true ensemble texture appeared in the string parts. But Beethoven's are also characterized by that treatment. Themes are given to violin and viola with great frequency, and all three string instruments take equal part in contributing figurations and development episodes. The conclusion is inescapable that even in his very first chamber-music works Beethoven was an innovator.

Stylistically, however, the works are not significant. They are in general full of Mannheim mannerisms, of Mannheim dynamic contrasts, and of Rococo figurations and ornaments. One theme, that of the slow movement of the C major quartet, was used again ten years later in the piano sonata, Opus 2, No. 1. Each of the three quartets contains three movements, as do most of the Mozart chamber-music works with piano. Beethoven did not employ the four-movement form in works with piano until he had moved to Vienna and adopted Haydn's forms.

About 1786–90 Beethoven wrote two trios, one in G major for flute, bassoon, and piano,[1] and one in E flat for violin, cello, and piano.[2] The latter is usually included in complete editions of Bee-

---

[1] In Vol. XXV of the *Werke*.

[2] According to Thayer, *The Life of Ludwig van Beethoven*, I, 136, who quotes from a contemporary catalogue, "composed *anno* 1791, and originally intended for the three trios Opus 1, but omitted as too weak by Beethoven."

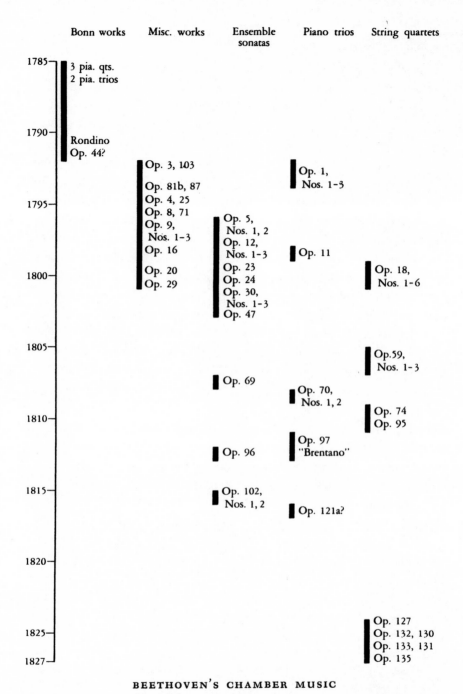

BEETHOVEN'S CHAMBER MUSIC

Dates of origin and composition according to Kinsky and Halm, *Das Werk Beethovens*

thoven's trios, hence is known to some extent; the G major trio is known hardly at all. Although the trios are roughly contemporary, there is little similarity between them.

The G major is a long, diffuse work with enough themes for several compositions. An extended allegro in sonata-form is followed by a loosely constructed adagio. The trio concludes with a set of eight variations on a moderately paced theme. The E flat trio, on the other hand, is a concise work; transitions are developed out of thematic fragments, and an air of economy prevails throughout. The second movement is noteworthy. Although it is a fast minuet, it is labeled "scherzo," just as similar fast minuets in Haydn's quartets of Opus 33 are given that name. This is not yet the presto movement in sonata-form that we shall find later in Beethoven, but its content points in that direction. A rondo in the style of Mozart's violin sonatas concludes the work. The trio was published posthumously in 1830.

A series of variations in E flat, for piano, violin, and cello, was written about 1792 and published in 1804 as Opus 44. The theme is a transparent melody based on rising and falling chord tones; the fourteen variations are concerned with slight rhythmic modifications of the theme. One or two of the variations have real emotional interest, but the work as a whole is merely pleasant. Also belonging to the music of the Bonn period is a single movement for an octet of wind instruments, in E flat. Written about 1792 and published posthumously in 1830, this *Rondino* is not an important work; it is mentioned solely in the interest of completeness.

Thus, three piano quartets, three piano trios, and a short octet for wind instruments are known to have been completed before Beethoven's twenty-second year, in Bonn.[3] Many other chamber-music works were begun in that city but were carried to Vienna by Beethoven in 1792. There they were completed or rewritten, supplied with opus numbers, and published. Those works will be discussed below.

---

[3] Scott, in *Beethoven*, p. 296, lists an additional trio in E flat, composed in 1792. I have been unable to find this work listed elsewhere; it is not included in the *Werke*.

THE PIANO TRIOS

Opus 1 and Opus 11. Among the works begun in Bonn were three piano trios. During his first months in Vienna Beethoven continued work on them, and he performed them at Prince Lichnowsky's in the fall of 1793, with Haydn present. The trios attracted considerable attention, were played often in Viennese aristocratic circles, and contributed to the ever-growing reputation of Beethoven as a promising composer. But not until the summer of 1795 did he allow them to be published; with them he made his debut as a professional composer, for he numbered them Opus 1. At least three years of polishing and perfecting went into these three trios in E flat, G major, and C minor.

That they are modeled upon contemporary works is evident in the general transparence of their style, in the contour of their melodies, in their four-movement form, and in their adherence to other formal restrictions. But there the similarity ends. At the very outset of the first trio Beethoven employed a device that he used throughout his lifetime: the theme is constructed out of repetitions of a short motive. In this case the motive is a rapidly ascending series of chord tones, similar to the so-called "Mannheim rocket" of earlier decades. It appears in transitions, and it creates almost a second development section out of the elaborate coda. Many of Beethoven's fast movements are constructed largely out of similar motives. It is the consistent use of this device that made possible his great contribution to musical form: the extension (one might almost say the development) of the development principle, perhaps the outstanding musical achievement of the post-1755 era.

Other examples of originality abound throughout the trios. Among the most important is Beethoven's expansion of the harmonic scheme. Sudden modulations, especially to the keys a third above and below the tonic, became characteristic. The slow movement of the G major trio and the finale of the C minor provide cases in point. Example 38 will illustrate the practice.

We shall see that similar modulations served Beethoven throughout his lifetime. They influenced later composers so strongly that in the

Example 38   Beethoven, Opus 1, No. 3, Finale (*condensed*)

Romantic period they became stock items. Here, in Opus 1, they immediately widened Beethoven's harmonic horizon far beyond that of his contemporaries. It was, indeed, significant that they appeared in the works with which he began his Viennese career. With these trios Beethoven established himself as an original and powerful composer.

The trios grew in popularity in the years following their publication. More than twenty years later, about 1817, an unauthorized and very poor arrangement of the C minor trio for string quintet appeared in print. Beethoven, greatly incensed at the mediocre quality of the arrangement, made his own. It was performed publicly in 1818 and published the following year as Opus 104, with the following whimsical description: "An arranged terzett as a four-voice quintet by Mr. Goodwill, brought from the illusion of five voices into the light of day with five real voices and lifted from the greatest miserableness to a degree of respectability by Mr. Wellwishing. Vienna, the fourteenth of August, 1817. *N.B.* The original three-voice quintet score has been consigned to the gods of the underworld as a festive burnt offering." [4]

In October, 1798, a trio for clarinet, cello, and piano, Opus 11, was announced by Beethoven's publisher as "wholly new." The trio was written for an obscure clarinetist whom Beethoven knew but who apparently did not inspire the composer to his best efforts. The first

[4] Kinsky and Halm, *Das Werk Beethovens*, p. 287.

movement is merely pleasant; its contrasting melodic fragments are developed at length but to no real purpose. The second is a highly ornamented adagio, superficially beautiful, but lacking in true sentiment. The finale, a set of ten variations on a little tune drawn from a contemporary opera, is a perfunctory movement; its variations do little more than modify the theme. On the whole, Opus 11 is a minor work; Beethoven was subject to better inspirations in 1798 than this work exhibits.

Opus 70. In the years after 1798 Beethoven passed through one of his great personal crises: the deafness he feared became actual. He realized that it was progressive and probably incurable. A period of despondency, when he was close to suicide, lasted for several years. In about 1802 the despondency gave way to acceptance and an outpouring of feeling. The somewhat restrained (for Beethoven) transparence of his style was replaced by an intense, subjective manner. Personal expression became the goal. The works of this second period show, in general, more heightened contrasts, greater harmonic freedom, more concentrated power. The two piano trios of Opus 70, in D and E flat, respectively, were written ten years after the Opus 11 work. They were published in 1809 and are typical of that period.

The D major trio is a unique work. Its first movement, one of the most tightly knit pieces Beethoven had written up to that time, is the peer of the first movement of the fifth symphony in its concentration on one idea. Two contrasting motives, one powerful and fast, the other lyric and sustained, appear at the very outset and provide the material out of which the entire movement is constructed. It is essentially a long development section, even though it contains contrasting harmonies and a recapitulation. Emotional contrasts are achieved by extreme changes in texture: a driving passage in unison or octaves gives way to tight contrapuntal imitations; a brief lyric moment is interrupted by a savage outburst of sound. The second movement, full of mysterious tremblings and passionate cries set opposite fragments of sublime melody, of thunderous chord progressions opposite delicate ornaments, has given the work its popular nickname, the "Ghost Trio." Like the first movement, it is constructed out of a minimum of materials, but here the effect is awe-inspiring. The finale, a large piece in sonata-form, is neither concentrated nor intense; the same inner compulsion to make much out of little is seen, however. Again the development principle steps out of its normal place and takes possession of the entire movement. The D major trio is one of the most passionate of all Beethoven's chamber-music compositions.

It was typical of Beethoven to provide startling contrasts within the same opus number. The second trio of Opus 70, in E flat, differs from the first in every essential respect. It begins with a slow, sustained introduction. The first movement proper contains graceful melodies and a well-defined form in which elements of the introduction appear. The second is a quiet set of six variations in C major and minor; here Beethoven's boundless imagination is given free play. And then the four-movement form, missing in his piano trios since the Opus 1 work of 1795, returns: the third movement is a minuet. It is a quiet, unassuming piece with broad melodies, and it contains a type of passage that Schubert was to employ a decade later. In the finale the impetuous Beethoven returns; rushing scale passages give way to reflective moments, bustling figures are succeeded by short recitations for each instrument in turn. The movement is outstanding in its climaxes and in the quality of its developments. It forms a fitting close to one of Beethoven's truly great works.

Opus 97. The trio in B flat, Opus 97, marks one of the highest points reached by Beethoven in his chamber music. In breadth, sublimity, and originality it is scarcely exceeded by any work in the nineteenth century. His sketch books of 1810 give evidence that the trio was in his mind during that year. But the theme fragments set down in sketch form were not utilized at once. It was not until March, 1811, and then within a period of three weeks, that the trio was written.[5] Publication was deferred until late in 1816, when the work appeared with a dedication to Beethoven's patron of long standing, Archduke Rudolph of Austria. The nickname, the "Archduke Trio," derives from this dedication.

The first movement is unique in the originality and logic of its de-

[5] Thayer, *The Life of Ludwig van Beethoven*, II, 199.

velopment. Although by this time we have come to expect striking
new departures in Beethoven, here are devices yet unthought of:
pizzicato string figures combined with staccato passages in the piano;
phrase extensions leading to unexpected changes of mood; new textures and new types of emotional contrast. Yet the entire movement
is pervaded with an air of nobility and a unity of expressive purpose
unmatched in the literature. The second movement is a fast scherzo
cast in a highly imaginative form. A sixteen-measure melody is presented; the first phrase of that melody returns four or five times, each
time leading in a new direction. It is developed; it modulates; counter-
melodies grow out of it. The trio combines mysterious phrases made
of syncopated chromatic lines and heavy-footed phrases of a coarse
bucolic dance. The movement as a whole is one of Beethoven's most
original and enjoyable scherzos.

But even this inspiration is overshadowed by the slow movement
that follows. Formally it is a theme with five variations and a coda;
musically it is one of the noblest pieces ever composed. The theme (see
Example 39), of great beauty and haunting simplicity, is not so much

Example 39   Beethoven, Opus 97

varied as transformed. The variations are based on successively smaller
note values: triplets, sixteenths, sextuplets. The harmonic framework
remains, and the melody is recognizable throughout. But the content

of the theme is refined, given new life and spirit. No description can hope to do justice to the sublimity of this movement. The spell it engenders is rudely broken by the finale, which is connected to the slow movement. Here is a lively, energetic, and humorous rondo, of a size and quality that only Beethoven ever achieved. It is said that Beethoven often ended his most moving improvisations with a loud chord and a louder laugh, in order to bring his listeners down to earth again. A similar device is employed here, and it succeeds admirably in restoring the listener's balance.

Other Piano Trios. In June, 1812, Beethoven wrote a single movement for piano trio, in B flat. The autograph is inscribed, "To my little friend Max [Maximiliane] Brentano, for her encouragement in piano playing. Vienna, June 2d, 1812." The trio was subsequently laid away. Found by the Brentanos after Beethoven's death, it was published without opus number in 1830. The movement is in sonata-form, with themes and development laid out on a small scale. But characteristic modulations and a masterful coda, longer than the exposition and in effect an additional development section, distinguish the work. Even in his miniatures Beethoven's sense of pace and expressive feeling are evident. While not a great work, it is a charming bit of music.

Beethoven's visitors at Baden in the summer of 1823 heard what they reported as "a new manuscript trio." [6] This work, a set of variations on a naïve tune from an opera originally produced in 1794 (and still being produced in 1813–14) was published in 1824 with the title, *Adagio, Variations, and Rondo—Opus 121a.* No information about the reason for writing the work exists. The theme, "Ich bin der Schneider Kakadu," is insignificant, but all else in the trio is of fine quality. A long adagio in G minor, serving as an introduction, is essentially a fantasy, or improvisation, on the first phrases of the variation theme. Dramatic movements are plentiful, and an air of brooding hangs over the whole. After so profound an introduction, the theme comes as a great shock. The ten variations are based on subdivisions of the note values: variations in sixteenth notes are set between variations in triplets, in thirty-second notes, and so on. An adagio, in

[6] Ibid., III, 135.

minor, provides a moment of repose before the final fast, major variation. A large and elaborate movement labeled "rondo" but having the
character of a development, concludes this fifteen-minute work. The
proportions of the three sections are unusual. The introduction itself,
quite apart from its musical weight, is five minutes long; the listener
is prepared for an equally large main movement. But the light, almost
childlike theme is heard instead; one sees the introduction in retrospect and becomes aware of its unusual quality. This work represents
a transition to third-period style.

THE ENSEMBLE SONATAS

   Beethoven composed fifteen ensemble sonatas—ten for violin and
piano and five for cello and piano. They may be divided into two
groups, according to their dates of composition. Twelve of the sonatas
(nine for violin and three for cello) were written in the period 1796–
1807, a period that included the passing of the first-period style and
the emergence of the second. The three remaining works (one for
violin and two for cello) appeared in the period 1812–15, that is, near
the end of the second period. In the eighteen years that intervened between the first and last of the fifteen sonatas, Beethoven's expressive
purposes and technical means changed markedly. These changes are
copiously reflected in the music.

   The Violin Sonatas. The first five sonatas for violin and piano
appeared as Opus 12, Nos. 1–3, Opus 23, and Opus 24 (the "Spring"
sonata), and were composed at intervals between 1797 and 1801.
Like the slightly earlier piano trios of Opus 1, they are full of the
spirit of Haydn, yet they bear the unmistakable marks of Beethoven
as well. Based largely on the technique of motive manipulation that he
was to make one of his outstanding characteristics, they also contain a
large share of lyric and eloquent melodies. Abrupt emotional contrasts,
striking modulations to mediant keys, and a wide dynamic range combine to give them an air of excitement and youthful exuberance.

   Those characteristics are shared by four sonatas of 1802–3: three in
Opus 30 and a single sonata in Opus 47. But now the greater pro-

fundity and larger scale of the second-period style add a new dimension to the music. A wider range in the piano part and more brilliant figurations in the violin are external symbols of the new style; but, in addition, contrapuntal textures become more common and moods of sublimity mark the slow movements. The first movement of Opus 30, No. 1, the finale of Opus 30, No. 3, and the slow variations of Opus 47 (the "Kreutzer" sonata) give striking evidence of the new direction Beethoven took in his second style-period.

The last violin sonata, Opus 96, from 1812, was composed shortly after the completion of the eighth symphony, but it contains little of the effervescent humor typical of that work. Somewhat austere at times and "formal" at others, it represents a reserved composer who is able to write melodiously and even eloquently but who keeps a tight rein on his emotions.

The Cello Sonatas. Two sonatas for cello and piano, Opus 5, were written in 1796 for Pierre Duport, famed cellist at the Prussian court, but were dedicated to Frederick William II, the cello-playing king for whom Haydn and Mozart had composed string quartets. The cello parts of these two works carry full responsibility for thematic statements and other essential material, in keeping with their purpose, and the two instruments are well balanced. In spite of this, Beethoven published the sonatas in 1797 with the old-fashioned designation, "For harpsichord or piano with violoncello obbligato." One may note here the strength of the tradition whereby the keyboard dominated in ensemble works, a tradition that had originated about fifty years earlier. Each sonata consists of a long, slow introduction leading into a fast sonata-form movement, which in turn is followed by a fast rondo.

The sonata in A major, Opus 69, was composed in 1807–8, a time during which Beethoven was also completing the fifth symphony and working on the sixth. In a sense the sonata represents a state halfway between the concise, intense utterance of the fifth symphony and the expressive, relaxed nature of the sixth. A fast movement, in which cello and piano engage in dialoguelike exchanges, is followed by a tightly knit scherzo based on a syncopated motive; and the fast finale

is prefaced by a short but moving adagio. Beethoven took full advantage of the cello's technical and lyric possibilities here, and the work
remains one of the masterpieces of the ensemble literature.

Two sonatas, Opus 102, were composed in 1815 and are virtually
the only large instrumental works written during that year. In their
concentration, varieties of texture, and emotional content they lie on
the very border of the third-period style. An increased use of counterpoint and a greater freedom of form were to become elements of that
style, and both elements are foreshadowed in these sonatas. The first,
in C major, consists of two fast movements, each preceded by a slow
section—twenty-seven measures in one and sixteen in the other. These
sections are by no means merely introductions, however, but are essential in providing mood contrasts, a degree of lyricism, and utmost
intensity of emotion. The second sonata, in D major, contains a
vigorous fast movement and a long, eloquent adagio, which is connected to a fast fugal finale. In both works a true partnership between
cello and piano is attained.

MISCELLANEOUS WORKS

We must now retrace our steps and return to Beethoven's first years
in Vienna in order to discuss another category of his works. His interest in chamber music during those years was not exhausted with the
writing of a few piano trios and sonatas. Beethoven also experimented,
while catering to the Viennese love for outdoor music or completing
commissions; he wrote a number of works for unusual combinations
of instruments. Thirteen compositions are in that category, and they
represent the tentative side of Beethoven's chamber-music activity.
These works have left the Bonn style far behind, but they have not
yet ascended to the richness and power of the second period. In a word,
they are typical of the style represented by the piano trios of Opus 1.
Exact dates of writing cannot be attached to these works. Some of the
thirteen were begun during Beethoven's last year at Bonn and completed later; others saw the light of day in Vienna. All, however, were
worked on and finished in the latter city between 1792 and 1801.

Probably the first of these compositions is the octet, in E flat, for pairs of oboes, clarinets, horns, and bassoons, written about 1792. Beethoven must not have thought too highly of the octet, for it was not published during his lifetime. Not until 1830 did it receive publication, and then it was given an irrelevant opus number, 103. But within a few years of its completion, about 1796, he rewrote the work for string quintet with two violas. It was published in that form in 1796 as Opus 4.

Opus 4 is in no sense an arrangement of the octet. External similarities between the two versions exist, true enough; the first themes of the four movements agree in most particulars. But secondary themes are completely different, developments are more carefully worked out in the string version, and its modulations roam much farther afield. The very phrase structure of one is unlike the other. Two words characterize the second version: expansion and maturity. Opus 4 is at least half again as large a work as Opus 103; the minuet of the former contains two trios in place of the one in the latter. Developments are expanded, elaborate transitions grow out of previously heard phrases. Yet the string version is a more concise work than the original octet. With all its greater length, it seems to move along tightly without any waste motion. Here is one example of Beethoven's increase in maturity in the period 1792–96. Another example is seen in the greater harmonic freedom of Opus 4. Modulations to the mediant, virtually unknown in Opus 103 and the earlier Bonn works, are characteristic in the quintet, as they were in their contemporaries, the piano trios of Opus 1. It is altogether fitting to regard Opus 4 as an original work on a level with other first-period compositions. One cannot raise Opus 103 to that level.

The String Trios. Contemporary with Opus 103 is the trio for violin, viola, and cello, also in E flat, also begun at Bonn in 1792. But the trio is far superior to the octet and cannot be considered a juvenile work in any sense. A first movement in sonata-form, with a masterful development and a highly original coda, gives way to a charming andante. A minuet is followed by one of the most moving works of Beethoven's youth—an expressive and dramatic adagio, like the first movement in sonata-form. Again one is astonished at Beethoven's skill

in handling development and transition details. A second minuet, with
the trio built a drone bass, intervenes between the adagio and the
lively rondo finale. Thayer gives evidence[7] that this work was played
from manuscript in England in 1793 and thus was probably the earliest
of Beethoven's compositions to be known abroad. It was published in
1796 as Opus 3.

But not all of his early instrumental works were in the larger forms;
Beethoven also tried his hand at writing serenades. Two trios, roughly
contemporary, resulted, both in D major. One is for violin, viola, and
cello, the other for flute, violin, and viola. The exact time of their
writing cannot be determined; Thayer believes[8] that both were composed about 1795–96. The date is probably correct, for both trios are
full of a light-heartedness and a secure mastery that were not always
present in earlier years. At any rate, the string trio was published in
1797 as Opus 8; the trio with flute was delayed until 1802, when it
appeared as Opus 25.

The string trio contains seven movements, the last one being a
repetition of the march with which the trio begins. Three of the
movements are quite regular: an adagio, a minuet, and an andante
with variations. But the fourth movement is unique. Essentially a
poignant adagio, it also contains two bright and sparkling sections
called scherzos. The contrasting bits appear alternately, in the form
ABABA, a form that Beethoven was to use subsequently to great advantage in his string quartets. In that form the principle of contrasting
themes within a movement is carried to its furthest limits, for here is
a contrast of tempos as well. Later in the century a considerable number of works, notably certain of Brahms's compositions, make use of
the device seen in Beethoven's Opus 8. Returning to the trio, we find
that the fifth movement, a sprightly dance "alla polacca," is distinguished by a daring episode for the cello, high and awkward (see Example 40). Thus Beethoven's habit of ignoring the instrumentalist's
comfort and convenience was shown very early in his career. Here is
probably the first example in his chamber music. The trio as a whole

[7] Ibid., I, 134.   [8] Ibid., p. 208.

Example 40   Beethoven, Opus 8

is not profound, but it seems quite appropriate to derive only entertainment from a piece cast in the old divertimento form.

The seven movements of the Opus 25 trio are equally light and diverting. But here the presence of the flute and the absence of the cello add a note of daintiness to the ensemble. Charm and delicacy characterize the work; one has the impression of hearing a full-size miniature, if such a thing is possible. The flute's graceful voice is not overly assertive, yet the work is conditioned, in style and content, by that instrument. The trio deserves more performances than it receives.

The three string trios of Opus 9—in G, D, and C minor—also belong roughly to the same years, 1796–97. Nothing is known of their genesis other than that they were given to a publisher early in 1798 and were published in the summer of that year. They are dedicated to Count Browne, a Russian officer who had given Beethoven a horse. In these trios the diverting content of Opus 8 and Opus 25 is missing, for these are serious works. Each of the trios contains four movements; the first trio has a slow introduction in addition.

In the G major trio one is struck first of all with the richness of texture. Sonorities such as a string quartet brings forth are everywhere evident. One does not feel that this trio, like so many trios, is merely an incomplete quartet. Particularly in the E major slow movement, with its pulsating figures and florid melodies, does the impression of completeness prevail. The scherzo, although fast and brilliant, is not a cheery piece. The finale, a long movement in sonata-form, with imaginative developments and beautifully contrasted themes, is the finest of the four.

The D major trio, the second of the set, is less successful. It is a long work, and for the first time in Beethoven's trios one feels that the composer was handicapped by having only three instruments. Although there are moments of interest and charm, there remains a general impression of dryness in the writing.

Perhaps the finest of all Beethoven works written up to this time is the third trio of Opus 9. Beethoven's affinity for the key of C minor is well known. The dramatic tensions and powerful emotions that key inspired in him are everywhere present in this trio, as they are later to be in the C minor symphony, in the slow movement of the "Eroica," in the piano sonata, Opus 111, and in the "Coriolanus" overture. Darkness dominates all but a few passages in the first movement, along with a degree of concentration not found earlier in Beethoven. The scherzo is in minor; its trio provides a moment of repose in a major key. The finale, an intense and passionate movement, is in sonata-form; both themes are in minor. But the great moments of the trio are found in the magnificent second movement, an adagio. Here, in C major, is a piece of music with repose, with noble sentiment, with dramatic utterance, and with reckless abandon. It alone would have been enough to lift the C minor trio to a high position among Beethoven's early works.

Works with Wind Instruments. Three other compositions from these productive years may be grouped together. Probably the first of the three to be composed was the sextet for string quartet and two horns, in E flat major, written about 1795 and published in 1810 as Opus 81b. Here we encounter a three-movement form again, a decided rarity in Beethoven's chamber music: allegro, adagio, rondo. The problems of texture that a mixed ensemble offers are neatly solved in this sextet. The horns are given the themes on occasion; at other times they accompany the quartet, play in thirds, or engage in imitations. And their ability to play lyric melodies is taken into account. Throughout the work their essential characteristics are kept in mind. An excellent blend of colors results.

Another sextet in E flat major, this time for pairs of clarinets, horns,

and bassoons, belongs to the same years, 1795–97. It was first performed in 1805 (one need not wonder at the delay), and was published in 1810 as Opus 71. Here the four-movement form returns. A
slow introduction is followed by a discursive movement in sonata-
form. A florid adagio, an orthodox minuet, and a marchlike rondo
follow in due course. The themes are appropriate to wind-instrument
style; they are in the main composed of short melodic fragments, with
breathing spaces between fragments. The form is clear, each instrument is given its share of melodies, and the tunes are suited to the
medium. More one cannot say. All the conventional devices appear,
and the composer's good taste is in evidence. What Beethoven hoped
to accomplish with this work is not clear.

A similar work is the trio for two oboes and English horn, in C
major. It, too, belongs to the prolific years of 1795–97; it, too, was
delayed in publication, for it appeared in print in 1806. Later the
irrelevant opus number 87 was given to the work. The usual four
movements occur. The first is rather too long for the quality of its
themes, and the second is overly sentimental. But the trio gains momentum as it progresses; the finale is a good, workmanlike piece of
music. Charming and light-hearted moments are found often. On the
whole, Opus 87 is a better work than either of the sextets, possibly
because Beethoven's resources were more limited in this trio and he
was inspired to do more with less.

And now the piano returns to his chamber music. A quintet for
oboe, clarinet, bassoon, horn, and piano, in E flat, was written before
1797 and was performed in April of that year. It was published in
1801, together with an arrangement, made by Beethoven himself, for
violin, viola, cello, and piano. Both versions were given the same number, Opus 16. The piano quartet piece is an arrangement in the truest
sense; Beethoven made only such changes as the new instrumentation
required.

A stately introduction precedes the first movement. Rich sonorities
and an air of largeness are characteristic. The following allegro is in
fully developed sonata-form and contains three themes; the development is exciting and does full justice to the contrasting melodic

groups. The andante is a long, melodious piece in large rondo form. Beautiful themes, delicious counterpoints, and delicate embroideries make it a charming movement. The finale (there is no minuet) is again a rondo—brilliant, fast, and full of humor. In a sense Opus 16 is the most Mozartean of Beethoven's early chamber-music works. Its transparent quality, its beautifully clear lines, and its general perfection are reminiscent of Mozart. But its vigor, humor, and size remove it from direct comparison with that master. It is the young Beethoven at his best. Straightforward in its emotional purposes, perfect in form and texture, richly endowed with satisfying melodies, it represents all that is best in first-period Beethoven.

When Beethoven's C major symphony, Opus 21, received its first performance, in the spring of 1800, the program included a septet for violin, viola, cello, bass, clarinet, bassoon, and horn, in E flat. In succeeding years the septet became enormously popular, so much so that Beethoven complained about its obscuring the fact that he had also written other works. It was published in 1802 as Opus 20. He arranged the work for piano trio, as Opus 38, some years after its completion, and in that form it is sometimes included among his trios. A version for string quintet was done commercially, without his approval. But the original is the only version worth considering.

It was not a new departure, even in Beethoven's time, to combine string and wind instruments into a chamber-music ensemble. Many works of Mozart, of the Mannheimers, and of earlier composers were for mixed instrumentation. But employing wind instruments in a work of large dimensions, treating them as integral parts of the structure, and lifting them out of their erstwhile orchestral anonymity had been done only rarely, notably in Mozart's clarinet quintet. And even there only a single wind instrument was added to the strings; the problems of manipulating three diverse colors is enormously more difficult. Beethoven's septet marks possibly the first successful attempt to write so skillfully and on such a scale for a mixed instrumental group in chamber music.

This work is a composite of several styles. Its six movements, including an adagio, an andante with variations, a minuet,[9] and a scherzo, point to a revival of the divertimento. Slow, dignified introductions to first and last movements are reminiscent of the Mozart of about 1780. The dominance of the first violin, plus an occasional cadenza for that instrument, bring the Rococo *style galant* alive again. Against such old-fashioned (even in 1800) characteristics one may place three sonata-form movements with large development sections, a true ensemble texture, and a general feeling of modernity. Beethoven's sense of pace and feeling for drama, present even in his less successful works, play important parts in lifting the septet well above the level of much wind-instrument music. Opus 20 is one of the truly great works of his first decade in Vienna.

The septet is no mere resurrection and expansion of the divertimento. It is a composition embodying everything Beethoven had learned up to his thirtieth year. It brings to an end the period of experimentation in chamber music. Gone was the vacillation between string- and wind-instrument works; gone, even, was all desire to include the winds in chamber music. With the exception of four sonatas mentioned above and one work contemporary with the septet, which will be discussed in the following paragraphs, Beethoven's chamber-music activity after 1802 was confined almost entirely to piano trio and string quartet.

The String Quintet, Opus 29. A string quintet in C major was begun about 1800 and published in 1802 as Opus 29. Even though it was written after the string quartets of Opus 18 were well on the way to completion and was indeed published after the quartets, the quintet retains certain of Beethoven's early characteristics. But it also quite definitely points to the future and gives an indication of what is to come after 1802. This is one of the transitional works that obscures the sharp boundary between periods.

Few of Beethoven's works flow as smoothly and easily as the first movement of the quintet. Its melodies move from cadence to cadence

---

[9] The theme of the minuet appears also in the piano sonata, Opus 49, No. 2, which dates from about 1796.

with a quality of repose that is delightful. The lyric, florid adagio, with its recitativelike middle section and its wealth of contrapuntal detail, is a charming inspiration worthy of comparison with the best works of Mozart. These two movements, taken together, are probably as closely akin to the mature Salzburg master as anything Beethoven wrote. But these beauties are echoes of the past.

Then the picture changes; at once we enter a new tonal world. The third movement, a pungent and concentrated scherzo, is generations removed from Beethoven's immediate predecessors. Its dominant feature is a one-measure motive, repeated ceaselessly in every instrument and on every scale step. This is a late Beethoven characteristic— the reiteration of a single figure (see Example 41). The scherzo

Example 41   Beethoven, Opus 29

moves forward relentlessly, and it clearly anticipates certain of the great scherzos of later decades. The finale is a surging, restless piece containing probably the most advanced contrapuntal passages Beethoven had composed up to that time. The form itself is enlarged; it includes three complete themes plus a codetta, and, in the development section, an entirely new theme that prepares for and justifies the final coda. Transitional details and modulations in this finale deserve careful study; the whole movement is a masterwork. In this fragmentary description of the third and fourth movements we see the Beethoven of the future.

In what respects, then, is the C major quintet a transitional work? In what sense is it merely anticipatory of second-period works and not one of them? The question cannot be answered fully until Beethoven reveals his later characteristics in the string quartets. But a phrase comes to mind, one that indicates in which direction the answer will lie: the generating power of the individual motive. We shall see in the pages to follow that Beethoven in his post-1802 compositions became able to endow his motives with life of their own. An organic growth, logical and controlled, and virtually unknown in music previous to that date, is disclosed. In Opus 29 that organic growth was not attained, even though other characteristics of the second period were. Thus the quintet came to the very border of the new style without crossing it. With all its qualities, it is essentially a first-period work.

THE STRING QUARTETS

He who knows only the nine symphonies of Beethoven can nevertheless acquire a deep understanding of that composer's art. Humor, power, drama, poignancy, majesty, great depth of feeling, and utter abandon—all are present in those compositions. Similarly, to one knowing only the thirty-two piano sonatas the secrets of Beethoven's music are very largely revealed. The symphonies, extending from about 1799 to 1823, embrace all three of his style changes; the sonatas, from 1795 to 1822, do likewise. A composer whose musical thought is called "orchestral" by some, who is described as "keyboard-minded" by others, could not help but disclose his innermost feelings in either or both of these categories.

Yet the strange fact remains that *all* of Beethoven is not to be found exclusively in symphonies or sonatas. Neither category embraces the subtleties and stark contrasts of post-1823 works. Nor is there in them the degree of intimacy or even the religious feeling one finds in other works. In only one series of compositions does one find all of Beethoven; in only one series is every shade of emotion, every technical refinement, every significant expressive musical purpose to be looked for. That series begins with works written in Beethoven's first maturity; it concludes with works written during his last months of life. The seventeen string quartets, from Opus 18 to Opus 135, form that series.

The quartets are variously described. They are the New Testament of music, or, more inclusively, they are its Bible; they are the backbone of musical literature; they are the first really modern music. Such characterizations, by sincere and thoughtful musicians, deserve recognition. They serve to show how highly regarded the quartets are, to how lofty a place the feeling of musicians has raised them. Generations of quartet players have marveled anew, with each replaying, at the greatness of these works. Informed contemporary opinion agrees that the seventeen quartets form a whole unmatched in the literature.

Opus 18. Beethoven was fully aware of his worth as a composer, even in his early Vienna years. But he was equally aware of his limitations. Self-criticism and complete objectivity in self-appraisal were strongly developed in him. He knew and admired the quartets of Haydn and Mozart; he had received a commission to compose some quartets in 1795. But with every incentive to do so, with great interest in the field of chamber music, he wrote no quartets until he was almost thirty. It seems plausible that only his high regard for quartet writing and his unwillingness to turn out mediocre works kept him from composing in that medium until he felt himself to be ready. Beginning in 1798 he spent more than a year in polishing and perfecting his first attempts in that field. In July and October of 1801 the results, six of them, were published in sets of threes as Opus 18. They are in F, G, D, C minor, A, and B flat, respectively.[10]

The six quartets give ample evidence of the "generating power of the individual motive," which was mentioned above as being present

[10] Beethoven's sketch books give evidence that the quartets were not written in their published order. The first and sixth, in D major and C minor, respectively, were placed third and fourth in the published version.

in the post-1800 works of Beethoven. Possibly the most illuminating examples are found in the F major, the very first quartet of the set. The first movement opens with a concentrated motive (see Example 42). Easily recognizable, rhythmically characteristic, and harmonically

Example 42   Beethoven, Opus 18, No. 1

clear, it dominates the entire movement. Out of it the first theme is constructed; in that theme's first twenty measures the motive appears eight times. The theme in the truest sense is generated out of the motive. But a single manifestation of growth is not enough for Beethoven; a small melodic strand occurring in the seventh and eighth measures of the theme is preserved for future use. Pages later the strand is used extensively in the recapitulation. And as though that were not enough, the strand there gives rise to another short melody that in turn becomes a transition based on the original motive. The cycle is complete and nothing has been wasted.

The scherzo is even more revealing. Usually the second of the scherzo's two parts is roughly twice as long as the first part. In this case it is almost eight times as long; extensive development of four fragments heard in the first part account for the unusual proportions. And furthermore, a small detail—an octave leap in the lower instrument, coupled with a grace note in the first violin—quite incidental in that development, becomes the generating motive out of which the passionate trio grows. In Example 43 the fragments are shown; reference to a score will disclose the use to which they are put.

This method of basing musical construction upon organic growth became Beethoven's lifelong characteristic. The great majority of his works after 1800 disclose a similar method. And even in the largest works, those containing dozens of melodic ideas—for example, the first movement of the "Eroica"—each idea, one might almost say each fragment, is exhaustively cultivated, is made to yield its full crop of derivative melodies.

Side by side with movements based on this type of organic life are

Example 43   Beethoven, Opus 18, No. 1

movements built out of series of tunes, similar to many earlier first-period works and similar to many works by Haydn and Mozart. Slow movements and rondos in general are less susceptible to motive manipulation, since their appeal is primarily a melodic one. Thus three of the slow movements in Opus 18 are traditional, and one, the andante of the A major quartet, is a set of variations. But in the adagio of the second quartet, in G major, there occurs the kind of extreme tempo contrast we saw in Opus 8: two slow and broad sections are separated by a sprightly allegro fragment. Here, again, is a forecast of third-period works, since such startling tempo contrasts became characteristic in the 1820s. And the slow movement of the C minor quartet is labeled "scherzo." Built upon fugal expositions, but in sonata-form nevertheless, it is a light and deft movement. It is difficult to see why Beethoven called the movement what he did, for there is not the slightest point of resemblance between this andante scherzoso and a true scherzo. Perhaps that is the joke.

The third quartet, in D major, is one of Beethoven's happiest inspirations. Pure joy and great beauty permeate the entire work. Joy and liveliness also dominate in the sixth quartet, in B flat, particularly in the marvelous syncopated scherzo. But here the joy is abruptly terminated; the fourth movement is prefaced by a moving adagio labeled "La Malinconia," which serves to restrain the finale to a great extent.

Opus 59. Taken together, the six quartets of Opus 18 are charming, beautifully proportioned, and at times noble and moving. What distinguishes them from other first-period works is their craftsmanship, their new techniques, and their emotional subtleties. They are six unrelated works that happen to share the same opus number. Their emotional content varies from movement to movement; only their consistency of style and their key relationships connect one with the others. But they are not profound. Not until Beethoven had passed through the crisis brought on by his deafness, with its great depression and subsequent moral victory, did he develop the profundity and largeness of vision that are so uniquely his contributions to music. Those attributes appear in his chamber music with the writing of the three quartets of Opus 59. Planned as early as 1804 and begun in May, 1806, they were completed in the latter year and were published in January, 1808, with a dedication to Count Rasoumowsky, the Russian nobleman who had commissioned them. The quartets are in F, E minor, and C, respectively. But no longer are they unrelated, as the quartets of Opus 18 had been; they are tied together in several ways.

The most obvious connection is furnished by the Russian element. Folk songs in the F and E minor quartets and a brooding slow movement in the C major (said by Scott to be a transformed folk song[11]) provide external links. Whether Rasoumowsky specified the inclusion of the Russian tunes or whether Beethoven employed them out of deference to the nobleman's nationality is not known. But a connection of that sort is scarcely a subtle one. A profound connection of an inner sort exists also, one that has so far not been generally recognized.

The F major quartet begins tentatively and in a restrained manner. Doubt is felt from the very beginning. The first phrase begins on the fifth note of the scale, returns to it time and again, and ends on an incomplete six-four chord—all of which provides a feeling of uncertainty (see Example 44). The recapitulation is unprepared; the theme returns shyly and a measure too soon. And the movement contains no real climax. The allegretto, which serves as a scherzo, is not joyful. With its hesitant style, its second theme (the movement is in

[11] *Beethoven,* p. 256.

Example 44   Beethoven, Opus 59, No. 1

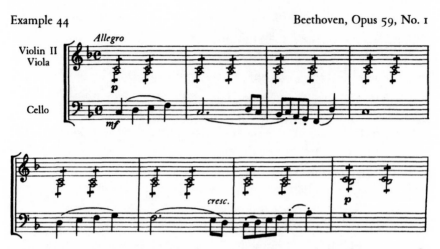

sonata-form) in minor, and its long development of the down-to-earth rhythmic motive, the movement does not generate momentum. It leads to tragedy, for the F minor adagio is, perhaps, the most tragic movement in all of Beethoven's works. Its gloom is not resolved; almost every moment of its eleven minutes is bathed in the deepest, most expressive pathos. Nor does it find relief in the Russian-tinged finale that is directly attached to the adagio; the quartet ends not triumphantly but with an air of resignation.

The first movement of the E minor quartet is intense and questioning: two abrupt chords, a short, doubting phrase in E minor, and, after a pause, a repetition of that phrase a half-tone higher—thus the beginning (see Example 45). The doubtful chords, the many short pauses, the strange shifting rhythms all strengthen the feeling of uncertain wandering, of indecision; only in the final coda is a decision reached. The E major adagio that follows is sublime and full of divine beauty. Deepest inspiration and celestial repose characterize this movement. One can well believe Beethoven's remark that he conceived it while contemplating the starry sky. Uncertainties are laid to rest; the movement is strong and clear. But it is not written on a note designed to relieve personal tragedy; the F minor adagio is not yet completed. The third movement, again tentative, with its shifting rhythms and abruptly contrasting trio (based on a Russian folk song), is moody

Example 45 Beethoven, Opus 59, No. 2

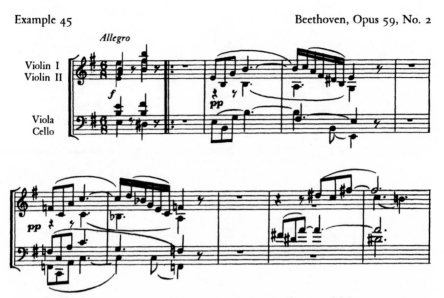

and impulsive. And the finale, an unrestrained, marchlike movement, is like a false dawn of hope. The very harmonies are false: a reiterated C major in an E minor movement. He who finds only humor in this movement has forgotten how Beethoven shouted raucously at the close of his tenderest improvisations—if only to conceal the depth of his feeling. So has he done here.

With the C major quartet the gloom lightens. A diminished chord (related to the final E minor chord of the previous quartet) introduces a series of shifting harmonies in which rhythm is virtually negated. The transition to C major requires thirty measures. The first movement proper, with crystal-clear themes, with pace and straightforwardness, prepares for an excursion into a kind of retrospective melancholy. This second movement contains none of the anguish of the F minor adagio, but rather a gentle reflective mood. The third movement, a minuet, bridges the gap between the andante and the enormous fugal finale. And then all creation breaks loose. The finale of the C major is the culmination of the whole of Opus 59, the crowning glory of the entire Rasoumowsky set. Its confidence, its unrestrained vitality, its dramatic climaxes, and its sheer *joie de vivre* make it one of the

Example 46   Beethoven, Opus 59, No. 3

most exciting pieces in the literature. The tragedy of the F minor adagio, transfigured by the heavenly repose and the sublime detachment of the E major slow movement, is here resolved, at the very end of the C major quartet. The uncertainty, tragedy, and questioning are answered and evaluated by light from above; renewed strength is found, and creative activity is again made possible. There lies the emotional connection between the three quartets of Opus 59.

Consider Beethoven. Filled with misgiving at signs of deafness; beset with the greatest tragedy a man such as he could suffer; plunged to the depths of despair and contemplating suicide; restored to balance through sheer strength of will and divine guidance; emerging from the valley of the shadow and restored to creative sanity in spite of his terrible affliction; composing all the more intensely and profoundly and joyously after the soul-searing experience. The parallel lies open to view: the quartets of Opus 59 are Beethoven's autobiography.

Opus 74. A single quartet in E flat was written in 1809 and published in 1810 as Opus 74. Its nickname, the "Harp Quartet," is derived from two short passages in the first movement; pizzicato arpeggios ascend through the three lower parts, in one case to lead to the recapitulation, in the other to form the coda. The unfortunate nickname has drawn more attention to those passages than they deserve. Many other details of the quartet are much more worthy of being singled out.

A slow, dreamy introduction leads into the first movement. A dramatic moment in the latter is the brilliant coda featuring a virtuosic passage for the first violin. It serves to rescue an otherwise placid movement from the threat of monotony. The high points of Opus 74 are supplied by the two middle movements. The romantic and intensely beautiful adagio, with its expressive, exquisitely ornamented melodies, realizes the perfect balance between sentiment and restraint. The diabolical scherzo, full of hammering figures and breathless scale passages, is a masterpiece. Its concentration and rhythmic drive are unmatched, even in Beethoven. The finale is a set of six variations based on a graceful theme. An increase in the speed of the variations provides the only dramatic note in the movement. On the whole the quartet, in spite of its many intense and beautiful moments, does not compare to the works that surround it.

Opus 95. The eleventh quartet of the series, in F minor, is in quite another class. Composed late in 1810 and published in 1816 as Opus 95, it is one of the great works of Beethoven's second period. But it also stands at the very gateway to the third; many features of the F minor relate it closely to the six quartets of his last years. The work is labeled "Quartet serioso," and a more terribly serious composition Beethoven never wrote. The first movement stands as a tonal incarnation of grim earnestness; its powerful, roughhewn phrases, its extreme drive and compactness, and its sharp contrasts of mood are unique. The second movement contains a quiet, brooding first theme and a mournful, undulating second; the latter is introduced fugally. The themes are held together by a descending melody given to the cello. Indeed, the whole movement is inflected downward, with a resulting air of pensiveness. The third movement is a scherzo in form only; a curt rhythmic figure and a choralelike trio are combined in a movement of restlessness and dissatisfaction. The agitated finale, prefaced by a short, poignant introduction, is magnificent in its concentration. To cancel out the quasi morbidity of the previous movements, an extreme contrast is required; and this Beethoven supplies in the coda. A boisterous new theme in major appears in the light and fleeting fragment with which this most intense and possibly briefest of Beethoven's quartets closes.

The Last Quartets. Fourteen years elapsed before Beethoven again turned to quartet writing. In the interval he had been brought low by family trouble, litigation, and the consequent emotional turmoil. A period of relative barrenness had set in, to be followed by renewed creative activity. But during the period of lessened productivity Beethoven had altered his position toward his fellow men: he learned to despise humans and to love humanity. The changed attitude resulted in marked changes in his musical style. Subjectivity disappeared, to be replaced by a spiritualization, by an objectivity that defies verbal description. Musical forms were expanded, extreme contrasts became characteristic, and a new world of stark, bare tonal lines was revealed.

It is almost impossible to describe the last Beethoven quartets. Music is a matter of moods, of emotional states, and to such states must be attached labels that are in common use. Quartets of the first and second period have been gloomy or joyful, pensive or abandoned, lighthearted or somber. But these are all personal, subjective terms. Here, in the works from Opus 127 onwards, such designations are no longer adequate. There is no poignancy or sentiment in these quartets, nor even gayety or charm. Rather, there is the spiritualized equivalent of those moods. The subjective, merely human emotions have been transformed into their objective, almost disembodied counterparts. Great strength becomes inexorable force; charm becomes austere beauty; extreme joy becomes divine abandon. Beethoven's last quartets become understandable, become one's own, only when one can go beyond everyday emotional experiences and ascend to the world in which he dwelt during his last six years of life. Sensuous beauty has no place in that world, nor has adherence to external forms. Everything in the quartets is flowing, plastic, newly formed; rigid concepts of harmony, form, or melody do not apply. To the extent that one can accept such fluidity, the works reveal themselves as the most divinely inspired music in the literature; by ordinary standards they are cold and unintelligible. Beethoven makes great demands upon his listeners in these quartets. One can meet them only with an open mind receptive to spiritual truths. It is not Beethoven who is being judged here, but we.

From this point of view, no attempt at a musical description of the works between Opus 127 and Opus 135 can make them understandable. It can only disclose the technical means whereby Beethoven achieved his results. But that in turn may be a step on the path toward such understanding. It is worth making, if only for that reason.

Opus 127. Six quartets were written between 1824 and Beethoven's death in 1827: Opera 127, 132, 130, 131, 133, and 135. The first three were dedicated to the man who had commissioned them in 1822, Prince Galitzin.[12] The quartets so dedicated would seem to belong together. Actually, however, Opus 127 stands alone. The two others, Opus 132 and Opus 130, are linked thematically with Opus 131, which is not one of the Galitzin quartets. For this reason we shall ignore the external connection provided by the dedication and discuss Opus 127 as a separate work.

That quartet, in E flat, was written mainly during 1824, received its first performance the following year, and was published in 1826. Its subtleties obscure the fact that its form is as regular and clear as any work of Beethoven's. The quartet begins with a few impersonal and majestic measures. The flowing first movement is in sonata-form, with orthodox themes and recapitulation. But the introductory measures twice appear in the development section and thus seem to divide the movement into three unequal parts. They serve really to unify and to stabilize its very free harmonic scheme. The second movement, a perfect example of Beethoven's depth of feeling even in the midst of this most objective work, is a set of five variations. The theme is born out of darkness, proceeds to grow and undergo transformation,

[12] Galitzin's commission from St. Petersburg was for "one, two, or three quartets"; Beethoven's acceptance is dated "January, 1823," according to Thayer, *The Life of Ludwig van Beethoven,* III, 87.

and dies away in the light of its new life. It is a plastic, vital, yet quietly impersonal movement that suggests a divine state. The stammering, fitful scherzo is combined with a swift, impulsive trio; abrupt changes of mood, tempo, and dynamics provide a feeling of unrest in this movement, a wavering between order and chaos. The clarity of the finale restores the order and supplies, perhaps, the only personal note in the quartet. The earlier movements are pervaded to a large extent by austerity, by a feeling of remoteness.

Opus 132. The four (or five) following quartets must be considered in the order of their writing, since opus numbers obscure the proper sequence. The A minor, Opus 132, was begun in the winter of 1824–25. Work on it was interrupted by Beethoven's serious illness in the spring of 1825, but the quartet was ready for rehearsal the following September. The B flat quartet, Opus 130, begun shortly after the A minor, was completed late in 1825 and performed early in 1826. Its gigantic fugal finale was felt, by publisher and friends, to be too long for the work. Beethoven accepted their judgment, withdrew it from the quartet, and allowed it to be published separately as Opus 133. Meanwhile, before the B flat was completed, work on the C sharp minor quartet, Opus 131, was well under way. It was finished by early summer of 1826, by which time the F major quartet, Opus 135, had been begun. The latter was completed in October. Finally, during those same summer and fall months the new finale for the B flat quartet, Opus 130, was written. Finished about November, 1826, it was destined to be Beethoven's last completed composition.

One must not suppose that Beethoven had lost control over his thematic material, that tight chronology alone was responsible for thematic similarities in these last quartets. It was quite possible for him to compose half a dozen works simultaneously without letting ideas from one leak into the others. In this case it was Beethoven's plan to connect the works through the use of a basic motive. The resulting cycle of three quartets and one fugue will be a perpetual monument to his genius.

The introduction of the A minor quartet presents the motive in its pure form (see Example 47: cello in measures 1 and 2, first violin

Example 47   Beethoven, Opus 132

in measures 3 and 4). The development section of the first movement of the quartet and the fugue theme of Opus 133 make use of the motive in that pure form. But dozens of modifications appear throughout the four works. The characteristic intervals of the motive are, of course, a half step at either end and a sixth in the middle. Those intervals are altered, expanded, inverted; new motives and phrases grow out of them. Example 48 will show a few of the developed forms.

Example 48   Beethoven

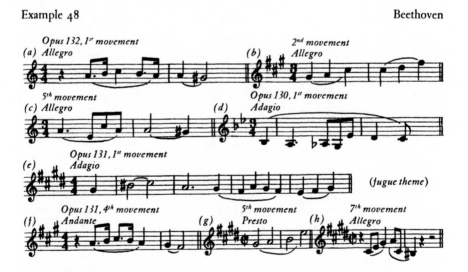

Beethoven's severe illness in the spring of 1825 and his consequent recovery provided the inspiration for the slow movement of the A minor quartet. Entitled "Holy Song of Thanksgiving to the Divinity by a Convalescent, in the Lydian Mode," the movement contains two

contrasting sections: a choralelike and prayerful passage and a more vigorous section, in which the invalid, according to the superscription, "feels new strength." The prayer is repeated, along with the vigorous passage, after which the prayer is heard again. During the course of the three prayerful sections the figurations become more syncopated, hence less definite. One has the feeling that the prayer gradually rises and dissolves, like a cloud high in the sky. Indeed, the chorale melody played by the first violin appears in successively higher octaves on each return. The movement, beginning on earth, becomes more and more filled with divine light as it progresses.

Opus 130. The five-movement scheme of the A minor quartet is expanded to six in the B flat. The first movement, with its duality of adagio and allegro tempos, is followed by a fleet and meaningful scherzo. A slow movement, willful and sublime in turn, leads to a German dance, which, originally designed for the A minor quartet, was shifted to the B flat to make room for the "song of thanksgiving." Then follows a fifth movement: an expressive cavatina filled with heavenly repose and superhuman pathos. The finale is a deceptively naïve movement whose wealth of melody and contrapuntal detail conceals certain subtle connections with the main motive of the cycle,[13] in spite of the fact that it was written later and has in general no organic connection with the quartet as a whole.

Opus 133. It is in the original finale of the B flat quartet, the "Great Fugue, sometimes free, sometimes sought for," Opus 133, that one must look for the culmination of the ideas contained in Opus 132 and Opus 130. This massive movement, possibly the most complex of Beethoven's compositions, deserves a full analysis. Lacking space for a complete account of its intricacies, we shall attempt only a brief description. The movement begins with an *Overtura,* in which several versions of the cycle's basic motive are passed in review. Then follows a fugue (allegro, 4/4), in which the motive becomes countersubject to a leaping and rhythmically forceful theme new to the cycle (see Example 49). After a stupendous development a quiet section (meno

[13] The interested reader is referred to the A flat major section, measures 109–145, and to the E flat–B flat section, measures 353–400, notably in the violin parts.

Example 49   Beethoven, Opus 133

mosso, 2/4) intervenes; the leaping theme is completely altered, and the motive theme disappears. Suddenly a fast and furious version of the motive (allegro molto, 6/8) is introduced, is expanded (A flat major) to several times its normal length, and is virtually developed out of existence; it dissolves until only a few trills remain. The leaping theme (E flat major), restored to some semblance of its original form, returns, as does the quiet section (meno mosso, 2/4), containing yet another version of the motive theme. This time it is the latter that remains; the leaping theme dissolves. The following section (allegro molto, 6/8) presents an early version of the motive theme again; now the development transpires quietly and confidently. A few retrospective measures, recalling the very beginning of the movement, are heard. The final section (allegro molto, 6/8) presents the expanded version of the motive, with the now subdued, erstwhile leaping theme serving modestly as countermelody.

The whole movement is an example of thematic conflict unsurpassed in the literature. It is the kind of conflict in which a theme, though beaten to earth, rises to fulfill its destiny. It is the conflict disclosed in the G major piano concerto, but raised to an intensity and profundity undreamed of in that work. In short, it is the kind of conflict Beethoven himself lived in; he, too, though beaten to earth, rose again to fulfill his destiny. No description can hope to do justice to the power, the overwhelming conviction, of this movement. A quality of growth, of organic development, pervades the entire work. Beethoven here reveals the actual life process of music—truly a stupendous achievement, even for a Beethoven.

Opus 131. The C sharp minor quartet, Opus 131, is tightly constructed; its seven movements are designed to be played without a break, for one connects with the next. The first is a slow fugue in C sharp minor. A comparison of Example 48e with Example 47 will show how the motive of the cycle is inverted to form the fugue theme. The fugue's somberness and detached air contrast greatly with the second movement, in D major, a movement full of restrained gayety. A short recitative in B minor leads to the fourth movement, an inspired set of variations in A major whose theme, divided between the two violins, again suggests a transformation of the motive (see Example 50). Then follows a long scherzo, full of humor; its thematic

Example 50   Beethoven, Opus 131, *4th movement*

connections with the motive are obvious. The sixth movement is short; its prayerful melodies lead directly into the finale, an involved movement in sonata-form whose thematic material is in large part based upon further transformations of the motive. In fact, the last four notes of the first thematic fragment (see Example 48h) present the basic motive in retrograde form.

The relationship of the melodic material of the quartets Opera 132, 130, 133, and 131 to the four notes with which the cycle begins (in Opus 132) is open to every observer. Not so obvious is the very largest expansion of which the motive is capable. Consider the keys of the first four movements of the C sharp minor quartet[14] and compare this key relationship with the original form of the motive (see Example 51).

Beethoven missed nothing. The three quartets together with the

---

[14] Adapted from Scott, *Beethoven*, p. 272, who in turn quotes D'Indy.

Example 51   Beethoven, Opus 131

Great Fugue form a related whole whose full significance cannot easily be grasped. This cycle, in its spiritual depth as well as in the technical mastery it discloses, represents the culmination of Beethoven's creative activity. It places him on a plane of musical achievement that perhaps only Bach, with *Die Kunst der Fuge,* attained before him.

Opus 135. There remains one work[15]—the quartet in F major, Opus 135, the seventeenth of the series. Begun in the summer of 1826, it was completed by October of that year; thus it is contemporary with the new finale for Opus 130.[16] Despite a few faint echoes of the previous cycle in the present quartet,[17] there is no thematic connection between this work and Opera 130–133. The F major quartet stands alone.

It is a relatively short work of four movements. The first begins, strangely enough, in B flat minor but quickly becomes established in F major. That harmonic fact sets the mood for the entire movement; a somewhat dark and pensive tone predominates. The scherzo is an impulsive, syncopated piece with a powerful and relentless trio. The music of the lento that follows is pure repose. The fourth movement bears the famous superscription, *"der schwer gefasste Entschluss."* Beethoven's biographers have discussed long and vainly the meaning of this "resolution reached with difficulty" and of the cryptic phrases that follow it: "Must it be? It must be!" It has not yet been determined to everyone's satisfaction whether the phrase refers to Bee-

---

[15] One other chamber-music work, published in 1827 as Opus 137, is a fragmentary fugue for string quintet, in D major. It occupied Beethoven briefly in 1817 but was laid aside with other fragments for the same combination, notably a piece beginning in C major, never to be completed.

[16] In the interest of filling the gap in the opus numbers involving the quartets— Opera 130, 131, 132, 133, 135—it may be mentioned that Opus 134 is an arrangement for piano (four hands) of the Great Fugue. Some doubt exists that the arrangement was made by, or even authorized by, Beethoven.

[17] Compare measures 17–18 of the last movement's allegro with measures 3–4 of the first movement of Opus 131.

thoven's need for paying his bills or to his knowledge that death was inevitable. A slow and dramatic introduction ("Must it be?") precedes the main allegro ("It must be"); it appears again in heightened form in the movement's development section. Again a conflict of themes results, as in the Great Fugue. In the present case the "must be," with its air of jauntiness, prevails. Whatever Beethoven's problem, it is solved bravely and with a light heart. If the movement really embodies his awareness of death's approach, it is quite in keeping with his character and moral greatness that he met death with a gay tune on his lips.

9. Schubert and the Romantic Period

AT CERTAIN TIMES in the history of music a close relationship develops between musical ideas and the principles under which the ideas are organized. During those times the ideas—melodies, harmonic types, rhythmic patterns, textures, and all the other factors of expression—develop characteristics that allow them to be utilized in accord with well-established aesthetic principles of proportion, symmetry, contrast, and variety. The great composers living during those times succeed in writing expressive and meaningful music while giving full recognition to the validity and force of the organizing principles. In their work they achieve a perfect balance between the ideas and the principles, between musical content and musical form. One is not separated from the other; a particular content is seen to require a particular form, and a certain form specifies its own content. Such a period is called classical; there have been several such periods in the history of music and the other arts.

During the course of a classical period its music may also achieve characteristics of transparence, clarity of purpose, perfection of detail, and complete objectivity. Minor composers, following in the path of the masters, may succeed in implanting those characteristics in their music; a pseudoclassical style arises, a style built upon detail, objectivity, and clear textures. But the essential element in classical style, namely, the interdependence of form and content, is missing, and a sterile, empty period may result. Formal principles turn into rigid forms and musical expression becomes burdened with mannerisms. All becomes hard and stylized, and the fluid life of true classicism becomes mere formalism.

Subsequently a period of reaction sets in; the rigid concepts of pseudoclassicism are abolished, great freedom is permitted, and the very nature of the musical content is changed. New organizing principles—forms—are established, lyricism and free melody substitute for conventional modes of expression, youthful enthusiasm takes the place of tradition, and a general air of liberty pervades the musical scene. Such a reaction from extreme classicism is called romanticism. In one sense the history of music is the history of the alternation between the two opposing styles. That alternation may be summarized as follows: a balance between form and content is first achieved, then misunderstood; a reaction against the dry formalism takes place, a reaction stressing lyricism and freedom, and it develops into a new style. In time the romantic characteristics of the new style develop their own classicism, the worship of the new classicism leads to new formalism, and the cycle is repeated.

Thus every cultural period may have its romantic beginnings, its classical maturity, and its pseudoclassical, or formalistic, decline. In some cases the mature section of the period seems most noteworthy; thus we speak of classic Greece. In others the beginnings attract the historian's eye; consequently the romantic Middle Ages are emphasized. Closer to our own time, we speak of the Classical period of the late eighteenth century and of the Romantic period of the early nineteenth.

ROMANTICISM

We are now concerned with the first half of the nineteenth century. The full flower of Classicism, represented by Haydn and Mozart, had faded. Beethoven, who in one sense bridged the gap between the periods and in another sense stood apart from them, was pursuing his own isolated way. The empty formalism of the rank and file of composers surrounding these giants had evoked the usual reaction. Adherence to traditional forms and worship of traditional musical content quickly became a thing of the past. A new expressiveness, new organizing principles, and a new aesthetic philosophy gave rise to the Romanticism of the decades between about 1820 and

1860. In its development the works of Schubert led the way, and those of Mendelssohn and Schumann became its outstanding examples.

The Romanticist, in his reaction against the formalized aspects of Classicism, looked around for new worlds to conquer. He discovered the world of the past and the world of nature. He became interested in the Orient, he read the mythology and folklore of all humanity, he rediscovered the chivalry and romance of the Middle Ages. Filled with youth and enthusiasm, he loved everything and tried to bring everything into his own life. He strove to master other art forms and to combine them with his own. Thus arose the fusion of drama and music that culminated in Wagner. Thus arose the preoccupation, in opera, with mythology and superstition. Thus arose, for the Romantic musician, the interest in activities other than music. Schumann was an editor and a critic; Wagner thought of himself as a dramatist who composed; Mendelssohn was an accomplished linguist. A movement so rich in interests and so alive with enthusiasms could not keep within bounds; indeed, it recognized no bounds. Enthusiasm became fanaticism, friendship became undying love, and noble sentiment eventually became sentimentality. To the Romanticist the world was a wonderful place; everything in it had inherent nobility, and the great variety of experience it offered him affected him vitally. Out of that feeling grew the intense subjectivity that is the outstanding characteristic of Romanticism. Out of the all-embracing love for the world grew the lyric expressiveness that is its musical counterpart.[1]

Evidence that definite boundaries cannot be set to style periods has been presented in earlier chapters. We have seen how periods overlap, how great composers have often produced their greatest works long after the style they represent has begun to decay in the world at large. So it is with the nineteenth-century shift from Classicism

[1] In a larger sense, however, Romanticism is not merely a reaction against Classicism. It is also a positive realization of ideas and ideals that had lain dormant or forgotten during the last decades of the eighteenth century. For a full account of these phenomena, with a complete analysis of the parts literature and philosophy played in their unfolding, see Lang, *Music in Western Civilization*, pp. 734–50, 801–9.

to Romanticism. At the time when Beethoven was composing his most Classical works, a number of poets, along with composers such as Weber, were concerned with the artistic principles that led to the Romantic movement. And during the decade when Beethoven was creating his terse, epigrammatic, third-period quartets, Schubert was establishing his own rules for Romantic expression. Thus the period from about 1815 to 1828 presents a mixture of several style tendencies. Minor composers occupied themselves with the formal shell of Classicism, Schubert laid the foundations of a style that the Romantic composers were unconsciously to follow, and the great Beethoven went his own way.

And for perhaps the first time since instrumental music began, major composers appeared who showed no interest in chamber music. Such great Romanticists as Berlioz, Chopin, Liszt, and Wagner will not be mentioned in these pages; they were too concerned with the piano, the orchestra, or the opera to write significant quartets or trios. Only Schubert, Mendelssohn, and Schumann can be singled out for their important contributions to the chamber-music literature.

SCHUBERT

A sketch of Schubert's life must by its very nature be unsatisfactory. Nothing of vital importance took place during his brief span of years, and one can report only a few external happenings. But three factors make that life of great importance to music history: Schubert's musical genius, his great zeal in composition, and his complete freedom from family responsibility.

Franz Peter Schubert was born in Vienna in January, 1797. The family situation was humble to an extreme degree, and he enjoyed few educational advantages during his early years. His father, a schoolmaster, was handicapped by a small income, long hours of work, and a large family. Schubert was taught the rudiments of violin, piano, organ, voice, and harmony at an early age. In his eleventh year he entered the Vienna court choir, where he remained until his voice broke in 1813. In order to avoid the compulsory military service to which he was subject he became a teacher of elementary subjects in his father's school. He remained in that position until 1816, his nineteenth year. But Schubert was not destined to be a teacher; indeed, he was not fitted for any "practical" activity. The teaching was drudgery—he was bored with his students and his subjects. About 1817 he left his home, and during the remainder of his life he enjoyed the meager hospitality of his friends in various parts of Vienna.

He had begun composing about 1811. Literally hundreds of songs, many Masses, piano pieces, and works for the stage were written before he was twenty. But the compositions were no source of income. Publishers, when they deigned to notice his works, exploited him shamefully. Always dependent upon his friends for financial assistance, never able to secure regular employment, he remained at the edge of destitution throughout his life.

Many of his friends were aware of his genius. Certain of his songs had attracted favorable attention and had been accepted. And from about 1826 his smaller instrumental compositions gained in popular esteem, to the extent that in 1828 he was able to give a concert of his own works. That concert was an artistic and financial success, but public recognition came slowly. When the quality of Schubert's compositions finally became known to the musical world it was too late to profit the unfortunate composer.

Moving from friend to friend, from room to room, as financial circumstances warranted, Schubert's physical existence was desultory. He lived only to compose, and he composed incessantly. But the irregular existence, coupled with the complete freedom from responsibilities, contributed to the undermining of his health. A serious illness early in 1828 was followed by an attack of typhus later in the same year. Schubert died in November, 1828, at the age of thirty-one. Mourned by the friends who appreciated his musical qualities, cherished his cheerful disposition, and admired his excellent character, he was almost unknown to the musical public at large. And he was one of the most prolific composers of all time. He composed more than six hundred songs, eight or more symphonies, two dozen piano sonatas, scores of smaller pieces for piano and for vocal groups, operettas and Masses, and finally about two dozen chamber-music works.

The great excellence of the majority of Schubert's compositions must be attributed to the quality of his musical instinct and to his keen awareness of aesthetic and dramatic values. His general and musical education was incomplete and unsatisfactory. Actually untrained in counterpoint and not too thoroughly grounded in other aspects of music, he depended largely on the inspiration of the moment. But that inspiration never failed him. He was gifted far beyond any previous composer as a creator of melodies, and he wrote with an ease and surety given to few more studied musicians. His outstanding characteristic is the charm of his lyricism.

The Early Quartets. Possibly the most formative musical influence in Schubert's early life was exerted by the chamber-music activity in his own household. Under that influence he made his first contributions to the literature. Six string quartets[2] and a one-movement sonata for piano trio[3] were written for the family group between 1812 and 1813, when Schubert was in his teens.

If Schubert intended to model his first efforts on the works of Haydn and Mozart, he fell considerably short of the mark. There is little trace of the proportion, texture, or even the self-discipline of those masters in the quartets. But if, as seems likely, he was experimenting to produce a style based upon his innate feeling for drama and color, he succeeded admirably. One has but to compare them with the great chamber-music works of 1824–28. Long, forceful passages rising to great climaxes of sound are present in the very first quartet of 1812, as they are in his last works. Orchestral effects of tremolo, sonorous unison, and widespread chordal writing are typical of early and late compositions alike. Schubert's apparently aimless harmonic wandering in the early quartets is merely a prelude to his lifelong preoccupation with colorful harmonies. The first quartet, for example, begins with a long introduction in C minor, D minor, and G minor, although the quartet as a whole is in B flat. The first movement proper, beginning in G minor, contains long sections in D major

[2] All fifteen of Schubert's quartets are in Vol. V of the *Werke*.
[3] Discovered about 1922.

and minor; other movements are in F and B flat. This extreme harmonic variety, extravagant as it is, served to develop in Schubert the surety of touch and the fertile harmonic imagination that are such large factors in his later style.

One must not dismiss these experimental works on the grounds that their form is faulty. True enough, they are overabundantly supplied with melodies, they ramble, and their proportions are obscure. But it was not Schubert's aim to restrict himself to formal patterns here. That he was able to discipline himself is seen in the single movement for piano trio, the 1812 work mentioned above. Here the clarity of form, the transitions, and the balance of themes all testify to the acuity of his formal perceptions. And in the first movement of the C major quartet of 1813 the form grows naturally out of the thematic content—as it did in earlier Classical works. That it is not the concise form of Mozart or the logical form of Beethoven is no defect. Schubert was not striving to imitate Classical form; his efforts were directed toward an expansion of color possibilities, toward a discovery of new textures and a warm lyricism. In short, Schubert was a Romanticist in the making, a composer breaking away from Classical models in his search for subjective expression.

The year 1813 also saw the writing of *Eine kleine Trauermusik,* for pairs of clarinets, horns, bassoons, and trombones plus a contrabassoon, and a minuet and finale for pairs of oboes, clarinets, horns, and bassoons.[4] They are mentioned here only as examples of Schubert's early interest in instrumental color.

We return now to the line of string quartets. The six of 1812–13 were followed by one ascribed to a period between late 1813 and 1817 and two written in 1814. The three are, respectively, in E flat, known today as Opus 125, No. 1; in D, without opus number; and in B flat, published as Opus 168. And now Schubert's mastery of sonata-form is disclosed, for the first movement of the E flat quartet is as well balanced and beautifully proportioned as one could wish. The middle movements are reminiscent of early Beethoven, and the sparkling, pulsating finale is a model of formal clarity. The D major

[4] Both are published in Vol. III of the *Werke.*

quartet is less successful; it represents a return to the experimental style of the earlier quartets.

In the B flat quartet of Opus 168, however, Schubert's progress toward a solution of his own formal problem is outstanding. The problem may be stated simply: to reconcile his essentially lyric themes with his feeling for dramatic utterance within a form that provided the possibility of extreme color contrasts. The solution, in the first movement of the B flat quartet, takes the form of a sectional structure; the contrasting sections, well marked by sustained notes, by pauses, and by holds, present in turn a melodious theme or an imaginative modulation or an exciting rhythm. The final synthesis of these diverse elements, brought together under the influence of a Romantic melancholy, is not found until the last great works after 1824; but here, in 1814, the solution of the problem is appreciably nearer. The slow movement is an early example of Schubert's sustained lyricism; the minuet is not unlike Haydn's. In the presto finale a single motive supplies the entire thematic material and provides the basis for a kind of harmonic development that only Schubert fully mastered. We shall see other examples of that process later in his chamber music.

Miscellaneous Works. A quartet for flute, guitar, viola, and cello, written about 1814 but not included in the *Werke,* has been attributed to Schubert since its discovery in 1918. Recent research has shown that the work is not by Schubert, however.[5] The fact is mentioned here in the interest of correcting the record in *Cobbett's Cyclopedic Survey,* where the work is described.

Schubert's tenth string quartet, in G minor, a one-movement string trio, and an adagio and rondo for piano quartet were written during 1815–16. Despite several dramatic and powerful themes, the G minor quartet marks no real advance for Schubert; Haydn casts a pale shadow over much of it. Nor is the fragment for string trio an important work.

The piano quartet is on a higher level. The introduction—for the adagio serves in that capacity—is highly imaginative and succeeds

[5] Deutsch and Wakeling, eds. *Schubert Thematic Catalogue,* p. 46.

in building up suspense and anticipation. The rondo is a brilliant piece, but it is not at all in the form we associate with that term. Instead of an alternation of thematic material (ABACA is a typical rondo diagram), Schubert presents a series of contrasting themes in various keys; a pattern of ABCD-development-ABCD-coda results. Again one may assume that his aim was not to imitate the old masters but to create a new form for the expression of his harmonic color interests. In that aim he succeeded admirably. In these early works of Schubert thematic material is of secondary importance and strict form falls by the wayside. The works must be evaluated from a different standpoint entirely, a standpoint that recognizes Schubert's lifelong search for color variety, both harmonic and instrumental.

Three small sonatas for violin and piano, composed in 1816, one large work for the same combination, written in 1817, and a sonata for arpeggione (most often performed on the cello) and piano, dating from 1824, represent Schubert's principal contributions to the field of the ensemble sonata. The works of 1816, often called "sonatinas," make small technical demands upon either performer; nevertheless they are typically Schubertian in their wide-ranging harmonies and their eloquent melodies. The sonata of 1817, in A major, is a full-scale and brilliant work. Its piano part especially reflects a mastery of idiomatic writing that earlier works of Schubert had not always revealed.

The E Major Quartet. The eleventh quartet, known today as Opus 125, No. 2, was composed in 1817. The publisher who caused the E flat quartet of 1813–17 to be paired in the same opus number with the present E major quartet was an excellent judge of values. For just as the E flat (Opus 125, No. 1) discloses Schubert's mastery of sonata-form, so the E major stands as the finest example thus far of his mastery of texture. Schubert's goal had never been precise four-part writing, nor did he often achieve it. He was much more concerned with a search for textures that were made attractive by the warmth of their instrumental color. In the E major quartet such a texture appears for the first time in his works. At times the violins are set opposite the lower instruments; at others, violin and viola appear in octaves against second violin and cello accompaniment. The resulting alternations of instrumental color must have satisfied Schubert, for they became characteristic in later compositions. The E major quartet is a brilliant work whose sparkle is in no wise lessened by the rapid shifts of interest from one instrumental line to another. On the contrary, the texture is so alive and flowing that a real vivaciousness pervades the whole quartet.

The Piano Quintet. In 1818 Schubert was engaged as music teacher to a branch of the Eszterházy family in nearby Hungary. Away from Vienna for the first time and confined to the plains of Zelész, he was not stimulated to write quartets. That year marks the first break in Schubert's chamber-music composition since 1812. But he returned to Vienna at the year's end and quickly regained his old interests. His first major chamber-music work was written in the summer of 1819—the famous *Forellen Quintet,* later published as Opus 114. The quintet, in A major, is for piano, violin, viola, cello, and bass. An acquaintance of Schubert's had suggested the work and asked that variations on the composer's song *Die Forelle* ("The Trout") be included in it. Schubert agreed and composed a work in five movements; the added movement, inserted between scherzo and finale, is a set of six variations on phrases from that song.

At first sight the instrumentation of the quintet is unique. One finds no similar work in Haydn, Mozart, or Beethoven; piano quintets by the minor Mannheimers usually include one or two wind instruments. But a possible model exists in the quintet arrangement of the septet for piano, three wind instruments, and three string instruments, Opus 74, by Johann Hummel (1778–1837).[9] The Hummel arrangement and Schubert quintet are alike in instrumentation, and there is a strong likelihood that Schubert knew the older man's work.

Even though his choice of instruments may have been suggested by Hummel's quintet, Schubert's use of them is original. For the

---

[9] According to Lang, *Music in Western Civilization,* p. 935, a quintet by Hummel (possibly the same work) appeared on the very first program of the Philharmonic Orchestra of New York, in 1842.

bass does more than double the cello; it is largely an independent voice that provides a foundation for the piano as well as for the string instruments. It is open to question whether the presence of the bass enabled Schubert to dispense with the usual six-octave range of the piano or whether the nature of the piano part made the bass necessary. At any rate, the piano plays in a high range throughout the quintet; only rarely are its two lowest octaves employed. The end result is that a new tone color is given to chamber music: octave passages and a general two-voice texture, both in the piano's upper range, are typical. Schubert's ceaseless preoccupation with color is again in evidence. Now, in addition to colorful harmonies and textures, he employs characteristic instrumental ranges. And the experiment is successful. Hardly any work of Schubert's, or of many another composer, is as brilliant, as sparkling, and as alive as the *Forellen Quintet.*

A fresh lyricism pervades the entire work. The second movement, a songful piece in Schubert's finest Romantic vein, provides an excellent illustration of his harmonic methods and may briefly be analyzed here. Three related sections, one lyric, one melancholy, and one restrained, are heard in F major, F sharp minor, and D major, respectively; but the last section ends in G major. The three sections are then repeated note for note, but a minor third higher: A flat major, A minor, and F major—with the insertion of only a single measure (the eighteenth from the end) in the last section to make possible the retention of F major in that section. Thus the themes are presented in different colors, are thrown into sharp harmonic contrast, but are otherwise unchanged. These are Romantic characteristics; yet the external tonal symmetry of Classicism is maintained, in that the piece begins and ends in F major.

The Satz-Quartett. In the following year, 1820, Schubert turned to quartet writing again. But the single chamber-music work of that year remained unfinished; a first movement in C minor (the so-called *Satz-Quartett,* which is bad German for *Quartettsatz*) and a fragment of a second movement are known. Here a new Schubert stands before us. The inner joy and vivacity that filled the earlier works is gone, and a restlessness and concern with more serious expression appear. A tortured, twisting chromatic theme is passed about from instrument to instrument over rapidly shifting harmonies. The second theme, more songful, offers but little relief from the dissatisfaction expressed by the first. With this C minor quartet movement, peace of mind and joy of spirit ceased to be typical components of Schubert's chamber music. When they reappear in later works, it is in company with darker moods.

The A Minor Quartet. After 1820 Schubert turned his thoughts to the writing of a "Grand Symphony." In a letter of 1824 [7] he declared that for him chamber music had become a means of developing a larger style in preparation for symphonic writing. It is true that the seven great chamber-music works written between 1824 and Schubert's death in 1828 are constructed on a larger scale than heretofore and contain many orchestral effects. But those works are not embryonic symphonies; they are merely more sonorous, more colorful, and more lengthy than earlier works and are still based on intimate, economical chamber-music techniques.

The first of these works is a string quartet in A minor—the thirteenth of the series. Written early in 1824, it was performed in March of that year and published in 1825 as Opus 29—the only one of Schubert's fifteen quartets to appear in print during his lifetime. The A minor is a gentle and modest work throughout; an occasional mild outburst in the first movement is quickly subdued and serves only to outline the prevailing melancholic serenity more clearly. The beautiful slow movement, employing a fragment of Schubert's own "Rosamunde" music, is at once lyric and resigned; it is as perfect in its way as any work of Mozart's, without the intensity that characterizes so many of that master's andantes. The minuet is restrained; its charm lies largely in its rich modulations and its deceptively simple phrase structure. The finale is in regular sonata-form, with a development section that approaches Classical perfection; in spite of its brilliant key of A major and its third theme in E, it is a delicate movement. The minor keys and subdued colors of the earlier movements are

[7] To Leopold Kupelweiser, dated March 31, 1824.

here beautifully transformed into brighter shades, but wistfulness and restraint are maintained to the very end. The quartet as a whole ranks as one of Schubert's finest achievements.

The Octet. Contemporary with the A minor quartet is an octet for wind and string instruments in F major, written in February, 1824, and known today as Opus 166. The work is in some respects similar to the Beethoven septet, Opus 20. It is written for string quartet, clarinet, horn, bassoon, and bass; in the Beethoven there are all these but the second violin. Like the Beethoven, it contains six movements, with slow introductions to first and last movements, a centrally placed slow movement with variations, and both a minuet and a scherzo; in the Schubert, however, the scherzo is placed third and the minuet fifth. Again like the Beethoven work, it exudes a general air of well-being. But there all similarity ends; the octet is typically Schubertian in its internal organization and Romantic color.

Now one may believe Schubert's remark about preparing for a "Grand Symphony," for the octet is laid out on orchestral lines. Forceful themes, brilliant figurations, and a wealth of instrumental detail characterize the work. A large and stately introduction leads into the impulsive first movement. The lyric, dreamy adagio contrasts with the solid, almost heavy scherzo. The andante, with eight variations on a simple theme, follows the usual course of Schubert's variation sets; concern with color and variety substitute for an interest in theme transformation, for nothing beyond figurations and embroideries is attempted. The minuet, with its delicacies, subtle phrase structure and charming melodies, is one of the finest movements in the octet. It contrasts strikingly with the powerful and dramatic introduction to the last movement. The finale itself recaptures the drive and force of the first movement and thus brings this long work to a brilliant conclusion.

The D Minor Quartet. The octet represents in many ways a reversion to Schubert's pre-1820 manner. Melodious, brilliant, and forthright as it is, it contains few of the soul-searching qualities that emerged in the C minor fragment of 1820 and developed so poignantly in the works of his last years. The resignation of the A minor quartet is not apparent here, nor any sign of the dramatic conflicts that occupied Schubert's mind after the spring of 1824. One has but to contrast the octet with another work of his, written within a month of the completion of the octet, to realize how wide is the distance that separates the melancholy Schubert from the vivacious one. That work is the fourteenth string quartet, in D minor.

Schubert's choice of a theme from one of his songs as the basis for the slow movement's variations has given the D minor quartet the nickname "Death and the Maiden." The subject of that song—death—plus the fact that a few phrases in the last movement are quotations from his *Erlkönig*—again a preoccupation with death—have inspired commentators to dwell on the inner unity of the quartet and to assert that death provides that unity.[8] Such an interpretation is pure speculation, even though it is made to sound plausible. Need the powerful and dramatic first movement be considered a struggle with death? Can it not also be seen as depicting Schubert's struggle with a refractory motive? What real evidence exists that the scherzo's theme is "Death, the demon fiddler," as Heuss has it, or that the andante "dwells on death's words," or that the last movement is a "dance of death"?[9]

It is both misleading and indefensible thus to attach an external program to so profound and pure a work as the D minor quartet. One may appropriately discuss the emotional effect of a movement, or bring to light the contrasting moods that underlie a series of movements, or even describe the composer's state of mind at the time of writing, but not to the extent of attaching external phenomena to the music, of burdening the music with a "program." It is much more to the point to indicate the nature of Schubert's handling of an obstinate motive in the first movement and to describe his success in creating a plastic, living development section in the finest Classical tradition—even though Romantic color and drama abound—and to call attention to the poignant slow movement, with its new technique

[8] See Kahl, in *Cobbett's Cyclopedic Survey of Chamber Music*, II, 359. Kahl in turn quotes Heuss, *Kammermusikabende*, pp. 85–90.

[9] Heuss, *Kammermusikabende*, p. 89.

(for Schubert) of transforming the simple theme in successive variations so that a series of contrasting moods is called up. The scherzo, as well, has no need of a program but stands on its own feet as a wonderfully wrought example of rhythmic intensity. The finale provides perhaps the finest of all illustrations of relentless drive and controlled power. In organization, expressive quality, and sheer emotional strength the D minor quartet is one of Schubert's greatest works.

The G Major Quartet. The fifteenth quartet, in G major, published as Opus 161 many years after Schubert's death, was written in 1826 within the space of ten days. It is in many ways the most orchestral of all his chamber music; tremolos, forceful unisons, and quantities of sound give the impression that the quartet is about to burst its bonds. Except for a few melodic fragments in the adagio and the tuneful trio, there is virtually none of the lyricism of the earlier—and later—Schubert. In place of the songfulness is a harmonic unrest, a ceaseless shift from one key to another. The quartet as a whole offers perhaps the most striking example of Schubert's departure from the lines of true Classicism. The clear part-writing of earlier decades is almost nonexistent here. A preoccupation with the composite sound of the individual chord, or measure, or harmonic progression, replaces the concern for linear clarity. The result is a degree of harmonic freedom that Schubert never again attained. The G major quartet points the way to the vertical conceptions of post-Romantic composers; it is generations in advance of Schubert's own time.

The Piano Trios. In 1827 Schubert became associated in friendship with three musicians who had formed a piano trio: Ignaz Schuppanzigh (1776–1830) and Joseph Linke (1783–1837), members of the Rasoumowsky Quartet and friends of Beethoven, and Carl von Bocklet (1801–81), an excellent pianist. Inspired by that friendship and moved to expand his newly achieved harmonic skill still further, he wrote two trios for piano, violin, and cello in the fall of 1827. The first, in B flat, was published in 1836 as Opus 99. The second, in E flat, performed at the only concert of his own works Schubert ever organized (early in 1828), was published a few months before his death; it is now known as Opus 100.

Never before had Schubert revealed himself as completely as he did in the two trios. All that is essentially Schubertian is found there: noble melodies, piquant rhythms, persevering figurations, Romantic melancholy, harmonic variety—and great length. The first movement of the B flat trio might be taken as a model of Schubert's formal practices: themes and theme fragments are not so much developed as repeated—but always in different keys and with different color effects. The second movement's theme contrasts greatly with the naïve and reiterated figures which surround it; a more serene piece is difficult to find anywhere in the literature. The buoyant scherzo and the delightful final rondo are pure joy. The E flat trio is more virile throughout. Schubert's practice of establishing contrasting tonal groups (strings opposed to the piano, in this case) here results in a general thickening of the texture and a certain heaviness of style. A march-like slow movement and a canonic scherzo are followed by one of the longest movements in the literature.[10] In the hands of a Beethoven such a movement might have achieved colossal stature. Schubert, a repeater of sections rather than a developer of themes, here gave full scope to his vivid harmonic and tonal color senses, but at the expense of listener interest and effective climax.

The String Quintet. It is seldom given to a composer to produce his most perfect work at the very end of his life. The C major quintet, for two violins, viola, and two cellos is such a work. Written in September, 1828, two months before Schubert's death, and published in 1854 as Opus 163, it has taken its place in chamber-music literature as one of the finest compositions of any period. In nobility of conception, beauty of melody, and variety of mood it is without equal. Instrumental color effects unknown in the earlier literature are scattered about in rich profusion. The added cello amplifies the texture and makes possible a quality of lyricism that a string quartet seldom achieves.

The first movement of the quintet contains two lyric themes and a

[10] The following solution of the formal problem offered by this movement may be

few derivative melodies. Out of them Schubert creates music of indescribable beauty and gentle pathos. Moments of dramatic tension are resolved with a degree of refinement and a technical skill that are truly wonderful. All possible groupings of instruments in twos and threes are employed; the variety of tonal effects results in a quality of texture no other work possesses. Probably nowhere else in chamber music are drama, serenity, and melancholy combined as they are in the recapitulation, whose beginning is shown in Example 52. This is one of the most eloquent passages in nineteenth-century music—and its technical means are of the simplest. If ever inspired genius was shown in music it is in those few measures.

The contrasts afforded in the slow movement are extreme: a sublime melody in E major is suddenly interrupted by a violent passage in F minor full of complex rhythms and dominated by a soaring melody of great emotional intensity. After a restrained transition the E major theme returns, now transformed by the addition of stumbling, un-

---

of interest. It illustrates the kind of sonata-form in which Schubert was most eloquent.

	Measure Number	*Key*	*Meter*	*Content*
EXPOSITION	1	E flat	6/8	1st theme
	73	C minor	2/2	2d theme
	125	B flat	6/8	2d theme modifi⌐ ˙
	163	C minor	2/2	2d theme developed
	193	B flat	6/8	1st theme developed
	275	B minor	6/8	3d theme, derived from second movement
DEVELOPMENT	315	B minor	6/8	
		D minor	2/2	
		D minor	6/8	development of 1st and 2d themes, with suggestions of 3d theme
		B minor / F major	2/2	
		E flat minor / B minor / E flat minor	6/8	
RECAPITULATION	441	E flat	6/8	1st theme
	519	F minor	2/2	2d theme
	551	E flat	6/8	2d theme modified
	593	F minor	2/2	2d theme developed
	623	E flat	6/8	1st theme developed
	693	E flat	6/8	3d theme and coda; end in measure 748

Example 52   Schubert, Opus 163

certain passages in the lowest voice. According to some commentators, it may have been Schubert's intention to express in this movement his emotional states before and during his severe illness of 1828, with its premonition of approaching death. The scherzo presents a similar set of contrasting moods. All is power, energy, and activity in the first section; the trio is dark, brooding, and altogether resigned. The finale has about it an air of false gaiety, of restless haste. Perhaps Schubert knew that his time was short.

Schubert would have been assured of a high position as a chamber-music composer had he written only the C major quintet. The two quartets of 1824 and the two piano trios of 1827, together with the quintet, mark him as one of the truly great. Departing from the Classical forms that resulted from the relationship between organizing principles and content, and faced with the need of creating new forms to encompass his enormous melodic gifts, he added a new element to musical form. The chief principles had been emotional contrast in clear and symmetrical forms, proportion, and organic growth. To them Schubert added the principle of harmonic and instrumental color contrasts. In most cases his works are held together by the unifying force of sustained lyricism. The world of music is a better place for having had Schubert dwell in it, even if briefly. A fresh, ever-youthful melodic quality, adorned with the most subtle color perceptions, will be his enduring monument.

MENDELSSOHN

Jacob Ludwig Felix Mendelssohn[11] was born in Hamburg in 1809. The son of wealthy and cultured parents, he enjoyed every advantage in education, environment, travel, and associations with famous people. The Mendelssohn home in Berlin, to which city the family moved about 1812, was a center of musical life. Small orchestra concerts were a feature of that life, and eminent musicians considered it a privilege to attend the bimonthly performances. The young Mendelssohn, a capable pianist from about his ninth year, began to compose in his twelfth. Many of his earliest compositions were written for and performed at the family concerts. There he had every opportunity to conduct and hear them and to profit from the expert criticisms he received.

By the time he had reached his sixteenth year Mendelssohn had achieved considerable fame for his improvisations at the piano and had dozens of worthwhile compositions to his credit. His maturity as a composer dates from about that time, for the famous overture to *A*

[11] The surname Mendelssohn-Bartholdy was adopted by the family when they renounced the Jewish faith and entered the Protestant Church.

Midsummer Night's Dream, the string octet, Opus 20, and similar works in which his style developed its later characteristics were written within a year or two of 1825. From about 1826 his style underwent little significant change. Confirmed in his espousal of a sweet lyricism, secure in his mastery of form in all details, he composed steadily.

The years from about 1827 to 1835 were filled with constant activity. Famed as a pianist and a conductor, known as a composer, and traveling widely, he enjoyed a large acquaintance with great men in all fields. Several trips to England established him in the affections of that country; his fame on the Continent increased from day to day. Among his great achievements were two performances of Bach's *St. Matthew Passion*, in Berlin in March, 1829—the first since Bach's death. With those performances began the modern recognition of Bach as one of the greatest of composers. The enthusiasm engendered there eventually led to the founding of the Bachgesellschaft and to the publication of that master's complete works. In that endeavor, as we shall see below, Schumann shared wholeheartedly.

In 1835 Mendelssohn accepted the directorship of the Leipzig Gewandhaus Orchestra; in 1842 he was largely instrumental in organizing the Leipzig Conservatory, which began its sessions in April, 1843, with Schumann as one of the faculty. The joint activities, carried out with the broad vision and attention to detail that were typical of Mendelssohn, soon made Leipzig the brightest spot in the musical sun. In addition to those responsibilities he made many concert tours, appeared as guest conductor, and composed unceasingly.

But Mendelssohn was also in constant demand at the court of Frederick William in Berlin. Performances, compositions, and the organization of festivals kept him occupied to such an extent that he was forced to relinquish a portion of the Leipzig responsibilities. Continued travels to England and about Europe, along with masses of correspondence and administrative work, kept him busy from morning to night. The years to 1847 were filled with such intense, almost feverish activity, and the resultant strain gradually undermined his rugged good health. Late in 1847, prematurely aged and completely exhausted, Mendelssohn died. His sterling moral qualities, his accomplishments as a musician, linguist, painter, and simple, unaffected human being had endeared him to all the musical world. Richly endowed, fortunate in his education, and warm in all his friendships, he stands for all that was noble in the Romantic period in which he lived.

Youthful Works. Mendelssohn's interest in chamber-music composition revealed itself at the very beginning of his career. His first attempts (and they are scarcely more than that) took the form of three piano quartets, Opera 1, 2, and 3, written between 1822 and 1824. The precocious Mendelssohn, hardly in his teens, here disclosed his awareness of musical form and his innate good taste. But the works as a whole give little evidence of the technical mastery and vivid imagination that were to illuminate later compositions. Themes are amenable to development to some extent, and mildly contrasting harmonies are in evidence. The three quartets are pale imitations of Classical formalism—except in one important feature. That feature, marking a definite departure from the earlier period, is the scherzo in duple measure. It is interesting to recall the eventful history of that form.

The minuet, it will be remembered, had been introduced into the sonata structure by the Viennese predecessors of Haydn in the divertimento decades, about 1740. Haydn faithfully wrote minuets until about 1781, when the famous quartets of Opus 33, those "written in an entirely new manner," were composed. In that set of works, possibly to balance the new seriousness of their first movements, Haydn increased the speed of the minuet and labeled the form "scherzo." In Beethoven's hands the speed was retained, but a light, deft, and humorous content drove out what was left of the minuet's courtly dance characteristics. It was also expanded, occasionally, almost to the size and proportions of sonata-form. The scherzo's trio, at first merely a contrasting section in a style similar to the scherzo proper, now became a section in contrasting meter: the trio of the ninth symphony's scherzo is in duple measure—but still in fast tempo. In Schubert the contrasting trio had undergone further change. The C major quintet, Opus 163, exhibits the most extreme contrast between a brilliant scherzo in triple measure and a somber andante in duple—the latter serving as a trio. Now, finally, in Mendelssohn further modifications are at hand: a new form results, bearing the name "scherzo" and containing somewhat the same style characteristics as the earlier form, but now distinguished by the use of duple measure throughout. The last trace of relationship with the minuet will be seen to have been eliminated when, later in these pages, subsequent scherzos of Mendelssohn reveal themselves in large rondo form; the trio and *da capo* features have disappeared entirely.

We return now to the survey of the works of Mendelssohn. A sextet for piano, violin, two violas, cello, and bass was written about 1824. Like the piano quartets, the sextet is a naïve work and exhibits no real originality. For even though the minuet is notated in 6/8 instead of 3/4, no significant musical difference results. Evidence of cyclical form exists in the finale: extended quotations of the minuet's theme are heard in that movement, without any real inner reason. The two movements are thus "unified" in an external way, but one is not convinced of the need for that unity. The odd instrumentation must be looked upon as experimental. The presence of two dark-toned violas and the doubling of the bass line by bass and cello make real tonal balance impossible. Schubert might have manipulated such a combination; indeed, the *Forellen Quintet* is somewhat similar in instrumentation. But the Mendelssohn of 1824 was not yet a Schubert. The best clue to the quality of the sextet is given by its publication date. The work appeared, as Opus 110, in 1868, decades after Mendelssohn's death. Had it been successful, or had the composer thought highly of it, he would have seen to its publication during his lifetime.

The Octet. Hardly a year after the composition of the sextet Mendelssohn suddenly stood at the very threshold of greatness. An octet for four violins, two violas, and two cellos, in E flat, was written in 1825 and published as Opus 20; that work is of altogether different quality. It differs greatly from the antiphonal double quartets of Louis Spohr (1784–1859), the first of which is roughly contemporaneous with the octet and is among the last flowerings of pseudo-Classical formalism. Mendelssohn's work is truly eight-voiced and shows his great skill in handling a large tonal body. The first violin dominates to some extent; the virtuosic brilliance of that instrument's part sets the mood for the whole work. The octet is conceived on orchestral lines; development sections are concerned in part with rhythmic modifications of themes, in part with their lyric transformations. The scherzo, played softly and swiftly throughout, is perhaps the finest movement. As a whole the work suffers from too orchestral a treatment, important thematic lines being sometimes obscured by the mass of tone. Nevertheless, in general content and effectiveness it ranks as one of Mendelssohn's masterpieces.

The Early Quartets. The first of Mendelssohn's string quartets,[12] in A major, was written in 1827; the second, in E flat, in 1829. They were published together in 1830 as Opus 12 and Opus 13; the E flat quartet, however, received the earlier number. In these two works the mature composer stands revealed. All the melodic charm, all the perfection of detail, all the deftness of touch we associate with the later works are present in these quartets from about his twentieth year. The first movement of the E flat quartet is melodious throughout. Its second theme partakes of the rhythmic nature of the first; no conflict of thematic materials, hence no drama, is possible. For thematic conflict—one of the essentials of true Classicism—Mendelssohn substitutes a lyric mood of great charm. The second movement is the well known "Canzonetta." It occupies an important place in the long line of light, fairylike pieces that represent Mendelssohn's greatest contribution to music. Evidences of cyclical form are present. The impetuous finale contains quotations from the themes of the first movement and concludes with a coda based on that movement. In the quartet of Opus 13, also, a similar attempt to achieve unity is seen; the quartet ends as it began, with material from one of Mendelssohn's own songs.

The Quintet, Opus 18. A string quintet (with two violas) in A major was begun in 1826, rewritten in 1832, and published in 1833

[12] An earlier effort, in E flat, and dating from about 1823, remained in manuscript until 1879; publication took place without an opus number. This quartet is not included in the thematic index of Mendelssohn's *Werke.* See Wilhelm Altmann, in *Cobbett's Cyclopedic Survey of Chamber Music,* II, 133.

as Opus 18. In this work Mendelssohn's power of invention seems weak. The themes in general are not noteworthy, in spite of their rather cheerful mood. Nor does the dramatic slow movement, with its detailed accompanying figures, flow with the ease and charm we have learned to expect from Mendelssohn. The contrapuntal scherzo is by far the finest movement—an observation one makes repeatedly in discussing Mendelssohn's music. A rather pretentious finale concludes a work that, on the whole, is not one of his great compositions.

The Quartets, Opus 44. The three string quartets of Opus 44, in D major, E minor, and E flat, were begun in 1837, finished during the following year, and published in 1839. During the ten years or so intervening between the writing of the Opus 12 quartet and those of Opus 44, Mendelssohn had grown more impetuous (perhaps nervous is a better word). The first and last movements of the D major quartet are models of enthusiasm and brilliance. But he had also gained in repose. The two middle movements are among the best representatives of that quality in all of his compositions. The E minor is a melodious work, distinguished by one of the most original and enchanting of all scherzos. Fleet, dainty, and lyric at once, it is Mendelssohn at his very best. Other movements stand in the shadow of this delightful piece.

With the E flat quartet Mendelssohn reached new heights of strength, surety of purpose, and technical perfection. From start to finish the work is perfect. The vibrant allegro is followed by a lively scherzo, by a deeply moving slow movement, and by an impetuous, brilliant finale. The quality of Mendelssohn's counterpoint had been improving through the years; in the quartets of Opus 44 we see its finest manifestation. Rich fugal passages, delightful imitations, and luscious countermelodies flow smoothly from his pen. And with the greater worth of his contrapuntal writing comes an increased clarity of form.

The Piano Trios. Mendelssohn's two piano trios, Opus 49, in D minor, and Opus 66, in C minor, were composed in 1839 and 1845, respectively. Neither conceived for the orchestra nor dominated by the piano, they represent the most enjoyable aspects of Mendelssohn's writing. Laid out on a large and flowing scale, full of beautiful lyric melodies and refined to the utmost degree, they are pure Romanticism. The scherzo of the D minor trio is one of his great inspirations, as is the lovely and serene andante. Seldom did Mendelssohn attain the level of technical perfection he reached in the first movement of the C minor; scarcely ever did he equal the tempestuousness of its finale. The exquisite finish and satisfying form that were Mendelssohn's outstanding characteristics are present throughout these two masterworks.

But with all their charm and beauty, they reveal Mendelssohn's weaknesses as well. Vigorous they may be, and impetuous, but there is little real strength or passion in them. Mendelssohn permits no harshness or driving emotion in his works. He is always refined, possibly a bit effeminate, even in his most striking moments. Depth of emotion, ability to feel strongly, reflection of significant experience are characteristics seldom found in his music. And it is precisely this lack of profundity that makes Mendelssohn fall short of being one of the eternal masters. All else was his: taste, technique, temperament, and imagination. To the extent to which those qualities shine through his works, we can enjoy them.

The Last Works. The second string quintet, Opus 87, in B flat, dates from 1845. In other categories Mendelssohn showed a steady growth in expressive power, in melodic invention, and in formal perceptions. In the string quintets the opposite is true. Opus 87 is even less distinguished than its predecessor, Opus 18. Orchestral tremolos, which here indicate a certain paucity of invention, characterize the quintet; the first violin, in its efforts to save the work, dominates with an air of bravado. Only in the rich adagio does Mendelssohn show that he has not regressed too far; that movement is outstanding in the beauty of its melodies and the quality of its figurations. The finale, except for several excellent contrapuntal passages, is rather weak.

Mendelssohn's last completed string quartet, Opus 80, in F minor, was written in 1847, the last year of his life and nine years after the quartets of Opus 44. It is a somber work throughout; even the scherzo and fast finale have about them an air of gloom. The adagio is subdued and dark in mood, in spite of its restful moments. The whole work is weakened by many orchestral effects, and the exquisite polish and perfection of earlier works is seldom in evidence. It is the least satisfactory of all his chamber-music compositions.

Four single movements for string quartet were found among Mendelssohn's papers after his death: the two middle movements of what was to be a quartet in A minor, from 1847, a capriccio from 1843, and a fugue from 1827. The four were assembled and published as Opus 81 in 1850. There is obviously no connection, in key or in content, between them: andante in E major, scherzo in A minor, capriccio in E minor, and fugue in E flat. But individually they are the purest Mendelssohn. The variations of the andante are highly imaginative; the scherzo is again one of the light, fairylike pieces. The capriccio, consisting of an introduction and a fast fugue, is more dramatic than Mendelssohn's fugues usually are. Certainly it is a more successful piece than the moderately paced fugue that serves as the finale of this uneven work.

SCHUMANN

Robert Schumann, a year younger than Mendelssohn, was born in Saxony in 1810. The literary influences to which he was subjected in his formative years turned his attention to the works of the Romantic writers, particularly to those of Jean Paul Richter (1763–1825). The sentimental, effusive, extravagant style of that writer left its lifelong mark on Schumann. Much of the latter's activity as a spokesman for the Romantic movement later in his life can be traced to the youthful fixation on Jean Paul.

Schumann's mother was opposed to his undertaking a career in music, in spite of his youthful accomplishments as a pianist and composer. She persuaded him to enter the University of Leipzig as a law student in 1828. But the free and attractive life there gave Schumann ample opportunity to work in music. He neglected his law studies, practiced piano assiduously—laming his hand with an ill-chosen mechanical device of his own invention—and steeped himself in Romantic literature. About 1830, having obtained his mother's grudging consent, he left the university, with the intention of embracing a musical career. Frederick Wieck became his piano teacher. Intimacy with the Wieck family led to an acquaintance with Wieck's daughter, Clara, a girl nine years Schumann's junior and already a remarkable pianist. Clara Wieck later became one of the finest pianists of Europe, a lifelong champion of Schumann's music and in 1840—after determined opposition from her father, which required a lawsuit to circumvent—Schumann's wife.

About 1833 Schumann and a group of like-minded friends made plans to establish a music paper, critical in purpose and designed to combat the bad taste and "Philistinism" then prevailing. Schumann became the editor, and for ten years, from 1834 to 1844, wielded an ever-increasing power over the cultural standards of Germany. His critical discernment and his literary skill made the paper, *Neue Zeitschrift für Musik*, a real influence in the musical life of the time. And his championship of new composers, of new ideas, and above all, of a higher standard of taste was, perhaps, his most important contribution to the musical scene up to that time.

When Mendelssohn moved to Leipzig in 1835 a long friendship between the two men began, one which was terminated only by Mendelssohn's death in 1847. The two men, so unlike in externals, temperament, and training, shared a great admiration for Bach. Mendelssohn's crusade to make Bach better known stimulated Schumann's interest in a project to republish all the works of that master. The founding of the Bachgesellschaft, together with the subsequent issuance of Bach's complete works, beginning about 1850, were in large part the result of Schumann's activity. Thus the latter deserves equal credit with Mendelssohn for initiating the present-day interest in Bach.

In the years following the Schumanns' marriage, in 1840, Clara undertook extensive concert tours, and Schumann often accompanied his more famous wife to distant parts of Europe. Within a short time the exertion of travel, the editorial responsibility, and the intense musical life of Leipzig combined to affect Schumann's disposition.

Never sociable, always preoccupied and introspective, he became irritable, absent-minded, and aloof. In 1844 the Schumanns moved to Dresden in an attempt to restore his health. The quieter life at Dresden, it was hoped, would bring about a change. The move turned out to be beneficial; Schumann was restored to creative vigor and apparent good health.

In 1850 he accepted the post of conductor of a singing society and within a few months that of musical director at Düsseldorf. But Schumann was not a capable conductor. His withdrawn manner, his absent-mindedness, and his strange inability to communicate his ideas verbally made him entirely unsuited for the post. In 1853 retirement was forced upon him. And in that year he met Johannes Brahms, then twenty years old, and prophesied for him a brilliant future. Schumann's negative characteristics grew stronger, and uncertainty concerning his health returned. In 1854 he attempted suicide and was placed in a private asylum near Bonn. Periods of lucidity alternated with fits of great depression. The melancholy moods grew stronger and finally clouded his whole consciousness. In July, 1856, at the age of forty-six and in a state of complete mental collapse, Schumann died.

The Quartets, Opus 41. Schumann's habit of concentrating on one musical medium for an extended period is well known. The years up to 1839, for example, saw only the composition of piano music; in 1840 Schumann was preoccupied with songs. With the same enthusiasm he showed for these categories, he turned to chamber music in 1842. Six of his ten compositions in that field were written in that year: three string quartets, Opus 41; the piano quintet, Opus 44; the piano quartet, Opus 47; and the *Fantasiestücke* for piano trio, Opus 88.

The three quartets of Opus 41—in A minor, F major, and A major —were written within a few weeks' time in the summer of 1842. From the very outset Schumann disclosed himself as a master of the gentler moods. Dreamy introductions to the first and third quartets, fervent or tender melodies in the slow movements, and an occasional introspective passage in the allegros all testify to his Romantic temper.

But the adagio of the A minor quartet is a model of eloquence—

until it is broken off by the uncertain agitation of the middle part. The adagio of the A major flows smoothly and richly—until interrupted by a pulsating dramatic episode. And these typify another of Schumann's characteristics: sudden contrasts of mood, impulsive changes of heart that bespeak the dual personalities with which he clothed himself. The Eusebius and Florestan personalities, creations of his imagination though they were, reveal themselves in almost every work of Schumann's. The dreamy Eusebius vein contrasts with the forthright Florestan on many a page. The moments of lyric tenderness in fast, rhythmic passages and the sharply accented or boisterous sections in melodious movements indicate that the personalities have momentarily changed places. But seldom does either achieve complete dominance within a single large movement. Acting on impulse or on inspiration, Schumann contrasts the most diverse elements in an episodic manner. Often unexpected, not always justified musically, these flights of undisciplined imagination give his music the great variety and charm it so often discloses. And it is the failure of performers to recognize this duality of moods that contributes to a certain misunderstanding of the real nature of Schumann's music.

Individual movements of the quartets are masterworks. The finale of the A minor, for example, is an exciting piece filled with boundless energy. The first movement of the F major gives us the soaring, passionate, and warm Schumann; the finale represents the youthful, exuberant young Romanticist. The second movement of the A major quartet, cast in variation form, is in a sense the most imaginative piece in the entire set. The theme undergoes subtle emotional transformations in successive variations, but ordinary variation techniques are noticeably absent. Forceful, agitated, and somber at once, the movement, with its Eusebius strains in the coda, represents a synthesis of Schumann's finest qualities.

The Piano Quintet. A few months after the quartets were finished Schumann conceived the idea that a string quartet might well be combined with the piano. (Twelve such works by Boccherini were most likely not known to him.) The piano quintet in E flat was the result. Begun about September, 1842, it was published in 1843 as

Opus 44. It is the first in a notable, if short, line of piano quintets by nineteenth-century composers and exhibits many features that were to influence subsequent works for this combination.

Scarcely any work of Schumann's is so noble, exuberant, and vital. The first movement is a model of formal clarity and perfection. The vigorous first theme—divided into six related phrases—is followed by a lyric second and by a short codetta based on phrases of the first theme. The development, in sectional form, is concerned entirely with material heard in the exposition; the recapitulation is regular in structure. Thus a Classical sonata-form results—an unusual achievement for Schumann. The second movement has about it the air of a funeral march; the scherzo is based on rapidly ascending scale passages. In the finale Schumann attained new heights of imagination and technical skill and created a kind of double sonata-form.[13] Here, also, is seen evidence of his adherence to the principle of cyclical form.

[13] Up to the 224th measure the finale is in regular sonata-form but is distinguished by great harmonic freedom; at that point a new theme is introduced. A second development section follows in which themes from the finale are combined with phrases from the first movement in a masterful way. A recapitulation of the new theme and a final coda conclude the movement. The following table will clarify the above description.

EXPOSITION	C minor Theme I 42 measures	G major Theme II 34 measures	B minor Codetta 19 measures
DEVELOPMENT	Theme I and Theme II 40 measures		
RECAPITULATION	C sharp minor Theme I 42 measures	E flat Theme II 34 measures	G minor Codetta 12 measures
NEW EXPOSITION	E flat Theme III 24 measures		
SECOND DEVELOPMENT	Elements of Theme I and a theme derived from the first movement by expansion 130 measures		
RECAPITULATION	E flat Theme III 24 measures		
CODA	E flat, based on Theme I 25 measures		

In many evaluations of this quintet one finds references to its orchestral quality, to the dominance of the piano, and to other factors that are taken to be defects. It is true that a large number of sonorous doublings occur and that the piano part is worked out in fuller detail than are the string parts. But a criticism that considers the piano as merely *one* of five equal instruments is wide of the mark. As a matter of fact, the piano opposes, or balances, or contrasts with, the quartet as a unit; it represents not one fifth but one half of the entire tonal body. From this point of view the quintet takes its high place among true chamber-music works and provides a sonority and effectiveness unmatched in the earlier literature. It is in every sense a unique work. The quality of its themes, the forms that result from their manipulation, and the instrumentation itself all contribute to making it one of Schumann's outstanding compositions.

The Piano Quartet. The last months of 1842 saw the completion of the piano quartet in E flat, published in 1845 as Opus 47. In this work the piano is again accused of dominating the texture, and now the charge is more justified. Here the piano is but one of four instruments rather than an entity opposed to the entity of the three string instruments; in that role its voice is too prominent. Rich accompaniments, unnecessary doublings, and a general thickness of texture in the piano part contribute to a loss of balance in the work as a whole. But that is a minor defect, after all; the quartet has its full share of musical beauty and significance.

It begins with a slow and solemn introduction that anticipates the motive of the first theme. Imitating a device employed by Beethoven in his E flat quartet of Opus 127, Schumann employs the introductory material again in the development section; thus the theme is heard in slow and fast tempos, is seen in different lights, as it were. The scherzo is a large piece with two greatly contrasting trios. The expansion that results from this extreme contrast represents one of Schumann's real contributions to the development of Romantic forms. The slow movement employs a dreamy, almost sentimental melody in Schumann's finest Eusebius vein. The finale, while containing some excellent contrapuntal writing and large melodic sections, is less successful; it seeks out the lower ranges of the instruments, thus achieving a darker color than the nature of the themes requires, and produces a general effect of restlessness and fragmentation.

Smaller Works. The last chamber-music work written in the prolific year of 1842 was a set of four pieces for piano, violin, and cello. It was published in 1850 as Opus 88, with the title *Fantasiestücke* ("Fantasy Pieces"). The work begins with a Romanza, a short piece based upon sequence repetitions of a single theme. The second movement, the Humoresque, is a long, loosely constructed movement containing four or five unrelated parts, each of which undergoes a certain amount of development. Then follows the Duet: cello and violin engage in mutual imitations of a lyric theme over a subdued accompaniment. The set ends with the March. The whole is one of Schumann's minor works; in spite of many delicate and songful moments, it discloses few of his finer qualities.

Similar in quality to the above work is the set of *Märchenerzählungen* ("Fairy Tales"), composed in 1853 and published a year later as Opus 132. This work is for an unusual combination: piano, clarinet, and viola. Even in this, the last of Schumann's chamber-music compositions, his Romantic interest in new tonal combinations is disclosed. But the rather dark tone color inherent in the combination is not reflected in the music. The first of the four pieces is lively; fanciful themes and a light, airy accompaniment create a real fairy-tale atmosphere. The second, almost as lively, suffers from considerable repetition of a short motive; no real continuity is established—and even a fairy tale must have continuity. In the third piece a charming duet between the clarinet and the viola over a freely flowing accompaniment creates an air of gentle nostalgia; it is written in Schumann's best narrative style. The fourth, again lively like the second, suffers from the same fragmentation. The four movements taken together give a good picture of Schumann's lighter side, a side not often disclosed in his larger chamber-music works. The composer was often most charming when talking to children; there was then no need to be anything but natural. And so he is in the *Märchenerzählungen*.

The Piano Trios. Between the two sets of miniatures just discussed

lie three full-size piano trios: Opus 63, in D minor, and Opus 80, in
F major, were written in 1847; Opus 110, in G minor, in 1851. The
first two reveal that the impulsiveness of Schumann's 1842 style has
developed into vagary. The sudden changes of mood, employed diffi-
dently in the string quartets of Opus 41, become characteristic in the
trios. The first movement of the D minor trio, for example, begins in
a veiled and subdued manner. The mood engendered by the opening
is then rudely broken off by a few measures of sharply accented
rhythms, after which the veiled mood returns. An ebb and flow of the
tempo, too, is characteristic of the movement; *ritardandi* and *a tempi*
occur at frequent intervals. Again, in the first movement of the F
major trio, a rugged, well-defined passage of great intensity is interrupted by a few dreamy, meditative measures in which rhythmic
motion virtually ceases. And in the last movement a similar situation
occurs.

But the impulsive dreamer is absent in other portions of these
works. Side by side with movements that can best be described as
vague and fragmentary are others whose vitality and straightforwardness do not fail. Of such quality are the finale of the D minor, a
vigorous movement in Schumann's most robust style, and the third
movement of the F major, whose delicacy and beauty of color are
superb. A further characteristic may be noted: Schumann's extensive
use of syncopated and compound rhythmic figures—at times employed
so copiously that the formal lines are obscured. The slow movement
of the F major trio provides a case in point; sections of that piece are
so written that the rhythmic beat is lost for measures at a time. The
resultant effect is formless, or at best impressionistic. That characteristic, of course, grew out of Schumann's preoccupation with effects
of sonority and tone color. But, like a number of his devices, it was
sometimes used to excess, and merely made the music unclear.

The G minor trio of 1851 is an uneven work. Along with moments
of genuine Schumannesque humor and energy are irrelevant sections
that wander aimlessly. As in so many of Schumann's works, many an
inspired detail loses its effectiveness by being overdone. The first
movement's undulating chord motive is heard throughout that move-

ment; scarcely changed on subsequent appearances and having within itself no power of growth, it succeeds only in creating an impression of fragmentation. The middle movements suffer from the same decline in Schumann's faculty of imagination.

The two sonatas for violin and piano may be mentioned briefly. Published as Opus 105 in 1852 and Opus 121 in 1855, both works were composed in 1851, and thus are contemporary with the G minor trio. All three compositions reflect an unfortunate period in Schumann's life. In 1851 he was still filled with creative energy, but his mental illness had begun to affect his power of concentration and logical thought. The results are apparent, especially in the sonatas. Themes are stated vaguely, lead aimlessly in one direction or another, and moods of depression are uppermost in the music.

A COMPARISON

Let us now review the principal characteristics of Classical music in order to appreciate the departures of Schubert, Mendelssohn, and Schumann from those characteristics. (1) The Classical composers accepted the validity of the development principle. To be amenable to the demands of that principle a musical theme had to be rhythmically characteristic, had to have within itself the power of growth, and had to be concise so that it could be perceived in its entirety. Beethoven recognized those demands to a greater degree than any previous composer. His solution took the form of motive manipulation, whose supreme manifestations are seen in the fifth and the ninth symphonies and in the last quartets, Opera 130–133. (2) An essential of Classical sonata-form was the conflict between two opposing elements, technically represented by the conflict between two themes contrasting in contour, harmony, and mood. This conflict took place in the development section of the form, indeed became the *raison d'être* for that section; and in turn it justified the recapitulation, for in the latter section the contrasting themes were reviewed in the light of their revealed opposition. (3) The requirement of unity loomed large in the minds of the great Classical composers. Unity was achieved by adherence to a basic tonality within a movement—with only such deviations as the thematic conflict made necessary—or by an emotional connection between several movements. The three characteristics, then, of organic growth of the material, of dramatic conflict, and of inner unity, determined both the content and the form of the greatest Classical music.

Schubert made little use of motive-laden themes. He was more concerned with large lyric melodies that, when manipulated (that is, developed), broke into fragments. Nor is there often in his works the dramatic conflict between themes; the drama in Schubert arises out of chance encounter, not out of calculated contrast. He reveals his melodies in various lights, in different harmonic colors, but leaves them essentially unchanged. And, having presented them in the exposition and illuminated them in the development, he has no real need of recapitulating them. When he does so—and most often he does—the themes return not as aesthetic necessities but as surfeits of beauty. Finally, his larger works are seldom connected within themselves. Movements stand side by side in isolation; only rarely, as in the E flat trio, is one piece organically bound to another.

Mendelssohn's chamber music conforms much more closely than does Schubert's to Classical principles. His solid education and musical background made him aware of the inner significance of musical form at an early age. At first in imitation, later from conviction, he chose Classical formal models and made Classical principles his own. This admiration for the formal practices of the past could easily have degenerated into rigid formalism. That it did not do so speaks highly for the vitality of Classical principles and for Mendelssohn's understanding of them. Hampered neither by slavish adherence to sets of rules (as many pseudo-Classicists were) nor by undisciplined imagination (which sometimes became an occupational disease among Romanticists), he remained true to his educational ideals and his sense of fitness. Only in the quality of his emotion did he fall below his models. Great depth of feeling and an awareness of the powerful tensions of human life were foreign to his temperament, nor are they reflected in his music.

Schumann reveals himself in his chamber music as a man of uncertain convictions caught between two opposing tendencies: not strong enough to make a complete break with the past and too strong to give way to every wayward impulse. One senses in Schumann the conflict between form and content—the conflict that was resolved by the great Classical composers and ignored by the typical Romantics. In his songs and his piano music he was as free as the wind; in chamber music, where he was subject to the restrictions imposed by the medium, he was thwarted. In miniatures and unpretentious works he was at his best; his inspirations were heaven-sent. But endurance, in a musical sense, was not in him. His inspirations were of a moment's duration; when he set to work on them, they vanished. Not as melodically gifted as Schubert, not as formally perceptive as Mendelssohn, Schumann represents to perfection one aspect of Romanticism. That period, seen now in retrospect, was concerned with the fleeting moment. It contained enthusiasm, feeling, humor, charm, exquisite taste—but no staying power. Its music was primarily enjoyable. And it remained for a later composer to add the ingredients of staying power and significance to the colorful, stimulating mixture that was Romanticism at its best. That composer was Johannes Brahms.

10. Brahms and the Decline of Romanticism

IN EARLIER chapters it has been possible to show, with due regard for overlapping, how one historical period flowed into the next. Each period has been seen, more or less accurately, as a self-contained unit concerned with its own musical problems and finding its own solutions. And it has been possible, through the admission of sufficiently large generalizations, to characterize one composer near the beginning of the period as the standard-bearer for the new, and one near the end as the great exponent of the old (in the sense that the new became old as the period ran its course). Baroque, Rococo, Classical, and early Romantic periods differed sufficiently from each other to make the selection of their representatives simple.

Very probably the historian of the future will have little difficulty in naming "the" composer of the last half of the nineteenth century. By emphasizing one of its aspects he will see that half century as a self-contained unit; but in so doing he must necessarily minimize or ignore certain sub-aspects. We, being closer to it, are confronted with at least three concurrent sets of characteristics, each set individual enough to constitute a separate aspect, and we see several significant composers representing each set of characteristics. Whom, then, shall we name as "the" composer of the period? What, first, are the various aspects?

1. The middle years of the nineteenth century were characterized by a growing amount of social unrest. The abortive revolution of German liberals against the Confederacy in 1848, the interest in socialism as a form of government, the definition of the new science of sociology, the Communist Manifesto of Karl Marx—all these indicate the temper

of the time: the common man was being discovered. And in that discovery lay one of the contributing causes to the decline of Romanticism. Romantic ideals, somewhat removed from everyday life, perforce became practical; realism, in art and literature as well as in music, was a logical consequence. Composers, in an effort to be as realistic as their brother artists, sought new means of expression, means that would accurately mirror what they had to express. Thus arose the preoccupation with storytelling in music, with extramusical devices, with messages or pictures that could be presented in compositions— in a word, with program music. In the development of program music Hector Berlioz (1803–69) and Franz Liszt (1811–86) were outstanding. And they, together with Richard Wagner (1813–83), were too concerned with the over-all scene to give any thought to chamber music.

2. In another group of composers the search for new means of expression led elsewhere. Possibly as a result of the Napoleonic Wars, a new awareness of national differences and a desire for national recognition arose in many parts of Europe. The establishment of the German Empire and a united Italy (both of which were achieved about 1870) strengthened those feelings. Artists turned their attention to the folklore, customs, and cultural heritage of their own people, and a period of nationalism in the arts developed. In music that development resulted in the use of folk music, national dances, and musical idioms, to the extent that Romantic music lost its universal characteristics (insofar as the western hemisphere can be considered the universe) and became Russian or Bohemian or Scandinavian music.

3. Thus Romanticism, transformed into realism, had developed along two parallel (but also intersecting) paths. Program music, concerned with the delineation of literary programs and unconcerned with "music for its own sake," eschewed traditional forms and methods and developed its own. The tone poem, the *idée fixe,* and the characteristic piece ("Butterflies," "The Mill," "The Last Spring," and the like) were among the new phenomena. National music, on the other hand, turned to folk songs, rhythms, and dances, and superimposed

them upon forms and a type of expression that were not essentially different from Romantic musical practices. But not all composers could hold with the new tenets. Some, too weak to overcome the inertia imposed by tradition, maintained the lyric content and idealistic aims of Romanticism; such composers were swallowed up in the rush of new events and contributed nothing of great value. Others, however, through temperament or aesthetic philosophy, were drawn strongly to the past. Equipped with contemporary techniques, affected by contemporary developments, but largely influenced by the works of earlier generations, these anomalous composers struggled against indifference or a feeling of loneliness throughout their lifetimes. With those words one has described César Franck and Johannes Brahms, the two greatest exponents of that aspect of the nineteenth century characterized neither by program music nor by nationalism.

BRAHMS

Life. Johannes Brahms was born in Hamburg in 1833. His father, a bass player, taught him the rudiments of music at an early age. The quality of the boy's talent soon made itself evident, and Johannes was placed with Eduard Marxsen, an excellent local musician. In his fourteenth year, when he made his debut as a pianist, he had gained local renown for the excellence of his playing. In 1853 he became the accompanist for a Hungarian violinist, Eduard Reményi. During the course of their tour Brahms met Joseph Joachim, who became his lifelong friend, and Robert Schumann, who hailed him as the hope of the future after seeing some of his compositions.

For parts of three years (1857–59) Brahms served as pianist and choral conductor at the court of Detmold. In 1860 he returned to Hamburg for further study, and in 1862 accepted a position as conductor of a singing society in Vienna. Between 1864 and 1869, becoming increasingly well known as a pianist, he made several successful concert tours. In the latter year he returned to Vienna, and he served for three years as conductor of the Friends of Music concerts.

Brahms's life was enriched by many beautiful and significant friendships. Joseph Joachim and Hans von Bülow were representative of the scores of musicians with whom he corresponded, whom he misunderstood, and whom he forgave throughout the greater part of his lifetime. His early acquaintance with Schumann soon ripened into friendship with the latter's entire family, particularly with his wife Clara. As an artist (Clara Wieck Schumann was one of the finest pianists of her generation) and as a woman she exerted a strong influence on him until her death. Brahms's love affairs with younger women usually came to the same unhappy conclusion: when he was all but committed to marriage he broke off the relationship in the fear (sometimes expressed to the girl in question, sometimes not) that domestic entanglements would deter him from the composing that had become the sole reason for his existence. The emotional turmoils into which Brahms plunged himself, plus his essentially reserved temperament, impelled him to adopt a mask of gruffness in most of his social encounters, which estranged him, at one time or another, from all who held him in highest respect and sincerest friendship. Lonely, misunderstood by many, Brahms was not a happy man. Much of his most deeply felt music is a reflection of his unhappy state.

His fame as a composer gradually extended to all parts of the musical world; he played or conducted performances of his own works in Holland and in Switzerland, as well as in all parts of Germany and Austria. Invitations to visit England were declined out of fear of the Channel crossing. Each year saw Brahms's reputation growing; it became customary to hold festivals devoted entirely to his works. This fame was established in the face of Wagner's domination of the musical scene, of the preoccupation with program music and with nationalistic elements—to all of which Brahms remained indifferent.

Clara Schumann's death in the spring of 1896 marked the beginning of Brahms's own decline. A summer of rest in the country under the care of physicians brought no improvement. Brahms returned to Vienna, which had been his permanent home since 1878, and attended a few concerts. Unable to maintain the active life he had led for decades, he sank rapidly. When he died, on April 3, 1897, all Europe was affected. Thousands marched in the funeral cortege, distant cities and foreign countries sent representatives, and musicians mourned the passing of a great master.

Brahms's contributions to chamber music total twenty-four works, written across the forty-one years from 1854 to 1895. The works include two cello sonatas, three for violin, and two for clarinet, all with piano; five piano trios, three piano quartets, and one piano quintet; three string quartets, two quintets, and two sextets; and one quintet for clarinet and strings. But that short list gives no indication of how prolific a composer Brahms actually was. He felt no regrets at destroying a completed work if it did not measure up to his own standard. Almost two dozen strings quartets were written; three remain. Other works were ruthlessly altered, transposed, or written for other media: the D minor piano concerto, originally designed as a symphony, passed through a two-piano phase before it emerged in its final form. Other examples of that practice will appear below. And in one notable case an early work was completely transformed late in Brahms's life—the B major trio, Opus 8, the first of his chamber-music compositions. We may begin our account with that work.

Opus 8. The trio, for piano, violin, and cello, was written in 1854. It was a large, extravagant work. The first movement contained five complete themes; after the adequate development section a second development in fugal style appeared in the recapitulation; the slow movement included a large section in fast tempo. In 1890, when the need for a second edition of the trio arose, Brahms undertook to revise it. But the revision took the form of extensive rewriting, so complete that a new work appeared having only its first themes and the scherzo in common with the earlier version. It is the 1890 version that is known today; the 1854 edition has all but disappeared from the repertoire. The later work is scarcely two-thirds as long as the earlier; its mood is much more concentrated and restrained.

Even in its condensed version the B major trio is a monumental work. The series of phrases constituting the first theme require some forty measures for their unfolding, and they rise to a great climax of sonority; later sections are laid out on an equally massive scale. The scherzo is at once light and boisterous; deft and fleeting passages alternate with thunderous outbursts of exuberance. The adagio is a sustained, intense movement filled with the richness of detail and clarity of purpose that are so uniquely Brahmsian. And the work as a whole discloses a texture that is typical of all Brahms's piano trios, quartets, and quintet. In those nine works a duality of tonal bodies is established: the piano is set opposite the two, three, or four string instruments (and woodwinds, in the case of the horn and clarinet trios), and carries half of the tonal burden. Thus a great number of string passages in unison, octaves, thirds, and sixths occur, or passages in two- or three-part counterpoint—all set opposite a full and magnificently written piano part. The resultant division of the tonal mass into two equally complete components, seen to some extent in the later Beethoven trios, provides Brahms with ample opportunity to develop a massive, multivoiced medium capable of carrying a detailed contrapuntal texture.

Opus 18. During his relatively happy sojourn at Detmold, about 1857, Brahms began work on a sextet for two violins, two violas, and two cellos, in B flat. The work was completed about 1859–60 and was published as Opus 18. The storm and stress characteristic of the B major trio are no longer in evidence; the sextet is one of Brahms's most cheerful and most Classical compositions. From the first tranquil melody to the humorous coda of the finale the work is serene and placid, except in those passages where Brahms's vitality and enthusiasm find expression.

The pairs of themes of the first movement unfold with an air of Classical repose. Never is one in doubt as to Brahms's harmonic or rhythmic intentions; all is transparent and intelligible. The variations of the second movement, lyric or dramatic in turn, make full use of the sextet's color combinations without becoming unduly extravagant in tonal variety. The scherzo is small but packed full of Beethovenesque energy. And the final rondo is a movement any of the great Classical composers might have written. Each phrase grows out of the previous one, short developments take the place of transitions, and masterful modulations are characteristic. In the importance given to the first cello throughout the work the sextet takes its place with those quartets of Haydn and Mozart that bear dedications to Frederick William II of Prussia.

Opus 25 and Opus 26. Two piano quartets, in G minor and A major, were published as Opus 25 and Opus 26, respectively. Brahms began the G minor in 1857, and both were performed in Vienna in November, 1862; no more exact information about their origin is available. With these works Brahms made his successful Viennese debut as a pianist. They are among the most expansive of all his chamber-music compositions.

The large scale that is characteristic of the first version of the B major trio is here again in evidence. Whole groups of melodies, in contrasting tonalities, of course, appear in place of first and second themes. The several movements disclose the power of invention and breadth of lyricism that were among Brahms's outstanding characteristics. Yet many of the themes are in themselves not lyric melodies: the first theme of the G minor quartet is founded on a one-measure motive; a two-measure figure is employed in a similar capacity in the A major. It is Brahms's consummate contrapuntal skill that enables him to derive ever-new melodies from these motives, to base transitional passages on them, and to invest them with dramatic power or gentle pathos at will.

Richness of thematic material such as is disclosed in the first movements of these quartets might have led to diffuseness and disunity in the hands of a less capable composer. Brahms, even in his twenties, was equal to the task of organizing the material, keeping it under control, and developing it in whatever direction his powerful imagination dictated. The charm and rich color content of the G minor quartet's intermezzo provide a fine contrast to the noble, full-bodied slow movement. The latter includes an animated, martial section in which new levels of sonority are established in chamber music; the vital, enthusiastic, almost orchestral Brahms is in evidence throughout the movement. But the climax of the quartet is reserved for the finale, "Rondo alla Zingarese." Brahms's fondness for Hungarian tunes here finds its first expression in his chamber music; Hungarian temperament pervades the entire piece, yet the melodies and texture are all of his own making. The coda, with its cadenzas, is magnificent. The A major quartet is an equally fine work; certain passages, notably those based on the short motive of the first movement, illustrate to a high degree Brahms's contrapuntal skill. The slow movement's serene melodies, the flowing scherzo, with its trio written in canon, and the sustained power of the finale are unsurpassed.

Opus 34. During the years that witnessed the writing of the two piano quartets Brahms completed a string quintet (with two cellos) in F minor. After 1862, convinced that the work was lacking in some respects, he rewrote it as a sonata for two pianos. But now the sustained lyricism that only string instruments could supply was gone. Again Brahms recast it, this time for string quartet and piano. In that form, completed in 1864 as the piano quintet in F minor, Opus 34, it was successful. It has since taken its place in the literature as one of Brahms's most characteristic works.

Built on broad lines similar to the piano quartets, the first movement of the F minor quintet includes pairs of first and second themes and several derivative melodies that are almost thematic in character. And again, as in the quartets, both motive manipulation and lyric melody are fundamental to the development of the themes. The slow movement, a shy yet characterful piece, contains moments of real inspiration, particularly in its coda. There a melodic fragment heard near the end of the first section is employed at the close of the movement (during the last nine measures) with particularly magical result. In Example 53 a portion of that passage is given. The powerful, intense scherzo reveals a miniature sonata-form in its first part: two contrasting themes are developed and in part recapitulated. The trio is a short, solid piece in Brahms's most eloquent vein. And in the finale his characteristic practice of modifying form to meet thematic requirements (a Classical characteristic, let it be noted) is exemplified. A slow, emotionally rich introduction leads into a sonata-form movement that contains no development section as such, but that in effect is a long development from beginning to end. The climax of the whole

Example 53   Brahms, Opus 34
2*d* movement

work is reserved for the coda, in which a masterful contrapuntal development of both themes simultaneously rises to heights of emotional intensity and musical significance.

Opus 36. A second string sextet, in G major, Opus 36, was written in the winter of 1864–65, the winter in which Brahms's mother died and in which he began to work on *Ein deutsches Requiem*. At the same time the last memories of one of his most serious love affairs— with Agathe von Siebold—flared up afresh and caused Brahms to relive many happier moments. Under the influence of contrasting moods, alternately moved by deep sadness and youthful joy, Brahms worked at the sextet. Essentially filled with sunshine, it has its moments of pathos and heartfelt emotion.

The massiveness and intensity of the F minor piano quintet, completed in the previous summer, are no longer present, nor is the great sonority that characterized the first sextet of 1860. In place of these are an ethereal quality and a mood of poetic restraint. The turbulence of Brahms's emotion is here transfigured; a delicate melancholy suffused with moments of deeply felt but quiet gloom pervades the work. His feeling for Agathe is reflected in the first movement, where her name is called out several times (see Example 54).

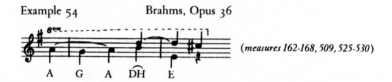

Example 54   Brahms, Opus 36

(*measures 162-168, 509, 525-530*)

A   G   A   DH   E

With the G major sextet Brahms left the tempestuousness of his youth behind. He began to draw around himself a veil of reticence. In later works he was as passionate, he felt as deeply, and he was moved as much by joy as in earlier works, but his emotions were restrained and somewhat concealed. It is as though an invisible barrier stood between composer and listener; only rarely is the barrier lifted entirely, and then only briefly. The essential loneliness of the man began to be reflected in his music.

Opus 40. About 1865 Brahms wrote a trio for piano, violin, and waldhorn (the natural horn, without valves), in E flat, published as Opus 40. The trio, when published, included an optional part for cello (to replace the horn); two decades later an optional viola part was added at Brahms's suggestion. But in his own mind both of the substitutions "sounded horrible"; only with the original instrumentation could his subtle color intentions be fully realized.

The inclusion of the wind instrument, the free forms characteristic of the trio, and the general air of Romantic melancholy in this work disclose certain of Brahms's suppressed Romantic feelings. For virtually the only time in his larger instrumental first movements, he departed from sonata-form. In its place he created a symmetrical five-part form in which two contrasting themes alternate. A unique characteristic of the movement is the subtlety of its cadence structure: one phrase flows into the next, cadences are hinted at, and basic harmonies are only half revealed. The end result is a fluidity and a mysterious quality seldom encountered in Brahms. But the scherzo is as vigorous and straightforward as anything in his works and reveals one of Brahms's later characteristics, the expansion of a phrase by the insertion of measures (see Example 55).

Example 55   Brahms, Opus 40

The adagio, in E flat minor, is a sustained, intense movement pervaded by the deepest sentiment. It contains one of the finest of Brahms's recapitulations; the second theme of the movement, transformed in the light of what has taken place in the development, returns in a radically modified form that enables it to prepare the way for the finale. Seldom is the inner connection between two contrasting movements revealed more subtly and more surely than here.

Opus 51. Eight years elapsed before Brahms turned to chamber music again. Two string quartets, in C minor and A minor, were written in 1873 and published as Opus 51. Thus, finally, in his fortieth year, after having written and destroyed almost two dozen quartets, Brahms achieved what he felt to be satisfactory results and allowed those results to be published. It is in general true of Brahms that we do not witness his gradual steps toward technical mastery; his self-criticism and his habit of destroying preparatory works have deprived us of the opportunity to observe his tentative, stumbling approach to musical heights. In all categories we are at once presented with mature masterworks; particularly is this true in the field of the string quartets.

The C minor is characterized by a sonority and a richness of tone seldom found in string quartets. Many double stops and a degree of elaborateness in the figurations provide a tonal framework well suited to the largeness of the quartet's musical ideas. But with all its richness, the work is not merely a condensed orchestral piece. Its details never serve as mere padding, nor do they in a single instance obscure the clarity of expressive intention. Brahms's feeling for dramatic utterance is in evidence on every page, as is the melancholy air that pervades so many of his works.

The A minor quartet, on the other hand, is a delicate and tender composition. Moments of lyric sweetness contrast with introspective passages; passionate cries are set opposite refined bits of melody, and an air of reserve is seldom absent. The charm of the quasi minuetto is matched only by the serenity that pours out of the slow movement in a gentle stream. Not until the finale does Brahms give way to a robust and forceful expression of energy.

Opus 60. An account of the next work must begin with the events of 1854–56. Those years were marked by the complete breakdown of Robert Schumann's health; they culminated in his insanity and death. During those years Brahms spent considerable time in the company of Clara Schumann; while hoping for his friend's recovery, he was filled with love for his friend's wife. The emotional turmoil and moodiness engendered by such unhappy circumstances found reflection in a piano quartet in C sharp minor, which Brahms began about 1855. A first and second movement, in C sharp minor and E major, respectively, and a finale were completed when he laid the work aside. Almost twenty years later, in 1874, Brahms became interested in the work again. But following his usual custom, he revised ruthlessly. The finale was discarded, the first movement was altered and transposed to C minor, and a scherzo and new finale were written. In that form, as the piano quartet in C minor, Opus 60, the work was published in 1875.

Like the B major trio, the C minor quartet reflects both the impulsive youth of twenty-two and the restrained, poised master. The first movement offers striking contrasts between a dark, moody first theme and a lyric second (remarkable in a technical sense for being a short set of variations). Wild sections in remote keys alternate with strong passages crystal-clear in their delineation of anguish. The scherzo is dramatic, fitful, and intense; only in its last few measures does it give way to a powerful abandon. The E major andante takes a high place among Brahms's slow movements. Glorious melodies accompanied by exquisite counterpoints soar to heights of Romantic expression. In the finale all is dark again; alternations of restraint and fury characterize a movement that closes one of the most despairing compositions in the literature.

Opus 67. A year or two after the piano quartet emerged Brahms composed a third string quartet, in B flat, published, about 1876, as Opus 67. And for virtually the first time since the A major piano quartet of Opus 26 (about 1862) a work of lightness, charm, and deft humor appeared among the chamber-music compositions. One need not look for the pensive, melancholy Brahms in this delightful quartet; this is the work of a good-natured, straightforward, and healthy composer. The first movement is characterized by changes from 6/8 to 2/4 meter; passages in one are bustling with activity, in the other are delightfully matter-of-fact. The slow movement is an appealing piece and contrasts well with the piquant, agitated third movement. The fourth movement's set of variations provides moments of great charm, particularly in its last section, in which phrases from the first movement are woven into the variation texture in a masterful way.

It is significant that the B flat quartet, in a sense the lightest of all Brahms's chamber-music works, was written during the time in which the first symphony, Opus 68, approached completion. The tragic mood and monumental scope of that great work made enormous demands on him from 1874 to 1876. Composing the quartet, so different in mood and intensity from the symphony, must have provided the needed moments of repose and relaxation. And in the following years some of the greatest of Brahms's works were written: the second symphony, about 1877; the violin concerto, 1878; the two overtures,

1880–81; the B flat piano concerto, from 1878 to 1881. During this extremely productive period, about 1875–81, Brahms found time for only one chamber-music work, a violin sonata, Opus 78. Not until 1882 did he complete a piano trio in C major, Opus 87, whose first two movements had been begun two years earlier.

Opus 87. In the C major trio Brahms reached new heights in mastery of thematic development, in the economical use of material. Virtually every scrap of melody gives rise to other melodies; every motive suggests new motives. The result, in the first movement, is a conciseness that borders on austerity. Terse and objective, the movement is also characterized by dignity and reserve. The second movement, a set of five variations, is an outstanding example of Brahms's skill; not lyrically inspired nor dramatically contrasted, the variations present different phases of the theme's character. The scherzo is turbulent in a mild way; the finale, in spite of its few outbursts, is essentially cool and reserved.

Opus 88. In the same year (1882) Brahms wrote a string quintet in F Major, Opus 88. As so often in his music, these two consecutive works differ completely in mood and content. Where the trio is austere, the quintet is ingratiating; where the trio is calculated, the quintet is alive with inspiration. The tuneful first movement of the quintet is filled with sunshine; its highly imaginative developments serve but to throw the general lightness of mood into better relief. And for the only time in Brahms's chamber music for three or more instruments we meet a three-movement form. The second movement contains alternating sections in slow and fast tempo and thus combines the functions of slow movement and scherzo. And the finale begins with a fugal exposition, again most unusual in Brahms. Modeled, perhaps, on the fugal finale of Beethoven's Opus 59, No. 3, it exhibits similar combinations of melodic developments and contrapuntal intricacies. The movement discloses an exuberance we have not seen in Brahms's chamber music since the A major piano quartet; a similar exuberance filled Beethoven's heart toward the end of the Opus 59 set. What is more natural than that Brahms should have made use of the free quasi-fugal style to give expression to his enthusiastic state? But the result is not as successful as Beethoven's.

Opus 101. A piano trio in C minor, Opus 101, was written during the prolific summer of 1886, which also saw the composition of the F major cello sonata, Opus 99, and the A major violin sonata, Opus 100. The first movement of the trio illustrates to an even greater degree than does the C major trio (Opus 87) Brahms's great economy of means. A three-note motive and a fragment of lyric melody are the materials out of which he constructed this most concise of movements. The second movement, light-hearted and melancholy at once, serves as the scherzo; although marked "presto," it is essentially a reflective piece. The charming andante, with its mixtures of 3/4 and 2/4 measures, exhibits an unusually thin texture; the string instruments are heard without the piano much of the time, and thus contribute to the great variety of tonal color the movement contains. The finale, beginning brusquely and in a restless mood, settles down to a rollicking gait in its last section. Short phrases, many cross rhythms, and abrupt modulations give the movement a dissatisfied air; it is not the finest of Brahms's finales.

Opus 111. In the summer of 1890, following a delightful visit to Italy, Brahms wrote a string quintet in G major, Opus 111. Full-bodied, strong, and cheerful, it is essentially a happy work. The first movement, with its energetic theme and bustling accompanying figures, is reminiscent of a younger Brahms. The wonderfully moving adagio, on the other hand, is one of the richest and most dramatic movements of his late period. The scherzo, filled with naïve charm, conceals a wealth of contrapuntal details and masterful craftsmanship. In the finale the power and energy of the first movement are repeated, but on a lower level of sonority. Altogether, the G major quintet vigorously belies Brahms's age: fifty-seven. All the youth and enthusiasm of the earlier Brahms are here, without the extravagance.

Opus 114. On so cheerful a note Brahms had planned to end his creative activity. Rather than fall below the level he had attained, he would forego further composition—such was his intention. But a visit to Meiningen early in 1891 caused him to postpone his retirement. For in the Meiningen orchestra he heard a clarinetist, Richard Mühlfeld (1856–1907). So accomplished was that artist and so beautifully did he reveal the possibilities of the clarinet that Brahms resolved to employ the instrument in chamber music. Two works were written in the summer of 1891: the trio for clarinet, cello, and piano, in A minor, Opus 114, and the quintet for clarinet and string quartet, in B minor, Opus 115. Two sonatas for clarinet and piano, written in 1894, will be discussed below; with those compositions Brahms's life work was virtually finished.

By comparison with his other works the trio is somewhat dry. Technically all is on as high a plane as ever; the clarity of form and contrapuntal workmanship disclose no lessening of creative skill. But the melodic charm of earlier works, which has shown a certain falling off since the C major trio of 1882, is present to a smaller degree. In its place has come a preoccupation with rhythmic development, to the advantage of structural interest, but at the cost of lyric beauty.

Opus 115. In the B minor clarinet quintet, Opus 115, the picture is changed radically. Imaginative details, variety of texture, and inspired developments are present, along with a beauty of melody and an air of nobility that even Brahms did not always achieve. The gentle melancholy of the first movement, undisturbed by a full sonority and a mass of figurations, is appealing to a high degree. The shy, reserved adagio, with its rhapsodic middle section, full of rich tremolos and richer harmonies, is a deeply felt, imaginative piece of exquisite music. The third movement contains two related parts, a melodious andantino and a bright, deft presto, thematically related to the first part. And the variations of the last movement bring to expression a variety of mood and color virtually unknown in earlier chamber music. The coda combines the theme of the variations with that of the first movement in a passage whose economy, reserve, and sheer beauty are unmatched in the literature.

It may have been Brahms's purpose here to display the clarinet to advantage. Certainly every opportunity is given that instrument: lyric melody, dramatic figuration, rhapsodic utterance, delicate passage work, and complete range are employed. But the quintet is in no sense merely a virtuoso display piece; it is an example of perfectly conceived, lovingly planned chamber music of the highest quality. Exquisite restraint, great variety of textures, and subtle changes of tone color characterize the musical content of the four movements. The clarinet is treated as one of five equal instruments throughout, but its essential lyric character finds reflection in the work as a whole and inspired Brahms to create one of his greatest masterpieces.

The Sonatas. Brahms's seven sonatas for piano and one instrument may be discussed together, for they reveal certain characteristics that are not common in his seventeen works for larger chamber-music ensembles. The sonatas include two for cello and piano, Opus 38, in E minor (1866), and Opus 99, in F (1887); three for violin and piano, Opus 78, in G (1880), Opus 100, in A (1887), and Opus 108, in D minor (1889); and two for clarinet and piano, Opus 120, No. 1, in F minor, and No. 2, in E flat (1895).

The usual four-movement form that Brahms employed in all but one of his seventeen larger chamber-music works is found in only three of the seven sonatas—Opus 99, Opus 108, and Opus 120, No. 1. Each of the remaining sonatas contains three movements, but only the violin sonatas Opera 78 and 100 appear with the normal fast-slow-fast sequence. In the cello sonata Opus 38 the middle slow movement is replaced by a quasi minuet; and the second of the Opus 120 clarinet sonatas consists of a fast movement, a scherzo, and a set of slow variations.

In other respects, too, the sonatas differ from their larger relatives. Textures are more varied and range from a largely homophonic finale in Opus 99 to a bristling fugal finale in Opus 38. Mood content is greatly varied in these sonatas; the simple, melodious quasi minuet of Opus 38 represents one extreme and the dramatic, brilliant finale of Opus 108 the other. A number of other unusual (for Brahms) details further set these works apart. For example, the two middle movements of Opus 120, No. 1, are both in the same key, and the fugal finale of Opus 38 resembles a form with contrasting "trio" and recapitulation.

It is likely that the violin, cello, and clarinet sonatas served the same purpose in Brahms's creative life that the piano sonatas did in Bee-thoven's. They provided an intimate medium for the expression of unusual or even rhapsodic ideas, and gave the composer ample scope to experiment with form, texture, and mood. Yet each of the seven works discloses a high level of craftsmanship and expresses warm sentiment in a dignified manner. In these respects the sonatas represent Brahms at his best.

Style Characteristics. It is appropriate at this point to cast a back-ward glance over Brahms's forty years of chamber-music writing. One is impressed by changes in the nature of his melodic line and in the quality of the rhythmic element. Earlier works, roughly those written before the horn trio of Opus 40, were characterized by long, sustained lyric melodies disclosing Brahms's kinship with Schubert. Melodies of that type are largely missing in the works after 1865. (The sublime melody of the slow movement of Opus 60, let us recall, was present in the first version from about 1855 and is not typical of the later Brahms.) Beginning about that year, a new type of melody was introduced: one that begins lyrically but that after a few measures dissolves into the contrapuntal structure or undergoes rhythmic devel-opment. Seldom does the melody of the later type have a definite cadence; it melts into the following passage and thus has a beginning, but no ending.

With the change in melodic type came a greater preoccupation with rhythmic details and rhythmic complexities. As Brahms approached his fifties he concerned himself less with bar lines and clear rhythmic patterns than with thick textures in which rhythmic detail was piled upon rhythmic detail. Such polyrhythms as seen in Example 56

Example 56   Brahms, Rhythmic Patterns

become typical. Melodic lines such as those found in the third move-ment of Opus 51, No. 1 (see Example 57), dot Brahms's pages in

Example 57   Brahms, Opus 51, No. 1

(*meas. 15-18*)

(*implied*): | 3/8 | 3/8 | 2/8 | 4/8 | 3/8 | 1/8

increasing numbers. Rarely does he shift bar lines to agree with
phrase structure, the most notable example being the C minor trio of
Opus 101 (third movement), shown in Example 58. Most often he is

Example 58   Brahms, Opus 101

etc.

content to ignore bar lines and to write phrases across the measures.

A third point has to do with the inclusion of two contrasting
tempos within a single movement. This device, found nowhere in
the chamber music through the sextet of Opus 36, appears nine times
in the eighteen works that follow that sextet.[1] In several cases the
melodies of the second tempo are developed out of those of the first;
in a sense they may be regarded as highly imaginative variations. In
that connection must be mentioned the fact that sets of variations
appear with somewhat greater frequency in the later works of Brahms
than they do in the earlier.

What is one to conclude from these observations? First, in his early
works Brahms was inspired to write long, lyric melodies of the kind
we have seen in Schubert's music. Such Romantic outpourings of
true lyricism as we find in profusion in the B flat sextet, the G minor
and A major piano quartets, and the slow movement of the C minor
piano quartet have much in common with Schubert—sturdy grace,
rhythmic flow, and an air of gentle nostalgia. Second, Brahms's melodic
inspiration failed him to some extent in his middle period and a
greater amount of rhythmic variety took its place. This stage is seen
in the C minor and A minor string quartets, in which a kind of

[1] In Opera 40, 51 (Nos. 1 and 2), 67, 88, 100, 101, and twice in Opus 115.

rhythmic development of melodies substitutes for purely lyric utterance. Finally, in those movements in which rhythmic development is not appropriate, a duality of tempos results (as in the third movements of the Opus 51 string quartets, the first movement of the B flat, Opus 67, and the middle movement of the violin sonata, Opus 100).

In later works such rhythmic manipulation of melodic fragments became a characteristic element of Brahms's style. The rhythmic profundity and great freedom of phrase structure that are so typically Brahmsian are seen in the first movement of Opus 87, the finale of Opus 101, and throughout Opus 111 and Opus 115. But occasionally even Brahms's mastery of rhythmic developments, usually so amazingly subtle, becomes a bit obvious. One is enabled to peer behind the scenes and see the mechanism at work; for a brief moment the passage loses its charm.[2]

May one conclude that inspired pure lyric melody is essentially a young man's concern? That it was only the power, the depth, and the energy of Brahms's musical intellect that enabled him to overcome the handicaps that increasing years brought with them? If a generalization about Brahms's life work may be made, it must recognize the dominant position of intellectual activity in his music. And that is not in the least incompatible with emotional significance, warmth, charm, humor, or strength. One may approach Brahms as one would any other major composer; one may revel in the manifold beauties and moving passages his music contains. But one may appreciate his full stature only when one takes into account the nature of his musical activity. Intellect, too, may be inspired, as it was in Brahms to a tremendous degree.

FRANCK

French instrumental music had suffered an almost total eclipse toward the middle of the nineteenth century. French musical culture, falling under the spell of an eloquent Wagnerianism, was dominated by the opera. Scores of operatic works from the pens of Massenet,

---

[2] Such lapses one finds, for example, in Opus 87, I, measures 80–89 and 258–267; in Opus 101, II, measures 89–94; and in IV, measures 191–212.

Gounod, and their lesser imitators became enormously popular. A welter of music that was merely lyric or dramatic, entertaining or sentimental, overwhelmed the more serious composers. It remained for a native Belgian to become the leader of a group of musicians who succeeded in restoring the integrity of instrumental music in France. César Franck (1822–90), born at Liége but educated in France, was doomed to a life of obscurity for the most part. For more than forty years he taught piano and organ in Paris; for more than fifty years he composed and found recognition, until late in life, only in a small circle composed of his pupils and friends. His music is characterized by a measure of contrapuntal excellence, formal innovation, and religious idealism. Such characteristics found no favor among the opera-loving Frenchmen of his time, and yet his influence on the course of French music was considerable. In proof, one has but to mention the names of a few of his pupils: Vincent d'Indy (1851–1931), Ernest Chausson (1855–99), and Gabriel Pierné (1863–97).

Franck's achievement is not reflected in a large quantity of works; in fact, he was among the least prolific of major composers. His one symphony is well known; his contributions to chamber music include only one piano quintet, one string quartet, and one violin sonata, in addition to four early piano trios, one of which has some slight historical significance.

Piano Trios. Three of the trios were written in 1840 and were later published as Opus 1. The first trio, in F sharp minor, bears within itself the seeds of cyclical form, the form that Beethoven had introduced so magnificently in the quartets of Opera 130–133, and the form that became the trademark of the last decades of the nineteenth century. Themes presented early in the first movement are heard again, somewhat transformed, in later movements; other themes are in turn derived from them, and a high degree of unity is thus attained. In other respects the F sharp trio and its two companions in Franck's Opus 1 are not important works; but the composer was only eighteen at the time of writing.[3] Nor is the one-movement fourth trio, Opus 2,

[3] Vincent d'Indy points out (in *Cobbett's Cyclopedic Survey of Chamber Music*, I, 420) that Franck's use of two contrasting trios in the scherzo and Schumann's

of great significance; that trio was originally planned as the finale of
Opus 1, No. 3, but was published separately at the suggestion of Liszt.

The Piano Quintet. Almost forty years elapsed before Franck turned
to chamber music again: the quintet for piano and strings, in F minor,
was written in 1878. During the long interval Franck had slowly been
developing his unique harmonic style, characterized by rich modulations and chromatic wandering. A restless, colorful, but somewhat
loose harmonic structure resulted. The quintet to a high degree contains such a structure.

But insofar as economy of thematic resources is concerned, few
works are so tightly knit. The cyclical principle is carried to its utmost
limits. One theme, the cyclical theme of the entire composition (see
Example 59b), appears in various guises throughout the work: as

Example 59   Franck, Piano Trio, Opus 1, No. 1

second theme and coda theme of the first movement, in the development section of the slow movement, and as the theme of the finale's
extended coda—each time appropriately altered in tempo and considerably modified rhythmically. That theme, playing so important a
part in providing inner unity between the contrasting, shifting
sections of the various movements of the quintet, is in turn derived
from one of the cyclical themes of the F sharp minor trio of 1840
(Example 59a). It was truly an example of thematic economy to utilize
in so masterful a fashion what had only been touched upon four
decades earlier.

Outwardly, each of the three movements (there is no movement

---

first employment of the same device—in the B flat Symphony—occurred in the same
year, 1840.

to correspond to the scherzo) is in sonata-form, with exposition, development, and recapitulation, plus introduction and elaborate coda in the outer movements. Yet so emphatically does Franck reiterate certain of his style characteristics throughout the work that one receives the impression that the quintet is episodic. Theme transformations accompanied by abrupt changes of tempo and mood, sequence modulations of melodic fragments, theme announcements in remote keys (E, G, F sharp minor, A and D flat are some of the keys dwelt upon in the F minor first movement), an abundance of *molto ritardandi* and *molto crescendi*—all these features contribute to an ebb and flow of the music, to a lack of continuity, to an absence of that sense of direction that was so strong a characteristic of Franck's contemporary, Brahms.

To the degree in which the quintet exhibits the same cyclical form principles that Beethoven employed in his last quartets, it testifies to Franck's avowed indebtedness to that composer. But in the sense that the harmonic scheme, the instrumental color, and the entire emotional content are so purely Franck's own, there is little relationship between this work and earlier ones. The quintet is a unique composition in its combination of outward adherence to formal models and of complete subjection to the peculiar nature of Franck's musical gifts. It has earned a place in the repertoire as one of the most popular of piano quintets.

The String Quartet. With Franck's single string quartet of 1889 we are, in the words of Vincent d'Indy, "surveying the most astonishing conception of the mind of this genius in tonal architecture." [4] The astonishment arises when the form of the first movement is examined; two separate yet related musical structures, one inscribed within the other, constitute the movement. A fully developed sonata-allegro is inserted between the parts of a slow, stately monothematic song form, with quasi trio and recapitulation; each structure is in itself completely unified and satisfying. A diagram may clarify the relationship between the six sections.

[4] In *Cobbett's Cyclopedic Survey of Chamber Music*, I, 426. Our analysis is based on that of D'Indy, which follows the quotation just made.

Section	Tempo	Key
Theme	Lento	D major
Exposition	Allegro	D minor and F major
Quasi trio	Poco lento	F minor and B flat minor
Development	Allegro	Various
Recapitulation	Allegro	D minor and major
Modified recapitulation	Lento	D major

Song Form brackets Theme, Quasi trio, Modified recapitulation; *Sonata-Form* brackets Exposition, Development, Recapitulation.

The slow, soaring theme of the first song form, along with its veiled, fugal transformations in the quasi trio, provide great contrast to the moderately fast, intense themes of the sonata-form. Yet the contrasts, along with the great emotional variety the movement affords, are wonderfully balanced; the inner unity of the movement is never threatened.

Magnificent in structure and completely enclosed within itself, the movement is closely connected with those that follow. The second is a charming scherzo containing a short quotation of the first movement's song-form theme. The sublime slow movement discloses less organic connection with earlier ones; rather is it an eloquent testimony to the depth of Franck's musical feeling and a monument to the essential nobility of his musical ideas. The finale begins with an introduction that reviews the themes of the two previous movements (much as Beethoven had done in his ninth symphony) and presents a new, contrasting, and agitated theme. The main movement begins with another transformation of the first movement's song-form theme, which thus becomes the cyclical theme of the entire quartet. And more evidence of cyclical structure is yet to be presented. The second theme of the finale is based on a short connecting motive that played an important part in the first movement; the coda contains a masterful passage in which melodies from the first are combined with the scherzo's theme; and, finally, the theme of the slow movement returns to pronounce a benediction at the very end of the quartet.

In all respects this is a major work, probably one of Franck's finest compositions. In it his rich modulation and wide-ranging chromatic wandering are kept at a minimum. In technical mastery, nobility of conception, and wealth of color the quartet represents one of the highest points yet attained by French music in the nineteenth century. All the concomitants of cyclical form—the *idée fixe,* the leitmotiv, theme transformation—are employed probably more consistently than in any chamber-music work since Beethoven. Thus the validity of that formal principle in nonprogram-music works is conclusively demonstrated. Berlioz, Wagner, and Liszt had, of course, conclusively demonstrated its efficacy in program-music contexts.

The Violin Sonata. Franck's single sonata for violin and piano, in A major, was composed in 1886, and thus is slightly earlier than the string quartet. Cyclical form is employed here again, as it was in the piano quintet and the string quartet; virtually all the themes in the four movements of the work are derived from three short motives. The first motive, appearing at the very beginning of the first movement, appears again in company with the second motive in the second movement and with the second and third motives in the third movement. The finale, a rondo in the unusual form of A—A^1—A^2—development—A, again makes use of two of the cyclical motives; thus the complete unity of the work is assured.

This reliance on a few melodic bits might suggest that Franck limited himself in his search for melodic variety. On the contrary, the four movements of the sonata (allegretto, allegro, fantasia, allegretto) contain many passages in which the cyclical motives are expanded by development, employed in different contexts, and presented in various harmonic colors. The end result is a work that is concise without being terse, that is concentrated even while it is eloquent, and that represents an economical approach toward the use of musical material. Few composers have equaled Franck in his ability to make much of little. The violin sonata ranks with the quartet in expressive power and variety.

SAINT-SAËNS

Camille Saint-Saëns (1835–1921) was a contemporary of Franck and Brahms, but he remained singularly unaffected by the rich,

Romantic expression of these men. In his chamber music one encounters a late flowering of Classical elements. His music exhibits a contrapuntal excellence, a clarity of form, and, in general, a restrained utterance that were more typical of composers a century before his time. Saint-Saëns during his long life—much of which was spent as a virtuoso pianist and organist—attempted almost every standard chamber-music combination. A piano quintet, Opus 14, was composed about 1855; a piano quartet, Opus 41, twenty years later. Two piano trios, Opus 18 and Opus 92, appeared in 1863 and 1892, respectively; a septet for string quartet, piano, trumpet, and bass, Opus 65, was published about 1881. His first string quartet, Opus 112, was written in 1900; his second, Opus 153, in 1919, when he was eighty-four years old. Interspersed between these works are about a dozen others for odd combinations or for piano and one instrument.

The eighteen works, written across the sixty-six-year span, 1855–1921, testify to Saint-Saëns' technical mastery of counterpoint, to his perception of delicate proportions, and to his great competence in all matters of musical composition. But they also disclose a lack of real inspiration in melodic writing, a certain sameness of style—indeed, the overuse of one accompanying figure throughout a movement is one of his chief characteristics—and a paucity of profound feeling. If music were to be measured only by its cleverness and originality, or even by its brilliance and effectiveness, the works of Saint-Saëns would hold a high place. Technical competence and fluency of expression are not enough, however, to insure a lasting place in the literature. The essential elements—emotional depth and musical significance—are for the most part lacking in the music of Saint-Saëns.

RUSSIAN COMPOSERS

At the beginning of this chapter, three parallel tendencies that characterize the music of the late nineteenth century were noted. The discussion of the music of Brahms, Franck, and, to a lesser degree, Saint-Saëns was designed to illustrate how that music had its strongest roots in the great Classical past and thus exemplifies one of the tendencies. The remainder of this chapter will be concerned with music illustrative of a second tendency: that which gave rise to the term *nationalism*. The works of Russian, Scandinavian, and Bohemian composers will be discussed, in that order. The third tendency, to make use of literary programs as a basis for musical composition, finds no expression in these pages, for the great exponents of that device, Berlioz, Liszt, and Wagner, were not chamber-music composers.

Musical life in Russia before the early years of the nineteenth century had been largely influenced by imported musicians. Germans and Italians, for the most part, dominated the musical scene in the few centers where music was actively cultivated. When, in the 1830s, Michael Glinka (1804–57) turned to Russian folk song as a source of musical inspiration, the seed for a national school was planted. Within a few decades Russia made up for her late arrival on the European musical stage. Glinka was followed by composers who dipped deeper into the fount whose musical treasures he had revealed. Such composers, making a feature of the folk-song elements in their music, were consciously nationalistic. But other composers appeared who for the most part eschewed folk material. Yet so closely were they related to the general stream of Russian expression and style that no great distance separates them from the avowed Nationalists. In the field of chamber music Tchaikovsky's name looms large. But Borodin, Arensky, and Glazunov are to be reckoned with also.

Tchaikovsky. Peter Ilyitch Tchaikovsky was born in Russia in 1840. His early education included music study, but his first positions were various government clerkships. In his early twenties he resumed the study of composition, wrote several large works, and in 1866 became a faculty member of the new conservatory that Nicholas Rubinstein had founded in Moscow. About 1878 he retired from teaching, having become the recipient of a generous pension offered him by Nadejda von Meck, a wealthy widow who was enamored of his compositions. Tchaikovsky spent much time in Switzerland, Italy, and elsewhere, and visited the United States and England as a conductor of his own works. He died in St. Petersburg (Petrograd or Leningrad, to our younger readers) in 1893, the victim of a cholera attack.

The String Quartets.—Tchaikovsky's chamber-music compositions are few in number, including only three string quartets, one piano trio, and a single string sextet. The first quartet, in D major, Opus 11, was completed in 1871 and became the work that first carried Tchaikovsky's name outside Russia. The first movement is filled with syncopated figures, a great amount of passage-work, and unrelieved sonority. The second movement, the famous "Andante Cantabile," known in dozens of arrangements, is in its original setting a charming piece that offers great contrast to both the sonorous first movement and the piquant scherzo that is placed third. The finale, like the andante, suggests Russian atmosphere through its irregular phrases and its sturdy rhythms.

In many ways the D major quartet is the best of Tchaikovsky's chamber-music works, for in later compositions long arid stretches are sometimes encountered. The ability to write interestingly at all times seems to have been a characteristic of all major composers before Tchaikovsky. In the latter's music that ability was not always revealed; he did not always develop his eloquent themes to their fullest extent. Had he restricted himself to the smaller forms, as many earlier Romantic composers had done, that tendency might have escaped notice. In the larger forms, however, his limited inspiration is sometimes evident. Technically all is well in these development sections; the fault was not an intellectual one. But real, detailed inspiration, of the kind Brahms was exhibiting so profusely at the very time Tchaikovsky was writing, is often absent.

The second quartet, in F major, was written early in 1874 and was published as Opus 22 in 1876. Three of its movements are typical of Tchaikovsky in his more restrained moods: themes are somewhat dry, transitions and developments are orthodox, and the workmanship throughout is excellent. In the scherzo, however, Tchaikovsky succeeded in writing a thoroughly enjoyable piece of music. Phrases that combine duple and triple measures to produce seven-beat melodies are typically Russian.

The third quartet, in E flat minor, Opus 30, was written early in

1875. It was planned as a memorial to his friend Ferdinand Laub, a violinist and colleague of Tchaikovsky's at the Moscow Conservatory and was dedicated to Laub's memory. The quartet is funereal in tone. A slow, elegiacal introduction precedes a sad, introspective first movement in which marchlike rhythms vie with great climaxes of sonority. The scherzo, rather subdued in its lightness, does no violence to the prevailing mood of the quartet. The third movement is outspokenly descriptive: elements of a chant are set between phrases of a chorale in a mirroring of the funeral service. After three movements, morbid, restrained, and elegiacal in turn, the bright finale in a major key comes as a relief.

The Piano Trio.—Nicholas Rubinstein, Tchaikovsky's teacher and friend, had died in 1881. Wishing to commemorate that artist as he had commemorated Laub, Tchaikovsky turned to chamber music again. This time, however, he did not employ the string quartet. Rubinstein had been a remarkable pianist (not to be confused with his more famous brother Anton), and a work with piano seemed more appropriate. The piano trio in A minor, Opus 50, written in 1882 and dedicated "to the memory of a great artist," resulted. In spite of its great length (its performance takes about fifty-five minutes) the trio contains only two movements.

The first movement includes four main themes and a number of derived motives. Each theme is developed to some extent after its announcement, an elaborate development section occurs in the usual place, and the recapitulation is as extended as the exposition. Noble or impassioned or lyric themes notwithstanding, the movement does not escape a certain amount of the dryness noted above in connection with the quartets. Orchestral sonorities, involved contrapuntal passages, and brilliant virtuosic writing throughout—especially in the piano part—add a new element to chamber music.

The second movement, a massive set of eleven variations (two of which are traditionally omitted in performance), plus an equally massive "Finale e coda," is more successful. Tchaikovsky's boundless imagination and technical fertility enable him to present the charming theme in a number of contrasting guises. Each variation assumes a characteristic form: mazurka, waltz, fugue, and scherzo are among those presented. The finale is a *tour de force* unlike anything else in the literature. The variation's theme is developed forcefully, at great length (Tchaikovsky himself authorized the omission of almost two-thirds of that development), and toward great climaxes. In the closing section of the movement the main theme of the first movement is reintroduced in the company of thunderous chords and flashing arpeggios, and only in the last few measures is a degree of restraint and deep feeling introduced. There, as in the comparable section at the end of the first movement, a dirgelike march restores an air of solemnity to this otherwise brilliant and sentimental trio.

A sextet for strings in D minor, Opus 70, was written between 1890 and early 1892. Bearing the title *Souvenir de Florence,* the piece recalls some of Tchaikovsky's pleasant memories of a stay in Italy early in 1890. It is one of his weakest works and deserves little serious attention.

Borodin. Alexander Borodin (1833–87), one of the avowed nationalists who called themselves "The Five," [5] wrote two string quartets (in A, 1884; in D, 1887) contributed separate movements to various omnibus quartets composed as a joint venture by several colleagues. On the basis of the two quartets alone, Borodin's place as an esteemed chamber-music composer is assured. The A major, influenced by a theme from Beethoven's B flat quartet, Opus 130, is remarkably free of Russian atmosphere, of nationalistic mannerisms. One or two phrases suggest native folk songs, but in the main the quartet is one of the most Classical of late nineteenth-century compositions. Throughout the work Borodin's lightness of touch and technical mastery— surprisingly great when one recalls that he was by profession a chemist—are revealed.

In the ever-popular D major quartet, as in his orchestral piece, *Sketch of the Steppes,* Borodin imbues the music with a spaciousness reminiscent of the vast plains of his native land. That effect, plus a rhythmic energy in the fast movements, may be considered nationalistic

[5] Nicholas Rimsky-Korsakov, César Cui, Mily Balakirev, and Modeste Moussorgsky were the others.

elements. For the rest, the quartet contains charming music, elegantly and effortlessly worked out in a mood of purest lyricism. The slow movement, the famous "Nocturne," remains a favorite of audiences and performers everywhere, in spite of its merely tuneful nature.

Other Composers. With the mention of Anton Arensky (1861–1906) we come to one of Tchaikovsky's numerous disciples, one who made use of nationalistic elements, who wrote somewhat sonorous chamber music, but who contributed nothing essentially new to the literature. Two string quartets, Opus 11 and Opus 35, two piano trios, Opus 32 and Opus 73, and a piano quintet, Opus 51, were written between 1889 and 1905.

Alexander Glazunov (1865–1936) was somewhat more prolific in the field of chamber music than his contemporary, having to his credit seven quartets, a string quintet, and several short pieces for quartet. He began writing under the influence of the nationalists; his earliest works, from about 1882, disclose themes based on Russian tunes. Later works show Glazunov turning away from the nationalists and adopting a more traditional expression.

SCANDINAVIAN COMPOSERS

Gade. The earliest significant composer among the Scandinavians was a Dane, Niels Gade (1817–90). Gade's numerous chamber-music works—a quartet, a quintet, a sextet, and an octet for strings, plus two piano trios, all published between 1846 and 1890—have much in common with the works of Mendelssohn, even though Gade was popularly called "the Chopin of the North." Elegance of form and ease of expression are characteristic of his works; their quality and sweetness of mood are agreeable but hardly moving. One must demand that music be more than sweet if it is to endure past its composer's lifetime.

Grieg. Edvard Grieg (1843–1907), Norwegian by birth but German by training, attained a degree of originality that has permitted his music to outlive the works of his Danish and Swedish (and some of his Norwegian) contemporaries. Educated largely in Leipzig, Grieg succeeded in freeing himself, after his return to Norway, from the somewhat saccharine influences that emanated from that seat of Mendelssohnian tradition. He turned to native folk tunes and dances, much as his Russian and Bohemian contemporaries were doing, and developed a manly, robust style of writing that embodied Norwegian melodic idioms and rhythms. Grieg's chamber-music compositions are few: three violin sonatas, one for cello, one string quartet, in G minor, two movements of another quartet, and two or three fragments for other combinations.

The G minor quartet was published in 1879 as Opus 27; thus it is contemporary with Franck's piano quintet. Like that quintet, Grieg's quartet is an embodiment of the cyclical-form principle; but here the similarity between the works ends. The quartet begins with a slow introduction; the phrases heard there appear again and again throughout the work. The second theme of the first movement, its coda, and large portions of the finale are based on the introductory phrases, and the latter's lyric breadth permeates the slow movement. Grieg, almost to a greater extent than any other nineteenth-century composer, succeeded in creating an individual style. His melodic mannerisms, his extensive use of sequences of short phrases, and his characteristic rhythms appear almost without alteration in the great majority of his works. The quartet is typical of that style. Its orchestral doublings and the somewhat pretentious expression do not detract from the value of the work. It is filled with beautiful melodies, great exuberance, and much poetic feeling.

Grieg's three violin sonatas (Opus 8, 1866; Opus 13, 1869; Opus 45, 1887) and one cello sonata (Opus 36, 1885) represent his dedication to the nationalistic impulse. Norwegian dances and dance rhythms—especially the triple-meter *springer* or *springdans*—play large parts in the sonatas, and Norwegian melodic idioms are prominent. In addition, however, Grieg's own melodic gifts and sense of drama and excitement are revealed. The style characteristics seen in the quartet appear in the sonatas also. Sequence repetitions, short phrases, and moods that range from wild exuberance to complete repose are represented.

BOHEMIAN COMPOSERS

For generations before 1850 Bohemia had sent her best musicians to the larger musical centers of Europe. One has but to recall the names of a few: Stamitz at Mannheim, Jiránek at Dresden, Gassmann at Vienna. In all cases these and other Bohemian musicians similarly placed wrote in the generally prevailing style; their music conformed to international patterns. Toward the middle of the nineteenth century the series of events mentioned earlier in this chapter, which culminated in Austria's granting Bohemia political independence (in 1860), caused Bohemian composers to follow the trend popular through large parts of Europe. Many of them turned to their own national culture for inspiration and musical content. Among the leading figures in the national school that developed was Smetana.

Smetana. Bedrich Smetana was born in 1824. He was largely self-trained as a pianist and composer, and his first professional ventures were in the field of private teaching. In 1856 he became conductor of the Philharmonic Society's concerts in Gothenburg and produced his first symphonic poems there. The political events in Prague led to the founding of a national opera there about 1860–62. Smetana, in his desire to contribute to the new movement, returned to Prague from Sweden, composed several operas for the new establishment (among them *The Bartered Bride,* 1866), and shortly thereafter became its chief conductor. But political opposition and severe criticism of later works undermined Smetana's health. In 1874, totally deaf, he resigned and returned to the composition of symphonic works. The cycle of tone poems *Ma Vlast* ("My Country"), depicting in music Bohemia's castles, woods, rivers, and mountains, was written between 1874 and 1879; of this cycle, "The Moldau" has become universally known. Two string quartets were written about the same time; they, with an earlier piano trio, are Smetana's only chamber-music works. The intensive writing did little to improve his health. When he died, in 1884, it was in a state of insanity.

The piano trio, in G minor, Opus 15, was written about 1855, when Smetana was still affected by the death of his young daughter. It is characterized by great variety of mood. The rather free and rhapsodic first movement is at times gloomy or pensive, at times vigorous and straightforward. The scherzo, with its two contrasting trios, tender and majestic in turn, is essentially reserved. The finale (there is no slow movement) begins brightly and with energy; during the course of the movement a chorale and a funeral march are heard. With so many contrasting elements, a lack of unity is inevitable. Yet the trio's many poignant passages and moments of real beauty and its excellence of technical detail make it a worthy example of Smetana's prenationalist style.

More than two decades later Smetana turned to chamber music again, to describe the course of his own life; both of his quartets bear the title *Aus meinem Leben* ("From My Life"). The first, in E minor, was written about 1876 and published in 1881 as Opus 115. Smetana supplied a complete program for the work.[6] The four movements depict the "romantic tendency and unsatisfied yearnings" of his early life, suggested in a restless but highly organized first movement; the lighter side of his youthful existence, in a charming polka; "the bliss of my first love for . . . my wife" in a moving and beautifully sustained slow movement; and "the discovery how to treat the national material in music" in the lively finale. But also reflected in the finale is "the beginning of my deafness, a glimpse into the melancholy future," mirrored in a sustained high E over a somber tremolo in the lower instruments.

The second quartet, considerably shorter than the first, and in a sense disorganized, is in D minor. Written about 1882–83, it was published posthumously in 1889 without opus number. "The new quartet takes up—after the catastrophe" of Smetana's deafness but goes no further in autobiographical detail. Composed during a time when Smetana was prey to intense morbidity and when his mental powers were fast waning, it is characterized by impulsive contrasts and lack of cohesion. Its four movements form a regrettably sad memorial to the unhappy fate suffered by the essentially cheerful

[6] Rosa Newmarch, in *Cobbett's Cyclopedic Survey of Chamber Music,* II, 427 ff.

Smetana. The first quartet, on the other hand, with its effective writing, brilliance, and nationalistic flavor, has won a commanding place in the literature. It stands as one of Smetana's characteristic works, one that combines program and nationalistic traits in a predominantly musical framework.

Dvořák. Far more prolific in chamber music than Smetana, and perhaps of greater musical importance, was Antonín Dvořák. He was born at Mülhausen, Bohemia, in 1841, and his early life was not a happy one. His father's wish to have him trained as a butcher scarcely comported with his own desire to become a musician. In the end he broke away, self-taught to some extent, and became a member of a theater orchestra in Prague. He played viola and composed, but not until he was in his thirties did his compositions attract any favorable attention. From about 1875 he devoted himself exclusively to composition, and his friendship with Brahms and von Bülow helped him to gain favorable hearings for his works. During the course of a few years he gained considerable fame as a teacher of composition. Dvořák visited England several times between 1884 and 1891, conducting his own works at various festivals; his success and the quality of his works added to his personal renown. From 1892 to 1895 he served as director of the National Conservatory in New York and visited a Bohemian community in Spillville, Iowa. He returned to Prague in 1895, resumed his post at the conservatory in that city, and in 1901 was made the director of the school. When he died, in 1904, he was secure in his position as Bohemia's greatest and best-loved composer.

Dvořák's chamber-music works include four piano trios, three piano quartets (one of them with two violins), a piano quintet, a trio for string instruments, eight string quartets, two string quintets, one sextet for strings, and almost a dozen (published and unpublished) early or smaller compositions—thirty works in all. In them we may see how Dvořák was influenced by one or another composer throughout his lifetime.

Early Works.—A series of early works written between 1861 and 1873 includes five string quartets, a string quintet, a piano quintet (not the more famous Opus 81), and *The Cypresses* (ten love songs arranged for string quartet as Opus 8). According to Ottokar Šoorek,[7] these unpublished works reflect at first Dvořák's adherence to Beethoven and Schubert, then, about 1870, a sudden infatuation with the methods and forms of Liszt and Wagner. That phase expired rather quickly; by 1874 Dvořák had returned to the path marked out by Classical models.

Between 1874 and 1877 lie three string quartets, Opera 16, 80, and 34, in A minor, E major, and D minor, respectively; a string quintet for two violins, viola, cello, and bass, in G major, originally planned as Opus 18 but eventually published as Opus 77; two piano trios in B flat and G minor, Opus 21 and Opus 26, respectively; and a piano quartet in D major, Opus 23. The B flat trio, lying about midway in the period, represents both the strength and the weaknesses of Dvořák's style at this time. Its first movement is clear in form and straightforward in expression. But some of its rhythmic figures are a bit obvious; phrase extensions and development episodes merely follow the usual course, and a general air of immaturity prevails. An otherwise beautiful slow movement is marred by the overuse of a few standard devices. The finale is likewise weakened: inane sequence passages destroy to some extent a forthright and vigorous movement. Only the third movement, a quasi intermezzo, is free from such structural weaknesses.

The works that lie between 1878 and about 1890, on the other hand, show that Dvořák had freed himself from the somewhat rigid expression derived from his Classical models and had entered on a period in which Slavonic elements predominated. Nine chamber-music works were written during those years, as follows:

String sextet, A major	Opus 48 (1878)
String quartet, E flat	Opus 51 (1878)
String quartet, C major	Opus 61 (1881)
Piano trio, F minor	Opus 65 (1883)
String trio, C major	Opus 74 (1887)
Piano quintet, A major	Opus 81 (1887)

[7] In *Cobbett's Cyclopedic Survey of Chamber Music*, I, 355–370.

Piano quartet, E flat	Opus 87 (1889)
Piano trio, E minor	Opus 90 (1890)
Bagatelles, G major	Opus 47 (c. 1878, published 1890)

Of these works the string quartet, Opus 51, the piano quintet, Opus 81, and the piano trio, Opus 90, may be accorded closer attention.

Opus 51.—The success of Dvořák's sextet, Opus 48, with its outspoken Slavonic elements, led to his being commissioned to write a string quartet embodying similar elements. The E flat quartet, Opus 51, was the result. The Slavonic touches are seen in the themes of the first movement, in the "Dumka" constituting the second movement, and in the brisk, dancelike finale. The *dumka* occurs so frequently in Dvořák's works that it may well be defined a bit more closely. A *dumka* is an elegy, hence may be expected to be melancholy in mood; but it also contains a middle section, usually in fast tempo and always contrasting sharply in mood with the elegiacal sections. Thus the *dumka* (*dumky* in plural) was a perfect vehicle for Dvořák, who was fond of abrupt emotional changes. But the E flat quartet as a whole is much more than an expression of nationalistic elements; it is the reflection of a capable, sensitive, imaginative, and humorous composer—for Dvořák was all these things. The first movement breathes an air of good nature that is in no way incompatible with its contrapuntal excellence. The "Dumka" offers great contrasts between the sentimental and scherzolike sections. The "Romanze" is a moving piece, and the finale delightfully boisterous.

Opus 81.—The A major piano quintet again reveals a Dvořák who is essentially happy. Its first movement is melodious, brilliant, and altogether an excellent piece of music. Many of the rhythmic devices one associates with Brahms are here evident; what might be called rhythmic counterpoint becomes characteristic. This rhythmic vitality, which forms an important element of Dvořák's later style, appears in constructions such as those seen in Example 60.

The second movement is again a *dumka;* its contrasting sections are poignant and lively in turn. The scherzo breathes the spirit of the *furiant,* an energetic triple-measure Slavonic dance. And the finale, a gay and boisterous dancelike movement, suggests a collection of

national airs without actually quoting such. airs. One is continually struck by the variety of Dvořák's means of expression. Lyric tunes, melodies dripping with sentiment, brisk fugal passages, and sections containing elaborate contrapuntal devices are all there. This variety is largely responsible for the charm and sterling qualities that his music possesses and always makes hearing it a pleasure.

Opus 90.—The E minor piano trio, Opus 90, lies near the close of Dvořák's Slavonic period. Its content is unique. For virtually the only time in his chamber-music works he departed from the conventional four-movement form and wrote a collection of six *dumky* (hence the popular nickname of "Dumky Trio"). Alternations of slow and fast tempo, of somberness and abandon, are characteristic of the trio— inevitably so, the *dumka* form being what it is. But in Dvořák's hands that form did not always retain a simple ABA pattern. The return of the A (slow) section is seldom exact; rather is it a greatly modified recapitulation embodying changes of tone color, of instrumental figuration, even of harmony. As a result the trio exhibits a certain lack of cohesion and gives the effect of being composed of many short fragments. Only the facts that the first three *dumky* are connected and harmonically related (E, C sharp minor, and A, respectively)— forming in effect one long movement—and that the fourth, fifth, and sixth are unrelated—thus completing the illusion of a four-movement form—save the trio from making a completely episodic effect. Inner threads of unity are provided by the contrasting moods that prevail: sentiment and pathos in the slow sections, abandon and forced gaiety in the fast.

The years 1892 to 1895 mark the dates of Dvořák's stay in the "new world." Two chamber-music works were written during that visit—a string quartet in F major, Opus 96 (the "American Quartet") and a string quintet in E flat, Opus 97. These works are characterized by his "impressions" of American folk music ("American" taken in its widest sense to include many of the European and extra-Caucasian elements that find expression in that music) and not by direct quotation of American tunes. Thus in the quartet one finds themes based on the Oriental pentatonic scale (F-G-A-C-D); in the quintet, rhythmic figures popularly associated with the American Indian; and in both works, a variety of mood that reflects the countless facets of life in the United States.

But apart from these local, quasi-descriptive elements, the works reveal Dvořák's depth of feeling, the resourcefulness of his technique, and his boundless imagination. Clear forms, subtle contrasts of texture and tone color, and great melodic charm combine to place these among his finest works. The "American Quartet" is deservedly one of the most popular of late nineteenth-century chamber-music compositions.

Late Works.—After his return to Bohemia, in 1895, Dvořák composed two more quartets: Opus 106 in G major and Opus 105 in A flat (obviously, the first written was the second to be published). With them his long activity as a chamber-music composer, extending across almost thirty-five years, came to an end. Filled with joy at returning to his native land, secure in the affections of his countrymen, and honored by all of Europe, Dvořák gave expression to his feelings of peace and contentment. No longer concerned with nationalistic expression or exposed to an alien culture, he reverted to a Classical purity of form. The two quartets, despite several passages that are devoid of deep feeling, are among his most successful works.

Seen in retrospect, the chamber-music compositions of Dvořák reveal a composer second to none in technical ability, in melodic invention, and in formal perception. Contrasting moods are typical; passages in which one is suddenly transported from the depths of melancholy to the heights of wild abandon are found frequently in his pages. In only one respect does he fail to warrant a place among the immortals of chamber music: his work is seldom profound. All other types of expression are reflected there: passages of deepest morbidity and most intense joy, and all shades between. But the universally significant kind of music, the music that enthralls or inspires the listener, is missing. In that respect Dvořák is akin to Mendelssohn. Both composers succeeded in writing charming, dignified, and even moving music, but it is always a surface emotion that is touched. Many chamber-music composers in the late nineteenth century were technically superb and musically inspired, but only Brahms was able to write profoundly.

11. The Contemporary World

ONE WHO WISHES to write convincingly about the direction of present-day music should be either a participant in the creation of that music or a critic proficient in prophecy. Only then can he unerringly underline this or that trend, style, or composition and persuade his readers that it contains within itself the germ of the future; only then can he name "the" composer of the age in whose shadow later generations will stand. It can hardly be denied that contemporary music has a direction. A backward glance over the music of the past few decades discloses a reaction to this, a counterreaction to that, and a return to something else. In short, music is always on the way to a new condition. Only the adherent of a particular style or the seer can venture to predict its path of development.

Being neither one nor the other, this author can do no more than report events, describe new techniques, and summarize trends. Twentieth-century chamber music exists in large quantities, and new composers emerge almost monthly. New compositions are hailed, performed once—and forgotten; new style tendencies are eagerly exploited, imitated—and heard of no more. This chapter attempts to survey that growing, changing field and to discuss its most significant aspects. Inevitably it is an incomplete and, perhaps, superficial account of contemporary developments. But first a brief summary of the entire period under discussion, namely, the period from about 1890 to the present, may be of help in clarifying the complex situation in which modern music finds itself.

We had reached the last decade of the nineteenth century. The subjectivity, the outpouring of emotion, the extravagance that often led to bad taste, the attention to sentimental detail—in short, all the elements of post-Romanticism were in fullest bloom, were at the height of their influence. The grandiloquent, sometimes pretentious expression of Wagner was emerging, in the orchestral field, in the tone poems of Richard Strauss (1864–1949). Brahms was still contending against that type of expression, as he had struggled against it during his lifetime. But Brahms reacted, not by going forward to something new, but by endeavoring to restore the balance and the clarity of the past. Such a negative reaction was bound to fail. Brahms was himself too much a Romanticist at heart successfully to avoid becoming infected by the extravagant harmony and personalized expression that surrounded him.

A stronger, positive reaction was needed; inevitably a forward-looking composer appeared, to give music a new direction. At the hands of Claude Debussy, in the 1890s, that new direction made itself apparent. Finding in Moussorgsky a freedom of melodic line and in Wagner a chromaticism that seemed to presage a new employment of tonal resources, Debussy seized upon those elements and created the musical style called impressionism.

The new style was strong in its appeal from the first, influenced many later composers, and did much to clear the air of post-Romantic excesses. But neither during Debussy's lifetime nor up to the present moment has the subjective Romantic style died out completely. In the field of chamber music its rearguard included, through the early decades of the twentieth century, such composers as Fauré, D'Indy, and Dohnányi. These men modified their techniques, of course, but they remained tied, in some degree, to Romanticism's subjective point of view.

Impressionism in its early stages was also subjective in its viewpoint. The very term adopted to characterize the new style gives evidence of its personal nature. It remained for later impressionists to become somewhat objective in their musical utterances, thus to employ the new style as a means of establishing a new aesthetic code. Influenced largely by Maurice Ravel, postimpressionistic composers appeared in France, England, and the United States.

In the years before World War I, about 1910 to 1913, Arnold Schoenberg, a Viennese composer who had begun his work in the traditional, advanced Romantic style then current in Vienna, reached an expressive impasse. Convinced that significant musical creation did not lie merely in an extension of that style, Schoenberg began his sensational development away from tradition. His experiments led to atonality, gave rise to spare, sparse tonal skeletons, and culminated in the twelve-tone technique that later developed into the style called serial writing. Simultaneously the music of a Hungarian, Béla Bartók, working independently of Schoenberg, was evolving in a related but only somewhat atonal direction, employing the additional element of Hungarian folk music.

About the same time Paris and the musical world were startled by the compositions—large ballet works for the most part—of a comparative newcomer, Igor Stravinsky. Characterized by a complete negation of accepted rhythmic, harmonic, and formal procedures, Stravinsky's works seemed unlike any music ever heard before. These negations were later seen to be logical extensions of customary procedures; the works were polyrhythmic, polytonal, and the like. In their use of a sentiment-free expression and in their air of stark primitivism, however, they pointed to a dissonant future.

The war years, to about 1920, put a temporary halt to international communication among musicians. When the smoke of battles had been dissipated the musical scene revealed itself as one of frank experiment. Schoenberg, Stravinsky, and Bartók went their several ways; Ravel and other postimpressionists were strongly opposed by a group of French composers headed by Darius Milhaud. Experiments with extreme dissonance, with jazz elements, with Oriental and primitive flavors led to a decade of wild extravagance and cacophony. Out of this period of experiment grew a desire to return—no one knew to what. The clarity of eighteenth-century music became one ideal, and a Neo-Classicism arose. And out of Germany came Paul Hindemith, to bend the Neo-Classicism to his own expressive purposes, one of which resulted in the style called linear counterpoint.

In the years after 1930, with political upheavals in Europe and with new war clouds looming over the horizon, many leading composers came to the United States. Here and elsewhere throughout the musical world each had developed a following among native composers. In England, throughout Latin America, and in the United States the influence of Stravinsky, Schoenberg, Bartók, Milhaud, and Hindemith has been felt. But native composers of the last three decades have also begun to write individually and to contribute to the formation of a definite, unique, and indigenous American music. Among chamber-music composers Bloch, Piston, Porter, and Harris represent the older generation.

The foregoing incomplete and generalized sketch of the years from about 1890 to the present will provide a basis for discussing the activities of chamber-music composers during the last half century. It will enable us to group together those works that disclose similarities of structure and style and to relate the works of one style tendency to those of another. It will hope to show that contemporary composers differ in their expressive aims, in their technical means, and in their aesthetic results. They are not easily lumped together into one dissonant pot and disposed of with the term *modern*.

POST-ROMANTIC COMPOSERS

Fauré. Gabriel Fauré (1845–1924) composed his first chamber-music work in 1876 and his last in 1924. In the almost half a century that intervened between the two, musical styles elsewhere had undergone violent and far-reaching changes, to which Fauré remained essentially immune. The work of 1876 is a violin and piano sonata, Opus 13; a second sonata for the same combination appeared as Opus 108 in 1917. Other works include two piano quartets, Opus 15 (1879) and Opus 45 (1886); two piano quintets, Opus 89 (1906) and Opus 115 (1921); two cello sonatas, Opus 109 (1918) and Opus 117

(1921); a piano trio, Opus 120 (about 1923); and the last work, a string quartet, Opus 121 (1924).

These ten works are in a category separate from other chamber music of the time. Their general harmonic content, their melodic types, and even their forms are not essentially different from other post-Romantic works. A vigorous expression of honest sentiment, a mood that is forthright, delicate, or merry in turn, a fluency of utterance are all to be found in Fauré. And yet such terms do not adequately describe the music, for over and above such characteristics is a poetic feeling, a combination of directness and reticence. What in Schumann was akin to moodiness must be called reflectiveness in Fauré; the dramatic passion of Brahms is transformed by Fauré into something disembodied, remote, and objective; the chromatic richness of Wagner becomes in Fauré a considered and controlled manipulation of the chromatic scale. Many other late Romantic devices are in evidence, yet all are refined and brought into balance. We are told that Fauré is so typically French that only a born Frenchman can enjoy his music. But surely anyone with an ear for sensitive expression and subtle shading of tone quality can profit by the serene and dignified poetry that is reflected in Fauré.

D'Indy. With Vincent d'Indy (1851–1931) the case is somewhat similar. D'Indy's contributions to the literature are two piano trios, Opus 29 and Opus 98; two piano quartets, Opus 7 and Opus 81; three string quartets, Opera 35, 45, and 96; a string sextet, Opus 92; plus a few minor works. The piano quartet Opus 7 was written in 1878; the piano trio Opus 98, about 1929. During those fifty-one years D'Indy remained faithful to a reserved and somewhat conservative style. As befitted a pupil of Franck, he made considerable use of cyclical-form principles; as a Frenchman, he strove for clarity of intention and refined expression.

But in that clarity itself lies a possible source of musical weakness. D'Indy's clear lines and forms appear as the result more of calculation than of expressive necessity. His cyclical themes are transformed under the influence of a dominating intellect, sometimes at the expense of warmth or even real musical interest. Reserve, austerity, and technical excellence characterize D'Indy's chamber music. Charming moments occur often, and the presence of considerable rhythmic inventiveness contributes to that charm. Surrounded however, by a half century of music that appeals either through its noble sentiment or technical innovation, the music of D'Indy appears dated and something less than eternal.

Dohnányi. The Hungarian Ernst Dohnányi (1877–1960) must be placed in a separate category from the two preceding composers. In his early works the influence of Brahms was strongly felt, as was also the case with Fauré. But Dohnányi's original melodic turn and his contrapuntal skill came to minimize the external influence. The result, even in his Opus 1, the C minor piano quintet, published in 1902, is a quality of music that need yield to no other for freshness of thematic material, formal clarity, and rhythmic interest. Dohnányi's melodies often leaned toward sentimentality, but invariably they were kept under control. In the quintet, as in many later works, Dohnányi wrote multivoiced passages that are unequaled for sheer melodiousness and unashamed emotional appeal.

The quintet of 1902 was followed by three string quartets: Opus 7, in A major, 1903; Opus 15, in D flat, 1907; Opus 33, in A minor, about 1926. A small but effective string trio in C major, Opus 10, was published about 1904; a second piano quintet, in E flat minor, Opus 26, in 1919. The quartets reveal in ever-increasing measure those of Dohnányi's style traits that were first seen in the C minor piano quintet. In addition we see a complete mastery of form and a greater pungency and variety in the harmonic scheme. Not essentially influenced by contemporary developments, Dohnányi nevertheless progressed toward a more rugged melodic line and greater freedom in key relationships. The new developments are most strikingly revealed in the second piano quintet.

The outstanding features of the quintet are its contrapuntal texture and its angular melodic lines. The fugal last movement contains a plethora of augmentations, diminutions, inversions, and the like, to a degree virtually unknown in other works contemporaneous with it.

True to his expressive code, Dohnányi does not allow his contrapuntal fluency to obscure the dramatic or colorful purposes to which it is applied. In form, also, the quintet is unique. Although not based on cyclical-form principles, first-movement themes are quoted in the intermezzo and the finale and serve as unifying material. The intermezzo is a masterpiece of theme transformation and varied moods.

Reger. How shall one treat Max Reger (1873–1916)? No composer held in such esteem by so many sincere and intelligent musicians can be ignored. No composer who has written almost three dozen massive chamber-music works containing passages of real musical worth should be neglected. No composer whose technical attainments and contrapuntal skill are so self-evident dare remain unmentioned. Yet the forbidding quality of much of Reger's chamber music makes even adequate reporting of its content and direction more than difficult. In a book such as this, whose second part is devoted so largely to works in the present-day repertoire, one may be justified in attempting little more than a catalogue of Reger's chamber music. Only a minute portion of its bulk has found a place in the permanent literature. For those readers who find his polyphonic massiveness appealing, the following list is given: five string quartets; one clarinet quintet; two each of piano quintets, quartets, and trios; one string sextet; two string trios; and more than a dozen sonatas for various pairs of instruments. This author must honestly admit his own temperamental inability to look beyond its dryness, its thickness of texture, and its obscure forms to find the musical worth that its admirers claim for it.

IMPRESSIONIST COMPOSERS

Debussy. The imaginative and influential Claude Debussy (1862–1918), founder of musical impressionism, made few contributions to the chamber-music literature. A string quartet in G minor, Opus 10 (1893) and three sonatas for various instruments (1915–17) were his only works in the field. Outwardly, the quartet owes much to Franck: the cyclical principle is at work in three of its four movements. And it owes as much to Russian contemporaries, of whose music Debussy had some knowledge: the whole-tone scale is an important element in the quartet's melodic line, as it is in certain Russian folk music. But the content of the quartet, its sensitivity, and its general atmosphere are Debussy's own. In the 1890s quantity of tone and variety of color were closely related to musical quality, as they are in Richard Strauss's early symphonic poems, and richness of emotional expression was deemed an essential. The quartet's cool restraint and lack of blatancy immediately showed the way to a new kind of music. Suggesting rather than stating, concerned more with the color of the fleeting moment than with form and structure, and characterized by shimmering arpeggios and tremolos, the new music reflected the aims of symbolist poets and painters who were called impressionists. The latter term stands in opposition to realism, the outstanding exponents of which were the post-Romanticists.

In later works Debussy's technique was expanded. Unprepared or unresolved dissonances made their appearance; a greater freedom of modulation based on enharmonic changes[1] became characteristic, and a texture became typical in which contrapuntal and outspokenly homophonic devices were freely alternated. The consistent use of the new technique created a style eminently suited to the aims of the impressionists. Preoccupation with isolated sounds and with new color effects achieved through the increased use of dissonance, employment of a greater variety of chords, rapid changes of harmony, and a departure from the accepted methods of thematic development all became characteristics of the new music.

In the G minor quartet, however, not all the new techniques are yet apparent. Orthodox methods of theme development are still in evidence; a variety of simple repetitions, of sequence modulation, of rhythmic transformations, and even some contrapuntal imitation are present. The forms of the individual movements, too, correspond rather closely to the traditional patterns: sonata-form, scherzo with trio, and song form. With the retention of all these customary devices, it is inevitable that one feels the quartet's kinship with earlier works. But there is also a feeling of great originality in Debussy's employment

---

[1] The device whereby a note, E flat, let us say, is transformed (in notation) to D sharp, and whereby a whole new range of keys is made available.

of short melodic figures, of sustained trills, of colorful tremolos and repeated notes. The general atmosphere of the music is new; it is characterized by a refinement and elegance, by a delicacy of expression, and by a variety of veiled colors virtually unknown in earlier music. The innovations that Debussy introduced into this quartet became commonplaces in the works of later composers who were influenced by him. Thus the quartet stands on the dividing line between the turgid, emotionally rich music of the late nineteenth century and the objective, somewhat intangible music of the early twentieth.

The three sonatas—lesser works in all respects—include one for cello and piano (1915), one for flute, viola, and harp (1916), and one for violin and piano (1917). Each contains three movements, and an air of spontaneity—almost of improvisation—dominates throughout, except in a few passages in the violin sonata. Themes are declamatory, pastoral, or piquant in turn; they are stated briefly, then elaborated in typical impressionist fashion, after which they give way to other themes. One of Debussy's purposes in his later years was to free his music from thralldom to Germanic idioms, to express himself strongly against the intrusion of programmatic materials (as in Wagner) and even predominantly intellectual activity (as in Strauss). Thus it is to be expected that he refrained from writing in conventional forms in these sonatas.

Ravel. The single string quartet of Maurice Ravel (1875–1937), like the quartet of Debussy, is an early work. Composed in 1902–3 and dedicated to Fauré, it represents an early period in Ravel's development. The later typical preoccupation with isolated, glistening colors—to the virtual exclusion of thematic or formal interest—is not always present. Singularly melodious and regular in its sonata-form, the first movement is precise and economical in its use of thematic material. The scherzo is agitated and broadly lyrical in turn. The final movement of the quartet, however, employs many of the devices that became characteristic in Ravel's later works. An expressive melody, for example, is suddenly interrupted by a vivid splash of colorful sound, introduced by means of rapid tremolos on a short melodic fragment. And again, sweeping arpeggio figures accompany a sustained phrase and serve to veil the underlying harmonies most effectively. The finale as a whole is a dramatic movement in which a variety of meters—5/4 and 5/8 among them—contribute to a restlessness of mood. It provides a striking preview of what the impressionistic style will later contain.

The Introduction and Allegro, for harp solo with accompaniment furnished by flute, clarinet, and string quartet, was written about 1906. Although it is sometimes found on chamber-music programs, the work is essentially an orchestral piece, hence requires no further mention here.

In 1915 Ravel composed a piano trio in A minor. That work reveals the full development of his impressionism. Extreme use of arpeggio figures, rapid repeated notes and tremolos through long passages, many harmonics (overtones) in the string parts, and increased range in the piano all contributed to the extension of Ravel's color palette. Harmonies based on parallel use of neighboring triads (akin to the old *faux bourdon*), added seconds and sixths in chords, and unresolved dissonances gave the work its quality of freshness. Themes based on modal formulas and scales that create pentatonic patterns supplied an exotic tinge to the melodic line. Free phrase structures, an avoidance of symmetry, and an absence of traditional development devices contributed to a breakdown of accepted forms. And above all, an avoidance of sentimental expression and emotional tumult gave rise to the cool, objective, colorful, and aloof utterance that is typical of Ravel's music.

SERIAL COMPOSERS

Schoenberg. Had Arnold Schoenberg (1874–1951) stopped composing in 1910, his place in the history of music would be easily defined. A string sextet, *Verklärte Nacht,* was written about 1899 and published as Opus 4 in 1905; two string quartets, Opus 7 and Opus 10, appeared in 1907 and 1910, respectively. In those works Schoenberg disclosed himself as a fluent, impassioned Romanticist. The one-movement sextet employed the technique and the form of the tone poem and became a masterpiece of dramatic expression and emotional variety in a rich, eloquent, and subjective texture. The quartets, equally subjective in content, but characterized by four-movement patterns, represent other aspects of late Romanticism. The first quartet contains suggestions of cyclical form, in that many of its first-movement themes occur in later sections of the work; the second includes a part for soprano voice. All three contain Wagnerian climaxes; chromatic harmonies and intense lyric melodies are found throughout. With these compositions the last step in the expansion of subjective emotional expression had been taken. Yet in some respects even these works contained within themselves tentative steps toward Schoenberg's future style development.

The path that development was to take was revealed in the *Kammersymphonie*, Opus 9, written about 1906. There Schoenberg abandoned the tonic triad to a large extent and based his themes on successions of fourths: the negation of tonality was made possible and the road to atonality was opened. In the quartets two further elements of his new style are to be seen: (a) a theme seldom appears in a concrete form, but is varied on each appearance, and (b) the melodic line becomes angular to an extreme degree, embraces leaps of major sevenths, minor ninths, and similar large intervals. Expansion of those elements, to the virtual exclusion of customary relationships between one tone and another, is seen in *Pierrot Lunaire*, Opus 21, written in 1912. In that work twenty-one short poems are set to music in a half-recited, half-sung style, to the accompaniment of piano, flute, clarinet, violin, and cello. Intricate contrapuntal passages, rhapsodic sections, and a wealth of new instrumental colors occur in the cycle.

Then followed a group of works in which Schoenberg's probing among tonal resources became systematized. A serenade for mandolin, guitar, two clarinets, and string trio, with a part for male voice in one of its seven movements, was published as Opus 24 about 1923. A woodwind quintet, Opus 26, appeared in 1924. In 1926, as Opus 29, came a suite for piano, three string, and three woodwind instruments. A third string quartet was published, as Opus 30, in 1927. With this group of four works the principles of the "twelve-tone system" were clarified. Schoenberg and his disciples became eloquent in their explantations of the system and have been of great influence on a whole generation of later composers.

The twelve tones refer to the complete chromatic scale. In the system, as finally laid down by several of Schoenberg's pupils, the notes of that scale are arranged in an arbitrary manner; the resulting series of tones, called a tone row, may be inverted, may be played backward, and that retrograde version may be inverted. Those four chromatic lines then become the basis for the construction of the desired piece. Melodies are drawn out of them, chords are constructed out of them (the first three tones of the row may form one "triad," the following three another, and so on), and various prescribed actions may be taken. Apparently in the strictest kind of writing the entire series must be heard before any portion may be repeated.

Example 61, drawn from the suite, Opus 29, will illustrate the procedure. The basic form of the row is given in Example 61a. Examples 61b, c, and d disclose the way in which the rules are applied in musical creation; and they disclose further the fascinating mathematical possibilities of this purely abstract system of composition.

It must be emphasized, however, that the twelve-tone system describes only the technical aspects of Schoenberg's music. Every variety of music has its own principles and formulas. Schoenberg has merely substituted his formulas for the diatonic, chords-built-on-thirds, tonic-dominant formulas that served music from the early seventeenth century to the late nineteenth. His compositions must be evaluated for their musical results, for the quality of the musical responses to which they give rise.

The experiments of Schoenberg and his school, which in two large steps led from post-Romanticism to the tone-row technique, were soon seen as a reaction against the impressionistic style. Impressionism was concerned with color; the new atonal music was at first not interested in that element. Impressionism had its roots in the tonal system; the new music led away from that system in an attempt to develop its own. Impressionism often took the form of program music; the new music was abstract and severe. Early impressionism provided an outlet for subjective sentiment; the new music, which soon came to be called

Example 61 Schoenberg, Opus 29

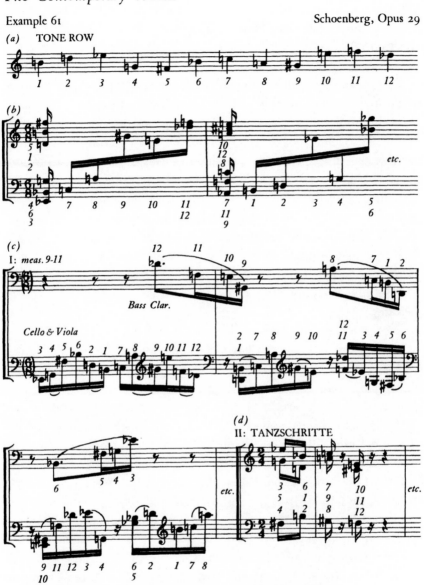

By permission of the copyright owners, Universal Edition, Vienna.

expressionistic, avoided emotional display and confined itself largely to bare, impersonal melodic lines. The term *expressionism* is obviously misleading, since it applies equally well to all music; it is no longer in general use.

Schoenberg's fourth quartet, Opus 37, was composed in 1936 and published in 1939. In this work a mood of relaxation may be sensed. The close imitations that were characteristic of the works of the middle period, from Opus 26 to Opus 36, are less in evidence. The lyric qualities of the music approach those of Romanticism, and the tone rows are employed much less rigidly than formerly. The quartet presents conventional forms in its four movements (sonata-form, minuet and trio, two-part slow movement, and sonata-rondo, respectively), but thematic restatements and recapitulations are virtually never exact. Indeed, perpetual variation and continuous development of themes became features of the system. The result is that the forms can be grasped only after thorough analysis, scarcely ever at first hearing.

Two single-movement works, a string trio, Opus 45 (1946), and a fantasy for violin with piano accompaniment, Opus 47 (1949), closed the series of Schoenberg's chamber-music works. Here again, derivations from conventional forms may be sensed but not aurally perceived. The devices of varied thematic statements, freely developing recapitulations, and constantly changing textures tend to conceal the formal divisions and give a rhapsodic, flowing character to the music.

Berg. Of the many composers who adopted the twelve-tone system, Alban Berg (1885–1935), Ernst Krenek (b. 1900), and Anton von Webern (1883–1945) may be singled out. Berg, one of Schoenberg's earliest disciples and pupils, was not primarily a chamber-music composer. Two early works, a quartet, Opus 3 (1909), and the Lyric Suite for quartet (1927), exhibit a tendency to introduce Wagnerian moods and melodic devices into the system. The evidence is strong that Berg attempted to combine the richness of late nineteenth-century Romantic expression with the twelve-tone technique. The greater amount of emotional warmth in his music reveals that to a large extent he succeeded in that attempt.

The Lyric Suite is in six movements and is based in large part on conventional forms treated freely. A sonata-form movement without a development section, a rondo, and a scherzo with trio are among the forms represented. The tone-row technique is adhered to rather consistently, yet Berg succeeds in expressing a greater variety of moods than his preceptor, Schoenberg. The movements of the suite are arranged in three contrasting pairs, and in each pair the contrast is widened. Thus an allegretto is followed by an andante, an allegro by an adagio, and a presto by a largo. Textures are full and sonorous throughout, and the technical excellence of the work is manifest on every page.

Krenek. Ernst Krenek was not a Schoenberg pupil, but the influence of Schoenberg's music is evident in his works from about 1935. His earliest compositions were based on a solid contrapuntal style; the Neo-Classical objectivity and dissonant harmonies also present in them did not quite conceal an undercurrent of Romantic expression. An interest in jazz idioms led to the writing of his famous jazz opera, *Jonny spielt auf* ("Johnny Strikes Up the Band"), in 1927. Three published string quartets—No. 1, Opus 6 (1922), No. 3, Opus 20 (1923), and No. 5, Opus 65 (1930)—represent these earlier styles. The quartet No. 6, Opus 78 (1936), reveals the impact of Schoenberg's style on Krenek. A seventh string quartet, Opus 96 (1944), three trios, and a few miscellaneous works composed (without opus numbers) in the following decade continue in the twelve-tone technique. In Krenek's compositions of this latest period the tone row is not always stated in its entirety; rather, several three- or four-tone motives are drawn from the row, and these short motives then provide the thematic material out of which the works are constructed.

Webern. Unlike Berg, who sought to develop the twelve-tone system in the direction of Romantic expression and expansion, Anton von Webern moved toward ever-greater concentration, refinement, and brevity. Two sets of pieces for string quartet—Opus 5 (1909)

and Opus 9 (1913)—reflect these characteristics. The first set of five
pieces requires less than nine minutes for the performance of its hundred thirty-five measures, while the second set of six pieces totals
fifty-six measures with performance time of about five minutes. Similarly, the three movements of a string quartet, Opus 28 (1938), require barely six minutes.

The extreme brevity and concentration are but two of the elements
that distinguish Webern's works from other contemporary compositions. The texture is thin to the point of sparseness, as Example 62,

Example 62   Webern, Opus 28
                                                     1ˢᵗ movement

By permission of the copyright owners, Boosey & Hawkes, London, and New York.

drawn from the quartet, Opus 28, reveals. In addition, that texture
consists essentially of a single melody, the tones of which are spread
consecutively among the various instruments; and virtually every
tone is differently inflected. One tone is executed pizzicato, another
col legno (played with the wood stick of the bow), a third *am Steg*
(near the bridge), and so on. A brief tremolo a fraction of a second
in duration may animate a single tone; a sharp accent may emphasize
another; and an artificial harmonic (whereby a flutelike tone of high
pitch is produced) may color yet another. Further, meticulously
marked dynamic indications serve to give each tone an individual
value. A brief crescendo and diminuendo marked across one short
tone, a range of dynamics from *piano* to *pianissississimo* across a two- or
three-tone passage, a subtle series of gradations in tempo across a

two-measure phrase are devices found regularly. With this complex of expressive aids at his command, Webern succeeded in imparting a constantly changing series of tone colors to his music.

The principle of canonic writing came to play an ever-increasing role in Webern's works, but the more complex devices of canon are employed far more frequently than the more usual means. For example, in his quartet for violin, clarinet, tenor saxophone, and piano, Opus 22 (1930), the first movement is filled with passages in which the second entrance of a canonic pair of themes is inverted. And in a chamber concerto, Opus 24 (1934), for nine instruments, short segments of the tone row are treated canonically—but in retrograde inversion. And in both works, canons at the third, sixth, or tritone are more common than canons at the octave.

Another principle, that of perpetual variation, looms large in Webern's works, as it does in Schoenberg's. Rarely is a thematic statement recapitulated in its original form; rarely does a rhythmic figure reappear unaltered. Thus, with constantly changing instrumental colors, with constantly changing dynamics, and with a constantly changing set of themes, Webern's music gives an over-all effect of ceaseless flow, plasticity, and kaleidoscopic color.

BARTÓK

The six quartets of Béla Bartók (1881–1945) are among the most successful of twentieth-century chamber-music works. In a tonal language that is unique in its flexibility, Bartók created a series of works that are unsurpassed in the variety of their sonorous effects, in the power of their rhythmic appeal, but more especially in the rich expressiveness they achieve in their dissonant, atonal idiom. Beginning with the second string quartet (the first, written about 1908, belongs to a style category that Bartók did not pursue in later works), published in 1920, each succeeding one disclosed new musical possibilities. Thus the second quartet contains moments of deepest gloom and frenzied energy in a sonorous and somewhat contrapuntal texture. Successions of fourths and fifths in the melodic line, considerable use of parallel seconds in the harmony, and complete modulatory freedom provide the work with a dissonant acridity that precludes any possibility of sentimental expression.

Contrapuntal writing is noticeably absent in the third quartet, published in 1927. In its place comes a preoccupation with brutal chords, with running scale passages, and with broken, hesitant rhythms. In spite of its apparent complexity of sound, much of the writing is two-part; octaves and unisons now became a characteristic of Bartók's quartet style. The fourth quartet was published in 1928. The great ability of Bartók to devise new instrumental effects, seen in the earlier works, here reaches new heights. Tight chordal formations, long glissandos, percussive bowing effects, concentrated tone clusters, new employment of pizzicato techniques—all are here in the fourth quartet, added to the emotional tension created by barbaric rhythms and unrelieved dissonance.

In the fifth and sixth quartets, written in 1934 and 1936, respectively, as in the *Contrasts*, for piano, violin, and clarinet, of 1938, Bartók turned away from the relentless, acrid dissonance of earlier works. The fifth quartet even bears some relationship to the key of B flat; but it is a key in which major and minor are employed simultaneously, in which modal implications are present, and one which Bartók does not hesitate to employ in its widest aspects. Certain outspoken diatonic chords and even extended diatonic passages occur. And in the sixth quartet the quantity of sheer dissonance is lessened. In its place comes a melodically derived dissonance; the progression of individual parts tends to absorb the tonal clashes, and a degree of warm sentiment almost completely missing in earlier works emerges.

From a late Romantic standpoint the quartets of Bartók seem cold, forbidding, and devoid of expression. From any standpoint they are reserved and impersonal. Yet their general quality, their indefinable air of sincerity, plus the magnificence of their purely instrumental effects and savage rhythms, combine to give them a deservedly high place in twentieth-century literature. One suspects that many of the barbaric rhythmic effects and exotic turns of phrase in the quartets are derived from eastern European folk music. Bartók's position as one of the most eminent of folklorists makes the surmise likely. But the variety of texture, the dignity of phrasing in the quieter moments, and the subtle form extensions are purely his own. Of all the many experiments that have led to a general widening of tonal possibilities in the twentieth century, those of Bartók seem to hold the greatest promise for the future.

NEO-CLASSICAL COMPOSERS

In the years immediately after World War I the style of impressionism was favored by a number of important composers. That style, introduced by Debussy and carried forward at first by Ravel, seemed for a time to be the perfect antidote for the extreme subjectivity and overemotionalism characteristic of the late Romantic period. By the 1920s, however, the realization came that impressionism, too, was but another phase of Romanticism. The vague and nebulous textures, the elaborate harmonic structures, and the free forms of impressionistic music did not satisfy a musical world that sought to rebuild a workable aesthetic basis for composition. Inevitably, reactions to impressionism set in. One reaction took shape in France itself, instigated by a group of young composers influenced by Erik Satie (1866–1925); another rose in Germany and was given impetus by disciples of Ferruccio Busoni (1866–1924). In both cases new musical ideals were sought—clarity of form and purpose, objectivity, economy, and a fresh approach to the diatonic scale and diatonic harmony. A similarity to the ideals of the late eighteenth century is at once apparent here. It was perhaps inevitable that the new styles that arose as results of these reactions were called Neo-Classical. And even though the styles thus grouped have many points of dissimilarity, the Neo-Classical label still serves as a convenient means of differentiating them from impressionism and other styles.

Milhaud. In a history of harmonic processes since the sixteenth century, one important topic concerns the enlarging of the basic harmonic unit, the chord. In the time of Palestrina that unit was most often a triad composed of thirds superimposed on each other. Each new development in harmonic complexity since that time has been accompanied, among other things, by the addition of another third to the basic unit. For a considerable period the major seventh chord, C-E-G-B, for example, represented the height of harmonic daring. Later the ninth, and still later the eleventh and thirteenth chords came into use. The latter—C-E-G-B-D-F-A in one version— was with difficulty perceived as one chord; its extreme spread and the fact that it contains within itself all the tones of the diatonic scale tend to divest it of any great chordal feeling. During the late nineteenth century the conviction arose that the thirteenth chord really contained the elements of several chords: the tonic triads of C major, G major, and D minor, respectively. Forward-looking composers made tentative use of such related chords, placing one harmony above another. Their use naturally suggested the employment of other unrelated chords. And so, in small steps and in full accord with historical precedent, the simultaneous use of two tonalities resulted. At the hands of Darius Milhaud (b. 1892) that expansion of harmonic resources received its most consistent employment. Polytonality, for so the practice is called, became an important element in Milhaud's style about 1918.

The early quartets of Milhaud have all but disappeared from general circulation. According to Edwin Evans,[2] the first three (1912, 1915, 1916) are distinguished by excellent contrapuntal writing in a strictly diatonic setting and by great clarity of form. During the course of a diplomatic visit to Brazil (1917–19) Milhaud composed his fourth quartet, in which polytonal devices received extended treatment. To make certain that the duality of keys was perceived, it became necessary to establish each tonality with the utmost clarity; diatonic writing in the several parts was essential. The latter, already a factor in Milhaud's earlier style, became even more pronounced in later works and led to the criticism that his melodic line was perfunctory and overly simple. No one denied its clarity and appeal nor Milhaud's technical competence.

Following his return to Paris and his association, about 1919, with the group of composers called "Les Six,"[3] Milhaud composed a fifth

[2] In *Cobbett's Cyclopedic Survey of Chamber Music*, II, 140–45.

[3] Arthur Honegger, Louis Durey, Georges Auric, Francis Poulenc, and Germaine Tailleferre were others of "Les Six."

quartet, dedicated to Arnold Schoenberg. Evans quotes passages from that work to illustrate the "uncompromising nature of the texture." The sixth quartet, 1922, and the seventh, 1925, mark a return to a relatively simple, unassuming, and melodious polytonality. Milhaud composed no fewer than eleven additional quartets between 1932 and 1951, for a total of eighteen (that is, one more than Beethoven). It was apparently Milhaud's intention to retire from string-quartet writing at that point, for the eighteenth quartet bears an inscription to that effect. And in spite of many individual differences between the early and late quartets, they form a stylistically consistent series. Impassioned or placid passages, quiet lyricism, and vigorous rhythms are basic to the works, and technical competence is characteristic of virtually all of them. Milhaud's forms and harmonies were mainly those of Neo-Classicism; the few excursions into jazz idioms and occasional experiments with acrid dissonance are neither numerous nor long-lasting enough to affect his normal style.

The fourteenth and fifteenth quartets, completed in 1949, mark a *tour de force* in Milhaud's work. Each quartet is thematically independent of the other and has its own distinctive moods and textures. Yet both quartets may be played simultaneously, to form an octet.

The string quartets stand at the center of Milhaud's chamber music, but he did not neglect other combinations. Four quintets, in each of which a different instrument (piano, bass, viola, cello) is added to the string quartet, were composed between 1951 and 1956; a string sextet followed in 1959. In addition, this extremely prolific composer wrote string trios, sonatas for various combinations, works for wind instruments, and the like.

Hindemith. An eighteenth-century musician was expected to be a complete master of his craft. It was normal to find composer, performer on several instruments, teacher, and musical administrator combined in one person. In the twentieth century, with its high degree of specialization, such universality is a decided exception. Of all modern musicians, probably Paul Hindemith (1895–1963) met eighteenth-century specifications most closely. Professionally active as a violinist and violist, he was a capable pianist and clarinetist as well, and he privately admitted his prowess on the bassoon. As a conductor and member of several university faculties he proved himself equally competent. Most important, his compositions gave him a leading place in the musical world during his lifetime.

Hindemith's early works disclosed his great skill in contrapuntal writing and his daring in harmonic innovation, even though some passages reveal conventional ideas that are post-Romantic in origin. Among these works is his first string quartet, Opus 10, in F minor.[4] With the second quartet, Opus 16, performed at a Donaueschingen festival in 1921, Hindemith's future path was revealed. Tendencies present in that work, notably the domination of melodic (horizontal) over harmonic (vertical) elements, led the way to the style of linear counterpoint with which Hindemith identified himself during the following decades. The third quartet (1922) revealed the full development of that style.

That work, making great technical demands on its performers, contains a degree of free contrapuntal writing not found in the earlier quartets. Fugal passages and close imitations appear in large numbers. The counterpoints exhibit little of the old relationship between parts. Each part follows its own destiny, realizes its own melodic implications quite independently of the others. The resulting dissonances are thus of another type than the dissonances, say, of Schoenberg, Bartók, or Milhaud. Hindemith's represent the logical completion of linear tendencies, while the others result from chordal complexes or melodic thickening. No concern with harmonious sound deflects the composer from his aim of making each voice really independent. In other sections of the quartet suggestions of polytonality, of thick chromaticism, or of merely expanded chordal writing provide the necessary contrasts of texture.

The fourth quartet, Opus 32, published in 1924, is the most con-

---

[4] The numbering of Hindemith's string quartets is ambiguous. He apparently discarded his actual first quartet, Opus 2, and numbered the second quartet, Opus 10, in F minor, as the "first"; Opus 16 became the second, and so on. In *Cobbett's* the quartets are so referred to, but in *Grove's Dictionary* the counting begins with Opus 2; consequently in the latter Opus 10 is "No. 2." In this book we have accepted Hindemith's own numbering.

sistent of Hindemith's chamber-music works in its employment of linear counterpoint. From beginning to end it embodies a polyphonic texture. The first movement contains a fugue (first theme) and a double fugue (second theme); one of that movement's episodes consists of a simultaneous development of all three themes. The second movement, whose inner voices are in canon with entrances an augmented octave (C flat-C) apart, contains a wealth of free contrapuntal weaving in the outer parts also. The polyphonic complex is lightened to some extent in the third movement, a march, but even there a full-bodied texture is employed. The fourth is a passacaglia: twenty-seven variations of a seven-measure theme lead to a fugal coda in fast tempo. Throughout the entire quartet an intensity of purpose is felt: in the sustained rhythmic drive of the first movement, in the almost sixty-measure crescendo from *pp* to *fff* in the march, in the inexorable tonal growth of the passacaglia, and in the relentless hammering of the final coda. In all respects the quartet reaches new heights of concentration and sonority.

Hindemith's fifth quartet, without opus number, was written in 1943 and carried on its title page an indication of tonality. Thus he, in company with Bartók, Stravinsky, and others, made the return to a tonal framework. But the tonality—E flat in this case—remained simply a point of departure. Modulations are abrupt, distant, and dissonant; major and minor modes occur simultaneously, and certain passages suggest polytonal writing. In earlier works dissonances were the inescapable results of strict contrapuntal writing; here, in the E flat quartet, they serve as elements of harmonic color. Possibly as a consequence of the new treatment of dissonance, the texture is lightened considerably. Consistent use of polyphony is no longer characteristic. Such contrapuntal passages as occur are incidental to Hindemith's processes of thematic development rather than essential elements of his style. With the return to tonality and the clarifying of texture come an increased directness and vitality in the music itself. Great energy had always been a characteristic of Hindemith's music; here the energy of earlier works has been translated into vitality and driving power, but these are made to contrast with moods of lyricism and serenity. A sixth quartet, composed in 1945, shows a still lighter mood and a lessening of the contrapuntal writing, although the finale of the work is written largely in canon in spite of a scherzolike style.

Almost two dozen sonatas for one instrument and piano were composed in two periods, about 1918–23 and 1935–49. Virtually every instrument had at least one sonata written for it, including, in the second period, one sonata for each woodwind and brass instrument from flute to tuba. The sonatas range from large four-movement works in an uncompromising quasi-atonal idiom (the cello sonata of 1923) to brief, two-movement works relaxed in character and comparatively mild in point of dissonance (the bassoon sonata of 1938). Sets of variations, short marches, elaborate fugues, and clear sonata-form pieces are among the separate movements found in the sonatas, and no two are alike in structure. Yet virtually all of them disclose Hindemith's technical mastery and quality of imagination, along with a gradual change of harmonic style from his harsh dissonance of the 1920s to the serene tonality of the late 1940s.

The six string quartets, the many sonatas, and a dozen other works for various combinations[5] disclose a composer second to none in tonal resourcefulness, expressive sensibility, and variety of mood. Hindemith's successive styles were of great influence on other composers; he became one of the most important of twentieth-century musicians. Having first shown the way to the logical expansion of polyphonic concepts and thereby leading the way to the dissonant style of linear counterpoint (that is, counterpoint freed from all vertical or harmonic restrictions), he then developed an equally vigorous but more restrained manner that again allowed subjective emotional expression to emerge.

Prokofieff. The major importance of Serge Prokofieff (1891–1953) was in fields other than chamber music. As one of the leading figures in contemporary music during his lifetime and one of the outstanding exponents of Neo-Classical style tendencies, Prokofieff became one of

---

[5] A quintet for clarinet and strings, two string trios, a quartet for clarinet and strings, a septet, an octet, and several other works for combinations of winds and strings are among the published and unpublished compositions not discussed here.

the best known and most frequently performed composers. While his contributions to the chamber-music literature are few, they are significant in their stylistic aspects.

Among the earliest of these contributions, a sextet in G minor called *Overture on Jewish Themes,* Opus 34 (1919), may be singled out. The work is for clarinet, string quartet, and piano, and it reflects Prokofieff's interest in folk rhythms and melodies. Humor, bizarre touches, and lyricism—all of which became essential elements of his later style—are here combined in an attractive way. A quintet for oboe, clarinet, violin, viola, and bass, Opus 39 (1924), also in G minor, provides marked contrast to the sextet. Complex forms, harsh dissonance, intricate rhythms, and complete objectivity are typical in this work. They represent a stylistic change that Prokofieff did not pursue in later works.

Two string quartets, B minor, Opus 50 (1930), and F major, Opus 92 (1942), mark a return of the folk influence in his chamber music. Although Caucasian folk melodies are suggested and even quoted in these quartets, the melodies are skillfully transformed and absorbed into Prokofieff's own melodic idiom. Both works are in three movements, but the first quartet is serene and even grave, while the second is colorful and at times brilliant.

Two sonatas for violin and piano, F minor, Opus 80 (1938–46), and D major, Opus 94 (originally composed for flute in 1943 but arranged for violin in 1944), and a sonata for cello and piano, C major, Opus 119 (1949), again show the wide contrasts typical of Prokofieff. Moods range from dry humor to fierce abandon, from suave lyricism to intense drama, and the quality of his imagination and technical achievements is everywhere apparent.

Prokofieff was seldom heavy or dull in his writing; a lightness of touch characterized even his slow movements. Lyric melodies abound, of a kind that at times suggest traces of Romantic sentiment. In spite of his free use of dissonance, he did not often stray too far or too long from established tonal centers. Early works (we speak here of compositions in other fields) were characterized by extreme instrumental range, by a fondness for the high registers, and by elements of grotesqueness and ironic humor. Later compositions, including those in the field of chamber music, disclosed a renewed interest in lyric melody, a less complex rhythmic scheme, and a partial abandonment of objective, remote expression.

Shostakovich. Dmitri Shostakovich (b. 1906) is in many respects similar to Prokofieff. His dozen chamber-music works disclose a Classical clarity of form, a mildly dissonant style, with strong elements of lyric grace and a marked tendency to employ humorous or ironic sentiments. His principal works in the field up to 1960 are eight string quartets, a piano quintet, a piano trio, and a cello sonata, virtually all conventional in form and idiom but widely different in expressive content.

The quietly melodious C major first quartet (Opus 49, 1938) is followed by an atmospheric and somewhat melancholy A major (Opus 69, 1944), a dramatic and moody F major (Opus 73, 1946), and a reposeful, lyric quartet in D major (Opus 83, 1949). With the fifth quartet, in B flat (Opus 91, 1951), the scope and size of Shostakovich's quartets change radically, for this work is symphonic in dimensions, intense in expression, and complex in structure. The cyclical-form principle plays a large part in the long and dramatic first and last movements, and a songful slow movement gives a moment of repose.

The sixth quartet, in D major (Opus 101, 1956), differs from the earlier quartets in its wide use of polyphonic texture—especially in a passacaglia that serves as the slow movement. The seventh quartet, in F sharp major (Opus 108, 1960), and the eighth, in C minor (Opus 110, 1960), show even more use of cyclical form than the fifth quartet; in addition, the two quartets are linked thematically. The common motive is based on the tones D-E flat-C-B, which in German nomenclature (D-Es-C-H) represent the composer's name (D. Sch.). The seventh quartet contains many variants of this motive, while in the eighth the motive is heard in its pure form and becomes basic to many of the themes in all four movements. To emphasize the autobiographical content of this quartet still further, Shostakovich here quotes themes from his own works.

The piano quintet, in G minor (Opus 57, 1940), and the piano trio, in E minor (Opus 67, 1944), represent yet other aspects of Shostakovich's style. The quintet, in five movements, contains a fugue whose theme is a melodious Russian folk song; the skill of the composer in combining lyric melody and rigorous polyphony in this movement is worthy of mention. The trio, written during the closing years of World War II, is filled with foreboding and deep melancholy; yet Shostakovich cancels these moods (in the finale) in a particularly noble and musically effective way. The variety of moods found in the quartets is continued in these works with piano, and the variety of harmonic devices likewise. In spite of sharp dissonances in many passages and hints of polytonality in others, Shostakovich remained largely within the confines of the tonal system.

Martinů. Bohuslav Martinů (1890–1959), after a hazardous existence in war-torn Europe, emerged in the 1940s as one of the most imposing of Czech composers. His long residence in Paris, where he was influenced by the successive styles of Stravinsky, perhaps accounts for the interest in rhythmic elements that his second quartet (1926) discloses. A play with cross accents and a variety of phrases written across measure lines became typical of those years. A piano trio (1930), on the other hand, is based on a solidly contrapuntal style. Other works show Martinů's tendency to employ first one, then the other of those styles. Thus a string quintet and a string sextet (1929 and 1932, respectively) embody the rhythmic characteristics of the second quartet. A third quartet (1932), with overt jazz devices, and a piano quintet (1934) continue the rhythmic style. On the other hand, the piano quartet of 1942 discloses a return to the polyphonic style of the 1930s. A similar type of stylistic alternation is to be observed in still later works; these include the fourth and fifth string quartets (1936 and 1938) and a second piano quintet (1944).

Other Composers. Almost every musical work, to whatever style period it may belong, can roughly be classified according to the following categories: (a) it contains new elements that lead in the direction of a new style; (b) it is one of the masterworks that realizes the full implications of its particular style; (c) it discloses evidence of the style's decline; (d) it is directly influenced by the works of a more powerful composer or is a pale imitation of those works; (e) it contains new elements that, seen in retrospect, lead nowhere; (f) it is purely of local interest. Obviously the categories are not mutually exclusive.

The chamber-music works discussed thus far in this book have in the main been representative of the first three categories. As such, their qualities are self-evident. But a sizable literature of contemporary works that must be placed in the minor categories (the last three) exists also. There are literally hundreds of such works ranging from those of Bax to Zemlinsky. Space limitations, among other things, forbid the discussion of this literature. One group of them is seen to reflect the style characteristics of Bartók, say; another embodies the twelve-tone system of Schoenberg or the Neo-Classicism of Hindemith; still another employs sterile experiment. Nor are these works confined to particular countries; the new developments in twentieth-century music have been world-wide in their effects.

A bare catalogue of names will illustrate the extent of this minor literature. Among the English, Arnold Bax (1883–1953), Frank Bridge (1879–1941), and Ralph Vaughan Williams (1872–1958) deserve mention. Italians include Alfredo Casella (1883–1947), Francesco Malipiero (b. 1882), and Ottorino Respighi (1879–1936). The Spanish Joaquin Turina (1882–1949), the Rumanian Georges Enesco (1881–1955), the French Jacques Ibert (1890–1962) and Arthur Honegger (1892–1955), and the Brazilian Heitor Villa-Lobos (1887–1959) all composed chamber music. This incomplete list includes only the more prominent composers and only those not primarily associated with the United States. With all due respect to the musical qualities of the works of these composers—insofar as they are known to the present author—it seems advisable to let a later generation of musicians decide, on the basis of repeated performances, which of them deserve to live and which had best be forgotten.

The full import of the appearance of Igor Stravinsky (b. 1882) on the musical scene in Paris about 1909 can be gathered only through a discussion of his music for the ballet. Since so full a treatment is not appropriate here, it must suffice to describe briefly the nature of Stravinsky's innovations. The works written between 1910 and 1914 (music to *L'Oiseau de feu* and *Le Sacre du printemps* is perhaps the best known) contain elements drawn from many sources. Impressionistic passages in *L'Oiseau* stand opposite sections based on almost primitive writing. Extreme dissonance derived from new relations between individual tones, as in parts of *Le Sacre,* is contrasted with diatonic, clear consonance, notably in certain of *Petrouchka's* passages. Suggestions of polytonality appear side by side with overt use of "old-fashioned" melodic devices. But several features dominate all these works: an avoidance of sentiment, a mechanized and impartial play with all the elements of the tonal system, and an experimentation with new concepts of instrumentation.

Out of this mixture of style tendencies came Stravinsky's early chamber-music works. *Three Japanese Lyrics,* a set for voice, four winds, piano, and string quartet, is roughly contemporary with *Le Sacre du printemps* (1913) and was Stravinsky's first published chamber-music work. Although basically impressionistic in mood, the work illustrates several elements that became characteristic in later compositions. The combination of voice and a few instruments was used again in other sets of songs in 1914 and 1916, and yet again in songs composed in 1953 and 1954. Another element in the early song groups was the attempt to obtain complete objectivity—even to the limit of impersonal or mechanical expression. Stravinsky's method here was to displace the normal textual accents so that the sense of the words was virtually lost. Three Pieces for String Quartet, composed about 1914, and a one-movement concertino, also for string quartet (1920), revealed nationalistic and modal touches in turn. Another work, the *Histoire du soldat,* scored for clarinet, bassoon, trumpet, trombone, violin, bass, and percussion, and requiring the services of a conductor and a narrator for its complete performance, was written about 1918. Here the search for objectivity and a purely impersonal tone was renewed.

The Octet for Wind Instruments, for flute, clarinet, and pairs of bassoons, trumpets, and trombones, was published in 1924. In that work the subjective element was expunged completely. Instrumental color (and the warm sentiment usually associated with it) plays no part in the octet. The separate parts are so calculated, and the calculations are so reflected in meticulously indicated dynamic markings, that the tonal lines themselves stand forth clearly and impersonally. There is no need to "interpret" this work; expressive changes in tonal volume, with which performers traditionally inflect phrases—sometimes arbitrarily, hence subjectively—are neither required nor desired. In 1932 Stravinsky composed a Duo Concertante for violin and piano, and revealed his continued adherence to the objective style coupled with the use of pandiatonicism[6] and, consequently, more pungent dissonance.

More than twenty years elapsed before Stravinsky turned to chamber music again. A septet for three strings, three winds, and piano was composed about 1953. The influence of serial writing had become marked in Stravinsky's work about the early 1950s; in the septet that stylistic change became even more apparent. The three movements, all thematically related, include an allegro in modified sonata-form, a passacaglia, and a gigue. The themes are based on tone rows and are angular in the Schoenbergian manner. But rarely is a theme divided up among several instruments, as became typical in later works by Schoenberg and Webern; thus a thick and sonorous texture, often consisting of five or more contrapuntal lines, is most usually evident.

A set of songs roughly contemporaneous with the septet marked a further step in Stravinsky's complete conversion to serial writing. That work, *Three Songs from William Shakespeare,* for mezzo soprano, flute, clarinet, and viola, was composed in 1953. The tone

---

[6] The practice of employing added seconds, sixths, sevenths, etc., in diatonic chords, thus using most of the tones of the diatonic scale simultaneously.

rows employed here vary in length from four to seven tones and are introduced freely—sometimes in company with other tones that are not parts of the rows. Strict contrapuntal writing is most often avoided. And two small one-movement pieces from 1959 completed Stravinsky's espousal of the serial style, including the Webern characteristic of extreme brevity.

In the relatively few chamber-music works composed by Stravinsky across an almost fifty-year period one may see a virtual panorama of twentieth-century styles. Beginning in an impressionistic, "neoprimitive" manner, Stravinsky systematically exploited various aspects of Neo-Classicism, explored both extreme atonality and polytonality, and finally arrived at his own highly individual version of serial writing.

AMERICAN COMPOSERS

For all practical purposes this survey of chamber music in the United States may well begin with compositions written after World War I. Much chamber music was composed in the late nineteenth and early twentieth centuries, but there is little need to speak here of its composers—American Romanticists, post-Romanticists, postimpressionists, and the like. Elements of their respective styles were derived largely from corresponding European models; their works in general did not lead to the styles of contemporary American music.

The compositions of Charles Ives (1874–1954) provide a notable exception to this general statement. Ives was experimenting with form and composing in a dissonant, highly original style several years before his European contemporaries had gained wide recognition. Polytonality, atonality, and elements of serial writing are found in his two string quartets, a piano trio, and several violin sonatas, all written between 1896 and about 1920.

Stylistic multiplicity has characterized American chamber music since about 1925. That music reflects many combinations of trends—from post-Romantic to serial writing—found in the music of the major European composers, most of whom moved to the United States in the years about 1930. American composers cannot easily be grouped; many have changed styles in consecutive works, others have changed slowly across several decades. In the following account they are arranged roughly in an order from post-Romantic to serial styles. Any attempt to categorize them more closely would be futile.

Bloch. Ernest Bloch (1880–1959) was born in Switzerland but lived in the United States intermittently from about 1917. Much of his chamber music was written and published here, and he was active as a teacher in this country. In certain respects, then, he may be considered an American composer. Bloch composed his first string quartet in 1916; then, after a thirty-year gap, he composed four more in the decade 1946–56. Two piano quintets are spaced almost as widely: The first was composed about 1923, the second in 1957. His other chamber-music works include a set of three nocturnes for piano trio (1925), two violin sonatas (1920 and 1924), and a few smaller works for various combinations. A richness of emotional expression that can be ascribed to Bloch's Jewish ancestry, a rhythmic vitality in the best American tradition, a trace of impressionistic concern with the sound of isolated harmonies, and a few digressions into the world of quarter tones are all represented.

Taken as a whole the works are based on a unified and individual style. Virtually every work contains melodies in which augmented fourths are prominent, and in many cases two tonalities an augmented fourth apart are employed simultaneously. They are further unified by Bloch's penchant for presenting short thematic statements with an air of proclamation. Further, vital rhythmic figures and sonorous chordal textures appear in all of them. And all are characterized by great emotional variety, with moods ranging from intense lamentation to wild abandon.

Bloch's later chamber-music compositions, however—that is, the second to fifth string quartets and the second piano quintet—contain other stylistic elements not present in the earlier works. He did not remain immune to the influence of Schoenberg, but at Bloch's hands twelve-tone writing took on an individual form. Each of the larger works composed after 1946 contains one or more themes in which all twelve tones appear, in the Schoenbergian manner; but the other devices of the system—inversion, retrograde forms, perpetual variation, and the like—are seldom employed. Thus while tone rows appear in thematic statements, they do not dominate or even greatly affect the transitions, developments, and other formal sections, nor do they become basic to Bloch's harmonic structures. And in respect to texture, the post-1946 works are based on contrapuntal writing to a greater extent than were his early works. The first quartet (1916), the violin sonatas (1920 and 1924), and the nocturnes (1925) typically contained short thematic statements presented in rhapsodic fashion. The later works, by contrast, contain sections in canon as well as complete fugues and other contrapuntal movements. Yet these two major late additions to Bloch's style—twelve-tone thematic construction and a use of contrapuntal textures—did not come at the expense of the energetic, emotionally rich, and rhythmically varied components of his style.

Barber. The cello sonata (1932) and two string quartets (1936 and 1948) by Samuel Barber (b. 1910) present in clear fashion the essence of American post-Romanticism. Barber's style is essentially diatonic, in spite of a few chromatic touches that verge on serial writing. His range of moods is wide and his rhythms are vigorous and varied. The basic element is lyricism, however; emotional, dramatic, and expressive passages predominate and provide a strong link with the past. One of his most widely performed orchestral works, both here and in Europe, is the "Adagio for Strings," which is actually a movement from the first string quartet.

Piston. Walter Piston (b. 1894) is among the most eclectic of American composers. Dissonant counterpoint in the style of Hindemith, tight chordal formations similar to those of Stravinsky's early period, a rhythmic vitality akin to Bartók's, and an occasional angular melodic line reminiscent of Schoenberg's—all are found in his music. Yet these diverse elements are combined in a texture that is unique in its clarity and transparence. Symmetrical forms and contrapuntal textures, along with excellent part-writing in a harmonic scheme that is clearly tonally centered, are most typical. Probably to no other contemporary American composer does the term *Neo-Classical* apply so aptly.

Four string quartets (1933, 1935, 1947, and 1953), a piano trio (1935), a quintet for flute and strings (1942), and a piano quintet (1949) are Piston's principal chamber-music works. The technical qualifications of an accomplished composer are everywhere apparent, and the intellectual aspect is uppermost. An austere, detached tone characterizes much of his music, relieved at times by relaxed dance movements or vigorous rhythmic pieces.

Porter. The chamber music of Quincy Porter (b. 1897), more conservative in its harmonic style than Piston's, reveals a lyric quality that contributes to a warm, personal expressiveness. Porter has composed nine string quartets (1923 to 1958), several quintets for various combinations of instruments, including one for harpsichord and string quartet (1961), and a number of smaller works. His style is basically tonal, and the composer's practical experience as a violist may account for the idiomatic writing that is characteristic. The string quartets reveal Porter's fondness for *ostinato* motives; a typical effect is created by the employment of two or three such motives at the same time to accompany a lyric melody. His thick part-writing sometimes gives rise to monochromatic effects, but it often develops into large, sonorous climaxes. A variety of moods emerge from the quartets, but on the whole, dramatic allegros, somber or serious slow movements, and agitated finales are typical.

Harris. A striking feature of the chamber music of Roy Harris (b. 1898) is its formal variety. In a style compounded largely of parallel writing, sixteenth-century modes used in pairs, and manipulated rhythmic figures, Harris' outstanding works in the field present several formal innovations. Thus his second quartet (1932) is entitled Three Variations on a Theme; the third (1938) consists of four preludes and four fugues; a piano quintet (1937) contains a passacaglia, a cadenza, and a fugue. His other works include a piano trio (1934), a string quintet (1940), a string sextet (about 1932), and several smaller works.

The piano quintet discloses Harris' strengths and weaknesses of style, perhaps to a greater degree than do his other works in the field. Its massive, concentrated, polyphonic first movement, with its long melodic lines, builds up at great length to an imposing climax that seems foreshortened. The second, in which the instruments singly and together engage in free rhapsodic development of the first movement's passacaglia theme, is not well proportioned. The third, a masterful and compelling fugue on the same theme, suffers from overdevelopment; a mass of unessential figuration obscures the lines of the fugue and leads to a noisy climax.

The third quartet, as noted above, contains a prelude and fugue in each of its four movements. In each case the prelude is cast in one of the old church modes, whereas the fugue employs two modes simultaneously. The resulting modal clashes create a new harmonic sound, redolent of the sixteenth and twentieth centuries at once. The prevailing contrapuntal texture is logical and precise, but thick writing and a lack of real climaxes lead to a certain monotony of color. Again the abrupt endings are encountered, as in the piano quintet. But the work as a whole—and this is still more true of the quintet—testifies to the vigor of Harris' writing, to its freedom from contemporary transatlantic influences, and to its directness.

Schuman. The four string quartets of William Schuman (b. 1910), composed between 1936 and 1950, represent yet another aspect of Neo-Classicism. Somewhat similar in style to the works of Harris, with whom he studied for a short time, Schuman's quartets are filled with harshly dissonant passages that are firmly based on tonality. His style is essentially polyphonic, but many unison passages and long lyric melodies chordally accompanied provide a variety of textures. Perhaps the outstanding characteristic of Schuman's music is its rhythmic vitality. Such devices as unmetrical rhythms, strongly syncopated passages, and sharp accents at irregular intervals give the music an air of nervous energy and great propulsive power.

Copland. Several prominent American composers, not primarily active in the field of chamber music, may be mentioned here for a few compositions. Aaron Copland (b. 1900) is represented by four works —a piano trio entitled *Vitebsk* (1929), a sextet for clarinet, string quartet and piano (1937), a violin sonata (1943), and a piano quartet (1950) that marks a radical departure from his earlier styles. The trio, with allusions to a Jewish folk song (hence its title), is warmly expressive; in a manner similar to Bloch's, Copland calls for the use of quarter tones as an added coloristic device. The sextet, arranged from the composer's Short Symphony of 1933 and dedicated to Carlos Chavez, contains many Latin-American rhythms and is a fine example of Copland's ability to absorb elements of an exotic style.

Riegger. Wallingford Riegger (1885–1961) did not gain recognition as a composer until the late 1940s. His numerous compositions, of which about half a dozen are in the field of chamber music, reveal a gradual change from a conservative, melodious style to one that embraced elements of serial writing combined with wide-ranging rhythmic experiments. An early piano trio (1919) discloses the traditional element in his work, but in it Riegger hinted at the rhythmic diversity that later became characteristic. A series of works for various combinations of woodwind instruments, two string quartets, a nonet for brass, a woodwind quintet, and a piano quintet—all composed between about 1930 and 1959—disclose a gradual adoption of serial technique. But Riegger did not hesitate to employ tone rows loosely, sometimes to the extent of introducing nonserial material into the tonal fabric.

Sessions. Roger Sessions (b. 1896) is a composer whose works are more often admired than performed. In a style that is Neo-Classical in form, atonal in harmonic idiom, and austere in mood, Sessions has composed relatively few chamber-music works, but each work is a monument to his uncompromising integrity and fine craftsmanship. Two string quartets (1936 and 1950) and a string quintet (1958) are his principal works in the field. He has not escaped the influence of serial writing, although his chief application of the system appears in themes that employ nonrepeated chromatic tones. The other techniques of the Schoenberg school are seldom apparent. Sessions has long been active as a teacher and an eloquent champion of contemporary music. His efforts on behalf of American composers have embraced those whose styles differ widely from his own.

Kirchner. One of Sessions' pupils, Leon Kirchner (b. 1919), has composed several significant chamber-music works in a style completely unlike his teacher's. In Kirchner's two string quartets (1949 and 1958), a violin sonata (1955), and a piano trio (1957) the element of unmetrical rhythm is characteristic. Measures of 5/16, 7/16, 9/16—up to 15/16 in a few cases—alternate with measures of customary length (6/8, 4/4, etc.), so that rhythmic asymmetry and tension come uppermost. Harmonically and formally Kirchner's music is stylistically diverse, for it contains elements of atonal, chromatic, and occasionally diatonic harmony. It includes conventional forms, such as a waltz with trio and *da capo,* but also movements that are entirely rhapsodic and virtually free of form. Underlying such stylistic multiplicity is a rich expressiveness not far removed from post-Romanticism in its warmth, intensity, and color.

Carter. The concern with rhythmic development reached a new level in a cello sonata (1948) and two string quartets (1951 and 1960) by Elliott Carter (b. 1908). Certain aspects of serial writing are evident, notably the principle of perpetual variation, but often the element being varied is an interval or chord rather than a tone row. The outstanding characteristics of Carter's music, however, are rhythmic complexity and concentrated texture. His rhythmic writing goes far beyond that of earlier composers, in whose music phrases were so written that bar lines were virtually negated at times. Syncopations, rhythmic anticipations of the beat, and asymmetrical phrases occur in a rhythmic texture that is itself unmetrical. Further, Carter often relies on polyrhythms, to the extent that groups containing three, four, five, and seven notes to a beat are heard simultaneously in the four parts. The second quartet provides a notable example.

In addition, with his concern for variety of tone color, Carter is meticulous in his use of dynamic indications and in idiomatic instrumental effects. Various kinds of pizzicati (with the fingernail, with the ball of the thumb, with a snap against the fingerboard, etc.) are specified. The placing of the players, in respect to distance from one another, concerns him also, for this bears on the spatial effect of his music. Such elements and devices take place in forms that are free, almost improvisational. The end result is a kind of chamber music that is distantly related to Stravinsky (in its rhythmic vitality), Schoenberg (in its constant variation), Webern (in tone-color effects), and Bartók (in instrumental effects), yet is purely individual and highly original.

The Future. In this brief survey of the chamber music of a few American composers it becomes apparent that no single musical style is characteristic of the twentieth century. Extreme emotional tension, much unrelieved dissonance, and a full use of the intellectual processes of composition are most usual. One may hear on occasion severe criticisms of the expressive aims and dissonant styles of contemporary composers. One learns that beauty has gone out of music, that noise and confusion are modern musical ideals, that expression of feeling is not to be found. One may grant, grudgingly, that contemporary music is clever, that it is inventive—in short, that it is "different." So, in general, run the comments.

Those who put forth these and similar criticisms sometimes fail to realize that in that very difference lies the hope for the well-being of music in the years ahead. Throughout the course of this book the author has attempted to show how music has always been on the march; how its forms, styles, and modes of expression have changed with each passing decade; how every new style has been derived from the old, has in a sense been an extension of the old. Chamber music was born amid diatribes and invectives; Artusi's pamphlet of 1600 was directed against the *nuove musiche* of his day. Out of that new music developed the forms and the styles of the late Baroque period. They in turn were outmoded while Bach was still alive, namely, before 1750, and another revolution in musical taste prepared the way for the style that culminated in the works of the late nineteenth century.

The conclusion is inescapable. Since the early 1900s still another musical revolution has been going on, one that in the last decade or two has shown signs of coming to a close. Out of that latest upheaval a new style emerged—is emerging—will emerge. It is the fate of progressive composers—and most great composers have been progressive —to stand some distance in advance of their audiences. It was true of Monteverdi, of Mozart, and of Beethoven; it is true of Stravinsky, of Bartók, and of Schoenberg.

It would be trite to point out that as the world has become smaller it has also increased its rate of change. A musical development that might have taken half a century in the past is now consummated within a decade. From Frescobaldi to Bach was a hundred years; from Debussy to Stravinsky is barely twenty. In that speed of development, in the rapidity with which new styles have encompassed the earth, lies the difficulty for many listeners to contemporary music.

The new styles are here to stay for several generations, even though they have probably not yet reached their definitive shapes. The gap that separates the most conservative listener from the most progressive composer has become noticeably smaller in recent decades. The expressive possibilities of the new music are vast, at least as great as they were in older music. Composers everywhere are tireless in their efforts to bring those possibilities to light. And in the future development of those possibilities the resources of chamber music will be called upon. Chamber music will play as vital and significant a role in music of the future as it has played in the music of the last three and a half centuries.

Bibliography

Abraham, Gerald, ed. Handel: A Symposium. New York, Oxford University Press, 1954.
———The Music of Schubert. New York, W. W. Norton & Co., 1947.
———Schumann: A Symposium. New York, Oxford University Press, 1952.
Adler, Guido, ed. Handbuch der Musikgeschichte. 2d ed., 2 vols. Berlin-Wilmersdorf, H. Keller, 1930.
Allen, Warren D. Philosophies of Music History. New York, American Book Co., 1939; reprinted, New York, Dover Publications, 1962.
Altmann, Wilhelm. Kammermusik-Katalog. 6th ed. Leipzig, Hofmeister, 1945.
Apel, Willi. Harvard Dictionary of Music. Cambridge, Mass., Harvard University Press, 1947.
Arnold, Franck Thomas. The Art of Accompaniment from a Thorough-Bass. London, Oxford University Press, 1931.
Artaria, Franz, and Hugo Botstiber. Joseph Haydn und das Verlagshaus Artaria. Vienna, Artaria & Co., 1909.
Artusi, Giovanni. Ovvero delle imperfezioni della moderna musica. Venice, Vicenti, 1600; reprinted in part in Strunk, Source Readings in Music History, pp. 393–404, q.v.
Attaignant, Pierre. Quatorze gaillardes, neuf pavennes, sept branles, et deux basses danses. Paris, Attaignant, c. 1530; facsimile ed. in Bernouilli, ed. Chansons und Tänze, Vol. IV, q.v.
Babbitt, Milton. "The String Quartets of Béla Bartók," The Musical Quarterly, XXXV, No. 3 (July, 1949), 377–85.
Bach, Johann Sebastian. Bachs Werke. 50 vols. to 1957. Leipzig, Der neuen Bachgesellschaft, 1901—.
———Musikalisches Opfer. Modern ed. by Hans T. David. New York, G. Schirmer, 1944.
——— Werke. Edited by Moritz Hauptmann and others. 47 vols. Leip-

zig, Bachgesellschaft, Breitkopf & Härtel, 1851–1926; reprinted, J. W. Edwards, Ann Arbor, 1947.

Bach, Karl Philipp Emanuel. Versuch über die wahre Art das Klavier zu spielen. Berlin, C. F. Henning, 1753. Translated from the German by William Mitchell as Essay on the True Art of Playing Keyboard Instruments. New York, W. W. Norton & Co., 1948.

Baker, Theodore. Baker's Biographical Dictionary of Musicians. 5th rev. ed. by Nicolas Slonimsky. New York, G. Schirmer, 1958.

Bauer, Marion E. Twentieth-Century Music. New York, G. P. Putnam's Sons, 1933.

Beckmann, Gustav, ed. Das Violinspiel in Deutschland vor 1700: 12 Sonaten. Leipzig, N. Simrock, 1918.

Beethoven, Ludwig van. Werke. Edited by Guido Adler and others. 25 vols. Leipzig, Breitkopf & Härtel, 1862–88; reprinted, J. W. Edwards, Ann Arbor, 1949.

Bernouilli, Eduard, ed. Chansons und Tänze. 5 vols. Munich, C. Kuhn, 1914.

Brahms, Johannes. Sämtliche Werke. Edited by Hans Gál and Eusebius Mandyczewski. 26 vols. Leipzig, Breitkopf & Härtel, 1926–28; reprinted, J. W. Edwards, Ann Arbor, 1949.

Brown, Maurice J. E. "Mozart's Recapitulations: A Point of Style," *Music and Letters,* XXX, No. 2 (April, 1949), 109–17.

Bücken, Ernst, ed. Handbuch der Musikwissenschaft. 13 vols. Wildpark-Potsdam, Athenaion-verlag, 1928–34.

Bukofzer, Manfred. Music in the Baroque Era. New York, W. W. Norton & Co., 1947.

Burney, Charles. A General History of Music. 2 vols. Revised ed., New York, Harcourt, Brace & Co., 1935; reprinted, Dover, New York, 1960.

——The Present State of Music in France and Italy. London, T. Beckett & Co., 1771.

Byrd, William. My Ladye Nevelles Booke (1591). Modern ed. by Hilda Andrews. London, J.Curwen Sons, 1926.

——Three Dances of William Byrd. Edited by Sir Granville Bantock. London, Novello & Co., n.d.

——, John Bull, and others. Fitzwilliam Virginal Book. New ed. by J. A. Fuller-Maitland and William B. Squire. 2 vols. London and Leipzig, Breitkopf & Härtel, 1899.

Castiglione, Baldassare. Libro del cortegiano. Florence, Giunta, 1531. English version: The Book of the Courtier, Done into English by Sir Thomas Hoby, anno 1561. New York, E. P. Dutton & Co., 1928.

Cobbett, Walter W. Cobbett's Cyclopedic Survey of Chamber Music.

2d ed. by Colin Mason. 3 vols. London, Oxford University Press, 1963.

Cohen, Albert. "The *Fantaisie* for Instrumental Ensemble in 17th-Century France," *The Musical Quarterly*, XLVIII, No. 2 (April, 1962), 234–43.

Collegium musicum. *See* Hugo Riemann, ed.

Corelli, Arcangelo. Œuvres. Edited by Joseph Joachim and Friedrich Chrysander. 5 vols. London, Augener, 1888–91.

Cowell, Henry and Sidney. Charles Ives and His Music. New York, Oxford University Press, 1955.

Crevel, Marcus van. Adrianus Petit Coclico. The Hague, M. Nijhoff, 1940.

Crocker, Eunice C. "An Introductory Study of the Italian Canzona for Instrumental Ensembles." 2 vols. Unpublished dissertation. Cambridge, Mass., Radcliffe College, 1943.

Cudworth, Charles. "Notes on the Instrumental Works Attributed to Pergolesi," *Music and Letters*, XXX, 4 (October, 1949), 321–28.

Dart, Thurston. "The Printed Fantasias of Orlando Gibbons," *Music and Letters*, XXXVII, No. 4 (October, 1956), 342–49.

Davison, Archibald T., and Willi Apel, eds. Historical Anthology of Music. 2 vols. Cambridge, Mass., Harvard University Press, 1947, 1950.

Denkmäler der Tonkunst. Edited by Friedrich Chrysander. 5 vols. Bergedorf, Weissenborn, 1869–71.

Denkmäler der Tonkunst in Österreich. 83 vols. Vienna, Universal Edition, 1894–1938. Abbreviation: DTÖ.

Denkmäler deutscher Tonkunst, erste Folge. 65 vols. Leipzig, Breitkopf & Härtel, 1892–1931. Abbreviation: DDT.

Denkmäler deutscher Tonkunst, zweite Folge: Denkmäler der Tonkunst in Bayern. 36 vols. Leipzig, Breitkopf & Härtel, 1900–1931. Abbreviation: DTB.

Deutsch, Otto Erich. Handel: A Documentary Biography. New York, W. W. Norton & Co., 1955.

——"The Schubert Catalogue: Corrections and Additions," *Music and Letters*, XXXIV, No. 1 (January, 1953), 25–32.

——, and Donald Wakeling, eds. Schubert Thematic Catalogue. New York, W. W. Norton & Co., 1951.

Donington, Robert, and Thurston Dart. "The Origins of the *In Nomine*," *Music and Letters*, XXX, No. 2 (April, 1949), 101–8.

Dorian, Frederick. The History of Music in Performance. New York, W. W. Norton & Co., 1942.

Drinker, Henry S., Jr. The Chamber Music of Brahms. Philadelphia, published by the author, 1932.

Ecorcheville, Jules, ed. Vingt suites d'orchestre du XVIIe siècle français. 2 vols. Paris, Fortin, 1906.

Einstein, Alfred. Mozart, His Character, His Work. Translated from the German by Arthur Mendel and Nathan Broder. London, Oxford University Press, 1945.

———Music in the Romantic Era. New York, W. W. Norton & Co., 1947.

———A Short History of Music. Translated from the German by Eric Blom and others. 4th American ed. New York, Random House, 1954.

Eitner, Robert. Biographisch-bibliographisches Quellen-Lexikon der Musiker und Musikgelehrten. 10 vols. Leipzig, Breitkopf & Härtel, 1900–1904; reprinted, 11 vols., Graz, Akademische Druck und Verlagsanstalt, 1960.

Encyclopédie de la Musique. Edited by Albert Lavignac. 11 vols. Paris, Delagrave, 1913–39.

Das Erbe deutscher Musik; erste Reihe. 49 vols. to date. Leipzig and Berlin, various publishers, 1935—.

Evans, Edwin, Sr. Handbook to the Works of Brahms. 4 vols. London, W. Reeves, 1933–35. Vols. II and III, Chamber and Orchestral Works.

Evans, Peter. "Seventeenth-Century Chamber Music Manuscripts at Durham," *Music and Letters*, XXXVI, No. 3 (July, 1955), 205–23.

Fitzwilliam Virginal Book. *See* William Byrd, John Bull, and others.

Frescobaldi, Girolamo. Werke. 5 vols. Cassel, Bärenreiter Verlag, 1957–59.

Gabrieli, Giovanni. Opera Omnia. Edited by Denis Arnold. Rome, American Institute of Musicology, 1956—.

Geiringer, Karl. Brahms: His Life and Work. 2d rev. ed. New York, Oxford University Press, 1947.

———Haydn: A Creative Life in Music. 2d ed. New York, Doubleday & Co., 1963.

Grove, Sir George. Grove's Dictionary of Music and Musicians. 9 vols. and supplement. 5th ed. by Eric Blom. London, The Macmillan Co., 1954, 1960.

Haas, Robert. "Aufführungspraxis der Musik," in Bücken, ed. Handbuch der Musikwissenschaft, Vol. VIII, *q.v.*

———"Die Musik des Barocks," in Bücken, Handbuch der Musikwissenschaft, Vol. IV, *q.v.*

Händel, Georg Friedrich. Werke. Edited by Friedrich Chrysander. 102 vols. (incomplete). Leipzig, Breitkopf & Härtel, 1858–1902.

Hansen, Peter. An Introduction to Twentieth-Century Music. Boston, Allyn & Bacon, 1961.

Haydn, Franz Joseph. Sämtliche Werke. Edited by Eusebius Mandyczewski. 10 vols. published. Leipzig, Breitkopf & Härtel, 1907–33. Edited by Jens Peter Larsen and others. 4 vols. published. Boston, Haydn Society, 1949–52. New ed. in preparation, Haydn Institute, Cologne, 1954—.

Heuss, Alfred. Kammermusikabende. Leipzig, Breitkopf & Härtel, 1919.

Heyer, Anna Harriet. Historical Sets, Collected Editions, and Monuments of Music: A Guide to Their Contents. Chicago, American Library Association, 1957.

Hoboken, Anthony. Joseph Haydn, thematisch-bibliographisches Werkverzeichnis. Mainz, Schott, 1957—. Vol. I, Instrumental Works.

Howard, John Tasker. Our American Music. 3d rev. ed. New York, Thomas Y. Crowell Co., 1946.

Jahn, Otto. W. A. Mozart. 2 vols. 6th ed. by Herman Abert. Leipzig, Breitkopf & Härtel, 1923–24.

Jahrbücher für musikalische Wissenschaft. Edited by Friedrich Chrysander. 2 vols. Leipzig, Breitkopf & Härtel, 1863, 1867.

Journal, American Musicological Society. Philadelphia, 1948—.

Kinkeldey, Otto. Orgel und Klavier in der Musik des 16ten Jahrhunderts. Leipzig, Breitkopf & Härtel, 1910.

Kinsky, Georg. A History of Music in Pictures. London, Dent, 1937.

———, and Hans Halm. Das Werk Beethovens; thematisch-bibliographisches Verzeichnis seiner sämtlichen vollendeten Kompositionen. Munich-Duisburg, G. Henle Verlag, 1955.

Klaviertänze des 16ten Jahrhunderts. Edited by H. Halbig. Stuttgart, J. G. Cotta, 1928.

Koechel, Ludwig Ritter von. Chronologisch-systematisches Verzeichnis sämtlicher Tonwerke Wolfgang Amadeus Mozarts. 6th rev. ed. by Franz Giegling and others. Wiesbaden, Breitkopf & Härtel, 1964.

Kolneder, Walter. Anton Webern: Einführung im Werk und Stil. Bodenkirchen am Rhein, Tonger, 1961.

Kretzschmar, Hermann. Führer durch den Concertsaal; I Abteilung, Sinfonie und Suite. 3d ed. Leipzig, Breitkopf & Härtel, 1898.

Lang, Paul Henry. Music in Western Civilization. New York, W. W. Norton & Co., 1941.

Leibowitz, René. Schoenberg and His School. Translated from the French by Dika Newlin. New York, Philosophical Library, 1949.

Leichtentritt, Hugo. Händel. Stuttgart, Deutsche Verlagsanstalt, 1924.

———"Was lehren uns die Bildwerke des 14ten-17ten Jahrhunderts," *Sammelbände der Internationalen Musikgesellschaft,* VII, Pt. 3 (May–June, 1906), 315–64.

Lenz, Wilhelm von. Beethoven et ses trois styles. New ed. by M. D. Calvocoressi. Paris, Legouix, 1909.

Das Locheimer (Lochamer) Liederbuch, and Conrad Paumann, Fundamentum organisandi. Facsimile ed. by Konrad Ameln. Berlin, Wölbing Verlag, 1925.

Lowinsky, Edward. "On Mozart's Rhythm," *The Musical Quarterly*, XLII, No. 2 (April, 1956), 162–86.

MacArdle, Donald W. "Beethoven, Artaria, and the C major Quintet," *The Musical Quarterly*, XXXIV, No. 4 (October, 1948), 567–74.

Machlis, Joseph. Introduction to Contemporary Music. New York, W. W. Norton & Co., 1961.

Mason, Colin. "The Chamber Music of Milhaud," *The Musical Quarterly*, XLIII, No. 3 (July, 1957), 326–41.

——"Some Aspects of Hindemith's Chamber Music," *Music and Letters*, XLI, No. 2 (April, 1960), 150–55.

—— "Webern's Late Chamber Music," *Music and Letters*, XXXVIII, No. 3 (July, 1957), 232–37.

Mason, Daniel Gregory. The Chamber Music of Brahms. New York, The Macmillan Co., 1933.

Mendelssohn, Felix. Werke. Edited by Julius Rietz. 36 vols. Leipzig, Breitkopf & Härtel, 1874–77.

Mersmann, Hans. Die Kammermusik. 4 vols. Leipzig, Breitkopf & Härtel, 1930–33.

Meyer, Ernst. English Chamber Music. London, Lawrence & Wishart, 1946; reprinted 1951.

Mishkin, Henry G. "Five Autograph String Quartets by G. B. Sammartini," *Journal*, American Musicological Society, VI, No. 2 (Summer, 1953), 136–47.

Modern Music. 23 vols. New York, League of Composers, 1924–46.

Moser, Hans Joachim. Geschichte der deutschen Musik. 5th ed., 3 vols. Stuttgart, J. G. Cotta, 1930.

—— Musiklexikon. 4th ed., 2 vols. Hamburg, Sikorski, 1955.

Mozart, Wolfgang Amadeus. Sämtliche Werke. Edited by Gustav Nottebohm and others. 24 series in 75 vols. Leipzig, Breitkopf & Härtel, 1877–1905; reprinted, J. W. Edwards, Ann Arbor, 1955.

Murrill, Herbert. "Walton's Viola Sonata," *Music and Letters*, XXXI, No. 3 (July, 1950), 208–15.

Music and Letters. London, 1920—.

Music Review. Cambridge, England, 1940—.

The Musical Quarterly. New York, G. Schirmer, 1915—.

Die Musik in Geschichte und Gegenwart. Edited by Friedrich Blume. 12 vols. to date. Cassel, Bärenreiter Verlag, 1949—.

Nef, Karl. Geschichte der Sinfonie und Suite. Leipzig, Breitkopf & Härtel, 1921.

―――― An Outline of the History of Music. Revised ed., translated from the German by Carl Pfatteicher. New York, Columbia University Press, 1957.

The New Oxford History of Music. Edited by Egon Wellesz and others. 3 vols. to date. London, Oxford University Press, 1957—.

Newman, William. "Ravenscroft and Corelli," *Music and Letters*, XXXVIII, No. 4 (October, 1957), 369–70.

―――― The Sonata in the Baroque Era. Chapel Hill, University of North Carolina Press, 1959.

―――― The Sonata in the Classical Era. Chapel Hill, University of North Carolina Press, 1963.

―――― "The Sonatas of Albinoni and Vivaldi," *Journal*, American Musicological Society, V, No. 1 (Spring, 1952), 99–113.

Nieman, Walter. Brahms. Translated from the German by C. A. Phillips. New York, Alfred A. Knopf, 1947.

Norlind, Tobias. "Zur Geschichte der Suite," *Sammelbände der Internationalen Musikgesellschaft*, VII, Pt. 2 (February–March, 1906), 172–203.

Notes. Washington, Music Library Association, 1943—.

The Oxford History of Music. 2d ed., rev. 7 vols. London, Oxford University Press, 1929–38.

Pincherle, Marc. Corelli, His Life, His Music. Translated from the French by Herbert E. M. Russell. New York, W. W. Norton & Co., 1956.

―――― Vivaldi: Genius of the Baroque. Translated from the French by Christopher Hatch. New York, W. W. Norton & Co., 1957.

Pohl, Karl Ferdinand. Joseph Haydn. 3 vols. Vols. I and II, Berlin, A. Sasso Nachfolger, 1875, 1882; Vol. III (completed by Hugo Botstiber), Leipzig, Breitkopf & Härtel, n.d.

Polyphonies du XIIIe siècle. Modern ed. by Yvonne Rokseth. 4 vols. Monaco, L'Oiseau-Lyre, 1935–39.

Prunières, Henry. A New History of Music. Translated from the French by Edward Lockspeiser. New York, The Macmillan Co., 1943.

Purcell, Henry. Complete Works. Ed. by J. A. Fuller-Maitland. 36 vols. London, Novello & Co., 1878–1928.

Redlich, Hans. "Bruckner and Brahms Quintets in F," *Music and Letters*, XXXVI, No. 3 (July, 1955), 253–58.

Riemann, Hugo. Beethovens Streichquartette. Berlin, Schlesinger'sche Buchhandlung, n.d.

————, ed. Collegium musicum. 50 vols. Leipzig, Breitkopf & Härtel, n.d.

———— Geschichte der Musik seit Beethoven. Berlin and Stuttgart, W. Spemann, 1901.

———— Handbuch der Musikgeschichte. 2d ed., 2 vols., 5 pts. Leipzig, Breitkopf & Härtel, 1920–23. Abbreviation: HM.

———— Musik-Lexikon. 12th ed. by Willibald Gurlitt. 2 vols. of biography published, 3d vol., general reference, in preparation. Mainz, Schott, 1959—.

————, ed. Old Chamber Music. 4 vols. London, Augener & Co., n.d.

Riezler, Walter. Beethoven. Translated from the German by C. D. Pidcock. New York, E. P. Dutton & Co., 1938.

Sadie, Stanley. "The Chamber Music of Boyce and Arne," *The Musical Quarterly*, XLVI, No. 4 (October, 1960), 425–36.

Salazar, Adolfo. Music in Our Time. Translated from the Spanish by Isabel Pope. New York, W. W. Norton & Co., 1946.

Sammelbände der Internationalen Musikgesellschaft. 15 vols. Leipzig, Breitkopf & Härtel, 1899–1914.

Sandberger, Adolf. "Zur Entstehungsgeschichte von Haydns sieben Worte des Erlösers am Kreuze," in his Ausgewählte Aufsätze zur Musikgeschichte. Munich, Drei Masken Verlag, 1921.

———— "Zur Geschichte des Haydnschen Streichquartetts," in his Ausgewählte Aufsätze zur Musikgeschichte. Munich, Drei Masken Verlag, 1921.

Schein, Johann Hermann. Werke. 7 vols., 8 pts. Leipzig, Breitkopf & Härtel, 1901–23.

Schering, Arnold. Geschichte der Musik in Beispielen. Leipzig, Breitkopf & Härtel, 1931; reprinted, Broude Bros., New York, 1950.

———— Tabellen zur Musikgeschichte. 4th rev. ed. Leipzig, Breitkopf & Härtel, 1934.

Schmieder, Wolfgang, ed. Thematisch-systematisches Verzeichnis der Werke von J. S. Bach. Leipzig, Breitkopf & Härtel, 1950.

Schnerich, Alfred. Joseph Haydn und seine Sendung. Zurich, Almathea-Verlag, 1922.

Schubert, Franz Peter. Werke. Edited by Johannes Brahms and others. 41 vols. Leipzig, Breitkopf & Härtel, 1884-97.

Schumann, Robert. Werke. Edited by Clara Schumann. 31 vols. Leipzig, Breitkopf & Härtel, 1881–93.

Schwebsch, Erich. Johann Sebastian Bach und Die Kunst der Fuge. Stuttgart, Orient-Occident-Verlag, 1931.

Scott, Marion M. Beethoven. 2d ed. London, J. M. Dent, 1937.

Silbert, Doris. "Ambiguity in the String Quartets of Joseph Haydn," *The Musical Quarterly*, XXXVI, No. 4 (October, 1950), 562–73.

Skempton, Alec. "The Instrumental Sonatas of the Loeillets," *Music and Letters*, XLIII, No. 3 (July, 1962), 206–17.

Spitta, Philipp. Johann Sebastian Bach. Translated from the German by Clara Bell and J. A. Fuller-Maitland. 3 vols. in 2. New York, Dover Publications, 1951.

Steiner, Rudolf. The Philosophy of Spiritual Activity. Translated from the German by R. F. Hoernlé. New York, The Anthroposophic Press, 1932.

Stevens, Denis. "Purcell's Art of Fantasia," *Music and Letters*, XXXIII, No. 4 (October, 1952), 341–45.

Stevens, Halsey. The Life and Music of Belá Bartók. New York, Oxford University Press, 1953.

Straeten, Edmund van der. The History of the Violin. 2 vols. London, Cassell & Co., 1933.

Strobel, Heinrich. Paul Hindemith. 3d ed. Mainz, Schott, 1948.

Strunk, Oliver, ed. Source Readings in Music History. New York, W. W. Norton & Co., 1950.

Studien zur Musikwissenschaft, Beihefte der Denkmäler der Tonkunst in Österreich. 21 vols. Vienna, Artaria & Co. and Universal Edition, 1913–34.

Sullivan, John William N. Beethoven: His Spiritual Development. New York, Alfred A. Knopf, 1927; reprinted, Random House (Vintage Press), New York, 1960.

Tagliapietra, Gino, ed. Antologia di musica antica e moderna. 18 vols. Milan, G. Ricordi, 1931–32.

Thayer, Alexander W. The Life of Ludwig van Beethoven. Revised and ed. by Elliot Forbes. 2 vols. Princeton, Princeton University Press, 1964.

Thompson, Oscar, ed. The International Cyclopedia of Music and Musicians. 9th ed. by Robert Sabin. New York, Dodd, Mead & Co., 1964.

Tilmouth, Michael. "The Technique and Forms of Purcell's Sonatas," *Music and Letters*, XL, No. 2 (April, 1959), 109–21.

Torchi, Luigi, ed. L'arte musicale in Italia. 7 vols. Milan, G. Ricordi, 1897–1903.

Tovey, Donald Francis. Beethoven. London, Oxford University Press, 1945.

———— Essays in Musical Analysis; Chamber Music. London, Oxford University Press, 1944.

Turner, W. J. Mozart: the Man and His Works. New York, Alfred A. Knopf, 1938.

Ulrich, Homer, and Paul A. Pisk. A History of Music and Musical Style. New York, Harcourt, Brace & World, 1963.

Vierteljahrschrift für Musikwissenschaft. 10 vols. Leipzig, Breitkopf & Härtel, 1885–94.

Vitali, Giovanni Battista. Sonate per 2, 3, 4, e 5 instromenti; Opus 5. 2d ed. Bologna, Monti, 1677.

Vivaldi, Antonio. Le opere. Edited by G. Francesco Malipiero. About 400 vols. published to date. Milan, G. Ricordi, 1947—.

Vlad, Roman. Stravinsky. London, Oxford University Press, 1960.

Walker, Frank. A History of Music in England. 3d rev. ed. by Jack Allan Westrup. Oxford, Clarendon Press, 1952.

—— "Two Centuries of Pergolesi Forgeries and Misattributions," *Music and Letters,* XXX, No. 4 (October, 1949), 297–320.

Walther, Johann Gottfried. Musikalisches Lexikon. Leipzig, W. Deer, 1732; facsimile reprint, Cassel, Bärenreiter Verlag, 1953.

Wasielewski, Joseph W. von. Die Violine und ihre Meister. Revised ed. Leipzig, Breitkopf & Härtel, 1927.

Webster, J. H. Douglas. "Golden Mean Form in Music," *Music and Letters,* XXXI, No. 3 (July, 1950), 238–48.

Werckmeister, Andreas. Harmonologia musica. Frankfurt and Leipzig, T. P. Calvisii, 1702.

Willetts, Pamela. "Sir Nicholas Le Strange and John Jenkins," *Music and Letters,* XLII, No. 1 (January, 1961), 30–43.

Williams, C. F. Abdy. G. F. Handel, Revised ed. New York, E. P. Dutton & Co., 1935.

Zeitschrift für Musikwissenschaft. 17 vols. Leipzig, Breitkopf & Härtel, 1918–35.

Index